UNITED STATES OF OLIGARCHY

Also by Casey Michel

American Kleptocracy

Foreign Agents

UNITED STATES of OLIGARCHY

HOW AMERICA'S WEALTHIEST ALLY WITH DICTATORS, WEAKEN THE U.S., AND DESTROY DEMOCRACY

CASEY MICHEL

ST. MARTIN'S PRESS
NEW YORK

First published in the United States by St. Martin's Press, an imprint of St. Martin's Publishing Group

EU Representative: Macmillan Publishers Ireland Ltd., 1st Floor, The Liffey Trust Centre, 117–126 Sheriff Street Upper, Dublin 1, D01 YC43

www.stmartins.com

Designed by Donna Sinisgalli Noetzel

The Library of Congress Cataloging-in-Publication Data is available upon request.

ISBN 978-1-250-43011-3 (hardcover)
ISBN 978-1-250-43012-0 (ebook)

First Edition: 2026

10 9 8 7 6 5 4 3 2 1

To Devi Rose—our Gudiya

My pride is my land
For I was born here
I don't love it because it is beautiful
I love it because it is mine.

—ENRIQUE ZORRILLA[1]

When you look too long into the abyss, the abyss looks back through you.

—KEVIN CONROY[2]

Contents

Oligarchs by the Numbers

- Amount of total wealth created for the nineteen richest American families in 2024: $1 trillion[1]
- Years in which the bottom 90 percent of America owned more than the top 1 percent: 1946–2005[2]
- First year the four hundred richest Americans had a lower tax rate than the bottom 50 percent of Americans: 2018[3]

- Change in the average tax rate for the top 0.1 percent of Americans, 1933–2020: decline of 50 percent[4]
- Change in the average tax rate for the bottom 90 percent of Americans, 1933–2020: increase of 150 percent[5]

- Net worth of John D. Rockefeller (adjusted for inflation): $30 billion[6]
- Net worth of Elon Musk (as of October 2025): $485 billion[7]

- Dark money expenditures on the 2006 American elections: less than $5 million[8]
- Dark money expenditures on the 2024 American elections: $1.9 billion[9]

- Date that a UN commission found Israel guilty of committing genocide in Gaza: September 16, 2025[10]
- Date that *Forbes* announced it had officially named Jared Kushner a billionaire: September 16, 2025[11]

- Growth of the Trump family's net worth since entering the White House: $3.4 billion[12]

UNITED STATES OF OLIGARCHY

Prologue

The Inauguration of the Oligarchs

I guess the trouble was that we didn't have any self-admitted proletarians. Everyone was a temporarily embarrassed capitalist.

—*John Steinbeck*[1]

In December 2016, a bearded, hawk-nosed man walked into an obsidian skyscraper in the middle of New York City. Clad in combat boots and jeans, the man rode the elevator up, past offices and hallways, as far toward the sky as he could go. He got off, entering the building's penthouse, walking with more swagger than his scrawny, bespectacled look would otherwise imply.[2]

Maybe that confidence shouldn't have been surprising. After all, the man wasn't alone. He'd traveled with an entourage—about thirty people total, all scrabbling behind him, all following his lead, including some with guns strapped to their bodies. More important, the man—Mohamed bin Zayed Al Nahyan (MBZ), the yearslong head of the United Arab Emirates' dictatorship—towered over a regime in the Middle East that was now breathtakingly, eye-wateringly wealthy. Hundreds of billions of dollars had flowed into his tiny nation's coffers year after year, pumped in thanks to his country's vast hydrocarbon holdings. Where just two generations prior had been mud-brick homes and sand-swept alleys now stood futuristic spires, terraformed lakes and dunes, and even the world's tallest building, all a testament to the supposed vision and savvy of this long-standing despot.[3]

Less obvious was the fact that much of the nation's wealth was never put toward anything that would benefit the average Emirati's life. Rather, as with every other kleptocratic regime around the world, much of that money found its way into MBZ's and his cronies' pockets. And in recent years, the wealth had begun spilling outward, buying off new allies and sycophants around the world, saturating places that were nominally opposed to things like dictatorship or kleptocracy. Some of that money went toward Western politicians and sports leagues, turning them into the UAE's playthings. Other Emirati wealth went toward luxury jets and mega-mansions in places like London and Paris and Miami. Some of it had even been used to finance one of the greatest political influence and interference schemes in U.S. history, with MBZ and his regime authoring a brand-new playbook for how antidemocratic regimes around the world could tilt American politics for their own ends—all while somehow remaining in the U.S.'s good graces.[4]

All that may have been fodder for MBZ's swagger. But there was another reason for his confidence as well. After all, just before arriving on that wintry day in Manhattan, MBZ had become one of the few global leaders to ever stiff-arm a sitting American president. According to later reporting, then-President Barack Obama had considered MBZ one of his allies—even, as one analysis read, one of his "friends."[5] It was an odd opinion, given that the Emirati despot oversaw a regime that not only tortured and disappeared opponents but opened its coffers to dirty money around the world, transforming into one of the go-to hubs for illicit wealth from tyrants decimating their nations across the globe.

But even with all his rampaging kleptocracy, MBZ was viewed by the U.S. government as one of the rare bright spots in a fractured, destabilized region. And the president wanted to host MBZ in Washington, breaking bread with the Emirati leader as one of his final acts in office.

But MBZ begged off. His schedule simply wouldn't allow it; surely Obama would understand. Left unsaid, however, was precisely *why* MBZ had to cancel his meal with the American president. It wasn't because of any regional crisis, nor any kind of domestic priority. It was because MBZ had gotten a whiff of how the incoming Trump administration was shaping up—and because there was one man in particular MBZ wanted to meet with.

Instead of dining at the White House in late 2016, MBZ rerouted to New York City. The change in plans was supposed to be a secret, but it didn't take American intelligence agents long to track MBZ's new path. As the redirect became clear—as well as the realization that he'd stood up the American president—Obama officials later said they were "shocked at the breach of protocol."[6] But MBZ calculated that the breach was worth it—and that his new conversation partner would lead to far greater, and far richer, outcomes for everyone involved.

It was, on paper, a bizarre gamble. Rather than dine with an American president, MBZ set up a clandestine meeting with a man whose résumé was wafer-thin. If anything, the man MBZ was meeting with was known more for his stupendous failures than anything else—of driving storied media outlets into the ground, of launching disastrous real estate investments that left gaping holes on his corporate ledger. Nor was MBZ's new interlocutor any kind of regional expert or academic savant; his "scant knowledge" and "ignorance" of the Middle East would soon become an open secret of regime after regime looking to take advantage.[7]

This was the man the Emirati dictator had slipped off to see: a naïf, struggling to find his footing, struggling to find any success at all. Yet MBZ couldn't say no to his new conversation partner for one simple reason: This man had married into the family of a new political dynasty, then rising to dominate and define American politics for years to come.

His name was Jared Kushner, and he was the waifish son-in-law of Donald Trump, the billionaire developer whom American voters had just elected as president. Improbably, Kushner would be Trump's point person for helping design and drive a policy to remake the Middle East, and much more. In the process, he would also open up the doors of dictatorial financing in ways that American politicians could never have imagined—and help usher in an age of oligarchy unlike anything seen in American history.

Kushner may have previously been a regional illiterate, an empty suit masquerading as a shrewd business operator. But when he sat down with MBZ—there in the penthouse of Trump Tower, there to plot out an entire future for the Middle East and far beyond—it was clear those days were done. Thanks to his father-in-law's recent election, Kushner had become, as one journalist dubbed it, an "American oligarch."[8]

And he was not alone.

A few years later—after Trump had launched an attempted coup to try to remain in office, and after Kushner had opened a spigot to billions of dollars more from tyrants and autocrats around the world—an American businessman named Elon Musk was in "regular contact" with someone far beyond Washington: Russian dictator Vladimir Putin.[9]

The fact that Musk was habitually speaking with Putin was, in some ways, surprising. After all, Musk had spent much of the previous few years actively aiding Ukrainian forces decimating Russian troops following Moscow's expanded 2022 invasion. With his Starlink satellite systems providing up-to-the-minute communications and logistics help for Ukrainian troops, Musk's technology had proved to be one of the game-changing services helping Kyiv beat back the Russian marauders, butchering more of Moscow's troops than in any war the Kremlin had seen in nearly a century. Throughout much of 2022, Musk praised the leadership of Ukrainian President Volodymyr Zelenskyy, with the Ukrainian government publicly thanking Musk for helping in their fight to preserve Ukrainian sovereignty, Ukrainian independence, and Ukrainian democracy.

But as the war dragged on, something began to change. The shift first arose on the battlefield. Despite his gung-ho attitude in public, in private Musk had started waffling, with reporters revealing that he'd personally refused Ukrainians' request to use Starlink to assist in an assault on Russian holdings in Crimea—concerned, apparently, that Putin would resort to nuclear weapons as a result. It was the first time one of Putin's nuclear bluffs had actually worked, with Musk buckling before the Russian dictator.

Soon, Musk began letting his rhetorical mask slip as well. On X (formerly Twitter), Musk began sinking into a morass of Russian propaganda, his feed transforming from pro-Ukrainian messages to a spew of pro-Kremlin talking points and fake Russian disinformation videos. Where he'd once backed Ukrainian forces with encouragement and logistics, he now peddled Putin's favorite narratives, claiming Russia's right to chunks of Ukraine. No longer was Zelenskyy some paragon of democratic values; to Musk, the Ukrainian president was now the one pushing war.[10] Musk even began floating a supposed "peace plan" for Ukraine—one that not only allowed Russia to retain much of the land seized from Ukraine but caved to further Kremlin demands on things like Ukrainian neutrality and NATO membership, without extracting any costs from Moscow itself.[11]

For those who'd followed Musk's career, it was a sudden, bizarre whiplash. Musk had transformed in just a few short months from one of Ukraine's key private-sector allies into the biggest bullhorn the Kremlin could have hoped to find. But for those familiar with Moscow's cultivation of allies abroad, the Kremlin's effort to turn Musk into a mouthpiece wasn't necessarily surprising. "It's very clear that Elon Musk is transmitting a message for Putin," Fiona Hill, one of the West's leading Russia experts—and one of Trump's former advisers on Russia—said. "Putin plays the egos of big men, gives them a sense that they can play a role. But in reality, they're just direct transmitters of messages from Vladimir Putin." It was a pattern that, as Hill and others had observed, Putin had shown previously. As Hill continued, Putin was "basically short-circuiting the diplomatic process"—and using billionaires like Musk as his tools.[12]

This transformation was dizzying, and only raised more questions: What happened? How had Musk shifted from a pioneering entrepreneur, and even a centrist liberal, into someone indistinguishable from the pro-Kremlin trolls flooding much of social media over the past decade? How had he gone from a tycoon praising Ukrainians' bravery to saluting Russian officials dedicated to carving up a neighboring nation, and even ending liberal democracy across the West?

There was, as Hill alluded above, clearly an element of ego. But there was something else, too—something far more concerning for any and all who'd wish to see democracy and American influence spread as far as possible. It had less to do with Musk's personality, per se, and more to do with the kinds of structural forces buffeting the rest of us in the contemporary United States. It centered directly on how some of America's billionaire class had become vehicles for antidemocratic forces around the world, helping despots and tyrants sink their teeth into the U.S., upending democracy wherever they saw fit.

Because it's not just Russia; as this book will detail, Musk has opened doors to regimes elsewhere—not least places like China, as Musk has become one of the most proudly, unmistakably pro-Beijing voices in America's corporate class, proclaiming everything from the fact that Taiwan is an "integral" part of China to hawking the idea that there are "two sides" to the Chinese Communist Party's ongoing genocide of Uyghurs. On the one hand, as a supposed lodestar of "free speech," Musk's silence on Beijing's suffocating censorship regime is galling. On the other hand, perhaps it shouldn't be—not only because of Musk's accelerating dependence on Chinese finance and remaining on the Chinese dictatorship's good side, but because of his clear embodiment of a kind of authoritarian messianism that has infected much of America's leading capitalists in recent years.[13]

To be fair to Musk, he's not the only corporate titan who's kowtowed over and over again to Beijing. At Google, corporate executives plotted out how to provide censorship tools to their Chinese counterparts. At Amazon, the online retailer followed edicts out of Beijing to whitewash the Chinese regime's image. At Apple, CEO Tim Cook praised China for being "so vibrant and so dynamic"—even as Beijing snuffed out Hong Kong democracy, decimated Tibetan sovereignty, and oversaw the most sprawling concentration camp the world has seen since the Nazis.[14] And at Facebook, the company not only worked "hand-in-glove" with Chinese counterparts on additional censorship programs, but founder Mark Zuckerberg—in what can only be described as a fit of mewling obsequiousness—directly asked Chinese despot Xi Jinping to name Zuckerberg's child.[15] (Xi declined; it's unclear what Zuckerberg's wife thought of her husband's request.)

Time and time again, America's leading corporate executives—figures like Facebook's Zuckerberg, Apple's Cook, Google's Sundar Pichai, Amazon's Jeff Bezos, and others—prostrated themselves before Chinese officials. It was less an ideological move per se; few American businessmen would claim to support Xi's Leninist economics or communist cant. The motivation, instead, was purely financial. Given the scope and the scale of the Chinese market, Chinese manufacturing capacities, and access to Chinese supply chains, America's corporate executives gladly peddled whatever pro-Beijing propaganda lines they needed to. As one critic said, when Xi and the CCP asked America's leading corporate heads to jump, they would simply ask, "How high?"[16]

Nor was this always metaphorical. On a visit to San Francisco in late 2023, Cook, Blackstone CEO Stephen Schwarzman, heads of companies like Boeing, Pfizer, FedEx, and many more all gave Xi a standing ovation—even before Xi had said a single word. It was, at the time, arguably the most fawning display of pro-authoritarian sentiment America's leading industrial figures had ever displayed, at least in living memory. There, in a banquet hall in northern California, America's most prominent businessmen unleashed a thundering round of applause for a man responsible for helping keep over one billion people under the thumb of a brutal, backbreaking dictatorship—of helping prevent nearly one-fifth of humanity from enjoying any basic freedoms of speech, of assembly, of religion, and of economic opportunity. It was, for many observers of America's corporate class, a startling display of slavish subservience—and a reminder that this corporate class couldn't care one whit about airy terms like "democracy," "human rights," or "freedom."[17]

Not long later, a different reception of sorts took place. Thousands of miles away, many of those same business leaders gathered in a rotunda, there to observe what had been for centuries a relatively staid affair: the inauguration of a new president. Except, this time, there was nothing routine about the process. Rather than a new administration, observers in the rotunda were welcoming an old face who they had spent hundreds of millions of dollars helping reelect. Standing in a line, these men swayed and smiled, heads bobbing like corks in a sea of suits, applauding a man regurgitating old conspiracies and threatening to unleash a more authoritarian state than anything the country had seen in decades—and pledging to unshackle these businessmen from both democratic checks and pro-transparency oversight, so long as they truckled to his message. At that moment, whatever barriers remaining between public goods and private interests collapsed, completing a half-century-long trajectory to privatize American politics.

The man frothing about conspiracies and enemies may have been the new president. But the entire affair, there in Washington in early 2025, was something the country had never seen before. It was, as one analysis read, the "inauguration of the oligarchs."[18]

The story of the rise of American oligarchy has multiple moving parts, shadowboxing across both decades and countries. This book not only details this oligarchy's rise, but also how some of these oligarchs became the middlemen in the broader sprawling fight to destroy American stability and American influence, used by forces both domestic and foreign to try to snuff out American democracy for good. It illustrates how these oligarchs have profited every step of the way, at the expense of the rest of us—and how, in the process, they have allied with some of America's greatest adversaries.

Much of this story may seem familiar: the demise of efforts to corral the power of money in American politics, culminating in the wealthiest men the world had ever seen directly bankrolling the wealthiest president America has ever known. It's hardly news that bottomless swills of money, much of it corporate, have corrupted and corroded the machinery of American politics. Some of the details may be a bit hazy (what was *Citizens United*, anyway?), but the thrust of the U.S.'s collapse into a fetid playground for the wealthiest Americans is impossible to miss. Gone are the days when American politicians were responsive to their broader constituents, who have been replaced by political donors with the deepest pockets—all of whom have a direct line to American politicians, all the way into the White House itself.

There is another component, however, that's been missed from this story, which much of this book tries to bring to the surface. For not only has the U.S. seen a new class of corporate greed emerge, propelled by things like slashed tax rates and swelling offshore services and decimated regulatory agencies. Some of these modern American oligarchs have also, crucially, proved willing to sell themselves to whichever regime may come calling. They have now become the most important vectors for modern authoritarians both at home and abroad—far beyond what any previous class of "robber barons" ever became. All the enemies of democracy on this planet have found willing handmaidens within the current crop of America's leading corporate figures.

That, then, is what this book is about: how many of America's leading corporate heads have become allies to autocracies around the world, and in the process flung America itself ever closer to an authoritarian abyss. How a crew of men who would style themselves as contemporary Carnegies and Vanderbilts have instead become some of the most oleaginous—even anti-American—actors now bestriding the world.

I've spent years writing about how foreign regimes and foreign oligarchs have manipulated the gears of American democracy, pocketing officials and tilting policies and meddling in ways far out of sight of most Americans. I've written books about how the U.S. developed into the world's leading financial secrecy jurisdiction, towering over the Caribbean islands and South Pacific archipelagos that we traditionally associate with offshore finance, and how the explosive rise of the foreign lobbying industry in Washington has fanned the flames of dictatorships around the globe. Time and again, I've written on how these industries first emerged as servants not of foreign regimes but of wealthy Americans—and then, in the post–Cold War world, how these industries realized that there was far more money to be made succoring and serving foreign kleptocrats.

It was, needless to say, a growth industry; modern kleptocracy has continued spiraling ever upward, allowing corrupt forces around the world to use American shell companies and American lawyers and American lobbyists to loot and launder trillions of dollars, drenching the United States in their dirty money, jousting with the overmatched investigators and prosecutors trying to keep them in check. And I was, I thought, doing some good with this work—or good enough, at least, to get sanctioned by the Kremlin for all my efforts. (So much for the Russian leg of my book tour.)

But by the early 2020s, it was clear that something had reversed. Where wealthy Russians and Chinese and Saudis had once learned how to hide and launder their wealth from their American counterparts, it was now the Americans' turn to learn something from their kleptocratic clients abroad. Where oligarchs in places like Turkey or Hungary or Kazakhstan had once leaned on American businessmen for advice about which consultants or spin-men or trust providers to use, by the early 2020s the information flows started to reverse. Not that some wealthy Americans were looking to, say, Azeri or Gabonese or Emirati oligarchs for where to set up particular shell companies. Instead, they were looking to them for something more elusive: how to dismantle democracy and destroy all those pesky regulators and investigators and journalists who were trying to gain access into their finances.

How, in other words, to eliminate anything that could hem in their finances, or prevent them from growing their pots of wealth for as long as they wanted, until the sun burned out of the sky. How they could do all this without any worries about being caught out, let alone facing any blowback. How they could emulate the kinds of antidemocratic success stories seen in country after country around the world. How they could become indistinguishable from oligarchs in places like Russia and elsewhere. And how, in the process, they could make the world safe for oligarchy, in America and far beyond.

Before we dive in, a few final notes about the book you're holding. *United States of Oligarchy* is not an exhaustive, encyclopedic rundown of anyone and everyone we could consider an American oligarch. Some figures flit in and out, such as Bezos and Pichai, while others, like Musk and Kushner, play far more starring roles. The book itself is generally chronological, tracing the origins of things like anti-corruption and anti-oligarchic efforts in the U.S., outlining the playbooks of some of the American oligarchs' greatest successes, and unearthing the subterranean links between certain American oligarchs and their foreign allies and their joint assaults on democracy in the U.S.

There are historical, economic, and ideological detours throughout this book; geographic swings through places like pre-American Hawaii and (pre-American?) Greenland; characters simultaneously farcical and formidable; and even a dispatch from a bizarre, boozy afternoon in a Moldovan wine cellar, when I was surrounded on all sides by far-right religious fundamentalists presenting the greatest bridge between Russian and American oligarchs. At its core is a search for a grand unified theory of how oligarchs both foreign and domestic began to work in tandem to dismantle American democracy. The book does not revolve around a single character, but rather a single story: how oligarchic forces in the U.S., aided by dictatorships abroad, are attempting to mount an antidemocratic assault on the U.S. like we've never seen before, trying to destroy the last, best bulwark against not only oligarchy but tyranny itself.

Welcome, then, to the *United States of Oligarchy*. Let's dive in, while we still can.

Section I

Capital

[There] is a natural inclination in mankind to Kingly Government. It sometimes relieves them from Aristocratic domination. They had rather have one tyrant than five hundred. It gives more of the appearance of equality among Citizens, and that they like.

—BENJAMIN FRANKLIN[1]

1

A Terrible Word

Power has to be handed over to our children; if not, our graves will be dug up later on.

—*Chen Yun*[1]

It's a slippery term, "oligarchy."

The root of the word itself is easy enough to identify. Combining the Greek roots of *oligoi* (few) and *arkhein* (rule), oligarchy means, quite literally, "the rule of the few."[2] In that sense, it should be easy to identify an oligarch, or even an oligarchy itself. Any polity—any nation, any country, any empire—in which a handful of individuals oversee political decisions and strategic policy is, then, an oligarchy. And those few steering the ship of state are, by definition, the oligarchs.

But even from the term's inception, thousands of years ago, the definition has been a contested one. After all, what comprises a "few"? Three? Five? More? Is that measurement static, or can it grow as a nation expands? Does the same definition hold for a place like ancient Athens, with its population of only a few hundred thousand, and modern America, with a population of hundreds of millions? And who defines what it means to "rule," anyway? Is it an official position? Can a president, a sultan, or a shah be an oligarch? Can a member of Congress, or someone who isn't even in office? Do those few who rule have to have the same amounts of sway, or the same antipathy toward democracy, or the same playbooks for clinging to power? And who's supposed to be in charge of all these definitions?

Needless to say, these are all impossible questions to answer.

There's no body dedicated to defining oligarchs or oligarchy. There's no firm threshold a businessman, a rising official, or a regime higher-up passes to become an oligarch; there's no technical point at which a democracy transitions into oligarchy. Oligarchy is, in a sense, in the eye of the beholder. To swipe a phrase about another contested term, you may have trouble defining "oligarchy," but odds are you know it when you see it.[3]

Much of that confused, blurred definition rests on the shoulders of one man: Aristotle, the ancient Greek philosopher who first popularized the term. Rather than simply leave "oligarchy" with its literal definition, Aristotle expanded the meaning.[4] Surveying the ruling class in Athens, Aristotle decided that the literal definition of oligarchy was too pat. To the philosopher, oligarchy was something more, beyond mere numbers and power. It was better understood as a system in which "men of property have the government in their hands."[5]

Notice the shift. It was no longer about the mere number of men in charge but about what those in control of a government *owned*. And even that wasn't sufficient for Aristotle. Oligarchy, overseen by this propertied ruling class, didn't exist in a vacuum. As Aristotle saw it, you could also define oligarchy by what it *wasn't*. To Aristotle, the antithesis of oligarchy was clear: democracy. As the philosopher continued, "Democracy [is] the opposite, when the indigent, and not the men of property, are the rulers."[6]

And yet, even then, Aristotle wasn't finished.[7] He concluded that it wasn't simply the number of rulers, or the acreage of property ownership, that defines an oligarchy. Rather, it was *wealth*—the amount of wealth associated with the oligarchs in question, and how that wealth can convince a group of oligarchs of their right to rule, solely because of the size of their pocketbooks. As Aristotle concluded, "Wherever men rule by reason of their wealth, whether they be few or many, that is an oligarchy."[8] Numbers, positions, even regime type—none of that necessarily mattered. Oligarchy was the rule of the *wealthiest*—and of those who see their wealth as reason enough for their rule.

It is a definition that, for the purposes of this book, we can utilize. States produce oligarchs and become oligarchies when their most affluent citizens reign, and when those residents are convinced that their wealth gives them the right to steer any nation, any country, any empire. An oligarchy emerges when the wealthiest control the levers of power not out of patriotism, or capacity, or intelligence—but because, in their eyes, their wealth alone rationalizes their rule. It is only wealth that matters, at least to these oligarchic forces. Let him who leads the race to the largest fortune also lead his nation.

Such is the logic Aristotle outlined thousands of years ago. Such is the logic that still dictates oligarchies around the world—including in the United States of America.

For such a contested, nebulous—yet still widely used—concept, there has been surprisingly little scholarship on oligarchy as a phenomenon, or on oligarchs as a type. Whereas other contentious terms like "democracy," "dictatorship," and "fascism" have all seen an abundance of analyses, books, conferences, and more in recent decades, the term "oligarch" itself has been something of an overlooked stepchild, huddled in the corner, waiting for just a bit of attention.

It's not as if there haven't been blazingly obvious forms of oligarchy throughout recorded history. In Aristotle's time, neighboring Sparta boasted a governing council of a few dozen individuals responsible for public policy—a clear sign of oligarchy for the philosopher. (As *Teen Vogue* noted, "One of history's most famous oligarchies was Sparta. . . . While it had two kings, real power arguably lay with the 'few' (*oligoi*)—a council of 28 aristocratic men over the age of 60 who shaped policy. . . . Citizen assemblies offered only a symbolic check to their power.")[9] And oligarchies abound in far more recent history. If you pick a one-party state or military junta, you're all but guaranteed to find an oligarchy. Mussolini's Italy, Pinochet's Chile, Castro's Cuba, Khamenei's Iran—all of them have presented forms of oligarchy, in which a ruling clique takes over a state, gathering as much wealth as it can for itself along the way. The enrichment at the heart of oligarchy overlaps neatly with kleptocracy, in which a ruling elite is dedicated to pillaging a society. Indeed, if you have a kleptocracy, you almost certainly have an oligarchy as well.

Odds are, if you've heard of the term "oligarchy" before, you associate it with places like Russia and other states that emerged from the

Soviet collapse. And you'd be right; the shattering of the Soviet Union bequeathed a range of new oligarchies, from Uzbekistan to Azerbaijan to, yes, Russia, in which rising oligarchs snatched up the state's crown jewels and watched their wealth blast into the stratosphere. Moscow's oligarchs may have been the most notorious of the bunch, but they weren't alone. Modern authoritarians around the world, from Viktor Orbán in Hungary to Recep Erdoğan in Turkey, now oversee their own oligarchies, as did Nicolás Maduro in Venezuela and Bashar al-Assad in Syria, with a wealthy elite capturing ever more power and ever more riches. Popular fiction is also littered with examples of oligarchies. George Orwell's *1984* introduces an "oligarchical collectivism" that stamps out democracy wherever and however it can.[10] Even Gotham City boasts its own oligarchy: the shadowy elite society of the Court of Owls, which secretly thwarts Batman at every turn.[11]

There is, in reality, a litany of examples of oligarchy all around us, scattered through history, saturating films and books, swirling the modern world. Yet despite oligarchies' prominence, you can count the scholars who've focused on oligarchy on one hand.

One of the few is Jeffrey Winters, who's carved out a career as an expert in oligarchy long before the term ever gained wide usage to describe contemporary American politics. Now the head of Northwestern University's Equality Development and Globalization Studies program, Winters has been the unofficial doyen of oligarch studies for years. And with good reason. Winters's 2011 book—titled, simply, *Oligarchy*—is still considered the go-to tract for sketching out the histories and shifting definitions of oligarchy in America and elsewhere. Drenched in details of everything from Suharto's decades-long dictatorship in Indonesia to the minutiae of intra-elite fighting in second-century Rome, the book is a sweeping, dense read. It is also the single best book that has ever been written on the topic of oligarchy.[12]

"I was going to write a book about oligarchs in Indonesia—that was the starting point," Winters told me, revisiting the birth of *Oligarchy*. "The first thing an academic does is ask, 'What does the literature say? What's the lay of the land?' I looked into it—and it was a mess. There was very little there."[13]

Much of that mess stemmed from just how to define "oligarchy" in the first place. "Oligarchy ranks among the most widely used yet poorly theorized concepts in the social sciences," he writes, pointing to other political scientists who've generously described the term as a "muddle" or "underspecified." Indeed, Winters admits that if you take oligarchy at its broadest definition, in which those in government are property owners, you risk watching the term crumble into meaninglessness, given that such a definition can describe so many governments around the world, both historic and contemporary. "The meaning of oligarchy is so incoherent that almost any political system or community that falls short of full and constant participation by its members arguably displays oligarchical tendencies," Winters writes. And he's right, both in his descriptions and his conclusion.[14] If a term can describe everything, then it describes nothing—hence why so many political scientists, for so long, have scratched their heads at oligarchy, preferring to work on other topics instead.[15]

Winters, though, wasn't satisfied with this befuddlement. Where others had looked at the term's etymology—its literal definition as the "rule of the few"—and tossed up their hands, Winters has attempted to provide some organization, some structure, to what oligarchy actually *is.* Instead of trying to reinvent anything, Winters points directly back to Aristotle's conclusion: that oligarchy is not about numbers, but about *wealth.* "'Rule by the few' simply will not do," Winters writes. "More than anything else, it is the conceptual drift away from this fundamental wealth-oligarch nexus that is the source of the chronic muddle."[16]

Put simply: It's about the money, and the towering amounts of wealth that those in power control. "Massive wealth in the hands of a small minority creates significant power advantages in the political realm," Winters adds. "Claiming otherwise ignores centuries of political analysis exploring the intimate association between wealth and power." Forget all this distracting claptrap about how many people are actually ruling, or how many people it takes to make up an oligarchy. If you live in a nation ruled by the *wealthiest,* then you live in an oligarchy, full stop.[17]

There's one further note that Winters highlighted when I spoke to him. As he pointed out, it doesn't matter where all that money at the highest rungs of power originally comes from. It could be through legitimate business, from selling computers to creating new social media platforms. It could be via wildly illegal means, from drug-running to human trafficking. It could be a mix, or it could be something else completely. The sources are irrelevant.

At least, that was the consensus for thousands of years. And then, in the early 1990s, American media began describing the wealthiest bankers and industrialists and financiers burbling around the former Soviet Union—the kinds rising to power in places like Russia, Kyrgyzstan, Ukraine, and elsewhere—as oligarchs. Not wrong, per se. But there was a pejorative slant to it: that these men were oligarchs not simply because of their wealth but because of how they'd corrupted the state and bilked populations, all for their personal profit. Their wealth all came with a whiff of illegitimacy, with an air of criminality to it.

As such, these men weren't tycoons, like those figures Americans knew during the Gilded Age. And they certainly weren't entrepreneurs or moguls, as America's wealthiest now posed.

They were something different. They were, the American media sniffed, *oligarchs*.

It was a bizarre mangling of what "oligarchy" actually meant. "The U.S. media was willing to use the word 'oligarch' when it came to Russians and Ukrainians, but went out of their way not to use it in the U.S. context," Winters told me. "And the question was, 'Why?' The short answer is that in the U.S., the term 'oligarch' got redefined as someone engaged in politics but who got rich illegally. . . . If you were wealthy, and even if you were engaged politically in the U.S., but your fortune was not the result of a crime, you would not be called an oligarch."[18] (As a pair of rotund businessmen said in a *New Yorker* cartoon, "'Oligarch'—terrible word, we'll need a new one.")[19]

It was all a strange swerve, as if "oligarchy" had taken on a new meaning completely. And it was a shift that confused an entire generation of Americans (and others) about what oligarchy truly was, and even where oligarchy could be found.[20] As one student told a bemused Winters, Russia might have oligarchs, but the U.S. merely had rich people.

But a quarter of the way into the twenty-first century, it's clear that that definitional detour has now ended. Oligarchy is once more understood the way Aristotle laid out thousands of years ago: as the rule of the wealthiest, regardless of where their funds came from. Including here, in the United States.

You might assume that oligarchs thrive best under antidemocratic regimes, under autocracies or juntas where a regime can prevent the huddled masses from limiting the oligarchs' wealth. And it's true that despotic regimes around the world, from Russia to North Korea to Cuba and beyond, have their own rosters of oligarchs.[21]

But as Winters details, oligarchs can also thrive in democracies themselves. For modern audiences, this may be self-evident. (Just look at Trump's 2025 inauguration, for instance.) But such a claim butts up against one of the key tenets of democratic theory: that voters are ultimately self-interested, especially when it comes to matters of personal economy. In other words, in modern democracies, why wouldn't voters simply vote for policies that could attenuate the power of modern oligarchs? Why wouldn't they choose policies that eliminate the oligarchs' wealth and power?

It's a question that—because of the way in which oligarchy as a phenomenon has itself been so long ignored—remains both under-discussed and under-theorized. It also points to a gaping hole in not only our understanding of democratic processes and democratic transitions but in everything from international relations to political science itself. These democratic oligarchies—"civil oligarchies," as Winters dubs them—carry all the basic elements of democracy: rule of law, property rights, free and fair elections, and the like. There are no warlords marauding across charred landscapes, no clans carving up entire regions, no sultans or shahs or kings acting as the mediator for rival businessmen. There are, at least outwardly, all the trappings of the kind of democratic policies that advocates and activists have long called for.[22]

And yet, even within the confines of these democracies, oligarchs rise. They don't necessarily rule, at least formally—but then again, they don't have to. So long as the democratic state provides the "strong and impersonal system of law" that oligarchs need to protect the wealth they have procured, they are happy to let the machinery of democracy chug along. It's not that these oligarchs are anti-democracy, necessarily; if anything, they're "indifferent to democracy," Winters concludes. "They neither require it to function nor are they seriously threatened by its existence." So long as voters and elected policymakers keep their hands off the oligarchs' wealth, they're happy to have democracy flourish, and even spread.[23]

But should voters begin making a move toward reclaiming some of the wealth the oligarchs have pocketed, such an arrangement suddenly risks falling apart, transforming a "civil oligarchy" into something different, and far worse. Should a population suddenly vote for, say, increased taxes on the oligarchs, or increased investigations into how and where these oligarchs are hiding their money, those same oligarchs would have no problem seizing a country's democracy by the throat, strangling it until it goes their way. As the oligarchs would say: It's a nice democracy you have there. Would be a shame if something happened to it.

Nor do these oligarchs have to rely on their own resources. Should a population rise up to reclaim the wealth the oligarchs have spent years hoarding, the oligarchs themselves can turn not only to the powers of their own state to crack down on the hoi polloi, but can even turn to other oligarchies for help. As Winters writes, this is a pattern—oligarchies aiding oligarchies, regardless of which state they're from—that traces back to antiquity, even among sworn enemies. "In the highly unlikely event that [Athenian citizens] were tempted to turn their weapons and overwhelming numbers as voters against [Athenian oligarchs], the oligarchs of Athens could, as a last resort, threaten to call for assistance from neighboring oligarchies, especially at Sparta."[24] Or as scholar John McCormick wrote, "Unless formally restrained, the richest citizens tended to use their power and privilege to . . . [subvert] republican governments, maneuvering them in more narrowly oligarchic or autocratic directions, even, on occasion, going so far as to deliver them to foreign powers."[25]

Oligarchic interests, in other words, would always trump national interests—a pattern that has come roaring back to relevance in the twenty-first century.

Of course, this is all theoretical—theoretical models, theoretical states, theoretical oligarchs. In order to fully digest some of Winters's conclusions, it's worth tracking not only the rise of the modern oligarchic class in the U.S. but how Americans have understood such a relationship between mass democracy and mass wealth throughout history. Because this is hardly a new discussion, or a new phenomenon. If anything, it's an update on a much older, and much more fundamental, fracture line in American politics, going all the way back to the country's creation.

The Founding Fathers themselves wrestled with these contradictions: of democracy, of oligarchy, of how to prevent a teeming populace from simply voting to seize the wealthiest Americans' assets. As James Madison worried, too much democracy could present "turbulence and contention," leading to a system "incompatible with personal security or the rights of property."[26] But the Founders were just as concerned with how to prevent those wealthiest individuals from simply dominating the new United States, and from transforming the U.S. into yet another oligarchic aristocracy—the kind that American revolutionaries rose up against in London.

It was a concern that motivated many of the leading American politicians and intellectuals. The Founders "feared a . . . source of power that could damage their grand experiment in popular government: extraordinarily rich Americans whose aims did not align with democracy," scholar George Thomas noted.[27] One early American official, Gouverneur Morris, worried that "the schemes of the rich" would take advantage of the passions of the people, resulting in "a violent aristocracy, or a more violent despotism." As Morris described, oligarchic wealth "tends to corrupt the mind and to nourish its love of power, and to stimulate it to oppression."[28] Oligarchy, in other words, was just as dangerous as any other form of tyranny. Another early American thinker, Noah Webster, concurred, pointing out that "when wealthy people centralize power, 'liberty expires' and republican government tends toward oligarchy."[29]

Despite the fact that many of America's Founders boasted their own towering wealth—much of it held in the form of enslaved humans—early policymakers were directly motivated to prevent the rise of an American oligarchy. Thomas Jefferson led efforts to ban practices like primogeniture (in which the eldest son inherits an entire estate) and entail (in which a specific child receives the family's entire property portfolio). Because "this enormous inequality produc[ed] so much misery to the bulk of mankind, legislators cannot invent too many devices for subdividing property," Jefferson wrote.[30] As Jefferson saw it, he and his colleagues were not only creating a new republic but attempting the wholesale elimination of "aristocracy founded on wealth," at least in the U.S.[31] Jefferson's strategy echoed Winters's recommendation centuries later: that if you want to rid a society of its oligarchs, you must eliminate extreme wealth inequality, and cut the oligarchs' fortunes down to size. "If extreme personal wealth is impossible or absent," Winters writes, "oligarchs are also absent."[32]

It was a push that, at least initially, bore considerable fruit in America's first decades. Topics like wealth inequality and concerns about the rise of an oligarchic class were never far from early American political discourse; indeed, much of the rise of Jacksonian populism, which launched Andrew Jackson to power—and launched the U.S.'s greatest ethnic cleansing campaigns, aimed at massive land theft from multiple Indigenous nations—centered directly on some of these topics. And on the whole, these anti-inequality reforms proved wildly successful, at least for the white male Americans comprising the American voting class. In his *Democracy in America*, Alexis de Tocqueville wrote that the elimination of things like primogeniture and entail had "unleashed a democratic 'revolution' in property, society, and government: It was a powerful means of tempering extreme or violent tendencies arising from equality of conditions and universal suffrage. . . . Extending the transmission and circulation of property to the lower classes provided the vital check and balance: It was the first precondition of democratic stability."[33]

It's no surprise, then, that as the country barreled toward the middle of the nineteenth century, the U.S.'s key political fractures circled around not just expansionism and slavery, but access to and ownership of land itself—and the kinds of labor practices such land could host. It's a truism to say that the American Civil War was "about slavery"; the Confederate secessionists said as much, blaring their desires to protect slavery in their own founding documents. But the U.S. Civil War was also about everything from access to the American West, and who would control the spoils of the land recently seized from Mexico, to the broader economic model of the United States moving forward—of who could own property, and who couldn't, and what that said about the future of the country itself.

Indeed, it was these topics, rather than any kind of humanitarian concerns about the rights of enslaved people, that drove broad swaths of small-scale farmers, business owners, manual laborers, ranchers, and others across the United States to enlist in the fight against treasonous Confederates. (It's also why, especially in places like eastern Tennessee and northern Alabama, you saw such an upswell of relatively poor white Southerners—those who'd watched slaveowners dominate the states and drive down labor costs through mass enslavement—remain loyal to the Union.) For analysts like Heather Cox Richardson, such a framing highlights the fact that in the Civil War, "The struggle between the free North and the slaveholding South was essentially a struggle between people and property"—between the broad masses of (white, male) laborers across much of the country, propelling Abraham Lincoln to the White House, and the (white, male) oligarchic classes responsible for execrable horrors against millions of Black Americans.[34]

It's a framing that politicians of the time recognized. A few years before war finally broke out, Massachusetts Senator Charles Sumner unleashed arguably the most important broadside against American oligarchy of anyone in the entire nineteenth century, targeting the slave-owning class that not only dominated American politics but threatened to eliminate any prohibitions on slavery throughout the country. Outlining the promise of the new Republican Party, founded only in 1854, Sumner railed against the "slave oligarchy" trying to make the entirety of North America—and potentially far more—safe for slavery.[35] "All who seek purity in the National Government must unite in this purpose," Sumner thundered, "for only by the overthrow of this corrupt oligarchy, which, beginning in the denial of all human rights, necessarily shows itself in barbarism and corruption of all kinds, can a better order of things prevail." For Sumner, the rise of an "Oligarchical Combination of slave masters, unknown to the Constitution, never anticipated by its founders, and existing in defiance of their example, has entered into and possessed the National Government, like an Evil Spirit."[36]

Sumner may have been too fawning of the Founders; after all, they'd authored a Constitution that went out of its way to favor slaveholders. But Sumner was ultimately correct when he proclaimed that "this Oligarchy" had seized "all the great posts of the Republic—the Presidency, the Vice-Presidency, seats in the Cabinet, seats in the Supreme Court"—positions that "seem to have been almost perpetually in their hands." As Sumner analyzed, "There is nothing in the National Government which the Oligarchy does not appropriate."[37] All of which left only one solution: overthrowing the oligarchy, with whatever tools stood available. If that meant basic political processes, fine. But if that meant war, so be it.

A few years would pass until Sumner had his result—and got his wish. After four years of rampaging warfare, the traitorous "Oligarchy"—a Confederacy that tried to splinter the U.S., leading to the unnecessary deaths of hundreds of thousands of Americans, all in pursuit of retaining and expanding both its wealth and the unspeakable crimes committed against Black Americans—stood defeated. It was a defeat that Sumner, and his anti-oligarchic allies, had foreseen. "Prostrated, exposed, and permanently expelled from ill-gotten power, the Oligarchy will soon cease to exist as a political combination," Sumner said before the war's outset. "Its final doom may be postponed, but it is certain. Languishing, it may live yet longer; but it will surely die."[38]

In the heady aftermath of the Civil War, with America left whole, free, and (largely) at peace, it was an understandable sentiment. The "Oligarchy" had died.

But it would rise again.

There have been reams of pages, hundreds of books, hagiographic biopics, and at least one glittering, high-budget television series dedicated to the era of American history we know as the Gilded Age. It was an era of conspicuous consumption: of marble mansions and long-tail tuxedos, of luxurious weddings and lavish parties, of private interests crashing into politics and making a mockery of things like democracy and transparency. It was an era of wild economic swings: of gold market manipulations leading to the original Great Depression in 1873, and of mismanaged monetary policy leading to a similar recession twenty years later. It was also an era that birthed the original political corruption scandals: of railroad barons using fake companies to cloak bribes to congressmen, stiffing American taxpayers and scarring the American landscape with railroad trunks neither used nor useful. It was, as historian Charles Calhoun has written, a "time of spectacular excess, of brass-knuckled business and shady politics, a long national carnival of fraud and bribery."[39]

It was also an era, despite the supposed defeat of the "Oligarchy" during the Civil War, of yawning wealth inequality, with the bottom lines of the country's wealthiest climbing ever higher. Roiling labor unrest and growing inflows of new immigrants, the accelerating rollbacks of basic civil rights, the capture of governmental organs by entrenched industrial interests—all of these defined the Gilded Age, all while a new kind of nouveau riche American elite swaggered over the entire era.

And what an elite it was. If there is a legacy of the Gilded Age that remains—and is ever more relevant in modern America—it is the gluttonous rise of a small group of men, many of whom have names familiar over a century later. These men all emerged from different trajectories. Some, like Andrew Carnegie, slung themselves out of impoverished childhoods, climbing to the top of the steel industry and far beyond. Others, like John D. Rockefeller, made a fortune in oil extraction—and perfected the art of corporate conglomerations that could hoover up much of the industry, benefiting him and him alone. Some even rose without any clear, distinct set of skills, such as the venal Jay Gould, a man largely responsible for the 1873 depression, collapsing an entire country's fortunes in the process—even while Gould himself died a spectacularly wealthy man.[40]

They were men known, colloquially, as the "robber barons." They favored other titles—"tycoons" was a preferred term of art, though they'd also settle for "captains of industry." But to modern eyes, it's clear that these men were something far more familiar: oligarchs.

Just look at how much these men owned and controlled. Cornelius Vanderbilt—a man who infamously boasted that the law had no influence on his "power"—was worth approximately $3 billion in modern dollars.[41] Carnegie—a man whose cheery public face helped mask his fierce anti-labor violence—was worth about $10 billion.[42] Rockefeller—whose backroom corporate restructurings decimated local economies and created arguably America's first monopoly—was the wealthiest of the bunch, at about $30 billion.[43]

Their portfolio was stupefying. The wealthiest 1 percent of the Gilded Age owned over *half* of all American property—compared with the bottom 44 percent of Americans at the time, who cumulatively owned only 1 percent of all American wealth.[44] Or if you want to slice it even further: by the end of the Gilded Age, the top 0.00001 percent of America's wealthiest—a handful of families like the Rockefellers, the Carnegies, and a few others—owned nearly 1 percent of the U.S.'s total wealth on their own.[45] Or broaden it back out, and you'll find that the wealthiest four thousand families of America's Gilded Age owned as much wealth as all other American families *combined*.[46] All this only a few decades after the Civil War had supposedly poleaxed America's oligarchy, killing it off once and for all.

Any way you look at it, the conclusion is inescapable: By the end of the nineteenth century, an American oligarchy had risen yet again. And they controlled the country in the gaudiest, most conspicuous, and most laughably corrupt ways imaginable: buying judges, bribing politicians, bankrolling anyone and everyone they needed to pile their wealth ever higher. It's no wonder that it's this era, and this agglomeration of "robber barons," that modern America is most often compared to.

That comparison is apt. But there are two key differences between those original oligarchs and their modern equivalents. First, America's current oligarchs make those Gilded Age fortunes look like a relative pittance. For as wealthy as the Carnegies and Vanderbilts were, their affluence still pales in comparison with figures like Musk and Bezos, who are each worth magnitudes more than their Gilded Age predecessors. Moreover, for as much as those robber barons steered American policy, they never called the White House itself home—a reality that figures like the Trumps and the Kushners would later enjoy, and profit immeasurably from.

Second, for as many faults and crimes as there are associated with the robber barons, they never outright allied with American adversaries. They never grew financially reliant on the doddering Spanish Empire, or opened doors for the kaiser's regime in Germany. Perhaps more important, there was at least a clear sense of noblesse oblige behind much of the Gilded Age oligarchs' later work. Figures like Vanderbilt, Leland Stanford, and William Marsh Rice left substantial parts of their fortunes to educational institutions, creating some of America's greatest universities in their name. Andrew Carnegie called not only for his fellow oligarchs to give away nearly all their gains to libraries, foundations, and hospitals, but for the state to actively step in to distribute any wealth remaining, especially via substantial estate taxes. "By taxing estates heavily at death, the state marks its condemnation of the selfish millionaire's unworthy life," Carnegie wrote in 1889. "The man who dies thus rich dies disgraced."[47] Or as Carnegie wrote in a private note to himself, "The amassing of wealth is one of the worst species of idolatry. No idol more debasing than the worship of money."[48]

It's difficult to imagine any contemporary American oligarch offering anything similar. But it's worth holding on to the precedent of these robber barons as this book proceeds. Not simply because their titanic wealth is the only thing we can compare to their modern variants, but because there was another group of American oligarchs, far from the Carnegies and Vanderbilts and Stanfords, who are often overlooked as key players in the rank rapaciousness of the Gilded Age. And it was this oft-forgotten group, thousands of miles from the shores of mainland America, who were arguably responsible for far more reprehensible acts than anything those more well-known robber barons ever participated in—and who set a far closer precedent for what some of America's modern oligarchs are now trying to do in the U.S., and far beyond.

2
Reign of Terror

If a big wave comes in, large fishes will come from the dark ocean which you never saw before, and when they see the small fishes they will eat them up.

—David Malo[1]

Sanford Dole is a name few would remember or recognize. A long-limbed, hatchet-faced man whose beard scraped his sternum, giving him the appearance of a mossy oak come to life, Dole was relatively unknown during the Gilded Age through which he lived, at least to most Americans. He was viewed by his friends as a quiet, thoughtful scholar, a man who always had his oblong nose tucked in a law book. He preferred comity to controversy, and never professed to having any enemies or rivals. or even adversaries. A poet and a legal expert, fully loyal to both his wife and his broader family, Dole was, in many ways, the epitome of an American gentleman of the era.[2]

And yet, underneath these trappings of manners and erudition, there was another side of Dole's personality that burned. A side that came through less in what he said, and more in how he acted—less in what he claimed, and more in what he actually did. In reading through both Dole's memoirs and the lone biography written about the man, it's clear that Dole never let a public mask of decorum and decency slip, even in private communiqués. Yet it's also clear that he was largely responsible for one of the greatest American crimes of the nineteenth century. Dole may not be remembered as anything or anyone in mainland America, but in Hawaii, they know his name. After all, how could they could forget the oligarch who gifted the Hawaiian islands to America, snuffing out Hawaiian independence forevermore, all for the sake of entrenched oligarchic interests in both Honolulu and Washington?

The seizure and desecration of Hawaii, part of America's broader imperialism in the Pacific, is a saga that is rarely included in the wider story of the American Gilded Age. But the two are inseparable: two complementary halves, each helping define the era. And those halves can be found in the person of Dole—a man who was himself split, claiming he was raised on "Hawaiian milk" but who nonetheless acted for the interests of his "American blood," and of the oligarchy he led.[3]

Dole himself descended from the earliest Americans who settled in the Hawaiian islands, those who arrived in the early nineteenth century not to cultivate crops but to cultivate souls. Landing in Hawaii as missionaries, sent in the service of both God and the U.S., this group of American settlers included Dole's father, a stern, puritanical man who saw Hawaii as a land of heathens just waiting for the guiding hand of Christian Americans. In many ways, as historian Stephen Hahn writes, it was in Hawaii that "Americans first act[ed] on the belief that they had a mission to transform foreign societies . . . reason[ing] that Christianity could hardly take root among people in thrall to illiteracy, superstition, pagan taboos, and feudal bondage."[4] This was a mission to which Dole's father, and eventually Dole himself, fully subscribed, viewing the island chain as little more than another potential jewel for America's imperial crown.

It didn't take long for the missionaries to make an impact, though not necessarily for the reasons they had anticipated. Within a few decades of their arrival, these Americans had already seen the population of native Hawaiians—those who'd called the island chain home for over a millennium—nose-dive, thanks almost entirely to a raft of diseases the new visitors brought. Smallpox, syphilis, measles: They all devastated the Indigenous Hawaiian population. Where there had been hundreds of thousands of Hawaiians at the end of the eighteenth century, a century later that population had plummeted by over 80 percent, in some places leaving swaths of the land abandoned entirely. It was, one analysis read, "an astonishing collapse."[5]

But what a boon that collapse was for the American settlers. Where ethnic Hawaiians had once tended the most fertile fields and quays across Hawaii, with towns and cities dotting every one of the major islands, those lands and harbors now stood open and available to all comers. Just as the early American colonialists viewed the openness and accessibility of North America as a supposed gift from heaven—instead of the result of their old-world diseases that, in addition to genocidal warfare, emptied many of the most productive parts of the new lands—the Americans swarming Hawaii throughout the nineteenth century saw the islands as a sign of God's grace, of His approval of their higher mission. Snapping up vast tracts of land from the reeling native Hawaiians, as historian Julia Flynn Siler writes, the Americans plowed under the small-scale taro farms and fish ponds Hawaiians had nurtured for generations, replacing them with commercial crops.[6]

The Americans focused on one crop in particular: sugar. Introducing sugar plantations—and all the brutal labor conditions that came with them—in the 1830s, Americans quickly made Hawaii into the center not only of Pacific sugar cultivation, but of global sugar supply. The explosive growth quickly shifted Hawaii into a monoculture economy, dependent not only on sugar exports but on the American plantation owners expanding their Hawaiian holdings. Developments elsewhere—including the U.S. Civil War, which cut off the sugar supply in the American South and made the U.S. that much more dependent on Hawaiian sugar as a result—only strengthened the plantation owners' grip on the islands. "The sugar boom, plus the assurance of secure property rights, produced a frenzy of land purchases," historian Warren Zimmermann found, meaning that "by the later years of the [nineteenth] century whites owned four times more acreage than native Hawaiians."[7]

For native Hawaiians, the changes—the population decimation, the rise of the American sugar barons, the complete makeover of the Hawaiian economy—were clearly disastrous. There was, however, one saving grace: Despite the economic stranglehold the Americans now had on the islands, Hawaii's politics still remained in Hawaiian hands. With the government overseen by a series of Hawaiian kings, native Hawaiians still retained some say, some sway, in their country's future. Not that Americans hadn't tried to change that before; all the way back in the 1850s, the U.S. had tried to annex the islands, with "several U.S. warships off Honolulu . . . set[ting] an example of gunboat diplomacy on behalf of American expansion."[8] Still, thanks to savvy Hawaiian diplomats, the kingdom managed to retain its sovereignty, sustaining an independence acknowledged the world over. As scholar Lorenz Gonschor told me, Hawaiian independence was recognized by dozens of nations around the world, from the U.S. and Spain to Thailand and Fiji.[9]

By the late nineteenth century, however, American policymakers chafed against Hawaii's independence once more. The key tool they used to begin suffocating Hawaiian sovereignty: tariffs. In Washington, American authorities threatened to slap crippling duties on Hawaii's sugar industry if the Hawaiian government didn't cede parts of its sovereignty, including control of Pearl Harbor, to the U.S. Hawaii's king was boxed in; with wealthy Americans gripping Hawaii's economy by the throat, the Hawaiian government had little choice but to accede to Washington's demand—to appease an imperial power still huffing the imperialist drug of "manifest destiny."[10]

Yet the Americans didn't stop there. In 1887, a group of American sugar barons—those who were now far and away the wealthiest residents of Hawaii—oversaw the creation of a new militia, an armed wing of the all-white social club known as the Hawaiian League. Cornering King Kalākaua, the American militia leaders threatened to assassinate him if he didn't agree to reform his country's constitution, stripping native Hawaiians of both voting and property rights and cementing "white rule in the islands."[11]

Aghast at the putsch, the king cast about for allies and aid. But with the native population in shambles and with the American oligarchs backed by Washington, his hands were tied. As a result, the militia "rammed through a white supremacy constitution," entrenching the sugar barons' rule, gutting the remaining Hawaiian voting rights in the process, and making a mockery of anything like native Hawaiians' political rights.[12] It was, for all intents and purposes, a coup at the point of a bayonet—with the result called, unsurprisingly, the Bayonet Constitution.[13] As Zimmermann, in his unrivaled history of America's Pacific expansion, writes, "In the end a determined drive for power by a local American minority—seeking profits from sugar, relying on Mammon as well as on God," had succeeded in overthrowing Hawaiian sovereignty, with the Americans "threaten[ing] the human rights of the native people by amassing political power at their expense."[14]

And at their head on this white supremacist putsch was one man: Dole, who had himself cofounded the paramilitary Hawaiian League, and who viewed control of Hawaii as his "birthright."[15] As Dole saw it, he was simply ensuring "democracy" on the island chain, ensuring the property rights of his fellow oligarchs, who had been threatened by the political rights of native Hawaiians. Stripping the Hawaiian king of any political power, Dole and his oligarchic allies placed control largely in their own hands. It was head-spinning for the remaining Hawaiians, who watched their country stripped bare by a small group of Americans—all of whom towered in wealth, and all of whom saw Hawaii as something that should be theirs, and theirs alone. By a group, in other words, of American oligarchs.[16]

Yet all was not lost. Thankfully for native Hawaiians, there was one person who saw these Americans for precisely what they were—and for what they wanted.

Lydia Kamakaʻeha never thought she would ascend to the top of Hawaii's politics. Born in 1838 on the island of Oahu, Kamakaʻeha took an early liking not to her native country's internal politics, but to both writing and musical composition. "Aloha ʻOe," possibly Hawaii's most famous song, came from her pen, as did plenty of other songs now considered part of Hawaii's musical pantheon. Even today, she's considered arguably Hawaii's greatest composer.[17]

But Hawaii's political turbulence and the rising power of the American sugar barons were never far from her mind. Not only because it was increasingly obvious how the Americans were strangling Hawaiian sovereignty but because, in 1874, Hawaii held its first elections for a constitutional monarch, with the legislature electing her brother Kalākaua as king. As his closest relative, Kamakaʻeha automatically became her brother's designated heir—and, as such, changed her name to Lili'uokalani, the name with which she's best remembered to this day.[18]

Initially, Lili'uokalani performed many of the rote duties as a court functionary, from glad-handing constituents to traveling throughout the islands to check on local investments. Serving as regent while her brother traveled abroad—and even traveling herself to events like the Golden Jubilee of Queen Victoria in London—gave her a close look not only at how the sugar barons dominated Hawaii's economy but also how Hawaii fit within the broader world of nations. And then, while traveling in 1887, she learned of the Bayonet Constitution that had suddenly threatened that independence, setting off a transformation in Lili'uokalani herself, one the sugar barons never anticipated.[19]

Returning to Hawaii, Lili'uokalani began growing her own support base throughout the islands, publicly castigating the American oligarchs for how they had demolished Hawaii's economy and Hawaiians' sovereignty. (In the process she developed "a most unfeminine tongue," one author sneered.)[20] With her brother still on the throne, there was little she could do, at least formally. But when he died in 1891, Lili'uokalani became queen of Hawaii, and she finally had the power and the position to affect the kind of change she wanted.

Quickly, Lili'uokalani submitted a new constitution for public consideration, traveling the islands on horseback to whip up support from native Hawaiians. Unlike the Bayonet Constitution, Lili'uokalani's constitution was remarkably democratic. Gone were the voting and property restrictions limiting native Hawaiians' political rights, all but cutting Hawaiians off from the country's government. Instead of being limited to a small number of Americans, electoral rights would once more be extended to all Hawaiian citizens, regardless of how much wealth they held.[21]

That, to the Americans, could not stand. Facing down the Hawaiian queen and her democratic proposals, the oligarchs formed a Committee of Safety, with Dole himself drafting their declaration of opposition to Lili'uokalani's reforms. In a comment that revealed more about themselves than anything else, Lili'uokalani's oligarchic opponents whined that her proposals "reduced white influence"—a reality they would do everything, and use as many tools as possible, to oppose.

But it wasn't just opposition. As Dole's lone biographer described, the oligarch and his coconspirators "began a campaign of attack upon every part of the [Hawaiian] government." As this Committee of Safety saw it, the time had come to end even the pretense of native Hawaiian rule, and to end any Hawaiian independence wholesale. The only option was for the oligarchs to finally overthrow the Hawaiian government—and for America to swallow Hawaii entirely.[22]

And this time, Dole and his coconspirators would not be alone. With the oligarchs confronting the queen in Hawaii's royal palace—declaring that they were formally abolishing the Hawaiian monarchy and announcing the creation of a new "provisional government"—John Stevens, the leading American official in Hawaii, ordered his U.S. Marines to swarm throughout Honolulu and across Oahu, preventing any Hawaiians from racing to defend their queen. Rather than come to the aid of the Hawaiian officials pleading for help, the U.S. added its full arsenal to the oligarchs' efforts.

Facing down the bootheel of American imperialism, with American troops now bivouacked around Oahu, there was little that Lili'uokalani could do. The Committee of Safety, with Dole at the head, proclaimed they were simply restoring Hawaiian stability, protecting property rights, and ensuring democracy on the islands. Knowing they had the backing of Washington, the oligarchs seemed almost nonchalant about the coup; in one photo from the overthrow, Dole could be seen in "an all-white suit and straw boater [hat] tilted forward . . . watching the American troops parade down King Street," wrote the historian Siler, one of the best chroniclers of the takeover. "Judged by his jaunty attire he might have been enjoying a Fourth of July day parade."[23]

But Lili'uokalani, as well as future historians and even contemporary journalists, saw the event for exactly what it was. As *The New York Times* reported, the entire coup was a "shameful conspiracy," the "political crime of the century" accomplished only through the "most shameful intervention" of the U.S.[24] And it was clear who profited from the overthrow: the sugar barons, now stealing the reins of power in Hawaii once and for all. It was a revolution, according to *The New York Herald*, "of, by, and for sugar," authored by a small group of American oligarchs who simply wanted to "plunder the land," added the *St. Louis Chronicle*.[25]

Filled with understandable rage, the now-deposed Liliʻuokalani didn't hold back on these men. "As they became wealthy, and acquired titles to lands through the simplicity of our people and their ignorance of values and of the new land laws, their greed and their love of power proportionately increased; and schemes for aggrandizing themselves still further . . . began to occupy their minds," she later wrote. "[They] desired above all things the extension of their power, and to carry out their own special plans of advancement, and to secure their own personal benefit."[26]

There was only one way to describe the coup plotters—these Americans who'd grown fat on Hawaii's wealth, so much so that they could then topple Hawaii entirely. They were, as Liliʻuokalani wrote, an "oligarchy . . . ruling Hawaii."[27] A century later, it's hard to conclude anything else. It was a "coup d'etat," Zimmermann added in 2004, led by—and for the benefit of—these American oligarchs.[28]

Still, this wasn't quite the end of the story, at least not entirely. Despite the oligarchs' request of American annexation, the U.S. initially turned them down. Much of this hesitation was due to the concomitant inauguration of Grover Cleveland, a man who, in a quirk of timing, had returned to the White House at nearly the same time that the American oligarchs, with the aid of the American military, claimed Hawaii's government as their own. Far more thoughtful and well-read than his predecessor, Benjamin Harrison, Cleveland immediately saw the coup as an "act of war," he later said, committed on behalf of a cadre of American oligarchs trying to steal an entire nation for themselves.[29]

In response, Cleveland sent an emissary, James Blount, to investigate the affair. Traveling around the islands, speaking with both former officials and new members of the so-called provisional government, Blount quickly came to a conclusion: The oligarchs and the Harrison administration had both conspired to strangle Hawaii's government. All the talk of restoring "democracy" and "stability" to Hawaii was a smoke screen for an oligarchic land grab of historic proportions, for the benefit of the few white businessmen now controlling the islands. Reading Blount's report, Cleveland realized that the U.S. had committed a "substantial wrong"—and that the "only honorable course [remaining] was to undo the wrong."[30]

Back in Hawaii, while the Cleveland administration tried to figure out how to reverse the coup, Lili'uokalani seethed. "Drove by the [Hawaiian] Palace and would not look at the American flag over the Government building," she wrote. "May heaven look down on these Missionaries and punish them for their deeds."[31] She wasn't under formal arrest, at least not yet. But the American oligarchs now controlling Hawaii's politics—led by Dole, who announced his new role as the president of the "Republic of Hawaii" in 1894—disabused her of any idea that she could ever reclaim power.[32]

And they said as much even after a representative from Cleveland's administration arrived in Honolulu, there to inform the oligarchs that they must restore Lili'uokalani as Hawaii's leader. In a remarkable display of gall, Dole suddenly proclaimed that the U.S. had "no right to interfere" in the Republic of Hawaii's internal affairs. The oligarchs would never return to a status quo ante. Hawaii was theirs.[33]

After all, why would the oligarchs cede power? They knew Cleveland wouldn't resort to war, risking both American bloodshed and his own political credibility. Moreover, with the final overthrow of the Hawaiian government, the oligarchs had also gained ownership of nearly two million acres of Hawaiian lands, now worth billions of dollars. Their own pots of wealth had just grown exponentially. There was no going back.[34]

Unfortunately for Hawaiians, the oligarchs weren't wrong. Cleveland eventually lost interest, put off by both domestic concerns and by the fact that Lili'uokalani reportedly said that, should she ever regain power, the oligarchs would be executed. In her memoir, Lili'uokalani claimed she was misquoted, potentially on purpose.[35] But that clarification came far too late, long after her reported comments scuppered support in Washington for her return. Cleveland still wouldn't annex the islands, but neither would he force the oligarchs from power.[36]

The oligarchs' grip on Hawaii tightened, illustrating how authoritarian a nation under American oligarchs could truly be. Pushing through yet another constitution in 1894, they restricted voting even further, limiting it to only the wealthiest, most propertied—and, needless to say, white—residents, with well over 90 percent of the population of the islands now unable to have any say in the country's politics. In the oligarchs' minds, "The Hawaiians . . . and any other non-Teutonic members must be prevented from voting." It was the equivalent of the mainland's Jim Crow regime, set in the middle of the Pacific.[37]

But it wasn't just the voting restrictions. Any residual evidence of Hawaiian nationality—language, culture, identity—would have to be eliminated. As Helena Allen, who authored the only biography of Dole, wrote, "The Republic—an oligarchy—saw the last remnants of Hawaiian culture being changed. Not only was the monarchy gone, [but so was] a great deal of former stability for the native Hawaiians. Schools ceased teaching the Hawaiian language and parents ceased speaking Hawaiian to their children—it took [decades] before the spark of Hawaiian culture was to be struck again."[38]

With the final ascent of the oligarchy, Hawaii had effectively collapsed into a white supremacist police state. Any dissent, any opposition, any criticism would not be brooked. As the *San Francisco Chronicle* reported, Hawaii had passed "into the hands of a military oligarchy," which censored and silenced Hawaii's previously freewheeling newspapers. "In a word, the freedom of the press of Honolulu is a myth" under the oligarchs. Anyone who criticized the new regime would be forced off the islands, with opposition journalists summarily deported.[39]

Nor was that all. Dole, with the assent of his fellow oligarchs, declared martial law and suspended the writ of habeas corpus, wielding the state against any remaining opposition from local Hawaiians. When anti-regime forces rose up in 1895, attempting to restore Hawaiian sovereignty, Dole's regime swiftly cracked down, arresting and frog-marching over a thousand Hawaiian rebels, "often in chained groups," forcing them into a "grim, coral-block prison known as the Reef," wrote Siler. There they would languish, many of the leaders sentenced to death as a result.[40]

As the years went on, the oligarchs' stranglehold on Hawaii only deepened. As one observer said, Dole's regime resembled "France under Robespierre"—an oligarchy that now lorded over Hawaii in a regime perhaps as "monstrous as the Reign of Terror."[41]

Eventually, of course, the American government came around. In 1898, in the middle of the Spanish–American War—a war that transformed the U.S. into a global power, snapping up colonies in places like Puerto Rico and Guam and the Philippines—the new administration of William McKinley agreed to absorb Hawaii, making the oligarchy finally, formally part of the United States itself. "We need Hawaii just as much and a good deal more than we did California," McKinley claimed. "It is manifest destiny."[42]

For native Hawaiians—the ones who'd watched American oligarchs thieve their entire nation, suffocate their culture, eliminate any pretense of democracy or civil rights—the dream of Hawaiian nationhood never died. With the U.S. announcing it would annex the islands, a "vast majority" of Hawaiians signed a petition protesting the move. But it was to no avail. In July 1898, a lavish ceremony inaugurated formal American rule over Hawaii. There were almost no native Hawaiians present, and those who witnessed the ceremony "wept audibly" at the lowering of the Hawaiian flag and the raising of the American standard. "Those who were present covered their eyes as their beloved flag was lowered, while tears streamed down their cheeks," one of Liliʻuokalani's friends later remembered. Back in New Jersey, now simply another retired president, Cleveland wrote, "I am ashamed of the whole affair."[43]

For the oligarchs, however, there was nothing but glee and glad tidings. Despite Hawaii now being a part of the U.S., Washington "did little to check the oligarchy's power" after annexation, scholar Kealani Cook wrote.[44] Hawaii's new status as an American territory meant that the oligarchs could import labor ever more cheaply and export their sugar products at ever greater profit. With little federal oversight, the oligarchs could continue their authoritarian rule. Even after Senate investigations later uncovered massive corruption—self-dealing, slush funds, and worse—little changed. First under the Bayonet Constitution, then during the era of the Republic of Hawaii, then as an American territory, the oligarchs' control of Hawaii continued untrammeled. Little would change for decades. And Hawaii would never recover its status as an independent, sovereign nation, instead becoming America's fiftieth state in 1959.

For Dole, the transitions amidst American annexation were easy. Shifting from Hawaii's president to Hawaii's territorial governor, Dole made sure that he and his oligarchic allies kept their hold on the islands' politics. A few years after annexation, he moved into a sinecure as a federal judge, where he could enjoy his final years deciding how his fellow oligarchs could continue dominating Hawaii's economy and politics both. He never expressed any regret over how he'd helped snuff out Hawaiian independence, or that, as his biographer wrote, he'd "headed an oligarchy that disenfranchised [Hawaiians]." When he died in 1926, he was feted as Hawaii's founding father—and as a man who'd finally brought Hawaii to its natural, and American, end point.[45]

Liliʻuokalani, however, never gave up her dream of restoring Hawaii's status as an independent force on the global stage. In a lucid, moving memoir published shortly after the American annexation, Liliʻuokalani castigated both the oligarchs and the American government alike for their corruption, for their malfeasance, for all the criminality used to topple and ransack her homeland. With the queen eventually jailed by the oligarchs for her opposition, it's difficult to disagree with Liliʻuokalani's conclusions: that the oligarchs' overthrow of Hawaii, and the later American annexation, were crimes of historic magnitude—and were arguably far worse than anything any other American oligarchs of the era ever engaged in.

"This great and powerful nation must go across two thousand miles of sea, and take from the poor Hawaiians their little spots in the broad Pacific, must covet our islands of [Hawaii], and extinguish the nationality of my poor people, many of whom have now not a foot of land which can be called their own," Liliʻuokalani wrote. "And for what? [. . .] Where would men . . . capable of changing [the U.S.'s] colonial and foreign policy at a single coup, stop in their schemes?"[46] It was a question that Liliʻuokalani, who died in 1917, never got an answer to. And it's a question that continues to stalk Hawaii's status to this day—and now, in the twenty-first century, spreads far beyond Hawaii itself.

In many ways, the seizure of Hawaii was the high point for American oligarchs during the entire Gilded Age. Some of them may have had their mansions and their monopolies on the mainland, but in Hawaii they'd succeeded in grabbing an entire *country*. It was a path to power far beyond what even Carnegie, Vanderbilt, Stanford, Rice, or many others ever achieved. A model of what oligarchs—unconcerned about things like democracy or any political opposition whatsoever—could achieve if given a chance. And with the 1898 annexation, that oligarchy was welcomed back into the warm embrace of a U.S. government happy to have Hawaii join the American family, and never let it go.

It's worth noting that there was at least some opposition to Hawaiian annexation in Washington—though not necessarily for the most upstanding reasons. One leading anti-imperialist of the era, Missouri Representative Champ Clark, publicly worried that Hawaii's annexation would alter the U.S.'s racial makeup, eroding the country's white majority—and potentially opening the door to more oligarchic-driven expansion in the future.

While other colleagues applauded the U.S. for the "rescue of these islands . . . in the onward march of liberty and civilization"—and for accelerating "the conquest of the world by the Aryan race"—Clark disagreed. Standing on the floor of Congress, Clark addressed his colleagues. "Mr. Speaker, should [you] preside here twenty years hence, it may be that you will have a polyglot House," Clark began.[47] It may be, Clark worried, that they would have to listen to new representatives from around the world, places that future American expansion might just target. Perhaps there would be a "gentleman from Cuba" in Congress someday. Or maybe a "gentleman from Fiji."[48]

Or, potentially, a "gentleman from Greenland"—there to represent another distant island that American oligarchs might someday covet, and that American officials might someday, far into the future, annex.[49]

But that's a ways off, and something we'll turn to later in this book. Because while the oligarchs may have plundered an entire nation in Hawaii, back in the mainland U.S. a counterreaction was already building. It was made up of farmers in the Midwest, miners and cattle ranchers across the West, the children of immigrants in East Coast tenements and urban hovels, lumberjacks and oilmen and sharecroppers watching their labor increasingly benefit their bosses. All of them added to the populist winds whipping through the country, sweeping across an economy increasingly captured by a handful of men, hurtling the country toward a breaking point in the ever-long American struggle against the rise of a domestic oligarchy. It was a time that would see the greatest burst of anti-oligarchic success since the Civil War—and the rise of a most unexpected man to steer the country toward an anti-oligarchic future.

3

Eaten Away

There are two things that are important in politics. The first is money, and I can't remember what the second one is.

—*Mark Hanna*[1]

Most Americans think they know the story of Teddy Roosevelt. A child of stupendous wealth, Roosevelt came from the kind of affluent background that other American oligarchs and their offspring enjoyed. Thanks to a range of real estate, sugar, and banking interests, the entire Roosevelt family rose through the ranks of New York's political establishment during the nineteenth century, joining others like the Vanderbilts and Astors along the way. By the time Teddy was born in 1858, growing up in a tony Manhattan town house, his family was firmly ensconced in New York's elite.[2]

But for Teddy, all that money meant little, at least initially. Suffering from devastating asthma attacks, Roosevelt was unable to enjoy any of the things boys his age could. There were no scrapes with neighborhood toughs, no backwoods treks with his father and friends, no games of baseball or rugby or anything that could strain a sickly child too much. Cosseted by his parents, subject to electric shocks and bloodletting, Roosevelt was effectively raised in a gilded cage, able to do little but watch the world spin past, prevented from enjoying the bounty his parents' deep pockets could purchase.[3]

And then, as a teenager, a transformation began. Days in the gym turned into weeks, into months, into years. A waifish boy steeled himself into a beefy, athletic young man, with stints as a rancher and hunter in the Dakota Territory turning that young man into a symbol of Western manhood. Returning to the East Coast, he rose through both New York and Washington politics, flinging himself into America's political firmament. There was the dusty, mythologized race up San Juan Hill in Cuba, Roosevelt leading his Rough Riders to an American victory in a war with Spain. Then the quick ascent to the vice presidency for William McKinley's second term, followed by the even quicker ascent to the presidency when a gunman murdered the president.[4]

What followed was one of the most momentous, muscular presidencies America has ever seen—a presidency that busted trusts and broke up conglomerates, ushered in new regulations that finally reformed America's filthy food and drug industries, and launched America's first efforts at conservation and environmental policy, creating policies and playbooks that remain with us to this day. All of it was led by a president in ceaseless motion, often caked in mud and sweat, whose calls for a "Square Deal" for Americans resonate over a century later: a pledge to deliver a decent life for a decent day's work for families across the country, regardless of the industry, regardless of their politics.[5]

All this, or at least the broad parameters, is familiar to most Americans. But there was another side of Roosevelt, both as president and after, that's been buried in the years since, as faded as one of those sepia-tinted photographs that commemorate him, all brawn and teeth and spectacles, waving his fist in the air in a blur of movement.[6] It was a side of Roosevelt's leadership and legacy that's been largely forgotten. But it's one that represented the high point in an American president's efforts to corral American oligarchy—and set a blueprint for American officials decades later as they faced down many of the exact same issues once more.

When Roosevelt rose to the presidency in 1901, he entered the White House at arguably the height of the Gilded Age. Dominating industry after industry, bankrolling politician after politician, the era's oligarchs initially celebrated Roosevelt's sprint into the White House, thinking that one of their own had finally taken the presidency for himself.[7]

They weren't wrong, at least initially. (After all, Roosevelt himself had celebrated the American seizure of Hawaii, praising the annexation as necessary for "the interests of the White race.")[8] But it didn't take long for the era's tycoons to realize their hopes may have been misplaced. Unleashing anti-bribery investigations and antitrust broadsides, Roosevelt shepherded through policy after policy that broke up monopolies in rail, oil, timber, finance, and other industries. It was a full-scale assault, the likes of which the country hadn't seen in decades, against the swelling monopolies devouring smaller businesses around the country.[9]

The president, however, wasn't content with simply splintering conglomerates. He wanted to do something further, something that would target the wallets of the oligarchs directly. There was one tool in particular that he wanted to implement—the one tool that, more than anything else, could trim the sails of oligarchs both then and now, and potentially even eliminate oligarchy entirely: taxes.[10]

Specifically, Roosevelt wanted two *types* of taxes. The first was an income tax—one that would disproportionately target the wealthiest Americans. The idea wasn't new; during the Civil War, Abraham Lincoln oversaw the country's first income taxes to generate much-needed revenue. Lincoln even ensured that such taxes were publicly disclosed, all in the name of "equity."[11] After the war's end, and after Lincoln himself was assassinated, the federal government repealed both the tax and the transparency—a sop to "the wealthy men of the dawning Gilded Age [who] did not like seeing their tax information in the pages of *The New York Times*," wrote journalist Jesse Eisinger.[12]

Others, though, picked up the baton, calling for renewed income taxes to help slow some of the spiraling rise of Gilded Age fortunes. By the early 1890s, sufficient momentum had built for Congress to finally introduce legislation implementing a new income tax. In 1894, the bill passed—only for the Supreme Court to immediately overturn the legislation, claiming income taxes were unconstitutional.[13]

Even then, though, income tax supporters pushed on. It took years more, but by the middle of the first decade of the twentieth century, they found a new opening: an economic downturn and a widening deficit, both of which necessitated the need for new revenue. Suddenly, the idea of an income tax—which could target the incomes of the wealthiest oligarchs especially—gained new relevance. And suddenly, unlike in the previous decades, there was a president who wanted it as well.

Roosevelt began refining his anti-oligarch pitch in late 1905. In the wake of a corporate financing scandal, in which a number of massive insurance firms were revealed to be covertly plowing money into American politics, the president called for an end not only to the practice but also to any corporate monies in American politics whatsoever. In his annual address to legislators, Roosevelt became the first American president to call for a ban on corporate funds wholesale. "All contributions by corporations to any political committee or for any political purpose should be forbidden by law," Roosevelt bellowed.[14] Following the president's lead, Congress soon passed a bill known as the Tillman Act, which "explicitly prohibited corporations and national banks from contributing money to federal campaigns."[15]

Roosevelt didn't stop there. The next year, in a rain-drenched speech in Harrisburg, Pennsylvania, he called for Americans to do everything they could to thwart a "civilization of a mere plutocracy."[16] It was a world that Roosevelt recognized intimately, given his upbringing. The "plutocrats"—the term Roosevelt used to describe the oligarchs—had already created a nation of "selfishness so appalling" that it could, if unchecked, usher in a "destruction hitherto unequaled."[17] It was language that seemed lifted from the socialists burgeoning throughout the era, but came from the mouth of a president attached to greater wealth than perhaps any before. It was also the start of a crusade that would last the rest of Roosevelt's life, through his years in the White House and far beyond.[18]

Just over a month later, in front of Congress, Roosevelt continued to rail against the robber barons. "The man of great wealth owes a peculiar obligation to the State, because he derives special advantages from the mere existence of government," the president thundered. All Americans, Roosevelt described, obtained some benefit from the government: rights and regulations, openings and opportunities. But the wealthiest Americans, if only by dint of their piles of assets, received the *most* rewards—and should thus be forced to pay the highest price for such benefits. As Roosevelt continued, "Not only should [a wealthy American] recognize this obligation in the way he leads his daily life and in the way he earns and spends his money, but it should also be recognized by the way in which he pays for the protection the State gives him."[19]

To Roosevelt—and to the populist crusaders and anti-oligarch reformers who'd longed for a president to side with them—there was one solution. The oligarchs must be taxed, and at a higher rate than the rest of America. After all, these oligarchs had all reaped tremendous benefit from America: from the protection of their property, from the largesse of America's lands, from the political stability that few nations outside America could offer. It was only fair—it was necessary—that the oligarchs pay their fair share, which was a share far higher than the rest of Americans. The federal government, Roosevelt said, should impose a "graduated income tax." It would be a tax that applied to all Americans—but most especially to those American oligarchs.[20]

Reaching back to figures like Jefferson, Roosevelt then called for something else: an inheritance tax that could break up the oligarchs' family fortunes, which were no longer found in land alone. Things like stock ownership, paper investments, and sprawling business holdings had all expanded the sources of wealth for American oligarchs. Yet because these assets weren't broken up upon a robber baron's death, they all passed to the oligarchs' heirs. All of it now threatened to create and entrench the kind of American aristocracy that the Founders had feared, of the wealthiest American families reigning over the U.S. like a smattering of feudal lords.[21]

American officials had toyed with the creation of a formal inheritance tax before. In addition to requiring landed estates to be broken up after death, Civil War–era legislators also implemented new taxes when wealthy Americans tried to transfer personal assets. But as with the income taxes of that era, those transfer taxes were soon repealed after the Civil War. When the Spanish–American War broke out in 1898, Congress implemented a "legacy tax" that was largely similar—but again, not long after the war's conclusion, that tax died once more.[22]

Which is when Roosevelt stepped into the breach. He mentioned a "graduated inheritance tax" in passing in his 1906 speech before Congress, but he made the idea a centerpiece of his 1907 address.[23] Rattling off similar examples and success in places like Britain, France, and Germany, Roosevelt highlighted time and again how such an inheritance tax was in no way unfair or unseemly; instead, it was about restoring an American ideal of opportunity, of striving, and of equality. "A heavy progressive tax upon a very large fortune is in no way such a tax upon thrift or industry as a [similar one] would be on a small fortune," Roosevelt said. "No advantage comes either to the country as a whole or to the individuals inheriting the money by permitting the transmission in their entirety of the enormous fortunes which would be affected by such a tax." Not only would a new inheritance tax help with "revenue raising, [but] such a tax would help to preserve a measurable equality of opportunity for the people of the generations growing to manhood."[24] It wasn't about robbing the rich to pay the poor; it was, Roosevelt repeated time and again, about what was fair—and what was, at its core, American.

Alas, for all his talents at the bully pulpit, even Roosevelt had his limits. Because of his truncated first term, Roosevelt ultimately ran out of time to push through the kinds of tax policies he'd called for. But his departure wasn't enough to stop the momentum he'd sparked. In speech after speech, in articles and books and memoirs, Roosevelt kept up the crusade. If anything, he only became more outspoken, more strident in his demands for taxes as the great solution to the problem of American oligarchs, and of economic fairness as the engine of American greatness.

In one 1910 speech, a year after leaving the White House—a speech to which we'll return at the close of this book—Roosevelt asserted that the "conflict between the men who possess more than they have earned and the men who have earned more than they possess is the central condition of progress."[25] It was a theme that Roosevelt never strayed from. In his 1913 autobiography, he wrote that America "had come to the stage where for our people what was needed was a real democracy; and of all forms of tyranny the least attractive and the most vulgar is the tyranny of mere wealth, the tyranny of a plutocracy."[26] And a year later he declared, "There can be no real political democracy unless there is something approaching economic democracy."[27]

By that time, Roosevelt could finally see the fruits of all his haranguing. In 1913, with the winds of war swirling around Europe, American states ratified the Sixteenth Amendment, which provided Congress with the explicit right to "collect taxes on incomes, from whatever source derived." A few years later, with the Great War in full tilt, legislators in Washington passed the Revenue Act of 1916, which created the country's first permanent estate tax.[28]

Roosevelt, of course, was not the president when these measures finally passed, nor does he deserve sole credit; populists like William Jennings Bryan and legislators like Cordell Hull, and even subsequent presidents like Woodrow Wilson, deserve measures of applause themselves, dragging the policies across the finish line.[29] But the example that Roosevelt modeled—of a president injecting his anti-oligarchic visions into the American body politic, pushing for them wherever and however he could, even if he wouldn't be the one to sign the legislation into law himself—was one that eventually proved successful. And it's a playbook that, a century later, still stands available to any president who would grab it.

It would take time for these new tax policies to bite. It would take a roaring, raging era that followed the First World War, followed by a Great Depression that ravaged a nation, unleashing more poverty than anything the country had seen before. It would eventually take another president—another Roosevelt—to push these policies as far as they could go, and to finally break the backs of the oligarchs lingering into the 1930s, including those who began looking abroad at fascism and totalitarianism with envy. But when the income and inheritance taxes were finally fully implemented, they devastated American oligarchy.

The data speaks for itself. As economists Gabriel Zucman and Emmanuel Saez calculated in 2019, whereas the average tax rates of

American oligarchs at the end of the Gilded Age stood at just over 10 percent, two decades later that rate had skyrocketed, peaking at approximately 60 percent—a breathtaking surge, resulting largely from the introduction of income and inheritance taxes (in addition to growing corporate taxes). As such, while the end of the Gilded Age saw the top 1 percent of America's richest owning nearly 50 percent of the country's total household wealth, a few decades later that number had been cut in half—a plunge so steep that the bottom 90 percent of Americans finally, perhaps for the first time in American history, controlled more wealth than American oligarchs. Thanks to income and inheritance taxes, America, wrote Zucman and Saez, was "a beacon of tax justice." In an era of fascists on the march and communists immiserating entire nations, the authors continued, "The United States was the democracy with perhaps the most steeply progressive system of taxation on the planet."[30]

By the mid-twentieth century, America's anti-oligarchic economy thrummed. A middle class broadened, swelling outward, welcoming new populations and new demographics into the American success story. Not everyone enjoyed the success, of course. Black Americans, those in the American colonies of Puerto Rico and Guam, Indigenous Americans who watched their supposed treaty rights trampled at every turn—millions and millions of American residents and citizens still stood on the outside, looking in. But on the whole, the kind of economy that Teddy Roosevelt and his allies envisaged—the kind that would cut off American plutocrats at their knees—brought more prosperity to more people across the country than anything before (or since, for that matter).

And yet, even with income taxes for the wealthiest Americans eventually reaching over 90 percent and estate taxes scraping nearly 80 percent, these weren't the only major anti-oligarchic successes of the twentieth century.[31] There was another victory, decades later, that stemmed directly from a bungled burglary on a balmy summer evening in Washington, DC, leading not only to the unprecedented resignation of a sitting American president but also to the greatest burst of anti-corruption and anti-oligarchy reforms the country had seen since Roosevelt—and has seen since.

In popular memory, Watergate is remembered as multiple things. Abuse of power. Breathtaking political cravenness. The lengths a sitting president would go to cling to the White House. The subsequent hearings in Congress revealed all this, and much more, ushering in the greatest presidential scandal the U.S. had seen to that point.

But the Watergate revelations were also about something else. Details hinted at throughout the related investigations—whispers and innuendo of American companies covertly backing Nixon's grip on power, secretly funding an administration that discussed everything from fire-bombing think tanks to assassinating critical journalists—spurred reformers in Congress to organize a series of post-Watergate hearings, even after Nixon left office.[32] Steered by a jowly, crusading senator from Idaho named Frank Church, these hearings examined everything from the CIA's pro-dictatorship coups to the U.S. Army's domestic surveillance programs.[33] But they focused on another topic as well: how some of America's most prestigious, most prominent companies and corporate executives had hidden significant funds off their books, using those funds not to benefit shareholders or even company officers but to instead bankroll any politician—or any dictator—they wanted, in any country around the world. How, in other words, America's leading companies and corporate heads had become the enemies of democracy, regardless of the cost.[34]

Hauled before a Senate subcommittee, American executive after American executive—including many who had covertly paid the Nixon administration—revealed that they'd secretly bribed any foreign regime they could. There was the head of Gulf Oil, testifying that his company had organized millions of dollars in bribes to South Korea's ruling dictatorship. There were Northrop Grumman and Lockheed Martin, America's leading defense contractors, admitting that they had both earmarked millions of dollars more for "foreign agents and officials around the world," including places like Saudi Arabia, just to land business. Over and over, America's most prominent executives revealed the head-spinning, globe-spanning bribery they'd been involved in. In just a single committee hearing, legislators discovered that over 20 percent of the U.S.'s Fortune 500 companies had engaged in this kind of overseas bribery—at least one hundred major American companies, and presumably many more.[35]

Nor were these simply bundles of cash in crumpled brown bags. In a hint of the spiraling offshore world to come, American corporate executives admitted that they'd set up shell companies in foreign jurisdictions as a means to hide their clandestine payments. Gulf Oil set up fraudulent companies in the Bahamas, marking the South Korean payments as expenses to their Caribbean shell corporations. Both Northrop and Lockheed kept their own pet shell companies to mask their own bribes. These shells did exactly as they were intended, and exactly as they've done in the half century since: hiding the true owners and beneficiaries, making it impossible to track the money's true path, all of it without breaking any laws. American officials stood in shock at the revelations, barely able to grasp how sprawling the bribery networks truly were. As one sitting senator said, "I am convinced that creative minds in the name of greed can concoct schemes faster than we can get legislation against them." It was all, added another, a "disgrace [to] our free enterprise system."[36]

By and large, America's corporate executives hunkered down, assuming they could wait out the revelations, that the news cycle would simply move on. Not all weathered the exposés; United Brands head Eli Black, outed as the secret paymaster behind Honduras's kleptocratic regime, couldn't handle the details of his bribery spilling out and leapt to his death from a Manhattan high-rise as a result. But while they acted contrite in public, in private America's leading corporate heads were confident. After all, according to American law, they'd committed no crimes. Remarkably, for all the stupendous corruption they'd engaged in—for all the theocrats and kleptocrats and autocrats they'd helped keep in power—these men had apparently broken no American laws.[37]

And they weren't wrong. Despite hiding all these payments from regulators and shareholders, there was "no federal law requiring publicly traded companies to keep honest books and records," journalist David Montero wrote in his history of the hearings. More important, there was somehow no law against American executives bribing foreign officials. Sure, they couldn't directly bribe *American* officials. But the second they crossed into international waters, anything—any payment, any bribe, no matter how big—was fair game. It was a grotesque, almost Kafkaesque situation. "We could prove bribery," said one official, "but we couldn't prosecute it as bribery."[38]

It's worth noting that this wasn't an especially American failure; no country, either then or before, had ever thought to criminalize something like foreign bribery. From the earliest days of Western joint stock companies operating abroad—the British East India Company and the Dutch East India Company landing on the shores of South and Southeast Asia and immediately swallowing as much land as they could—this kind of foreign bribery was "something that endured as an inevitable global evil," wrote author John Noonan.[39] Even the earliest corporations seeking and seizing land in North America, from the Massachusetts Bay Company to the Hudson's Bay Company, thought nothing of this kind of underhanded payment, all in the service of amplifying shareholders' returns. It was just the cost of doing business.

It wasn't until the Watergate hearings, though, that the extent of this corporate bribery became clear. As one American official said, "None of us dreamed that there were the millions, the tens of millions, the hundreds of millions, that we found."[40]

It wasn't just that these companies were helping keep crooked regimes in power, all so they could continue extracting their oil or dredging their lands or shipping them tanks and artillery batteries. For whatever short-term gains these companies thought they were accruing, they were not only decimating democracy in those countries, keeping kleptocrats in power, and enriching autocrats around the world. They were also weakening American foreign policy overall.

Just look at what happened as a result of the hearings themselves. In Honduras, the pro-American autocracy quickly disintegrated, with the bribery revelations cementing a generation of anti-American animus in the country. The government of Venezuela, meanwhile, cut off all discussion about compensating the U.S. for previously nationalized property, a priority for Washington. In Italy, another country exposed as a target of American corporate bribery, the clearest beneficiaries were the communists, who could point to their capitalist opponents as little more than bought-off American puppets. Again and again, the corporate bribery set back the cause of American interests and American allies in country after country, doing "grievous damage" to U.S. foreign policy—damage that was perhaps even "irreversible."[41]

For those overseeing the hearings, the damage was unmistakable. "These very practices have extremely serious consequences both for the conduct of U.S. foreign policy and the reception U.S. business receives abroad," Church growled. "U.S.-based corporations should not be allowed to weaken a friendly government through bribery and corruption while the United States is relying on that government as a stable, sure friend in supporting our policies. . . . The Communist bloc chortles with glee at the sight of corrupt capitalism." As the senator added elsewhere, thanks to this kind of American corporate bribery, "This country and its major allies are going to wake up one morning and find that the basis of stable democratic government has been eaten away."[42]

The solution, then, was simple. If legislators couldn't prosecute America's corporate executives for previous bribery and for all the damage they'd already done to American foreign policy, they would have to enact new legislation to prevent anything similar from happening in the future. It took a bit of legislative fine-tuning, but within a short time Congress hit upon a solution. Dubbed the Foreign Corrupt Practices Act (FCPA), the new legislation was deceptively simple. At its core, it prevented one thing: the bribing of a foreign official by an American businessman or company, or by any company listed on a U.S. stock exchange.

But that simplicity belied the ambition of the law itself. After all, given that the bill targeted specifically *foreign* corruption, it therefore implied that the U.S. had a right to target crimes taking place on *foreign* soil—an element of extraterritorial justice that, quite frankly, no country had ever tried before.[43] Suddenly, so long as an American was involved, the U.S. gave itself the right to prosecute any bribe taking place anywhere in the world. Moreover, given that multiple foreign companies were listed on U.S. stock exchanges, that meant the U.S. was suddenly arrogating to itself the right to prosecute *foreign* companies engaging in foreign bribery—even if those countries themselves didn't ban foreign bribery.[44]

The sprawling impact of the legislation was a colossal blow to oligarchs both foreign and domestic. While America's corporate heads of the 1970s may not have quite resembled the oligarchs of the Gilded Age or early twenty-first-century America, they nonetheless represented some of the wealthiest individuals in the country. Moreover, their bribery—whether in Honduras, Saudi Arabia, South Korea, or elsewhere—was likewise keeping some of the wealthiest individuals in *other* countries in power as well, seeding and cultivating oligarchies and dictatorships around the world. Now, with the FCPA, that carousel of corporate bribery was shut off. So long as the law was now enforced, American corporate bribery—and the ways that America's wealthiest corporate executives could keep authoritarians in power—was over.

On its own, the FCPA was the greatest piece of anti-oligarchic legislation the U.S. had passed in decades, at least since the First World War. And if legislators in the 1970s, led by figures like Church, had stopped there, they would have already presented the greatest burst of reform since the days of Teddy Roosevelt and his allies. But there was another legislative accomplishment worth pausing on, if only to consider what was in America's grasp—and what, after quickly falling apart, set America once more on a path to oligarchy, and to potentially far worse.

In addition to foreign bribery scandals, the Watergate revelations also pulled back the curtain on how many of those same American companies had skirted the U.S.'s existing campaign finance regulations to aid Nixon's presidency. Multiple companies revealed that they'd "channeled cash through foreign countries" in order to hide their off-the-books payments to Nixon's reelection effort, using fake checks and Swiss bank accounts to circumvent America's bare-bones transparency requirements.[45] Others simply "flew into Washington with suitcases filled with cash," dropping their payments off next door to the White House.[46] Many corporate heads were happy to see Nixon remain in office. (Though not necessarily all; as one former

American Airlines executive said, his company had bundled secret payments to Nixon out of "'fear' of what would happen to his company if it did not contribute" to Nixon's reelection.)[47] It all added up to tens of millions of dollars in funds for Nixon to use in his 1972 campaign—a campaign that appeared to cement his leadership, and his legacy, for years to come.[48]

Of course, it didn't take long for things to fall apart. And when they did—when legislators and audiences across America heard the lengths that America's corporate heads would go to help entrench a man as authoritarian as Nixon—reformers spied an opening. Not just in terms of cracking down on foreign bribery, but potentially even in ending the role of corporate money in American politics entirely.

It's not like this was the first time Americans had dreamed of a democracy free of this kind of corporate funding. As we saw earlier, Teddy Roosevelt himself said as much during his second term, signing into law the 1907 Tillman Act, which banned this kind of direct corporate funding outright.[49] But for decades, the topic was largely an afterthought, with few scandals propelling any kinds of effective reforms. Nixon himself signed a largely toothless Federal Election Campaign Act in 1971, requiring greater disclosures and transparency for campaign contributions.[50] (Left unsaid was the fact that Nixon's legislation didn't come with anyone to actually enforce the campaign finance reforms.)

But shortly afterward, undone by his own avarice, Nixon imploded. And an opening yawned in front of reformers, who realized they could finally implement the kind of corporate funding limits long needed—and even prevent the wealthiest Americans from simply purchasing American politics forevermore.

They began in 1974, just after Nixon's resignation. Legislators added language to the bill the president had signed only a few years before, placing formal limits on contributions for federal candidates. No longer could individuals, organizations, or corporations plow as much money as they wanted into the pockets of presidential candidates or those running for Congress. Now, such expenditures would be capped, limited to things like $1,000 in donations to any single campaign and $25,000 total to all candidates or related committees. Moreover, all contributions over $100 had to be publicly disclosed, allowing any and all to trace how much an individual American spent on individual candidates.[51] The new language also capped *expenditures* from candidates and campaigns. No longer could would-be presidents, senators, or congresspeople spend as much as they'd like during their campaigns. Now, they had to act far more strategically, with the new regulations limiting campaign expenditures to $20 million for presidential campaigns and only $70,000 on House elections.[52]

Yet the linchpin of the new language was not the limits on donations, or the caps on expenditures. It was the fact that there were finally enforcers involved. Dubbed the Federal Election Commission (FEC), the new body would be comprised of six members—four appointed by Congress, two by the president—and their task would be simple: "enforce the law."[53]

For the first time in American history, there would be actual supervision—actual teeth—to America's campaign finance reforms. The regulations "open[ed] a new era in the nation's politics," the *New York Times* editorial page wrote in 1975. "If the nation's politics are to be lifted out of this [morass], these subterranean rivers of cash have to be dried up and political finance brought wholly above ground."[54] As President Gerald Ford, in signing the new regulations into law, said at the time, the limits and enforcement would "stand as a landmark of campaign reform legislation. . . . The unpleasant truth is that big money influence has come to play an unseeming role in our electoral process. This bill will help to right that wrong."[55]

And he wasn't incorrect, at least theoretically. If anything, all these campaign finance developments—the caps on donations and expenditures, the threats of investigations and penalties, the fact that the momentum remained in the reformers' corner—seemed to be something of the final nail in the coffin for any remaining oligarchic forces trying to swamp American politics with cash and corruption alike.

It was also confirmation that this post-Watergate era was just as monumental, and just as important, as the era of Teddy Roosevelt's and his successors' reforms—and that, when looking at America's anti-oligarchic successes, those two eras have to be paired together. Thanks to things like the income and inheritance taxes, America's hemmed-in oligarchs already watched their grip on the American economy fade, their relative hold on American assets decline year after year. Thanks to the FCPA, they could no longer even go abroad to bribe their way to power or profit. And now, thanks to the new FEC and the related restrictions on what American politicians could spend or on what any would-be oligarch could even donate, the opening for money in American politics appeared to shrink into nothing.

It was, in hindsight, the apex of efforts to keep American oligarchs at bay. And it didn't take long for a new era to emerge—one that is still with us, and one that has seen American democracy, to swipe a phrase from Church, eaten away, devoured by the oligarchs who may have been down, but were never fully out.

4

Worse Than Useless

False and evil systems have crept in through defects in the Constitution, by which the natural rights of the people have been taken from them, resulting in an unequal distribution of wealth in the country.

—Omer Kem[1]

The first crack to form in the new campaign finance restrictions came barely a year later.

Almost immediately after Congress had passed the new regulations limiting how much Americans could donate and how much candidates could spend on any campaign, the opposition began. Unlike later assaults on campaign finance restrictions, the initial blow to the post-Watergate reforms came from a strangely bipartisan direction, bringing together a pair of bedfellows who otherwise had little in common.[2]

In one corner stood James Buckley, a right-wing senator from New York who would later hold several positions in the Reagan administration, a man considered one of the flag-bearers of conservativism of the time.[3] In the other corner stood Eugene McCarthy, long considered one of the most liberal Democratic senators of the entire era. In Washington, the two shared almost no common ground: not on foreign policy, not on health care or education reforms, not even on basic civil rights provisions for all Americans. But when it came to campaign finance—and when it came to the limits their congressional colleagues had just placed on money in American politics—Buckley and McCarthy formed an unexpected alliance.[4]

Their union wasn't ideological per se; Buckley, emerging from the kind of small-government stew then dominating the American right, preferred to strip away all major regulations, while McCarthy was perfectly fine with wielding the power of the federal government for his own political ends. Instead, they came together because of what they thought the new regulations meant for the U.S. Constitution's First Amendment—and, specifically, whether or not the new caps limited Americans' free speech rights, and even the right to run for office themselves.[5]

Combining forces (and joined by a hodgepodge of others), Buckley and McCarthy filed a lawsuit challenging the constitutionality of the new campaign finance restrictions, taking their case all the way to the Supreme Court. They focused in particular on the limits Congress had passed on what campaigns and candidates could spend. As Buckley saw it, Congress had "offended the basic idea of a sovereign, self-governing people."[6] Rather than helping American democracy thrive on an even playing field, Congress had instead limited candidates' abilities to best reflect their constituents' wishes—namely, by spending all the money they received from supporters, even if it blew past the new expenditure caps.

McCarthy agreed. Drifting further and further left as the 1970s continued on, McCarthy claimed that the new caps had unwittingly helped incumbents and well-known candidates; since third-party and lesser-known figures could spend only as much as their competitors, they were at an automatic disadvantage in an electorate who barely knew who they were.[7]

If you squint, you could see the logic to the arguments. (If a third-party candidate somehow received magnitudes more donations from magnitudes more donors, but was allowed to spend only the same as their incumbent opponent, was that necessarily fair?) But if you pull back, the implications quickly become clear. Lifting the expenditure caps wouldn't help only theoretical third-party figures but also oligarchs' favorite candidates—those who, if limits were eliminated, could spend far more than opponents relying on small-dollar, grassroots supporters. In other words, if expenditure caps were removed, it would open a spigot of campaign expenses that had no end in sight, and that could flood American political campaigns with more money than the country had ever seen before.

Which, on January 30, 1976, is precisely what happened. In its infamous *Buckley v. Valeo* ruling, the Supreme Court eliminated the just-passed expenditure caps, declaring them unconstitutional. Rather than limit presidential campaigns to spending $20 million per candidate, or congressional races to just $70,000 per campaign, the Supreme Court declared that these caps limited "the quantity of political speech" available to Americans.[8] Given the variety in the "size and intensity" of campaigns around the country, it was only right that certain candidates could spend more than their opponents.[9]

Plus, as the court found, even if certain candidates could spend more, it wasn't as if that automatically meant corruption could seep into American politics. The Supreme Court wrote that the "absence of prearrangement or coordination of the expenditure with the candidate or his agent alleviates the danger that expenditures will be given as a quid pro quo for improper commitments from the candidates." Cutting through the legal jargon, the Brennan Center described the ruling as one where the Supreme Court "upheld contribution restrictions, reasoning that limits help control corruption. And it struck campaign spending restrictions, reasoning that spending money does not involve a transaction between a donor and a candidate, and thus there is no possibility of corruption."[10] In other words, since donation caps were still in place, and since even the wealthiest Americans could only contribute as much as anyone else, it's not like candidates would be in hock to them or their interests, right?[11]

The Supreme Court didn't stop there. In addition to removing the caps on how much candidates could spend, the court ruled that Congress had no right to appoint any members of the newly formed Federal Election Commission. Those appointees were members of the executive branch; ergo, they had to be appointed by the president himself. Suddenly, the FEC became the plaything of the White House entirely. Yes, the Senate should still consent to appointees, just like it did with ambassadors, members of the president's cabinet, and others. But the body tasked with enforcing America's campaign finance laws was, according to the Supreme Court, controlled by one man alone—a man who, surely, would never twist or gut the FEC for his own ends. Coming immediately on the heels of Nixon's resignation, it was a vexing, shockingly naive assumption.[12]

All told, the ruling took a sledgehammer to the post-Watergate reforms that were supposed to help stem the tide of massive wealth swilling around American politics. It was, one legal analyst wrote, "dubious from the day it was decided."[13] It also created a whole new series of perverse incentives. For instance, didn't this ruling mean that candidates should now try to spend as much as they could—if only out of fear that their opponents might be spending more? And if individual donors were still capped, wouldn't candidates and parties spend all their time trying to tap as many individuals as possible in order to get money into their coffers? Or look at the FEC: Didn't this ruling mean that future presidents should only ever appoint FEC commissioners who would rule in their favor, and block investigations the president didn't like? Didn't this effectively guarantee that the FEC would be a toothless, gridlocked body, without much point or power whatsoever?[14]

The answer to all these questions was a resounding yes. Because of the ruling, candidates "turn[ed] themselves into full-time fundraisers," analyst Jeffrey Rosen wrote, with political parties following suit.[15] So much for the days of crafting policy, of organizing constituents, of sifting the lessons of history for the best paths forward. American politicians instantly became little more than magnets for as much money as they could find. Meanwhile, the FEC quickly became an afterthought—a backwater of inactivity, a case study in how even the best reforms can immediately go sideways. It still exists, and can even find itself issuing key rulings (as we'll see later in this chapter). But the notion that it is some grand enforcer of American political financing regulations would be laughable if it weren't so tragic. As one write-up found, the FEC is now "worse than useless because its failure to enforce campaign finance laws encourages [law-breaking] while making suckers of candidates or donors who, for reasons of conscience, opt to respect the law."[16]

There was a further question that the *Buckley* ruling raised, which had even bigger implications for American politics than knifing the FEC or transforming candidates into funding machines. For the deepest pockets around America, if the Supreme Court could find limits on campaign expenditures unconstitutional, then could it someday eliminate the caps on donations for the same reasons? And what would it take to make that happen?

For those reading this in the early twenty-first century, you almost certainly know what transpired following the *Buckley* ruling. In the half century since, the cascade of money sloshing around American politics has only grown and grown, a monster wave cresting and crashing down on every election cycle, every campaign, every turn that Americans take at the voting booth. The idea of campaign finance restrictions in the U.S. is now risible, with existing regulations worth little more than the paper they're written on. Much of American politics is now swamped in anonymous dark money, casting a shroud over almost every candidate. And now, in the 2020s, there's an additional element at play: It's no longer simply American wealth corrupting American politics but the dirty money erupting in regime after regime around the world—often finding willing accomplices within the American oligarchy who first trampled existing regulations, opening the doors for foreign regimes in the process.

But that story, true as it is, is too easy, too neat, almost to the point of being uninteresting. Far more revealing is the story of precisely *how* we got to this point in the twenty-first century, in which all the remaining guardrails on money in American politics have apparently disappeared.[17]

This story begins, strangely enough, in 1819 with Dartmouth College, then as now one of the country's most prestigious universities. Despite being a private institution, Dartmouth's corporate charter—just as every other corporate charter in America at the time—was authorized by its state government, in this case New Hampshire. Such practice dated back to the colonial era when U.S. states, building on British precedent, authorized and issued specific charters for all companies and corporations. Dartmouth—along with all other nascent American universities, joint stock organizations, private companies, and more—was no different.[18]

The university's trustees, however, thought it should be. Suing the state, the trustees claimed the state should no longer be the arbiter of Dartmouth's charter—that the state "had no right to interfere with private contracts," as historian Kim Phillips-Fein wrote. The case eventually reached the Supreme Court, which found that American corporations were, indeed, "private entities with their own legal rights," and did not have to be betrothed or beholden to any state government. It was an earthquake of a ruling. Bucking all precedent, corporations were no longer simply bodies tethered to ruling governments but instead had certain rights themselves—rights that from that point on began a slow, fitful march forward, slouching their way to all the same rights that any other American enjoyed.[19]

As the decades passed, corporations transformed into the convoluted conglomerates of the Gilded Age. The increase in size had a kind of gravitational pull on legal minds eager to see corporations expand their own rights as well. One figure, the lawyer and former Republican leader Roscoe Conkling, even went so far as to argue before the Supreme Court in 1886 that corporations were eligible for all the rights prescribed and protected in the Fourteenth Amendment, which had previously provided citizenship to formerly enslaved Americans. Conkling claimed that corporations should likewise be granted something approximating citizenship, with all the "privileges and immunities" attendant therein. That corporations were, in another word, people.[20]

Conkling may not have succeeded—even for a court greenlighting all the pro-segregation and antidemocratic policies of the era, claiming that corporations were citizens was a bridge too far—but he'd advanced an idea that would in time flower. After all, if a corporation was merely a collection of people, did that eliminate the rights that those people all held as individuals? Did those rights dissolve as soon as those citizens gathered in a group, organized into a company, and declared themselves a corporation?[21]

Such arguments are, then and now, generally considered ridiculous. Corporations and individuals are identical in the same way that, say, Willie Mays or Ken Griffey Jr. and any Little Leaguer could be considered talented baseball players, or a Michelin-starred restaurant on the Amalfi coast and Domino's Pizza could both be said to provide fine Italian cuisine. Not only can corporations long outlive any of the individuals participating in their founding, but as law professor Joel Bakan has outlined, corporations should be considered similar only to psychopaths, since they "act as pathological, fantastical 'individuals' shorn of any moral compunction, driven by the absolute imperative of profit alone."[22]

Still, the momentum was clearly pointing in one direction. Even though Conkling and his corporate allies lost their case, the lines between corporations and citizens continued to blur. Soon, bedrock rights reserved for individuals—things like due process and the ability to not be searched without a warrant—bled over to corporations. So, too, did First Amendment rights, when the Supreme Court ruled in 1936 that Louisiana Governor Huey Long's efforts to impose a new tax on newspapers critical of him violated the "circulation of information to which the public is entitled in virtue of the constitutional guaranties." A few decades later, in 1975, the court strengthened corporations' free speech rights even further, ruling that states could not place undue limits on corporations' abilities to advertise their wares—and that American citizens had a right to hear what corporations thought.[23]

With each ruling, with each right, the civil rights of corporations grew and grew. They often expanded not because corporations were viewed as distinct entities (or "persons") per se, but because American judges claimed that corporations were simply agglomerations of citizens themselves—and thus maintained all the rights enjoyed by individual citizens. It was darkly ironic—especially given how corporations and their wealthy benefactors would soon dominate American politics—that many of these rulings were themselves driven by progressives and anti-oligarchic forces. Protecting American organizations from unfair searches and seizures, preventing would-be autocrats like Long from targeting American media with punitive taxes—there were clear pro-democratic interests at every turn. Even the 1975 advertising case (which made it easier for pharmacies to publicize their prices) was viewed as "a significant victory for consumers," *The New York Times* noted.[24]

And yet, with each supposed shift in favor of Americans' democratic rights, alternative opportunities emerged. Openings that could allow pro-oligarchic forces to take full advantage of these new rights that corporations continued to gain. That transformed American corporations into a sort of golem—not quite human, but not quite the inanimate, managed entities they once were. And that could help corporations become tools to detonate the final protections against oligarchs, and even foreign regimes, from stealing American elections outright.

We the Corporations, UCLA law professor Adam Winkler's seminal history of the rise of corporate personhood, points to a moment when the march to corporate rights took a distinctly rightward lurch. It was in November 1977, almost immediately after the Supreme Court invalidated the expenditure caps that Congress had just passed, when corporate America opted to test just how far its First Amendment protections truly went.[25]

The case was led by First National Bank of Boston, which joined a number of other corporations in demanding the right to "fund a campaign against a ballot referendum" set to take place in Massachusetts. The referendum, fittingly enough, would have introduced a statewide graduated income tax, allowing the state government to augment federal efforts to make sure the wealthiest individuals in Massachusetts paid their fair share. The key wrinkle, and the key legal issue at play, was that even though the new tax would only apply to individuals (rather than corporations) the state's leading corporations nonetheless wanted to block it—not least because many of the wealthy individuals targeted also happened to run organizations like First National Bank of Boston.[26]

The bank's higher-ups wanted to bankroll a media blitz opposing the referendum, but state law prohibited corporations from spending funds "to influence the outcome of a vote that [did not] materially affect their assets and holdings." In other words, since these corporations had no skin in the game—even if their presidents and boards might—they couldn't spend any corporate funds opposing the referendum. But as the bank's lawyers saw it, this was a clear violation of their First Amendment rights as an American corporation. They sued, and brought the case all the way to the Supreme Court, asking one simple question: "Does the First Amendment protect the rights of corporations to attempt to influence the outcome of elections in which they have no direct monetary interest?"[27]

It didn't take long for them to get their answer. The justices found that Massachusetts "could not restrict the bank's spending and the speech it financed, because people had the right to hear what the bank might say." The bank couldn't produce outright advertisements opposing the referendum, but it could help finance the opposition, even if it wasn't directly affected by the referendum. To the court, this was "the type of speech indispensable to decision-making in a democracy, and this is no less true because the speech comes from a corporation rather than an individual."[28]

There was no explanation for why the bank's position was "indispensable" to Massachusetts voters' abilities to decide on the referendum—or any more "indispensable" than, say, the positions of the Boston Red Sox, Dunkin' Donuts, or any other Massachusetts organization. But that question was beside the point. For the court, all that mattered was that American corporations could not be muzzled on any topic, anywhere. They had the right, just as any other American individual, to opine on—and fund—any campaign, candidate, or election they wanted. It was a remarkable extension of First Amendment protections to American corporations. And it wasn't much of a leap to the next step: that corporations should also be allowed to spend whatever they liked to back whichever referendum, whichever candidate, and whichever campaign they wanted.

Which is precisely what happened next. It took a bit of time, but soon these pro-corporate forces coalesced into, as Phillips-Fein recounted, a "tremendous intellectual and political effort to shift the political culture toward support for the interests" not only of American corporations but of the "very wealthy" individuals overseeing them. They already knew that the Supreme Court had jettisoned the expenditure caps, meaning that their preferred candidates—those who, for instance, would strip away basic environmental or labor regulations, or hammer the U.S.'s existing tax regime into nothing—could spend as much as they wanted. All that was left was to make sure those candidates and their allies had access to the ever-growing pots of money that America's corporations and America's wealthiest could provide, with no questions asked.[29]

The term "Citizens United" has become such a shorthand for the tsunami of dark money drenching American politics that it's easy to forget where the name came from. Citizens United itself is a conservative nonprofit organization, overseen by former GOP congressional staffer David Bossie. Founded in 1988 and dedicated to anti-Democratic smear campaigns, in 2007 the group was busy attempting to take down then–presidential candidate Hillary Clinton. The centerpiece of their campaign was Citizens United's new, on-demand cable television movie, a schlock of anti-Clinton dreck with the stupendously banal title of *Hillary: The Movie*. Since the movie was scheduled for release in 2008—and since Citizens United had received significant corporate donations for producing it—the organization was theoretically banned from promoting the film, as it could have been seen as "corporate-sponsored political advertising."[30]

Yet that didn't stop the organization. Filing a lawsuit protesting the prohibitions, Citizens United eventually took its case to the Supreme Court, arguing that it should be allowed to promote its film during an election year, regardless of who its donors were. Moreover, those donors should not have to disclose their identities, because they didn't actually donate to any candidates directly—and therefore didn't have to reveal who they were.[31]

It was, on its face, a ridiculous line of reasoning. Even if Citizens United should be permitted to air the film itself, pushing the boundaries of corporations' First Amendment rights further than ever before, there was nothing in legal or political precedent that should allow Citizens United to keep its donors secret. Legally speaking, the Supreme Court should have upheld the FEC's prohibitions.

But that's not what happened. In a close 5–4 decision, the conservative majority, led by Justice Anthony Kennedy, not only sided with Citizens United but blasted the doors apart for any further efforts to check money—whether corporate or oligarchic—in American politics. While the Roosevelt-era prohibitions on corporations giving outright to candidates would remain, that didn't mean corporations shouldn't be able to spend any amount promoting the candidates and the causes they wanted. As Justice Kennedy wrote in the majority opinion, the U.S. government didn't actually have any interest in preventing anyone, anywhere, from promoting whichever candidates or campaigns they wanted. Individuals, groups, corporations—it didn't matter. To the court, money could and should be spent on elections, regardless of the source.[32] As Winkler summed up, "*Citizens United* would extend to corporations the same right to make unlimited independent expenditures."[33]

Reaching back to the *Buckley* decision, Kennedy wrote that even those previous concerns about corruption—that certain oligarchs might donate to certain candidates because they wanted to see certain policies passed or rolled back—were moot. "When *Buckley* identified a sufficiently important governmental interest in preventing corruption or the appearance of corruption, that interest was limited to quid pro quo corruption," Kennedy wrote. "The fact that speakers may have influence over or access to elected officials does not mean that these officials are corrupt. . . . In fact, there is only scant evidence that independent expenditures even ingratiate [donors and public officials]. Ingratiation and access, in any event, are not corruption."[34]

If anything, Kennedy wrote, the kinds of donation limits passed decades earlier simply denied reality. Individuals and groups will always favor certain candidates, and candidates will always favor certain individuals and groups. Such is the nature of American politics. Such is the nature of humanity. Why bother trying to prevent that? "It is in the nature of an elected representative to favor certain policies, and, by necessary corollary, to favor the voters and contributors who support those policies," Kennedy continued. "It is well understood that a substantial and legitimate reason, if not the only reason, to cast a vote for, or to make a contribution to, one candidate over another is that the candidate will respond by producing those political outcomes the supporter favors." As Kennedy concluded, in perhaps the most myopic line written in the entire history of the Supreme Court, "The appearance of influence or access will not cause the electorate to lose faith in our democracy."[35]

It was all a jumble of contradiction, a confused mess of sloppy logic and sloppier history. As analyst Matt Ford wrote, Kennedy's reasoning was "a stark and somewhat blasphemous vision for the American republic."[36] Rather than an electorate of informed citizenry and republican virtue, Kennedy claimed that the constitutional framers had outlined a nation of pure transactionalism—one in which money would buy political favor, and vice versa. And as the Supreme Court saw it, given that such transactionalism reigned supreme, it followed that any limits on the ability to use one's money for certain political outcomes was unconstitutional, even un-American. This was true for all individuals, all groups, and all corporations, who could now spend as much money as they could want in pursuit of a specific political outcome. What could be more American than that?[37]

John Paul Stevens, writing for the minority, disagreed vehemently. Kennedy and the majority "declare[d] by fiat that the appearance of undue influence by high-spending corporations 'will not cause the electorate to lose faith in our democracy,'" Justice Stevens wrote. "The electorate itself has consistently indicated otherwise, both in opinion polls and in the laws its representatives have passed, and our colleagues have no basis for elevating their own optimism into a tenet of constitutional law." It was plain for any and all to see: The wealthiest Americans' resources, whether corporate or otherwise, would always trounce any other Americans'—hence why both Roosevelt and legislators in the post-Watergate era tried to hem in American oligarchs' impact. The court's ruling, Stevens continued, was "a rejection of the common sense of the American people, who have recognized a need to prevent corporations from undermining self-government since the founding, and who have fought against the distinctive corrupting potential of corporate electioneering since the days of Theodore Roosevelt."[38]

Even at the time, the implications of the *Citizens United* ruling were obvious. If donation caps were now demolished—and if the expenditure caps were already undone, decades prior—then American corporations and oligarchs could unleash as much money as they wanted on American politics. There were still particular barriers and regulations; this unlimited floodtide of finance could only be directed to entities supporting candidates (rather than the candidates themselves), and those entities could not coordinate with the candidates they backed. And technically, Kennedy and the majority called for donor disclosures to remain intact, citing the belief that transparency could help keep the electorate informed, even if American elections were soon sucking in billions of dollars at every turn.

But those supposed barriers were wafer-thin, and almost immediately shredded. Take the barriers on coordination. Even if an organization couldn't *technically* communicate and strategize with the candidate directly, all the candidate had to do was give a public interview outlining what they thought their allies and supporters should be doing or spending money on, and—*poof!*—everyone was suddenly on the same page, with no laws broken.[39]

Or look at the disclosure requirements that Kennedy had apparently put so much faith in. By the time the court handed down its *Citizens United* ruling, disclosure requirements had already been watered down so much that they were almost meaningless. For instance, the FEC had already announced it would require disclosures under one rule only when a donation was specifically earmarked for "electioneering communications"—which almost none ever were. All of which meant that, as the Campaign Legal Center wrote in 2011, "there is no required donor disclosure."[40] Not for oligarchs. Not for corporations. Not for the foreign regimes suddenly realizing there was a way to get their illicit wealth directly into American elections.

None of that apparently mattered for Kennedy and the rest of the court's majority, who instantly obliterated any remaining efforts to keep the world's wealth out of American politics. Taken together, the implications of their ruling were staggering. Suddenly, any limits on corporate or oligarchic money in American politics were undone. Any transparency requirements, any mechanisms of tracking funds swamping American politics, any ability for regular Americans to match American oligarchs' access to resources and to politicians—all of it was annihilated. American politics were suddenly for sale in ways not seen in a century, or potentially ever.[41]

If tossing significant sums at politicians had once been unseemly, something to be publicly downplayed, the Supreme Court had just brought down the curtain on that era. It was as if the court had slapped a bright neon sign atop the Capitol Building, blazing "Oligarchs welcome here!"

"We are still only beginning to grasp what the impact of that decision was," Winters, the leading scholar focusing on oligarchy, told me. "Among the many things it did was embolden oligarchs. It gave them a sense of legitimacy. It made them think it was okay to be way more visible."[42]

There was no going back, even if it was easy to guess what would come next. After all, thanks to a separate, seminal Supreme Court ruling nearly a century prior, corporations in America were legally required to operate in the best interests of their shareholders rather than for the benefit of customers, employees, or others.[43] That is, according to American law, corporations must maximize shareholder value and profit over all other costs—even over silly things like democracy or national security. Now, thanks to the *Citizens United* ruling, corporations had a new way to maximize profits by helping elect the kinds of legislators and regulators who could wrench open new profits in the future. Corporations were suddenly under what was effectively a fiduciary duty to take as much advantage as possible of the Supreme Court's ruling—to flood American politics with as much of their wealth as they could in pursuit of ever greater profit share.[44]

Justice Stevens wrote, "The court's ruling threatens to undermine the integrity of elected institutions across the nation."[45] It was a prediction that soon became an understatement. As Matt Ford noted in 2025, "Rarely has a prophecy from [a] dissenting justice been proven so obviously correct."[46]

Yet that wasn't the only prediction that would in time prove correct. In late January 2010, less than a week after the *Citizens United* ruling, President Barack Obama strode to the dais in the U.S. Capitol, there to deliver his first State of the Union address before both houses of Congress. Outlining his policy blueprints, Obama ran through everything from economic and housing plans to new trade deals and health care policy reforms.[47]

About two-thirds of the way through his speech, the new president turned to something timelier. With the *Citizens United* decision still fresh, Obama addressed the ruling head-on. "With all due deference to separation of powers," Obama said, scanning the audience, "last week the Supreme Court reversed a century of law that I believe will open the floodgates for special interests—including foreign corporations—to spend without limit in our elections." In case the audience, both in Congress and around the country, missed his point, the president continued, "I don't think American elections should be bankrolled by America's most powerful interests, or worse, by foreign entities. They should be decided by the American people."[48]

Obama wasn't alone in airing this concern. Stevens himself had specifically cited the court's new belief that the corporate identity of the speaker (or donor) didn't matter as something that would blast apart protections against foreign meddling in U.S. elections. The decision "would have accorded the propaganda broadcasts to our troops by [Japanese propagandist] 'Tokyo Rose' during World War II the same protection as speech by Allied commanders," Stevens warned. It would even "afford the same protection to multinational corporations controlled by foreigners as to individual Americans."[49] After all, what was to stop a foreign regime from suddenly setting up an American corporation and routing as much money as it wanted directly into American politics, without anyone to stop it?

For those listening, Obama's comment was fleeting, less than a minute in an hour-long speech. But for those watching on TV, the camera promptly panned to the members of the Supreme Court, sitting at the front of the audience, berobed and stoic. In keeping with tradition, they were all entirely motionless, sitting quietly—save for one. In the back, Justice Samuel Alito was caught by the camera grimacing, shaking his head, and mouthing two words:

"Not true."[50]

How wrong he would be.

Section II

Alliance

Greed for power, like love, will permit no rival.

—GASPAR DE VILLAGRÁ[1]

5

How Greedy Can You Get?

Poor people protest—rich people lobby.

—Leon Garber[1]

In early 2014, a pair of political scientists published a striking study on the health, or lack thereof, of American democracy. Authored by Princeton University's Martin Gilens and Northwestern University's Benjamin Page, the study combed through decades of data to try to answer a single question: When it comes to American politics, who truly governs?[2]

The U.S. still had, at least for the time, all the trappings of a free and fair democracy. Elections were still routinely held, largely free from undue burdens or autocratic manipulation. American media still remained pointed and punchy, free from debilitating lawsuits or destabilizing pressures. The political opposition could still freely canvass, freely campaign, freely corral new voters into their camps. By all traditional metrics, American democracy appeared perfectly fine.

Yet as Gilens and Page discovered, that didn't mean that the American people steered American politics. Instead, as their data laid bare, the levers of American political control remained in the hands of a group of "economically elite Americans." This was a tiny group whose political influence stood out of all proportion to the size of their cohort—but which rose instead in direct relation to the size of their wealth. As the authors wrote, "Economic elites and organized groups representing business interests have substantial independent impacts on U.S. government policy, while mass-based interest groups and average citizens have little or no independent influence." Broken down, the authors discovered that policies with "high support" from a strong majority of these "economic elites" had remarkably high odds of succeeding. It wasn't that such "economic elites" always got what they wanted, necessarily; rather, it was that their say and their sway dominated anything else in the American body politic. Even when a "majority of citizens" disagreed with the wealthiest Americans' policy preferences, "they generally lose."[3]

Coming in at around ten thousand words and littered with political science jargon, the study from Gilens and Page was an unfortunate example of academic overwriting. (When was the last time you enjoyed reading about "quadratic logistic regression" or "bivariate results"?) At its core, though, was one clear conclusion: American democracy was an oxymoron—a sham steered by the wealthiest Americans. "In the United States, our findings indicate, the majority does not rule," the authors concluded. "[Our] analyses suggest that majorities of the American public actually have little influence over the policies our government adopts."[4] By the mid-2010s, as a BBC headline reported, the "U.S. [was] an oligarchy, not a democracy."[5]

At the time, the study caused few ripples. Issues like wealth inequality were far from the center of political discourse in the U.S.; the Occupy Wall Street movement had long ago petered out, while the rise of figures like Senator Bernie Sanders was still over the horizon. Gilens and Page's study came and went, and little changed. It's only in hindsight that the study proved both remarkably prescient and analytically accurate—a signal flare of where the U.S. was, and where it was headed.

Of course, as scholars like Winters wrote, this kind of oligarchy-hiding-in-plain-sight was part of the package of modern oligarchy—a kind of conscious cloaking that helped these figures rise in the first place, without any kind of public pushback. "The absence of the more frontal and visible aspects of oligarchy lead to the mistaken impression that there are no longer any oligarchs—only ordinary citizens who happen for the first time in history to enjoy politically neutral fortunes," Winters wrote in 2011. Moreover, most Americans maintained the outdated notion that oligarchies couldn't exist in nations that were at least nominally democratic. But in Winters's schematic, the kinds of "civil oligarchies" described in chapter 1 were perfectly compatible with nations that still held routine elections, that still maintained whole fleets of investigative journalists and opposition politicians and civil society groups banging on about policies and scandals and political preferences. There was no distinction between "civil oligarchies" and democracies; both could exist simultaneously.[6]

Still, there was always the latent threat that someday, even in the distant future, the broader mass of American citizenry would elect politicians and pass policies to explicitly target the oligarchs' assets. "Civil oligarchies" and democracies were compatible, until they weren't—until a figure like Teddy Roosevelt rose, or until one like Richard Nixon flamed out, leaving nothing but angry egalitarian reformists in his wake. It was that future that, in oligarchs' eyes, had to be prevented at all costs—regardless of what that meant for democracy in America or anywhere else.

But the new oligarchs had little to fear. By the 2010s it was clear they had already digested the Supreme Court rulings we saw in the previous chapter, the ones that pried the world of American politics wide open to the wealthiest Americans. As Gilens and Page discerned, those "economic elites" had already started using their wealth to effectively bid on American policies and politicians, all for their own benefit. It's not that this hadn't happened before, of course; American history is littered with previous examples of wealthy forces and factions pushing their policy preferences. This time around, though, these figures had one factor working in their favor that none of their predecessors had ever enjoyed: levels of wealth inequality that had spiraled far further than the Founders could have ever imagined, and beyond anything the world had ever seen.[7]

If we were to focus only on the statistics of modern wealth inequality in America, this book would barely include anything else. Indeed, the past decade has seen an entire cottage industry of books erupt about wealth inequality accelerating not just in the U.S. but around much of the world. Sparked in large part by the publication of Thomas Piketty's 2013 *Capital in the Twenty-First Century*, there's now an entire library of material available on the topic, much of which touches on the rise and roles of many of the oligarchs detailed in this book. For the sake of brevity, let's let a handful of data points highlight how monstrous American wealth inequality has become in recent decades—and how it's now surpassed anything the country has ever known.[8]

For instance, there's the fact that between 1980 and 2014, the incomes of the top 0.001 percent of Americans exploded, rising by over 600 percent—even as the incomes of the millions of Americans in the bottom 50 percent flatlined.[9] There's the fact that America's billionaire class, representing a fraction of a fraction of the nation, now holds more wealth than the bottom 50 percent of America *combined*.[10] There's the fact that the top 1 percent of Americans now make over twenty-six times more money than all the rest of the country.[11] There's the fact that the share of the national income that the country's wealthiest controlled by the end of the 2010s had nearly doubled since the 1970s—but for the bottom 50 percent of Americans, it had been cut nearly in half.[12] And there's the fact that, in 2024 alone, the net worth of the nineteen wealthiest families in America expanded by about $1 trillion total, hashing out to approximately $53 billion per family.[13]

The examples run on and on, and at a certain point the numbers begin blurring together. For those more visually inclined, just imagine a graph charting out the total assets held by Americans. Picture it as a boomerang lying on one side, with the flat, nearly horizontal edge representing the wealth holdings of America's lower and middle classes; the boomerang's joint, curving slightly upward, representing the American upper class's holdings; and the vertical line, running up as high as the eye can reach, representing the wealth now held by the richest American figures and families. The wealth of the richest Americans has torqued upward, bursting through the top of the graph, with no end in sight, completely untethered from the rest of the United States.[14]

Inequality has accelerated at an ever-growing pace, blowing past that of any previous eras, including the Gilded Age. By the early 2020s, it was clear that the wealthiest American cohorts now controlled a greater slice of the American economy than even the robber barons and plutocrats of the late nineteenth and early twentieth centuries. As

Zucman calculated in 2025, the share of total American household wealth that modern American oligarchs owned was now more than double the size of the wealth owned by the Rockefellers, Carnegies, and others combined.[15] As the most popular comment on an article summarizing Zucman's 2025 research—written in *The Wall Street Journal*, never a bastion of leftist thought—read, "You don't have to be a socialist to see there's a problem here."[16]

This wasn't just an American phenomenon. Such skyrocketing wealth inequality could be found in nation after nation in the modern world, whether Russia, China, Saudi Arabia, or elsewhere. Scratch a modern tyrant, and you'll often find a billionaire, whether Vladimir Putin, Xi Jinping, Mohammed bin Salman, or plenty of others.[17] Indeed, this spiraling wealth inequality seemed a distinctly *global* pattern in the early twenty-first century, infecting even places like Britain (where the top 1 percent owned 21.3 percent of the country's total wealth), France (27.2 percent), and Germany (27.6 percent).[18]

But this is an American book, focused on an especially American story (even with its global resonance), so it's worth asking: What happened in the U.S. in the twenty-first century to rocket American oligarchs' wealth into the stratosphere? Just how did these individuals—now worth not just billions, but *hundreds* of billions of dollars—break free from the gravitational pull of America's previous efforts at reining them in?

The answer spans decades' worth of policy shifts, both within and without the U.S. It involves thousands of lobbyists and analysts and middlemen looking to carve out entire careers for themselves to help the rich become richer, and protect their wealth from any and all. It's also connected to the rise of the world we've dubbed "offshore," of spiderwebs of shell companies and anonymous investments and financial secrecy, of tax havens and hidden bank accounts and impenetrable trusts, all of which have sucked generations' worth of wealth out of country after country around the world, hiding it from any journalist, tax authority, or regulator who may come knocking.

The rise of this offshore economy over the past few decades is worth a book in and of itself. And, indeed, there are some phenomenal ones written in recent years: Oliver Bullough's *Moneyland*, Nicholas Shaxson's *Treasure Islands*, Atossa Araxia Abrahamian's *The Hidden Globe*, and plenty more.[19] For right now, though, just know the ease of access to these shell companies, these financial secrecy networks, these entire policies and industries and nations that comprise the offshore world helped the wealthiest stash ever more resources into their own kitties, beyond the reach of the rest of us. Thanks to the rise of this offshore world in recent decades, tens of trillions of dollars have simply disappeared from ledgers around the globe, slipping into a world that is largely untouchable and untraceable. It created, as Brooke Harrington, the Dartmouth University expert on the offshore world wrote, "the platform for an elite insurgency opposed to basic principles like equality before the law, economic stability, free markets, and social solidarity."[20]

Even then, the simple existence of such an offshore economy doesn't necessarily explain how American oligarchs' wealth drove to suffocating heights. The rise of this offshore world—in which wealthy forces can keep their lucre safe from any kind of transparency or democratic oversight—also sparked a global revolution in how to undo existing checks on oligarchs' wealth. It wasn't just that shell companies in the Cayman Islands or bought-off bank regulators in Germany or Denmark allowed oligarchs to safely stash and launder their money. It was that the rise of the offshore world also jump-started a shift in incentive structures—political, legal, social, and more—that began to prefer and prioritize the interests and whims of the wealthiest, to try to attract and protect their riches, at the expense of the rest of us. In the process, the rise of this offshore world also led directly to the undoing of all the efforts to hold oligarchs and their wealth to account.[21]

In the U.S., this shift began decades ago. Despite the successes of income taxes—which reached over 90 percent under Franklin D. Roosevelt, Harry Truman, and Dwight Eisenhower—a new anti-tax sentiment began swirling in the 1960s, beginning under John F. Kennedy.[22] Looking for a means to boost a flagging economy, Kennedy proposed gutting the income tax rates. As he saw it, the mile-high rates "exert[ed] too heavy a drag on growth in peace time," and needed to be slashed. It was, in hindsight, a bizarre claim, given that the years before Kennedy's speech saw some of the greatest economic growth America had ever known—and far greater than anything seen in the decades since. But no matter.[23] After Kennedy's assassination his successor, Lyndon B. Johnson, pushed through legislation paring back the requirements, bringing the income tax rates on wealthy Americans, which had been 91 percent the year Kennedy was murdered, down to some 70 percent in just a few years.[24]

The bottom hadn't quite dropped out, and wealthy Americans still paid taxes at a notably higher clip than the rest of the country. But the move was a watershed. For the first time since the Second World War, wealthy Americans watched their tax rates plunge, unleashing a genie that, in time, would shake loose any remaining restrictions on American oligarchs' wealth.[25]

As the years following Kennedy's proposal wore on, the downward pressures on wealthy Americans' tax rates only accelerated. By the time Ronald Reagan entered the White House in 1981, the right man met the right moment for the kinds of right-wing policies that wealthy Americans had long championed—including, most especially, the slashing of their tax receipts. Spun as a means for oligarchs' wealth to "trickle down" to others, Reagan pulverized the tool that Teddy Roosevelt had once helped push for. When Reagan took office, income tax rates on wealthy Americans stood at 69 percent. By the time he left office, they had collapsed, coming in at a meager 28 percent—where they have largely stood ever since. Thanks to the combination of Kennedy and Reagan, income taxes were suddenly shadows of their former selves, eradicating any promise they once held as key tools in the anti-oligarch arsenal.[26]

As if that weren't enough, inheritance (or estate) taxes, that other pillar of Rooseveltian reforms to corral oligarchs, soon had their turn in the barrel. Where top inheritance tax rates had stood at nearly 80 percent for decades, helping dissolve the U.S.'s most significant estates and preventing the rise of a feudal aristocracy, Reagan's rise once more shattered the consensus. Thanks to Reagan's pro-oligarch leanings, his administration drove down inheritance tax requirements, pushing rates down to nearly 50 percent—leaving the heirs of oligarchs with more than enough to quickly rebuild their families' financial empires.[27]

And yet, if income tax cuts culminated with Reagan, inheritance tax cuts only began with him. By the end of the 2000s, those rates had crashed even further, allowing the wealthiest families to keep nearly two-thirds of an estate after a tycoon's passing. Additionally, with the rise of a so-called estate tax exemption, which allowed certain wealthy families to skip inheritance taxes altogether, the number of Americans who had to pay *any* kind of inheritance tax took an even steeper nosedive, coming in by the end of the 2010s at a resounding 0.08 percent of the total population. The inheritance tax had become little more than a rounding error.[28]

Charted out, the twin collapses of the income and inheritance taxes look like a roller coaster careening downhill, picking up speed toward and through the twenty-first century. It's not that other Americans weren't also seeing tax receipts slashed; administration after administration pushed tax cuts across the board while America's federal debt ballooned beyond control. But time and again, all these cuts redounded to only one cohort's benefit: the wealthiest Americans, watching opportunities to retain and entrench their lucre expand and expand.[29]

And yet that still wasn't all. As we saw above, downward pressures on the wealthiest cohort's tax rates took place in tandem with the outward pressures to take advantage of the swelling world of offshore finance. Secret accounts, secret companies, secret rosters of attorneys and accountants in the Caribbean, in the Mediterranean, in the South Pacific—all of it drained even more money from the till, hiding it from the American authorities charged with trying to collect taxes owed. By the dawn of the twenty-first century, American jurisdictions themselves—primarily states like Delaware, Wyoming, and South Dakota—had begun offering their own offshore services, crafting corporate secrecy tools that would allow money to effectively disappear, for as long as clients would like. Instead of complying with declining tax rates, wealthy Americans could simply hide their wealth behind a facade of shell companies, anonymous trusts, and untraceable investments, confident that their offshore networks would never be discovered, relying on growing teams of corporate providers and legal experts and accounting teams to keep their offshore wealth safe.[30]

These states, these islands, these policies, these middlemen—all of it created what Winters dubbed the "Wealth Defense Industry." Comprised of asset managers, leading lawyers, financial experts overseeing so-called family offices, and much more, this Wealth Defense Industry included all those white-collar professionals who wanted to provide their services and expertise to help their richest clients hide and protect as much of their wealth as humanly, and as legally, as possible. "When you're in a certain class of wealth, people are marketing their services to you," author Chuck Collins said in 2021. "If you have money and it is in a bank or it is invested somewhere, there are investment advisors, and pretty soon they're saying: Have you done tax planning? How do we minimize your taxes? Have you used any partnerships or trusts? Are you preparing to avoid estate taxes? How can we set up trusts for your children and unborn grandchildren? So there's a lot of money to be made working with these clients. There's a whole culture and industry surrounding wealthy families."[31]

Indeed, an entire political-economic model has arisen in recent decades to service and succor the wealthiest figures across the U.S. As more and more money has raced upward, draining public services and straining local economies, more and more opportunities have emerged to provide financial secrecy and financial protection services to help hide oligarchs' wealth. To swipe a term from political science, a "race to the bottom" has emerged among law firms, wealth and asset managers, accountants, and others looking to provide the greatest number of services in pursuit of defending their clients' money. It's a simple formula: As more and more wealth agglomerated to oligarchs in the U.S. (and elsewhere), more and more white-collar professionals wanted to help hide it—and, in the process, get a piece of that wealth for themselves. These Wealth Defense Industry professionals became the hangers-on of the oligarchic class, competing for crumbs from their billionaire clients and doing everything they can to keep the spigot open and the offshore world spinning.[32]

This all points to one inescapable conclusion. For many of the wealthiest figures in twenty-first-century America, there is no longer any functional difference between tax *minimization* and tax *evasion*. The former is technically legal, allowable to the fullest extent of the law, while the latter remains a crime, punishable by years in prison (but only if there's the will and the means to prosecute). But in practice—with tax receipts of wealthy Americans plummeting, and with ever more opportunities to dodge taxes year in and year out—they are almost indistinguishable. Whatever line may have once existed in practice between tax minimization and tax evasion has effectively collapsed.[33]

There are thousands of examples of this phenomenon available, but it's worth focusing on just one case study to get an idea of both the practices and the kinds of people we'll spend much of the rest of this book discussing. Venture capitalist Peter Thiel is a man of many talents: eyeing successful investments, backing successful political campaigns, sketching out potential futures that have a funny way of coming to fruition.[34] He is also, among other things, one of the leading antidemocratic faces of modern American oligarchy. We'll detail Thiel's illiberalism later in this book—and how that pro-authoritarian streak stems directly from a desire to protect his and his oligarchic allies' wealth—but for now, it's worth looking at one of the ways Thiel has managed to violate the spirit of American taxes, accruing billions of dollars in the process, all without committing any crimes.

It has to do directly with something known as a Roth Investment Retirement Account, or Roth IRA for short. Introduced in 1997, a Roth IRA was a tool that was supposed to help "hard-working, middle-class Americans" build out bigger retirement savings. The way it did so was easy: Instead of Americans paying taxes on money they withdrew from their retirement accounts, as was traditionally done, with a Roth IRA they would have to pay taxes only on what was *deposited* into their retirement accounts. Since all the assets in retirement accounts should theoretically grow over the decades, the taxes would be significantly less at the beginning (when assets are deposited) versus at the end (when those assets, which have grown by leaps and bounds, are withdrawn).[35]

The theory is sound, which is part of the reason these Roth IRAs have exploded in popularity in previous decades. For millions of Americans, they've been a phenomenal tool to build out retirement nest eggs, especially while other resources like pension funds have atrophied elsewhere.[36]

Indeed, they've proven so popular that wealthy Americans across the country have tried to take full advantage—even though legislators specifically prevented them from ever getting their own Roth IRAs in the first place. Since these tools are supposed to be available only for middle-class Americans, policymakers put specific backstops on the legislation to make sure the richest Americans couldn't take advantage. Blocking individual Americans who make more than $110,000 annually from operating a Roth IRA, and limiting annual contributions to only a few thousand dollars, legislators thought they'd successfully walled off Roth IRAs from a new class of oligarch then emerging across the country.[37]

But they were wrong—spectacularly so. A quarter century after their introduction, a series of IRS tax returns for the wealthiest Americans revealed that Roth IRAs had become the favorite tools of those budding oligarchs. Rather than helping middle-class Americans relieve some of their tax burdens on their retirement accounts, they'd helped oligarchs dodge billions of dollars in taxes that should have otherwise been paid.[38]

As *ProPublica* reported, the documents, which spanned some fifteen years, revealed that billionaire after billionaire took full advantage of these tools. There was Warren Buffett, widely considered one of America's savviest investors—and a man who routinely calls for wealthy Americans to pay more in taxes—stuffing tens of millions of dollars into a Roth IRA. There was Buffett's deputy Ted Weschler, managing hundreds of millions of dollars in his own Roth IRA, with millions more controlled by figures like hedge fund manager Robert Mercer, investment manager Randall Smith, and others.

Few, though, took as much advantage of these new tools as Thiel, who'd somehow managed to stash some $5 billion into his Roth IRA—all of which will never be taxed.[39] One of the cofounders of PayPal and an early investor in Facebook, Thiel is a billionaire, and has been for years. Yet as *ProPublica* discovered, Thiel has built a massive nest egg—all of it now tax-free—thanks to one tool alone: a Roth IRA. Thiel, and many of his other billionaire allies, had discovered a convenient loophole for these Roth IRAs, sitting like a black hole in the middle of the legislation.[40]

The loophole was simple. While those who made over $110,000 in annual income couldn't set up a Roth IRA account themselves, they could, if they oversaw a start-up—say, a place like PayPal—keep their income below that threshold. Likewise, while they couldn't contribute more than a few thousand dollars into the account annually, they could purchase a number of shares in their start-up, at fractions of a penny, while never breaching that Roth IRA contribution threshold. From there, all you had to do was sit back and watch your start-up and all those shares now inside your Roth IRA take off like a rocket, growing bigger and bigger by the year, and rest easy knowing you'll never have to pay a cent of tax on any of that growth.[41]

Which is precisely what happened with Thiel. Claiming an income of less than $110,000, Thiel opened a Roth IRA. He then proceeded to purchase 1.7 million shares in PayPal for only $0.001 per share, coming in well below the Roth IRA contribution limit. All Thiel then had to do was wait for PayPal's share price to take off—which, needless to say, it immediately did—and watch his account begin ballooning. By the early 2020s, Thiel's Roth IRA was worth billions.[42]

And this was only one example of one tool, linked to one multibillionaire. And it was all done without breaking any laws whatsoever. "That's a huge scandal," University of California, Irvine, tax law professor Victor Fleischer said after reviewing Thiel's documents. "How greedy can you get?"[43]

Still, it wasn't just these tax loopholes that allowed oligarchs to maximize their net worths, obliterating efforts to keep them in check. Nor was it just the story of imploded tax rates, the growth of the Wealth Defense Industry, or the rise of the offshore world more broadly. The story of the rise of oligarchic wealth in America, and the rise of unprecedented wealth inequality as a result, has an additional factor worth pausing on: the implosion of the Internal Revenue Service

(IRS), whose demise has demolished the remaining barriers to the rise of American oligarchs.[44]

The IRS, which dates its earliest iteration to the Civil War, typically has few public supporters in Washington (or elsewhere). Which is a shame, since the IRS is one of the few tools available for investigating those oligarchs obsessed with dodging taxes, and also one of the few bodies in Washington that routinely takes in far more revenue than what taxpayers spend on keeping it afloat. At last check, according to Massachusetts Institute of Technology economics professor Nathan Hendren, for every dollar taxpayers expend on the IRS—paying for agents, investigations, and the like—the IRS returns twelve dollars, payable directly to the U.S. Treasury.[45] If the IRS were a private entity, it would be routinely hailed as one of the most profitable organizations in the country.[46]

And yet, for all that success, the IRS has been little more than a punching bag in recent years, largely from the right. While part of that has to do with largely fabricated scandals—including instances of the IRS supposedly targeting conservative nonprofits—much of it stems from one primary motive: protecting the wealth of the richest Americans, especially those bankrolling the same American politicians busy gutting the IRS.[47]

As such, rather than receiving the bipartisan celebration it rightly deserves, the IRS has in recent years seen its budget and personnel slashed. In the 2010s alone, the IRS's budget fell by nearly a quarter, a decline that has only continued through the 2020s. By the end of the 2010s, the number of IRS auditors had been cut by a third, leaving it with fewer agents than at any point since the early 1950s. At the same time, the overall number of IRS audits had been sliced by over 40 percent, gouging efforts to actually make sure wealthy Americans were paying what they owed. Most spectacularly, new IRS investigations into "nonfilers," or those who didn't even bother to pay a single cent in taxes, collapsed by nearly 90 percent over less than a decade—a catastrophic drop-off that alone cost American taxpayers billions in lost revenue.[48]

It's not difficult to see who's benefited most from the IRS's slow-motion strangulation. "Corporations and the wealthy are the biggest beneficiaries of the IRS's decay," one analysis from ProPublica found.

"Most Americans' interaction with the IRS is largely automated. But it takes specialized, well-trained personnel to audit a business or a billionaire or to unravel a tax scheme—and those employees are leaving in droves and taking their expertise with them. . . . For the rich, who research shows evade taxes the most, the IRS has become less and less of a force to be feared." This was especially true for those who took full advantage of offshore services; as ProPublica added, "Given a list of American accounts in a tax haven, the IRS would often be able to audit only 10 to 15 percent of them."[49] Thanks to these Republican-led cuts, it was as if the IRS was supposed to somehow find tax cheats in a dark maze, without a flashlight, while also blindfolded and with both hands tied behind its back.

Even then, on the off chance that the IRS successfully identified a wealthy tax evader, there was still no guarantee of a successful investigation. By the end of the 2010s, white-collar prosecutions into tax fraud and other related crimes were already at a multi-decade low, on track to soon become the lowest rate the U.S. had ever seen. It was a spiral downward, with no bottom—all for the benefit of the oligarchs ascendant in the U.S. Small wonder that, by the end of the decade, the best estimates pegged the wealthiest Americans as evading at least 25 percent of their total taxes owed—a far higher clip than anyone else, and a number that has almost certainly only grown since.[50]

All of which brings us back to 2014, and to that paper from Gilens and Page. At the time, their analysis appeared surprising, even preposterous (though significantly less so in hindsight). But taken together with the other trends evident throughout the decade, it was simply laying out a reality that was there the entire time, if anyone had cared to notice. By the mid-2010s, and certainly by the end of the decade, the U.S. had transformed into a full-bore oligarchy.

Everywhere you looked, the evidence was inescapable. Anti-oligarch tax policies were hollowed out, shells of their former selves. An expanding Wealth Defense Industry swelled by the year, finding ever more ingenious ways to slip their clients' wealth into the world of hidden offshore finance, whether in the U.S. or elsewhere. Wealthy Americans were evading taxes at an ever-expanding clip, unafraid of a shattered, demoralized IRS. Whatever efforts to retain the anti-oligarchic policies of years past were being pried apart, ground to dust.

All of it culminated in perhaps the most shocking statistic of all: By the end of the 2010s, the wealthiest Americans now paid lower tax rates than *any other Americans*. Lower than cops or coal miners. Lower than teachers or secretaries. Lower than pastors or plumbers or even the politicians groveling for a bit of their wealth, pledging to do the oligarchs' bidding.[51]

It was as if the entire American economy had been tilted on its head like an hourglass, with all the nation's wealth slipping steadily into the hands of those who already controlled more than anyone else. And it was beyond anything seen in American history, far worse than anything Americans ever experienced in the Gilded Age. Indeed, it's unclear quite what to compare the current reign of the oligarchic class in America to, even beyond American history. The U.S. economy is now more stratified than ancient Greece, when the average Athenian oligarch was worth a meager $31 million. It's more unequal than even ancient Rome; figures like Julius Caesar may have themselves been worth the modern equivalent of tens of billions of dollars, but this was pocket change compared with Elon Musk, Jeff Bezos, and Mark Zuckerberg.[52]

And all this has taken place while any remaining barriers to wealth in American politics have crumbled, undone by an onslaught of court cases and lobbying and politicians reading which way the economic winds were blowing. Corporations had their rights. Oligarchs had their wealth. And American politics were suddenly being sold in ways the country had never known before—all while certain American oligarchs were, by the mid-2010s, beginning to look for allies in the most authoritarian places they could find.

6

Liberty Means Order

It is the essence of revolutions of the more silent sort that they are unrecognized until they are far advanced.

—Adolf Berle and Gardiner Means[1]

In late 2014, shortly after Gilens and Page published their paper declaring America an oligarchy, a rumply middle-aged man entered a building just south of San Francisco. Opening the door to an airy, bustling workplace, the man waddled in, dodging the scooters and skateboards swirling all around him—all part of the millennial aesthetic that the company he was visiting embodied. But this man wasn't there to enjoy any of the ping-pong matches or lounge in any of the beanbag chairs he tottered past. He was there to meet with the executive overseeing this company: a corporate head who preferred hoodies and T-shirts to pressed suits or coiffed hair, and who claimed that he had an idea for how to help this visitor.[2]

The company was called Facebook—and the executive the man was there to meet with was none other than Mark Zuckerberg. It was still a heady time at Facebook, coming before the onrush of scandals—of Russian interference, of genocides in Myanmar, of the rise of tailored disinformation and the fracturing of societies—that would define the company's later years. At the time, Facebook and Zuckerberg were still liberal darlings, feted by Obama-era officials as a company charting a path toward a more open, more democratic future.[3]

But when that paunchy man in a slightly wrinkled blazer walked into Facebook's office that day, that facade—of Facebook as a company interested in a supposedly liberal, or even America-led, future—cracked. And for a moment, for those paying attention, one could snatch a glimpse of what the next decade would have in store: for Zuckerberg, for American politics, and American foreign policy, and even for democracy on this planet.[4]

The man there to meet Zuckerberg and the rest of the Facebook brass was named Lu Wei. He was a largely unknown figure, either then or now, but for Zuckerberg and his team, Lu was more than a simple visitor; if anything, he was the key to Facebook's path forward.[5]

Lu's technical title was director of the Cyberspace Administration of China. But he was known more colloquially as China's "internet czar"—as the man charged with overseeing the Chinese Communist Party's censorship regime, tasked with barring over a billion people from reading news from around the globe, feeding one-fifth of the world's humanity only the propaganda that China's brutal dictatorship wanted them to see. Given his position, it's entirely likely that Lu was single-handedly responsible for more censorship and pro-dictatorial propaganda than any human at the time—and potentially ever.[6]

You never would have guessed that from Lu's interactions with Zuckerberg that day. As photos later published on Chinese state media showed, Lu stood at Zuckerberg's desk, rubbing his hands as he surveyed the Facebook CEO's office. One photo showed a beaming Zuckerberg standing next to Lu, the two of them—Facebook's top official and China's top censor—caught in a moment of laughter. (Whatever comment sparked the chuckles has been lost to time, or perhaps just censored.)[7]

On its face, the meeting could have been dismissed as a simple one-off, as little more than a polite move on Zuckerberg's part to spend a few moments with a foreign official. But there, in the bottom corner of one image, just out of focus, is a photo of another man smiling back up at Zuckerberg and Lu. It was the man Lu ultimately reported to, and whom Zuckerberg, according to later reporting and congressional testimony, would do everything he could to placate. The photo is of Xi Jinping: the man who has spent years overseeing China's sprawling, suffocating kleptocracy, responsible for keeping one in every five humans on the planet in the grip of a decades-long dictatorship, and for constructing the largest system of concentration camps the world has seen since the days of the Nazis.[8]

Xi's photo, grinning up at Zuckerberg and Lu, graced the cover of a book the Facebook head had specifically posed on his desk: a copy of the Chinese dictator's new publication, compiling dozens of Xi's speeches, interviews, and analyses.[9] The book itself is as wooden and stilted as you might imagine (one quote from the tome reads, "Exchanges and mutual learning form an important driver for human progress and global peace and development.")[10] But Zuckerberg didn't buy the book for the content. Instead, it was yet another tool to suck up to Lu, to ingratiate himself with Beijing, and to do whatever was needed to open up China to Facebook. To align, in other words, with the most powerful autocracy in the world—and become a force that other autocrats around the world could use for themselves.[11]

Lu's meeting with Zuckerberg was brief. Not long after he arrived, the Chinese official shook hands with the Facebook chief, and doddered back out of the office, past the scooters and the skateboards and the bustling millennials once more. There were no formal agreements that day. But the meeting sparked a strategy for Facebook that would, in time, become clear. Zuckerberg wanted Facebook to be able to tap China's market. And if that meant providing whatever services the Chinese Communist Party and Xi Jinping asked for, whenever they wanted, so be it.[12]

It's not as if Zuckerberg was the first American executive to court China. Indeed, by the time Lu shuffled into Facebook's offices, there were already innumerable scandals of American corporate heads looking the other way about basic human rights crimes in China, buttering up to the Chinese dictatorship at every turn.

There was, for instance, the cozy relationship between companies like Nike and China, overseen for years by billionaire Phil Knight. Concerns about Nike's usage of child labor and so-called sweatshops in China dated all the way back to the 1990s, when the shoe company was discovered running factories that employed young teens, some paid as little as two dollars a day for their labor. (Not to be outdone, Nike set up similar sweatshops around Asia, from Vietnam to Cambodia to India.)[13] Much of Nike's and Knight's wealth was built on the broken backs of Chinese youths, showing other American companies a path toward profitability, and a path toward escaping things like basic labor or environmental regulations.

American companies like Apple likewise built their empires thanks to ruthlessness in China. In one notorious example, Apple relied on China's Foxconn manufacturing plant to turn out its cutting-edge products. Conditions at the plant were so horrendous that, by the early 2010s, assembly-line workers began killing themselves in such droves that it generated international news coverage. "Worker after worker threw themselves off the towering dorm buildings, sometimes in broad daylight, in tragic displays of desperation—and in protest at the work conditions inside," *The Guardian* reported, with "suicides and sweatshop conditions [reigning] in the House of iPhone."[14] That didn't stop Apple's corporate executives—starting with Steve Jobs, and flowering especially under current CEO Tim Cook—from constantly praising their Chinese partners, including the country's ruling one-party dictatorship. Nor did it stop Apple from continuing to rely on the good graces of China's dictatorship to keep its manufacturing going, even to this day.

And yet, by the mid-2010s, something had qualitatively shifted. It wasn't just that America's corporate heads relied on Chinese labor and leadership for their profitability, or even similar programs in other autocratic nations like Vietnam, Cambodia, and Bangladesh. It was that many of America's corporate heads began to realize around this time that, if they wanted to continue turning a profit, they would have to begin pushing the Chinese Communist Party's interests wherever and however they could. No longer could they simply strike manufacturing or supply chain agreements with Beijing. Now, they needed to help the Chinese Communist Party go on the offensive, both at home and abroad.

Part of the reason for this shift was purely economic; thanks to an overreliance on Chinese labor, resources, supply chains, and more, these companies had grown ever more dependent on Chinese services and manufacturing as the twenty-first century continued. Providing Beijing with increased leverage, the Chinese Communist Party began to discover new pressure points it could exert on American businesses, who were all looking to maximize profit however they could.[15]

But much of this shift—this eventual willingness to not only bend the knee to Beijing but to search out ways to expand and entrench the Chinese Communist Party's rule—stemmed also from domestic developments in China itself. Shortly after ascending to leadership in 2012, it was obvious that Xi had shifted the structure of power in Beijing. Rather than return to the days of rotating leadership, Xi had eliminated all rivals for power, cementing a personal dictatorship the likes of which China had not seen since the days of Mao Zedong.

China has obviously never been a democracy under the party's leadership. But by the mid-2010s, it was clear that any hopes of ousting Xi from power and replacing him with another party official had shriveled. If certain American corporate heads wanted to continue profiting from their relationship with Beijing, they would now have to not only back the Chinese Communist Party in things like labor and economic disputes, but specifically provide Xi with whatever he'd need.

This, then, was the situation when Zuckerberg met with Lu on that chilly December day in 2014. Unlike Nike or Apple, Facebook had not yet cracked the Chinese market. Beijing remained wary of allowing a service that could potentially lead to domestic destabilization, or even democratic reforms. But for Zuckerberg, China remained something of a holy grail of corporate expansion—a kind of final challenge for a company that had already recruited over a billion customers elsewhere. Zuckerberg realized that China presented another potential billion customers, and billions upon billions of dollars in potential ad revenue, if only he could get the Chinese dictatorship to sign off.[16]

"In our mission to connect the world, there have always been a few difficult problems we've always said we'd get to eventually: connecting those who can't afford the internet, building satellites for those who don't have any connectivity infra[structure], and connecting countries where we're blocked like China," Zuckerberg wrote in an internal email to other Facebook executives in the summer of 2014. "We've now made progress on every single other major problem, and the last one on the list is China." Entering China would be, as Facebook whistleblower Sarah Wynn-Williams would later write, Zuckerberg's "number one priority." The cost didn't matter, nor the fact that the Chinese dictatorship stood for everything that Facebook supposedly opposed. All that mattered was the potential revenue, just sitting there, waiting for Zuckerberg to take advantage. And it wouldn't take long to reveal the depths to which Zuckerberg would stoop to succor the Chinese dictatorship—and what that would mean for American democracy, the American economy, and even American national security.[17]

Zuckerberg's campaign to cultivate China's totalitarian leaders began with Lu's visit, with the Facebook head shepherding the Chinese censorship chief around Facebook's office, making sure that Lu saw Xi's book sitting prominently on his desk. As Chinese state media later reported, Zuckerberg told Lu that he'd purchased multiple copies of Xi's book for his colleagues. "I wanted them to understand socialism with Chinese characteristics," Zuckerberg claimed.[18]

Indeed, it was the Facebook chief who took the lead on cultivating China and its higher-ups. He made multiple trips to Beijing, part of a "charm offensive" that saw him speak Mandarin with a group of students and post photos of himself jogging around Beijing, despite the debilitating air pollution.[19] Zuckerberg also took his efforts directly to Xi himself. In late 2015, he met Xi during a visit in Seattle, where the two shared a conversation in Mandarin.[20] But it wasn't just pleasantries. In a display of remarkable groveling Zuckerberg asked the Chinese despot if he would name the baby he was expecting with his wife, Priscilla.[21]

It's not as if folks couldn't see what was happening. Online, social media accounts mocked Zuckerberg's sycophancy, drawing up images of him as part of Xi's communist cadre. Pro-democracy activists in Beijing slammed Zuckerberg, comparing his knowledge of China's domestic politics to that of a toddler.[22] Many watched with a mix of befuddlement, wondering why Facebook thought Xi would ever open his country up to the social media platform, and secondhand embarrassment, mocking the depths to which Zuckerberg lowered himself for Beijing. It all added up to, as one analysis in the Council on Foreign Relations wrote, "Zuckerberg's Love Affair with Xi Jinping."[23]

Years later, though, we know that Facebook's campaign to cultivate China wasn't simply about public glad-handing and requests for Xi to name Zuckerberg's child. Behind the scenes, according to Wynn-Williams, Zuckerberg and Facebook's leadership were drafting plans to become a secret tool in the Chinese Communist Party's strategy to continue, and even expand, their dictatorship for decades more. (Meta, Facebook's parent company, has said that Wynn-Williams's allegations were "false and defamatory.")

While he was meeting with Xi and other party officials, Zuckerberg was also overseeing a mission to transform Facebook into whatever China needed, so long as it meant the company could enter the Chinese market. Zuckerberg directed his colleagues to focus almost exclusively on providing Beijing with a suite of services and assurance, telling his staff that "everyone need[ed] to tackle this intensively right away, if Facebook's going to get into China anytime soon." To that end, Zuckerberg laid out a three-year plan to have Facebook "fully operational" in China, from opening a sales office to partnering with a "senior Chinese leader" in order to build out a formal "partnership" with the Chinese government.[24]

The rest of Facebook's leadership apparently had few qualms about the strategy. Nor did they have to guess at the lengths Zuckerberg was willing to go to help China's regime—a regime that was then in the middle not only of overseeing a genocide of Uyghurs but also bloodying Hong Kong protesters demanding a modicum of democracy. As one Facebook staffer laid out, "In exchange for the ability to establish operations in China, [Facebook] will agree to grant the Chinese government access to Chinese users' data—including Hongkongese users' data." In other words, Facebook would provide Beijing with every scintilla of information on its Chinese users, including those the regime was then in the middle of bashing.[25]

The only hesitation appeared to come in how Facebook would publicly spin its pro-China efforts. When the team lead heading up the China project suggested defending the Chinese Communist Party's efforts to supposedly uphold "the rule of law" in Hong Kong—even while the regime cracked skulls and unleashed oceans of tear gas on pro-democracy protesters there—another Facebook colleague pointed out that this was the same defense that Nazi officials had used at the Nuremberg trials. ("I think the point at which you have to explain Nuremberg to the head of the team leading your China entry is probably a red flag," Wynn-Williams, who witnessed many of these moves firsthand, later deadpanned.)[26]

By 2017, Facebook had formalized its pitch to China's dictatorship. Dubbing it "China—Our Value Proposition," the document is a heap of corporate pablum, paeans to how Facebook will help China "boost your economy" and "help you prosper." But the document went beyond just this kind of PR-speak. As Zuckerberg proposed, Facebook would "promise to help [the Chinese Communist Party] increase its global influence" and "promote [a] safe and secure social order." Facebook, in other words, was actively offering to aid the efforts of a regime—and, specifically, a dictator in Xi—that had already declared designs on hegemony not just in China, and not just in Asia or the Western Pacific, but potentially globally as well. A regime that, needless to say, would brook no dissent or deviation from what Xi viewed as his historical mission to restore Chinese primacy, with the Chinese Communist Party—and Xi himself—remaining in power for as far as the future could hold. A regime that, by the mid-2010s, was clearly chafing against anything that could prevent the party's expansion and entrenchment, regardless of the human cost.[27]

According to Wynn-Williams, the primary service Facebook pitched to aid Xi and his regime was simple: surveillance. "Facebook is saying: Millions of your citizens will post information about themselves publicly that you can view and collect if you want," Wynn-Williams later summarized. "Facebook is dangling the possibility that it'll give China special access to users' data," an "intent to work hand-in-glove with the [Chinese Communist Party] to help enforce its will on its people." As the pitch approvingly quoted Lu, the Chinese official who'd visited the Facebook office years before, "Liberty means order."[28]

The pitch itself was about as far a divergence from Facebook's public-facing claims as you could find. This was a company, after all, that promised to lead to a more open, freer world. Not only was it led by a man who remained a liberal icon, but Zuckerberg had even gone so far as to publicly castigate the White House when it was revealed that the Obama administration had secretly spied on allies. Now, just a few years later, that same company and that same leader were allegedly pledging to work as a furtive, undeclared surveillance tool for arguably the most repressive regime on the planet.[29]

To be fair to Zuckerberg, he wasn't the only American corporate leader of the era who was covertly plotting with forces in China about how to aid the CCP's and Xi's grip on power. If anything, you could even argue that Zuckerberg—who was at least humiliating himself in *public*, in addition to his private scheming, all on China's behalf—wasn't nearly as furtive as some of the others.

Take Google, then as now overseen by chief executive Sundar Pichai. Long held up as a paragon of corporate responsibility, Pichai had helped publicize Google's "Don't be evil" ethos. Through the mid-2010s, Google's reputation as an upstanding corporate citizen even appeared well-earned; not only did the company regularly speak out against surveillance-related policies but it even went so far as to actively leave China entirely in 2010 following the Chinese Communist Party's moves to censor Google's search results.[30]

But then, by 2018, the company appeared to have second thoughts. As China's market expanded, and as Xi's standing both domestically and internationally increased, Pichai and Google began to search out ways to reenter China—and, as with Facebook, provide the Chinese dictatorship with the kinds of tools needed to cement its reign for years to come.[31]

Mulling ways to return to Beijing's good side Google's leadership and engineers soon hit on a potential tool they could provide to China's dictatorship. Code-named "Dragonfly," Google's project was right in the company's wheelhouse. It would be a new search engine—but one that would directly censor all the results that Xi and his autocratic allies wanted removed, such as information about human rights, the 1989 Tiananmen Square massacre, or even accurate air quality data.[32] Nor was that all. Dragonfly would link search queries directly to Chinese users' phone numbers, and even track the live locations of Chinese users—handy bits of information for a regime trying to retain totalitarian control.[33] "In terms of the most worrying aspects [of the Dragonfly project], I think it's the fact that Google would seemingly be giving pretty open access to Chinese authorities, giving them info and data on all Chinese users," Joe Westby, a researcher on technology and human rights at Amnesty International, told me.[34] It would, in other words, be precisely what Google claimed it wouldn't stomach: a censorship and surveillance tool more insidious than anything previous, available to a dictatorship throttling the freedoms of over a billion people.[35]

Only a few dozen employees at Google had any idea about the project; one former employee said the information was kept purposely "siloed," with communication often verbal (rather than written) in order to "reduce the paper trail," per one report.[36] As one journalist noted, "The secrecy surrounding the work was unheard of at Google." *The Intercept* reported that Google leadership had even "forced employees to delete a confidential memo . . . that revealed explosive details" about the program.[37]

But it didn't take long for the details of the project to spill out. When information about the proposed censorship engine began circulating within Google, a mass of employees was immediately up in arms. An internal open letter demanded that "Google employees need to know what we're building."[38] One former engineer who'd contributed to Dragonfly even went public with his contrition, saying the project "did nothing but benefit me and my career, and so it fits the classic definition of morally heedless behavior: I got things and in return it probably made some other people's life worse."[39] Another former senior researcher publicly blasted Google as well, saying the company's leadership had obliterated its supposed "ethical red lines."[40] And Congress wasn't far behind; once word of Dragonfly leaked, a series of bipartisan letters to Pichai accused him of leading a "coup for the Chinese government and Communist Party."[41]

They weren't wrong. Indeed, when faced head-on with questions about the program, Pichai ducked and dodged, claiming that Dragonfly was simply an "experiment" without any firm plans to launch—a claim that not only contradicted reporting on the project but even Google employees' own understanding of the project.[42] As one Google employee said, Pichai's defense that Dragonfly was simply an experiment "was ultimately horse shit. This was run with 100 percent intention of launch from day one."[43]

As with Facebook's and Zuckerberg's sudden pro-China lurch,

Google's and Pichai's decision to race to service China was a remarkable about-face for a company that supposedly cared about things like human rights and basic freedoms. "We've seen this with [Mark] Zuckerberg and Facebook: countless apologies, and then policies and practices that are in direct contradiction to those [apologies]," Courtney Radsch, advocacy director at the Committee to Protect Journalists, told me. "Their motto used to be 'Don't be evil'—but maybe they've left that to the wayside."[44]

It was also whiplash for observers, who'd long assumed that Google and Pichai were also interested in charting a stable, democratic—and, it went without saying, American-led—future. "This has much wider implications for Google, and for human rights online more generally," Westby added. "We're talking about the world's largest search engine caving in to a model of the internet that is probably the most repressive in the world. . . . [Google's] willingness to so demonstrably compromise on its human rights commitment will mean that it's very difficult to trust Google on its statements on human rights, and on its own commitments to human rights in the future."[45]

If it were only Zuckerberg and Pichai sprinting to aid the Chinese Communist Party, that would be one thing. But at the time Zuckerberg was proposing a new surveillance tool and Pichai was drafting a new instrument for censorship, all for Beijing's benefit, another company and another figure—and yet another erstwhile liberal darling—were also targeting China for business, without any concerns for the cost, for the implications, or for what the relationship may one day mean for American national security.

In 2014, the electric vehicle company Tesla announced that it was moving into the Chinese market. At the time, electric vehicles were still in their relative infancy, their market share a fraction of an automotive industry still dominated by internal combustion engines. Tesla's founder and chief, however, could see which way the world was shifting—and how to best place himself and his carbon-minimal company at the center of a transformation about to take off.[46]

Elon Musk, a sui generis inventor and corporate visionary—a

man who at one time fielded comparisons to Tony Stark, and not without reason—has single-handedly ushered industry after industry into a new chapter.[47] Private space travel was a far-off dream, until Musk used SpaceX to prove that the rockets blasting past Earth's atmosphere could also return in one piece. Private networks of linked satellites bringing high-speed internet to the farthest reaches of the planet were the stuff of fantasy, until Musk proved that Starlink could do just that. And brain-machine interfaces were relegated to science fiction—some optimistic, some utterly terrifying in their implications—until Musk's Neuralink revealed that patients could use computers or play video games with their thoughts alone.[48]

But it was with Tesla that, throughout much of the 2010s, Musk witnessed his greatest success and his greatest impact. The South African native helped transform electric vehicles into not only something viable and appealing for consumers but something that could even be scaled—making both owner and company billions of dollars in the process. It would be Tesla that would usher in the electric vehicle revolution, with Musk at the wheel.

Still, as Musk well knew, those electric vehicles not only had to be manufactured somewhere, they also had to be marketed to ever-growing audiences if the company was to remain in the black, especially with new competitors coming online. Which is when Musk discovered the appeal and the promise of the one market and the one government that Zuckerberg and Pichai had also recognized: China.

Musk's relationship with China began simply enough, with Tesla announcing the opening of a number of retail stores in places like Shanghai and Beijing in the mid-2010s.[49] It quickly became apparent that, as Walter Isaacson reported in his 2022 biography of Musk, China was "key to Tesla's global ambitions"—not only because China was now a larger market for passenger vehicles but because its manufacturing prowess was key to turning out Tesla's products.[50] In 2018, Musk and Tesla announced a new arrangement with the city of Shanghai. Identifying hundreds of acres of "grassy fields" near the city, the local government green-lit the creation of a sprawling, behemoth manufacturing plant for Tesla alone. Coming in at approximately $7 billion, it would be Tesla's first overseas manufacturing plant, creating approximately a half-million cars per year.[51]

In and of itself, there was nothing especially unique about these arrangements. There was, however, one element that stood out, perplexing observers. Rather than require Tesla to partner with a local company—the kind of joint-venture agreement the Chinese regime almost always requires of foreign companies setting up shop in China—the government allowed Tesla to go its own way. "Tesla is doing something that no foreign auto maker has done before: build a factory and a network of suppliers in China without the support of a local joint venture partner," *The Wall Street Journal* reported.[52]

It was all so sudden, almost haphazard. In one meeting between Musk and his colleague Robin Ren, Isaacson writes:

> Ren started to go through a slide deck with maps, financing commitments, and deal terms [in China], but Musk did not look at them. Instead, he stared out of the window of his plane for almost a full minute. Then he looked Ren directly in the eye. "Do you believe this is the right thing?" Ren was so taken aback that he paused for a few seconds before saying yes. "Okay, let's do it," Musk said.[53]

Shortly thereafter, Musk flew to Shanghai, where he met with Chinese officials at a signing ceremony, formalizing Tesla's presence in China. He stood in a "red-draped banquet hall," toasting to a brighter future ahead. There was no reason to think his time in and ties to China wouldn't be beneficial for everyone involved.[54] And in a way, as he stood there in that state room, surrounded by suits and clinking glasses, he was right—but not for any of the reasons he thought.

On its face, the arrangement appeared almost exclusively for Tesla's benefit, allowing the company to retain all the revenue generated from its Chinese operations. But if you tilt the agreement, looking at it in a slightly different light, something else emerges. In pulling Tesla in—and in providing the company with what appeared to be a sweetheart deal to both tap the Chinese market and take advantage of Chinese manufacturing—Beijing put an offer on the table that was, for a company like Tesla, too good to refuse.[55] And in so doing, the

Chinese regime was able to entice a man in Musk whose importance to the American economy was not only swelling but who appeared to have increasing political leanings, preferences, and connections—all of which a foreign regime could, if it played its cards right, eventually take full advantage of.

At first, the arrangement was a galloping success for everyone involved. The behemoth Tesla factory in Shanghai was completed within a year, quickly churning out over half of Tesla's total vehicles, well on its way to meeting its goal of a half-million Teslas produced each year—and already representing "the bulk of [Tesla's] profits."[56] China's growing domestic market couldn't get enough of Tesla, with the company "ignit[ing] demand for electric cars among consumers."[57] Tesla and Musk couldn't have asked for more.[58]

Musk himself traveled routinely to the country, spending "more time walking assembly lines [there] than he did walking around the design studio."[59] And he kept up an increasingly chummy relationship with Chinese officials. His closest link was with a man named Li Qiang, who was elevated to the position of premier in 2023 and widely viewed as a close ally of Xi, even arguably the second-most-powerful man in China. In one meeting between them, Li referred to Musk as an "old friend," going out of his way to praise Musk's toddler son as a "handsome little boy." Footage of the two of them meeting shows a pair of smiling men, apparently tickled with one another.[60]

For most observers, Tesla clearly appeared to get the better end of the deal. But as the years went by, it became obvious to those both outside and inside China that the balance in the relationship was shifting. Tesla may have turned out record profits, and jump-started demand for electric vehicles in China itself, but the company was also becoming betrothed to Beijing in a way it almost certainly never intended.[61] Rather than diversifying its output and target markets, Tesla glided ever more toward dependence on China, and on outright reliance on remaining on the Chinese regime's side.[62]

Some of that soon started to seep into Musk's public comments about the relationship. It didn't take long for Musk, a supposed "free speech warrior," to start singing the Chinese Communist Party's praises—and, like corporate heads before him, playing down all the human rights abuses, crimes against humanity, and rank brutality the regime itself is accused of.[63] One 2020 interview is worth quoting at length, showing how Musk had begun laundering Beijing's propaganda for audiences. As he said:

> [My] experience with the government of China is that they actually are very responsive to the people, in fact, possibly more responsive to the happiness of people than in the U.S. And when I meet with Chinese government officials, they're always very concerned about this. Are people going to be happy about a thing? Is this going to actually serve the benefit of the people? It seems ironic, but even though you have sort of a single-party system, they really actually seem to care a lot about the well-being of the people. In fact, they're maybe even more sensitive to public opinion than what I see in the U.S.[64]

But it wasn't simply rhetoric. Because by the early 2020s, Musk had begun undergoing his own transformation, collapsing from a celebrated entrepreneur into a fetid, conspiracy- and allegedly drug-addled force in American politics—from a man who once relied on scientific research and high-quality output to a sewer of misinformation and fascist behavior. And it wouldn't be long before foreign governments, not least China, realized that in that collapse stood an opportunity—and that American oligarchs had transformed into potential pawns for whichever regime came calling.

7
Hit Job

Families are always rising and falling in America.
—Billy Costigan[1]

In the late 1990s, a wealthy New Jersey banker named Charles Kushner invited a young, up-and-coming Israeli politician to his office in New Jersey. Kushner, who had long supported Israel, was eager to cultivate ties with like-minded officials in Jerusalem—with those who saw Israel as a port in the storm, and with those who were willing to stretch the outer bounds of the law in pursuit of their interests. This Israeli politician he'd invited fit the bill: He not only viewed Israel as a state blessed by a higher power but in the years to come he would be accused of everything from ethnic cleansing and war crimes to even genocide, all in pursuit of Israeli expansionism. This was a man whom, in other words, Kushner wanted to support—so much so that Kushner gave him a $10,000 check to help his political chances.[2]

But it wasn't just about the money, at least not that day. In addition to hosting the politician at his office, Kushner later invited him to spend the night at the Kushners' home, about an hour's drive outside New York City. While there—an expansive seven-bedroom estate in northern New Jersey with an atrium, a floor-to-ceiling fireplace, and much more—this Israeli met Kushner's lanky, athletic son, an affable teenager eager to please his father.[3] The younger Kushner gave up his bedroom for the politician, opting to sleep in the basement of his parents' house for the night. He also, according to later reporting, joined the politician in the driveway, where the two of them played basketball, dribbling and driving under the New Jersey sky.[4]

The politician in the driveway that day was a once-and-future Israeli prime minister named Benjamin Netanyahu, a man later at the heart of Israel's lurch toward authoritarianism, eventually wanted by the International Criminal Court for crimes against humanity in Palestine.[5] And the boy he played basketball with was Jared Kushner, who would later marry Ivanka Trump, daughter of a real estate and reality television magnate named Donald Trump.

It was a quick visit, and it's unclear what the teenage Kushner made of it all, distracted as he likely was by all the other things teenage boys prefer to focus on. But it was an interaction that set a crucial precedent for young Jared's future. Because while Netanyahu at least had a clear set of skills—however malign, and even potentially criminal, they may have been—Jared didn't have many apparent skills at all, on or off the basketball court.[6]

But that lack of discernible talent didn't necessarily matter. Because as Jared learned that day, he could, through family connections alone, attach himself to a man who would become one of the world's most notorious politicians. It was a pattern that would play out, time and again, in the decades to come, launching Jared himself to greater prominence than he'd ever imagined, injecting him directly into the heart of the American policymaking process and showing how, in the twenty-first century, American oligarchs didn't actually need any skills at all, just the right family links. How, in other words, you could ride on the coattails of other oligarchs before you—and eventually become one yourself.[7]

As Kushner grew into adulthood, his track record remained unimpressive. Where the other oligarchs detailed in this book all exhibited clear scholastic success, passing through Ivy League universities before moving on to bigger things, Kushner scuffled through school in New Jersey. Kushner may have been a perfectly pleasant, perfectly sociable kid, but he also proved a middling student. Not inept, per se, but obviously not destined for any kind of academic glory. "Jared was not in [his high] school's highest academic track in all courses, and his test scores were below Ivy League standard," writer Daniel Golden noted, revisiting Kushner's early years.[8] Students at his high school were split into a trio of classifications: "L" was highest honors; "K" was honors; and "H" was everyone else. When later asked, no one in either the "L" or "K" tracks could "recall ever sharing classes with" Kushner.[9] As one school official said, "There was no way anybody in the administrative office of the school thought [Kushner] would on the merits get into Harvard."[10]

And yet, when he graduated in 1999, that's precisely what happened. It was a remarkable turnabout for a forgettable student. Kushner's admission, however, happened to coincide with one thing in particular: A year before he applied, his father, Charles, had pledged a $2.5 million donation to Harvard University—payment that only started "after Jared matriculated." While Harvard has never admitted that the younger Kushner's acceptance was in any way tied to his father's donation, it's not much of a stretch to see the connection, especially given that Harvard's acceptance rate was at that point the lowest in the school's multi-century history.[11]

Or look at Kushner's track record as a businessman. Where Zuckerberg built Facebook, Pichai shepherded Google, and Musk oversaw an entire suite of companies, Jared struggled time and again to get a single venture off the ground after his college years. There was, for instance, his takeover of *The New York Observer* in 2006, with Kushner only twenty-five years old at the time. While the paper was known for its splashy mix of society coverage and industry insights, it didn't take long for Kushner to begin prioritizing his own preferences, whether personal, business, or otherwise.[12]

Multiple editors reported that Kushner was less interested in the trappings of successful journalism, and more in what *The Observer* could do to score personal vendettas and elevate Kushner's own business interests. (It's unclear if Kushner even enjoyed the paper; as he said at one point, he found the paper "unbearable to read," comparing it to "homework.")[13] One editor, Peter Kaplan, told people that Jared wanted to specifically run a "hit job" on a prosecutor who had previously convicted the elder Kushner on a range of charges, including using a sex worker to both entrap and blackmail his own brother.[14] Another former editor, Kyle Pope, echoed the claims that Kushner pushed for "hit jobs" against opponents, including one involving a banker. Pope even wrote an entire essay in the *Columbia Journalism Review* detailing Kushner's biases and pressures atop the *Observer*. As Pope noted:

> I came to believe that Kushner wanted the *Observer* to succeed not because he believed in what it was, but because he needed it as a bullhorn for his own business interests. The episode with the banker "hit job" was only the most egregious of many more minor examples of him using the paper to prop up himself and his family, ranging from a dubious annual listing of the top people in New York real estate (which was dominated by his clients and business partners) to favorable treatment for other people in his business circle.[15]

The *Observer's* reputation was soon in tatters. Kushner turned the outlet into a tabloid, purposely deleting articles that painted friends and allies in a bad light, and then canceled the paper's print run in 2016—but not before using the paper to endorse Trump as the Republican nominee for president.[16] In the process, Kushner transformed the "once-proud" outlet into a "Potemkin village" of a publication, more interested in listicles and celebrity gossip than anything approaching real journalism.[17] Whatever role *The New York Observer* may have once played in the city's goings-on is long gone, a shadow of a formerly great newspaper, limping along with little readership and less impact.

The paper was far from Kushner's only business fiasco—nor was it even his most spectacular bust. That honor belongs to a forty-one-story glass-and-steel office building in midtown Manhattan known as 666 Fifth Avenue.[18] Originally constructed in 1957, the skyscraper has been a staple of the area for decades, with tenants ranging from Warner Brothers to Xerox to Citigroup.[19] (The building is featured in the opening scene of *The Wolf of Wall Street*, in which Matthew McConaughey's character drunkenly thumps a song on his chest.)[20]

In 2007, 666 Fifth Avenue went on the market and soon attracted Kushner Properties, the real estate portfolio company overseen by

Jared and founded by his father. With Jared's leadership, the company purchased 666 Fifth Avenue for nearly $2 billion—a staggering markup, given the building had sold for only $518 million seven years prior.[21] It was, even for New York, an astounding sum, representing the "biggest deal of its kind in the United States at the time," as journalist Andrea Bernstein wrote.[22] Investing $50 million of the Kushners' own money, the company borrowed some $1.75 billion to cover the remaining purchase fee.[23] It was a remarkable risk, even at the best of times.

But a few months later, the bottom fell out—first of the global economy, and then of Kushner's fortunes. The building at 666 Fifth Avenue suddenly appeared like an albatross around Kushner's neck, getting bigger by the minute, threatening to drown not just the investment itself but the Kushners' entire net worth. Vacancy rates in the building spiked, draining rents, even as interest on the ten-figure loan climbed and climbed. Forced to restructure the loan, Kushner soon had to sell a chunk of the building just to cover costs.[24] But with the skyscraper still bleeding both tenants and money, it had become a "crippling liability" for the entire Kushner family—one more failure not just for Kushner Properties but for Jared Kushner himself, who had imploded yet another storied part of New York's landscape.[25]

And then, in November 2016, the American people elected Donald Trump president. And everything—for Jared, and for American oligarchy—changed.

When Jared married Ivanka in 2009, there was little sign that his new father-in-law would ever return to a former glory he once claimed.[26] The real estate impresario had become a reality television punching bag, a supposed billionaire whose companies had declared bankruptcy multiple times over, resorting to shilling for projects—Trump University, Trump Steaks—that swung between fraudulent and farcical. In time, Trump's business ventures would be exposed as destinations for kleptocatic wealth from across the globe, all while Trump bilked contractors and clients alike. Not only would the Trump Organization later be convicted of massive tax fraud but Trump himself would soon become a convicted felon: a white-collar criminal whose onetime business empire had been exposed as little more than a dirty money laundromat.[27]

And yet, for anyone living through the twenty-first century, you know that's only half the story. Because shortly after Kushner married Trump's favorite daughter in a New Jersey ceremony—at a Trump golf course, naturally—his new father-in-law became the face of a racist conspiracy theory, positing that the new President Barack Obama was never born in the United States and was thus ineligible for the presidency.[28] It was that lie that would soon restart Trump's rise, this time not in business but in politics.[29] Becoming the face of the racial revanchism rising around the U.S.—of largely white voters unable to stomach that a Black man had become the president—Trump soon congealed enough support that he launched his own presidential campaign in 2015. He slapped down any Republican challengers, taking the nomination, then eked past Democratic nominee Hillary Clinton, losing the popular vote but landing an Electoral College victory.

And then he was president. And he needed people around him he could trust. People who'd stood in his corner every step of the way. People who'd never wavered, even when others turned their backs.

People like Kushner. And it didn't take long for Kushner to take full advantage of the fact that his father-in-law was suddenly president-elect—or for regimes around the world to suddenly look to Kushner as their gateway to the incoming president and all the policy potentials that could come with it, if only they could recruit Kushner to their side.

The first regime to hit upon the idea of using Kushner as their wedge into the new Trump administration was Russia. While much of the supposed nexus of Russian infiltration in Trump's 2016 campaign was overblown—Trump's former campaign manager, Paul Manafort, maintained a clandestine back channel with at least one Russian intelligence officer, but there's no evidence that Trump himself was ever a Russian asset—the Kremlin immediately looked for new avenues into the new administration.[30] The most appealing was a type they, and plenty of other dictatorships around the world, recognized: a family member close to the ruling leader, a wealthy intimate of a wealthier patron who didn't have any kind of ideological scruples about things like "democracy" or "human rights."

Kushner fit the bill. As Bernstein wrote, "The Russians had figured out that Jared had rare influence over his father-in-law." It was an apt insight—one that would pay dividends not just for Moscow but for plenty of dictatorships elsewhere.[31]

Pursuing Kushner, Vladimir Putin tasked a specific underling with connecting with the new president's son-in-law. Kirill Dmitriev is a balding, bespectacled Russian national, whose most memorable feature is a head that slightly resembles an overcooked egg. He's also a man who has seen one of the most meteoric rises in the Russian system, perhaps more than anyone else over the past two decades in Russia. As the current head of Russia's sovereign wealth fund, Dmitriev—who, alongside the fund itself, would later be directly sanctioned by the U.S.—is nominally in charge of perhaps a greater pot of Russian state assets than any other figure in Moscow.[32] More important, Dmitriev studied at both Stanford and Harvard, in addition to working at the consulting firm McKinsey & Company, meaning that he is the only member of Putin's regime who can speak the same social language—understanding the same topics, navigating the same jargon—as the Americans produced by these nominally prestigious institutions.[33] Americans such as Kushner.

As investigators and analyses like the Mueller Report would later reveal, Dmitriev pitched himself as someone who was simply "interested in improved economic cooperation between the United States and Russia," and that, if only the U.S. "approached [Russia] with respect and willingness to understand our position, we can have major breakthroughs quickly."[34] Dmitriev connected with another intermediary, a hedge fund magnate and Kushner friend named Rick Gerson, knowing that Gerson could be trusted to pass along information from Moscow to Kushner himself—such as a memo from Dmitriev outlining a potential rapprochement between Russia and the U.S. Kushner at the time still hadn't met Dmitriev, and didn't yet know who he was. But when Gerson passed him Dmitriev's memo, Kushner "said he would get it to the right people," soon passing it along to Trump's cabinet—a remarkable feat for a figure who had neither any foreign policy experience nor any formal position in the new administration.[35]

Dmitriev wasn't the only channel Putin used to get to Kushner; the Russian dictator also directed another oligarch, Petr Aven, as well as the Russian ambassador in Washington to set up multiple lines of communication with the new president's son-in-law.[36] Kushner even held a "secret meeting" with the head of another sanctioned Russian bank, trusting the bank chief to outline the "best ways [for Moscow and Washington] to work together."[37] But it was with Dmitriev—a man who, in time, would become the main figure Putin looked to in order to influence Washington—that Kushner developed the strongest rapport. "It was with Kushner that Dmitriev established the closest and most trusting relationship," the Russian outlet *Novaya Gazeta* would later write.[38] And it was a relationship that, in years to come, would be more fruitful than either Dmitriev or Kushner could have ever hoped for.

While Dmitriev was looking for ways to orbit Kushner, Trump had different ideas for the direction he wanted his son-in-law to lean in. Immediately after the election, Trump tapped Kushner to be the person in charge of Middle East policy. Despite his lack of experience, and his absence of any expertise in the region or in foreign policy more generally, this was the man Trump selected to oversee a new path forward for one of the most important regions in the world. It was a move both head-turning and head-scratching, launching Kushner to a more prestigious role than he'd ever known. And a role that dictators in the region eagerly took advantage of.

First up was the United Arab Emirates. Overseen by dictator Mohammed bin Zayed Al Nahyan, whom we met in the prologue, the UAE had grown in recent years into one of the most brutal, rapacious regimes in the region, accused of everything from rank torture to inflaming genocide bloodshed in Sudan.[39] In 2016, MBZ himself directed a broad-based and wildly successful political interference and influence operation in the U.S.—one that not only bankrolled multiple American think tanks, but that controlled fleets of lobbyists both legal and illicit, siccing them throughout Washington to improve the

UAE's image, all of which helped tamp down criticism in the U.S. of Emirati cruelty.[40]

Almost immediately after the election, MBZ eyed Kushner as a potential ally. Shunting President Obama to the side, MBZ pivoted to schedule a meeting with Kushner in New York, identifying the new president's son-in-law as the key point of entry to influence the new administration. As Kushner himself later admitted, MBZ "wanted to create a relationship with the incoming [Trump] administration, discuss [the UAE's] views of the world, and to hear our views of the world."[41]

The meeting itself was supposed to be secret, but American intelligence agencies easily followed MBZ's path to New York. It was a move—snubbing the sitting president in favor of the president-elect's son-in-law—that left Obama officials "shocked at the breach of protocol."[42] Little matter for the Emiratis, though; for them, Kushner was suddenly a man for whom foreign leaders should cancel meals with the sitting president.

Meeting at a penthouse in New York's Trump Tower, the two jumped into discussion. MBZ began unspooling complaints about how the Obama administration handled relations with the UAE, and how the "situation in the Middle East" could be "different."[43] Ninety minutes sped by, with the conversation growing more and more "animated."[44] It didn't take long for the two to realize they were simpatico, especially when it came to Iran, which MBZ and Kushner detested in equal measure.[45] Small wonder that, throughout the Trump administration, MBZ "received almost everything he sought from the White House."[46]

But all that was in the future. Because at the outset of Trump's first term, there was one additional regime that Kushner specifically wanted to build bridges with. One even more inhumane than the Emiratis, known not just for mass state-sanctioned executions and for tossing women in prison for the crime of driving cars, but for shearing apart opposition journalists with bone saws, tearing tendons and limbs from prone bodies, all because they exposed the regime's criminality and corruption.[47]

It was Saudi Arabia, a dictatorship overseen both then and now by a tyrannical, even messianic, figure named Mohammad bin Salman (also known by his initials MBS). By 2016, MBS was in the middle of sidelining any potential rivals for power in Saudi Arabia, all while launching devastating bombing raids on civilians in Yemen, ordering the killing of journalist Jamal Khashoggi, and entrenching arguably the most anti-female dictatorship this side of the Taliban.[48] He also oversaw a regime that had already identified Kushner as someone who combined a "transactional mind-set" with "scant knowledge about the region," and specifically "ignorance of Saudi Arabia."[49] Still, as the Saudis determined, Kushner was "a crucial focal point in the courtship" of the Trump administration. It was Kushner whom MBS would lure, and whom MBS would use as a wedge to leverage American policy for his own benefit.[50]

The dance between Kushner and MBS began quickly. Part of that was geostrategic; sharing a mutual loathing of Iran and a clear antipathy toward anything resembling democracy, the two figures, only a few years apart in age, immediately hit it off. But there was something else, another tether that linked Kushner and MBS and many of the other figures their circles would soon expand to include: money. Money for them. Money for their families. Bottomless pots of money, even if it also meant bottomless pits of bodies, full of journalists and opposition politicians who'd dared to stand up to the Saudi regime. "They see the world in the same way—they see themselves as being in the tech-savvy money world," one former official observed.[51] It was that money that would soon make Kushner effectively a sock puppet for MBS, along with a number of other American oligarchs eager to earn just a bit of the Saudis' wealth. And it all started almost immediately after Trump's first election.

Following Trump's 2017 inauguration, Kushner helped organize his father-in-law's first foreign trip—not to an ally or other democracy, but to Riyadh. It was an idea that was all Kushner's; as one former official said, "Jared was the engine for all this." Despite widespread opposition even within his administration—"The whole establishment was opposed to it: State, [Defense], Treasury, everyone," said one official—Trump agreed, shining a bright, unmistakable signal on his administration's priorities.[52]

But Trump wasn't the only member of his family to travel to Saudi Arabia. Within the first year of the new presidency, Kushner himself made at least three trips to the country, holding "private, informal conversations" with the Saudi head, including spells where he and MBS "stayed up until nearly 4 a.m. several nights, swapping stories and planning strategy," according to *The Washington Post*.[53] Emails transformed into phone calls, which transformed into texts on WhatsApp, with the two growing so close that they soon started referring to each other as "Jared" and "Mohammad."[54]

It was enough to make the heart glow, were it not for the horrific crimes MBS's regime stood accused of. But it was soon clear that the chummy relationship between Jared and Mohammad "constitute[d] the foundation of the Trump policy not just toward Saudi Arabia but toward the region," as one former official added—the most important relationship, in perhaps the most important region in the world, all overseen by a man whose most notable accomplishment to date had been marrying the president's daughter.[55]

It didn't take long for rumors to begin swirling, especially that this naïf had fallen hard for a man widely regarded as a master manipulator. Soon, reports emerged that Kushner had not only offered MBS advice on how to further entrench his dictatorship but that the Saudi regime had purposely "cultivated the relationship with Mr. Kushner for more than two years."[56] MBS even bragged to MBZ, the Emirati chief, that the Saudi despot had Kushner "in his pocket."[57]

It was difficult to conclude otherwise. Intelligence officials grew increasingly alarmed by Kushner's willingness to fly to Riyadh for private confabs with MBS, even as the Saudi tyrant was in the midst of one of his latest bloody sprees. "There was a risk the Saudis were playing him," said one former White House official, stating the obvious.[58] Things reached such a breaking point that Kushner's application for top-secret clearance was denied, primarily because of "concerns about potential foreign influence on him."[59] Kushner, though, didn't need to worry; Trump soon reportedly overruled his intelligence officials, granting Kushner top-secret clearance and allowing him access to all information that would cause "exceptionally grave damage" to American national security if it ever leaked—or if a foreign dictator ever got his hands on it.[60]

As MBS tucked Kushner further and further into his pocket, other regimes began to try to replicate his success. A year into the Trump administration, American intelligence analysts reported that officials in a range of foreign countries had also "privately discussed ways they can manipulate Jared Kushner . . . by taking advantage of his complex business arrangements, financial difficulties, and lack of foreign policy experience."[61] They'd hit on the same conclusion as MBS did: Kushner was both gullible and tractable—and continued to serve as perhaps the key vector for reaching Trump himself.[62]

One of the countries that came to this realization was Israel. Such a conclusion was unsurprising: For years, Kushner and his family had supported Israeli imperialism in Palestine, helping bankroll so-called settler organizations stealing Palestinian lands in the West Bank, accelerating efforts to eliminate Palestinian sovereignty wholesale. With Kushner now in the American president's ear, the Israeli government—led by Kushner's former basketball buddy, Benjamin Netanyahu—realized it had a direct line in the White House whenever it needed it.

Nor were the Israelis alone. China reportedly came to the same conclusion, as did Mexico.[63] Indeed, it was the latter that sparked perhaps the greatest internal hand-wringing during Trump's first administration—and highlighted the lengths Kushner would go to short-circuit American diplomacy. At one point in his tenure, Secretary of State Rex Tillerson—America's top diplomat, lauded across American politics for his geopolitical know-how—went out to eat at a local Washington restaurant. There, he discovered Kushner sharing a meal with someone Tillerson had no idea was in town: the Mexican foreign secretary.[64]

Ambling up to the table, Tillerson watched the Mexican official blanch. "I could see the color go out of the face of the Foreign Secretary of Mexico," Tillerson remembered. "I smiled big, and I said, 'Welcome to Washington. . . . Give me a call next time you're coming to town.'" It was a breathtaking diplomatic faux pas, with a foreign country's leading diplomat flying to the American capital and not even bothering to inform the American secretary of state.[65]

Still, this wasn't necessarily the Mexican official's fault. "As it turned out later, the Foreign Secretary was operating on the assumption that everything he was talking to Mr. Kushner about had been run through the State Department and that I was fully on board with it," Tillerson continued. "And he was rather shocked to find out that when he started telling me all these things that were news to me, I told him this is the first time I'm hearing of it."[66] Back in his office, Tillerson fumed, watching his role as America's chief diplomat slip away to a man whose only credential was being in-laws with the president. As Tillerson asked his staff in a fit of frustration, "Who is the secretary of state here?"[67]

Cozying up with a Saudi despot, covertly dining with the Mexican foreign secretary, aiding Israel's devastating imperialism, all while placing himself at the mercy of foreign regimes who knew a mark when they saw one—what, exactly, was Kushner doing? And what kind of effect was he having on American policy?

There is still a mountain of unknowns about Kushner's impact, his motivations, how he tipped American foreign policy for his own benefit. This will take decades to unravel, only when—or if—archives are finally opened.

More broadly, though, Kushner confirmed what foreign regimes had long suspected about America's ruling families: The best way to get into their ears was through family members. This was a practice that long predated Kushner or Trump. Stretching all the way back to the days of Jimmy Carter, foreign regimes had hired or recruited family members of sitting presidents or other executive branch officials to do their bidding for decades. Jimmy Carter's brother lobbied on behalf of the Gaddafi regime in Libya; Joe Biden's son moonlighted for oligarchs in places like Ukraine and Romania; the Clinton family opened their foundation to dictatorship after dictatorship. In a certain sense, Kushner is just a continuation of a trend decades in the making.[68]

But Kushner represented something else: a new variation on an older theme, one that had its own particular characteristics, and which pointed to the utter collapse of any distance between American policy and private interests that we would see explode in Trump's second administration. Hanging behind all Kushner's international foibles—the secret meals, texts, and flights, all without any kind of transparency or oversight—was another reality, circling all the way back to Kushner's pre-administration days, when he was little more than a struggling businessman. Because even as a key player in the Trump administration, Kushner still had that albatross slung around his neck: that skyscraper at 666 Fifth Avenue, dragging Kushner's corporate wealth like an anchor, down into the deepest red.

There had been one moment, right before the election, when Kushner thought he'd found a lifeline. Joining his father, Kushner sought out a half-billion-dollar investment in the building from a leading figure in another Middle Eastern nation: Qatar.[69] Connecting with Sheikh Hamad bin Jassim al-Thani, the former head of Qatar's sovereign wealth fund (and a man also known by his own initials, HBJ), the Kushners thought they'd initially found success, with HBJ pledging $500 million on the condition that the Kushners could raise the rest of the needed financing elsewhere. Negotiations bled into 2017, well into the new Trump era—an era in which Jared Kushner was suddenly America's chief diplomat, in practice if not in name. However, after revelations about a number of other potential investors in the building sparked public criticism, the Qataris pulled out—leaving the Kushners once more on the hook for spiraling debt payments.[70]

And then, the blockade began. In early June 2017, the Saudis, Emiratis, and a number of other regional regimes severed both diplomatic and economic ties with Qatar. Invasion hung in the air, with Saudi and Emirati troops massing at Qatar's border. A tinderbox looked set to explode.[71]

Even more shocking than the blockade, however, was Washington's response. Rather than act as the neutral arbiter many expected, the Trump administration immediately threw its weight behind the Saudi and Emirati moves—a stance led by none other than Kushner, who, according to CNN journalist Vicky Ward, "greenlit" the entire operation in the first place.[72] "The Saudis would not have risked moving forward without permission from somebody," one Tillerson aide said. The conclusion was inescapable: "That person must have been Jared."[73]

While there's no direct evidence connecting the blockade and Kushner's investment, the financial entanglements raised legitimate questions about his motivation. He had already "reamed the Qatari ruling family for not doing the deal" on the 666 Fifth Avenue property, Ward reported. Now, with the U.S. siding with Saudi Arabia and the UAE, would the Qataris have looked at the sudden destabilization "as Kushner saying, 'If you don't pay my father [for 666 Fifth Avenue], the Americans are going to sanction an invasion of your country'"?[74]

Months wound by, and the blockade remained in place, alongside the ever-present threat of invasion. And then, suddenly, a report emerged that Kushner's company was in "advanced talks" about 666 Fifth Avenue with a company owned in part by Qatar.[75] Shortly afterward, Kushner himself flew to Qatar to hold "intergovernmental meetings" with the regime.[76] A few weeks later, confirmation: The Kushners and the Qatar-backed company had reached a deal that would "remove the [Kushner] family's biggest financial headache," opening an onrush of funding and rescuing them from the sinkhole that was 666 Fifth Avenue.[77]

Everyone involved denied any kind of quid pro quo, shooting down the idea that the new financing was in any way related to anything Jared may or may not have been doing in the White House. But the outcome was clear. (For good measure, around the same time *The New York Times* reported that Kushner's personal wealth had quintupled in recent years, rising to over $300 million—and yet he "appears to have paid almost no federal income taxes," using a number of handy tax minimization schemes to dodge any payments otherwise due.)[78]

It was a remarkable turnabout for both the family and the building. And it was a complete dissolution of any distinction between public and private interests, all for Kushner's benefit—one that arose not because of any inherent skill set, but simply because of who Kushner was and the family he had married into. It was all enough to make him, as Bernstein said, an "American oligarch."[79]

And Jared was just getting started.

8

Homophobic Fascists

How can I even begin to explain this to the kids,
that the state they live in has become a monster?
—*Paul Lynch*[1]

In the summer of 2018, while Kushner was reportedly wielding American foreign policy against those who wouldn't bankroll his family's properties, I was in the middle of Moldova, hundreds of feet belowground and surrounded by millions of bottles of wine, trying to hold my own against a dozen Christian fundamentalists drinking me under the table.

I'd arrived in Moldova to report on the annual conference of the World Congress of Families (WCF). The WCF was itself the foremost fundamentalist group anywhere in the world: a transnational organization dedicated to rolling back as many of the basic elements of liberal society—abortion access, same-sex marriage, even individual rights writ large—as it could find. It was, then as now, the leading bridge between hard-right American Evangelicals and fundamentalist counterparts in Russia, receiving funding from oligarchs on both sides of the Atlantic, linking pro-Putin billionaires wherever they could be found. The group's annual flagship conference, held that year in Moldova's cozy capital of Chisinau, was a celebration of everything authoritarian: of stripping away the basic rights, protections, and allowances that both the American Constitution and democracy provide.[2]

But that would all start later. Because on that night, in a musky, expansive wine cellar, next to the personal wine collections of people like Putin (and, bizarrely, American politician John Kerry), the WCF wanted to treat me to a multi-course and multi-bottle feast, celebrating all the momentum swirling in the U.S., in Russia, and around the world to eliminate liberal rights as we knew them.[3]

I never hid who I was; I'd properly identified myself as a journalist with the left-leaning publication that had sent me. But whatever tension may have existed soon receded into the background, with glasses constantly refilling and plates of polenta and stuffed cabbage and steaming sausages somehow never emptying. Representatives from France and Mexico, Uganda and Poland, the U.S. and Russia, as well as local Moldovans—all of them slowly turned flushed and slurry. The WCF's own press spokesperson, a man no older than thirty, tipped into drunkenness, the salmon color slowly spreading from his cheeks under his beard and down toward his neck.[4]

The chatter veered around the table, hopping from theology to Moldovan soccer to marveling that we'd somehow all ended up in the world's biggest wine cellar. Eventually, the conversation tilted into geopolitics, and to how Russia had started carving up Ukraine. It wasn't necessarily a surprising shift in topic; given that the Kremlin has occupied a chunk of Moldova for over three decades, Russian imperialism is an everyday reality for those in the country.[5]

Opinions pinballed, with some wondering about Putin's end goal, others admiring his supposed restoration of masculinity, still others losing their comments behind a fourth or fifth glass of wine. One older man, a white-haired septuagenarian from Switzerland, leaned over to me. He said he didn't necessarily approve of Putin's expansionism. But Putin was hardly his only concern.

"Putin is an imperialist," he said, wiping his mouth. "But what's worse: Imperialism, which will kill your body, or the gender ideologies that the [West] pushes, which will kill your soul?"[6]

It was a comment that swerved between biblical and bizarre. (Would he ask a Ukrainian recently bombed by Russia the same question?) But it helped explain how the WCF had transformed into a vehicle for Russian oligarchs to find allies across the spectrum of the American hard right—and how and why groups like the WCF had become spear tips for bringing the kind of autocracy Russia has long suffered directly into the U.S., dismantling any of the remaining democratic checks that could keep oligarchs, or even dictatorship itself, at bay.

While the WCF gained a certain amount of notoriety throughout the 2010s—I may have been one of the few journalists getting blotto in a Moldovan wine cellar with them, but I was certainly not the only one covering them—the group itself actually extended far back, into the earliest days after the fall of the Soviet Union. At the time, Russia was little more than an open wound: a country with shaky borders, with tens of millions of nationals watching both their savings and the empire implode, with colony after colony seeking freedom far from the Kremlin.

It was, as later Russian politicians would claim, the lowest point in the history of the Russian nation. But it was also a time of ripe opportunity. Which is what an American named Allan Carlson discovered when he arrived in early 1995, stepping into the freeze of another Moscow winter, there to collaborate with a pair of Russian political scientists on a new project that might not only restore Russian influence but even roll back some of the liberal gains then spreading across the entire post-communist space.[7]

Carlson was no novice on these topics. A former historian, he'd served on the Reagan administration's National Commission on Children, where he fine-tuned so-called family policy—the kind that made sure families were overseen by a working, domineering husband and a submissive, stay-at-home wife. The work had gotten the attention of a Russian sociology professor named Anatoly Antonov, who invited Carlson to Moscow to share some of his findings. Carlson didn't hesitate. "Family life [in Russia] just was in shambles," he later told me. "They're coming out of communism, and communism had done its damage to family life, to social life. But then on top of that, rushing in in the 1990s was the Western sexual revolution, and the two kind of combined in a whirlwind." So he packed his bags and set off.[8]

Carlson kept a diary of his trip to Russia—a record of this first meeting between the American far right and Russian interlocutors, which he later shared with me. Much of the diary is filled with minutiae: bags not appearing on the runway, the lack of potable water, "bad soup." Along the way he met with members of Russia's parliament, even visiting the embalmed body of Soviet leader Vladimir Lenin.[9]

In one entry, though—dated January 16, 1995—Carlson describes the meeting that eventually opened the door for collaboration between American social conservatives and the oligarchs close to Putin. Joining an "Orthodox mystic" named Ivan Shevchenko, Carlson writes not only about the "antique Russian furniture" and the "photos of American jazz greats" peppering the Russian's apartment but about what Shevchenko wanted from him. As Carlson wrote:

> Shevchenko wanted to talk "business." He sought help in organizing/recruiting for an international conference on the family planned that summer at an Orthodox monastery, near Moscow. I replied that I had been thinking, myself, about working to convene a conference of fairly compatible "pro family" groups from across the globe, to serve as a kind of informal Congress of Families with the purpose of (1) defining the common pressures on families in modern countries, vis-a-vis state and economy, and (2) drafting an "appeal" or "declaration" to the governments of the world, including common demands.[10]

This initial agreement—a "Congress of Families" dedicated to "pro family" policy—formed the basis for the WCF. Initially, the group met with little success; formally founded in 1997, Carlson launched the organization at a time when the ascendance of liberal values was taken for granted, especially in the U.S. Outsiders paid them little mind, viewing the WCF as little more than a reactionary, retrograde organization whose time had already passed.[11]

That assessment wasn't wrong, at least at the time. But it also bordered on the myopic, failing to imagine a world in which the WCF's views would only grow more and more popular—and would build bridges between fundamentalists and oligarchs around the world, disseminating lessons and resources for destroying democracy wherever it went.[12]

Konstantin Malofeev is a ruddy, rotund man, a bit like a bowling ball with some scraggly facial hair slapped on. He is also one of Russia's most notorious oligarchs, a billionaire henchman for Putin, dedicated to obliterating democracy wherever and however he can, whether in Russia or elsewhere. Malofeev was one of the key figures behind Russia's initial invasion of Ukraine in 2014, overseeing much of the post-invasion investment in occupied Ukraine—including, memorably, a theme park dedicated to Russian history.[13]

In a certain sense, Malofeev is little different from the other oligarchs undergirding Putin's regime, building out his financial empire on rank corruption and proximity to power. There is, however, one key difference that sets Malofeev apart: an avowed desire for theocracy, and for a restoration of outright monarchy in Russia. Nicknamed "God's oligarch," Malofeev has been linked to any number of religious-right funding operations in Russia and abroad, from churches to children's groups to fascistic television channels spouting pro-Putin propaganda.[14] He is unapologetic in his pursuit of restoring monarchy in Russia, and for doing anything and everything he can to spread oligarchic rule.[15]

And those efforts aren't limited to Russia. Because as reporting and revelations elsewhere reveal, Malofeev is one of the sources of funding for the WCF itself—despite the fact that the Russian oligarch has been sanctioned for years by Washington, specifically for his role as a proxy for Putin. It's unclear how much Malofeev has given to the group; neither he nor the WCF have ever revealed the total amounts.[16] But it's clear that Malofeev has taken an especial interest in the group, so much so that he has assigned his right-hand man, a young, urbane associate named Alexey Komov, as his representative to the WCF—and to many other far-right groups in America, all of whom have opened their doors to Moscow in the process.[17]

Indeed, it was Komov I was there in Moldova specifically to speak with. After surviving the far-too-boozy night with the fundamentalists,

I stumbled to Chisinau's grand Republican Palace, trying to keep my hangover at arm's length. Finding an empty seat in the main hall, I slumped through the conference's opening ceremony, unclear if what I was seeing was real or another wine-sotted hallucination.

A gilded string orchestra opened the festivities, playing acoustic renditions of Coldplay and the Black Eyed Peas, while opening speakers railed against the "aggressive invasion of radical liberalism." Shortly afterward, a young couple walked down the main aisle, hoisting a confused, bow-topped baby above their heads. Ascending the stage, they spent nearly five minutes swaying the infant back and forth for the audience, all while baby photos cycled in the background and ballet dancers twirled alongside. They were soon replaced by two dozen young girls who sang a Romanian version of "We Are the World," serenading the approximately two thousand people who had turned out for the conference. Speaker after speaker then took the dais, railing about "perverted marriages" and the "promotion of pornography." In a fit of spiritual mathematics, one speaker even claimed that when "one devil is taken out of a body, seven others enter." At a certain point, I began praying for my hangover to take over, if only to distract me for the rest of the conference.[18]

Eventually, as the breakout sessions began, I shifted toward the hallway hosting the midmorning snacks. And there, standing next to the crudités, was the man I was looking for: Komov. He was of average height, lithe, with his hair slicked back and in a tan suit, speaking fluent English to a group of rapt listeners. I knew a few facts about Komov at that point. He was, for instance, a former nightclub owner from Moscow, who also maintained an outsized interest in yoga. He'd apparently tired of the lothario lifestyle, turning by the end of the 2000s to fundamentalist Christianity—and toward providing whatever services he could to Malofeev, who hired him as his lead assistant.[19]

The Russian oligarch didn't waste any time, immediately assigning the debonair Komov to a new project. As an extension of Malofeev, who was in turn an extension of the Kremlin, Komov would target fundamentalist Americans and their benefactors, many of whom were looking for inspiration for how to dismantle liberal democracy and restore so-called traditional values across the country, eliminating any limits on oligarchs in the process.[20]

Komov's initial entry point was the WCF. With the group accepting Malofeev's funding, the oligarch appointed Komov as his official representative on the WCF's board.[21] Soon, the group began expanding, reaching out far beyond just the U.S. to sign up partners around the world, forming a network of allies dedicated to decimating liberal democracy wherever they could. In the process, the WCF became not only the largest international group propounding fundamentalist values across the globe but also a kind of clearinghouse for autocracy.[22]

And Komov was along for the ride. Using the group as a springboard, he was soon glad-handing with fundamentalists around the world, in the Balkans and South America, Western Europe and Africa. But it was in America that, time and again, Komov and Malofeev found their greatest successes—and the greatest appetite for lessons on how oligarchic wealth could help drive a stake through democracy.[23]

In the early 2010s, Komov began a series of trips to the U.S. to recruit more and more allies to his and Malofeev's side. In early 2014, he arrived in Los Angeles to speak at a gala event for Movieguide, the U.S.'s leading Christian filmmaking group, dubbed by *The New Yorker* the "Christian Oscars." Komov strolled the red carpet, kitted out in a black tuxedo.[24] Movieguide allowed him to take the stage as one of the event's presenters, announcing him as a "Christian family advocate."[25]

Shortly thereafter, Komov traveled to the U.S. once more to attend the annual soiree for the National Organization for Marriage, the leading organization dedicated to eliminating same-sex rights. This time, Komov was there to cheer on his fundamentalist allies and to pledge his support. In one photo from the event, Komov can be seen smiling next to an up-and-coming Republican politician named Ben Carson—a man who would, in short order, become a member of Donald Trump's cabinet and one of Trump's most outspoken supporters.[26]

From his perch as perhaps fundamentalist America's favorite foreigner, Komov then turned toward recruiting the leaders of America's Christian homeschool movement. He began schmoozing with Mike Donnelly, the head of the Home School Legal Defense Association (HSLDA), America's most prominent homeschooling association. As Kathryn Brightbill, a legislative analyst with a nonprofit that advocates for accountability in homeschooling, told me, the HSLDA "is probably the major player who's driven American homeschooling in the last thirty years, and they've always been a very far-right, religious-right organization." Thanks to Komov, they also became something else: an organization willing to partner with a sanctioned foreign oligarch, opening the doors for the Kremlin in the process.[27]

In 2018, the HSLDA helped host the annual Global Home Education Conference in Russia, the largest gathering of its kind anywhere in the world. While Donnelly played down his and his group's involvement, Carlson told me that the main American group sponsoring the conference was, indeed, the HSLDA. And all that was due directly to Komov, who had successfully convinced Donnelly that he and the Russian government wanted to do what they could to back his movement—a movement dedicated to "creat[ing] that next generation of soldiers for the religious right to train up kids to take over in politics," as Brightbill told me.[28] (Donnelly has denied there is anything untoward in his organization's relationship with Russia, and has said their mission is to "advance homeschooling everywhere.")

In one video from the conference, Donnelly and Komov can be seen standing in the slowly falling snow. "Our movements have the same issues, the same challenges, and as parents we really want what's best for children," Donnelly claims. "Would you agree that that's what's motivating Russian homeschooling?"[29]

"Absolutely," Komov purrs in response, a Cheshire Cat smile slowly spreading over his face. "I think we have very similar issues—and we should be close together."[30]

This, then, was Komov: a representative of Russia's most theocratic oligarch, assigned to recruit as many American fundamentalists to his—and to the Kremlin's—side as he could, finding success time and again, tallying allies across America's religious right. And there, on that day in Moldova, Komov wandered over to me, Cheshire Cat smile once more unfurling, and struck up a conversation.

I asked him initially about the WCF: this group that not only brought fundamentalist forces together from around the world, but that specifically married the kinds of fascistic fanatics in both Russia and America who had no time for niceties like liberalism and democracy. "The World Congress of Families is the platform that definitely can help to bring [people] closer, especially conservatives in the U.S. and Russia, and overcome this madness of sanctions and demonization of Russia—which is very sad, really," Komov told me.[31]

He continued on, his English punctuated with only a slight accent, eyes flitting behind his glasses, taking in both me and the room at the same time. Relations between Moscow and Washington, he said, would only be repaired over the long term. Things had "changed for the worse" in recent years, he added—not because of Russia's invasions and brutality in places like Ukraine but "because of the Deep State and the U.S. establishment," citing a canard that right-wing forces across the U.S. regularly use. "The Deep State, all the departments and bureaucrats and neocons—they put so much pressure on Trump that despite his will . . . he cannot change things," he added, listing all the reasons the White House and the Kremlin were still at odds.[32]

I wanted to keep the conversation going, asking him about other points of entry in the U.S., about how and why the forces of theocracy and oligarchy had become so entwined. But someone else had caught his eye, and he began to beg off. But before walking away, he turned back to me and offered one last thought.

"We're often shown as a strange people," he said, "like we're homophobic fascists or something." At that, he wandered back into a sea of suits, lost among a crowd of fundamentalists waiting to hear more from him.[33]

Despite Komov's denials, calling him and his allies fascists is a fair description for not only many of his oligarchic patrons in Russia but for the phenomenon of oligarchy more broadly. Modern oligarchs might not all be homophobic—even in the U.S., demolishing same-sex marriage is far from the top priority for many oligarchs—but for some the undergirding of their movements, their beliefs, and their political projects is clearly fascistic in both intent and outcome. Putin and his regime may not be traditionally fascist, organized around a single-party-state structure dedicated to an ethnically pure polity at home. But it is certainly *fascistic*, worshipful of a masculine dictator and warfare beyond its borders. The same could be said for China, or for Azerbaijan, or for Turkey, or for any of the other regimes dedicated to expansionist dictatorship. Leaders like Hungary's Viktor Orbán, Belarus's Aleksandr Lukashenko, Serbia's Aleksandar Vučić, and other right-wing authoritarians have clearly displayed tendencies *toward* fascism, if they haven't collapsed into outright fascism itself.

And, needless to say, the same is true of Trump's U.S. The jutted chin and the hypermasculine imagery, the comfort with political violence and the thirst for constant accolade, the dismissal of any political or judicial opposition and threats against any who would expose any of his or his government's corruption—all of it smacks of the kind of fascistic patterns we've seen play out elsewhere. The constant identification between both person and state—the ideology of "l'état, c'est moi"—is a kind of fascistic approach the U.S. has never seen before, not even under the Confederacy, not even under the likes of Richard Nixon and Andrew Jackson.[34]

It is this antidemocratic ethos that tethers oligarchic movements around the world. Part of it is ideological, as seen in the revanchist forces pushing Israeli or Russian expansionism. But much of that slouching toward fascism is likewise driven by the defense of wealth from any threats whatsoever. The pursuit of ever-greater riches—and the protections of such lucre from any kind of oversight, transparency, or taxation—has braided oligarchic forces together, convincing them to ally with fascistic leaders who pledge to protect their wealth from the democratic masses demanding change.

It's not as if certain American oligarchs are coy about this antidemocratic ideology. Turn back to Peter Thiel, for instance. The multibillionaire not only exploded his wealth on the backs of loopholes that were never meant for him but has been conspicuously tied to nearly every other oligarchic figure detailed in this book, from serving as an early investor in Facebook to initially partnering with Musk decades ago.[35] He is, indeed, so well-connected that one writer even dubbed those authoritarian forces arrayed around the U.S. as part of a broader "Thiel-verse."[36]

All the while, Thiel provided perhaps the greatest clarion call for why modern American oligarchs must do away with democracy, subverting and circumventing it, demolishing it however they can—and in the process became, as *The New York Times* wrote, perhaps "the most influential right-wing intellectual of the last 20 years."[37] In a notorious blog post in 2009, Thiel laid out all his antidemocratic views. "I no longer believe that freedom and democracy are compatible," he wrote. For Thiel, the last time "one could be genuinely optimistic about [American] politics" was the early twentieth century: an era that not only represented the height of Jim Crow but likewise prohibited American women from voting.[38]

Throughout the blog post, Thiel claims his antipathy toward democracy is directly related to his love of "freedom." But it's not difficult to see that this supposed "freedom" is indistinguishable from the pursuit and protection of one thing alone: wealth. In the post, Thiel lays out his opposition to "confiscatory taxes" and the "vast increase in welfare beneficiaries," claiming that "the notion of 'capitalist democracy'" has become "an oxymoron." As a result, Thiel says, he and his allies must "create a new space for freedom," whether in cyberspace, at sea, or even in leaving America—and earth itself—entirely.[39]

Thiel's entire write-up is a dense exercise in grievance: about people on Social Security or Medicare, about entire genders who don't support Thiel's preferred policies, about the expansion of American voting and economic rights over the past century. But it's also something else—a call to do away with democracy, to "exit" a political system that threatens to slow oligarchic wealth accumulation and to hem in some of those billionaires barreling through the loopholes of the American financial system that the rest of the country will never have access to.

Thiel and the oligarchic allies who "advocate 'exit' from democratic accountability imagine themselves natural rulers, reasserting hierarchies that protect their privilege," author Sarah Churchwell wrote. "Ironically, of course, it is the very democratic and economic infrastructures they scorn as obsolete that enabled their rise."[40] They were, as Dartmouth's Brooke Harrington wrote, "*noblesse* without the *oblige*"—and they want nothing less than "representation without taxation."[41]

Thiel has long denied that he wants to disenfranchise anyone, or that he's even necessarily opposed to voting in general. But it's easy to discern the kinds of antidemocratic outcomes that he and his allies prefer. It's not just in his writing. Just look at the man Thiel has tapped as his in-house philosopher. Curtis Yarvin is a lumpy, middle-aged divorcé, a former software developer with a penchant for leather jackets and convoluted, overwritten essays. He's also perhaps America's greatest advocate for dictatorship, all for the sake of an oligarchic class that has gravitated to him more and more in recent years. Yarvin himself plays down his thirst for dictatorship, preferring to cloak his beliefs as a call for "techno-monarchism."[42] Claiming that "democracy is bunk," Yarvin has demanded that Americans "get over their dictator-phobia," pushing the notion that only a supposedly enlightened autocrat could cut through the clutter and chatter drowning democracies and provide an elevated form of government that benefits all of America.[43]

It's a complete fantasy—the term "enlightened autocrat" is itself an oxymoron—and one that grates against the entire history of American politics. (Is there anything more American than opposition to monarchy?) Yarvin himself also has little use for historical accuracy or factual bases for his claims, saturating his writing in obvious errors and rampant mistruths. In one notorious example, Yarvin claimed that "European civilization" wasn't responsible for any genocides before the Holocaust, as if European-enacted genocides in places like Africa, North America, or even Ireland and Ukraine never took place.[44] Inexplicably, Yarvin has further claimed not only that places like China are bastions of free speech but that dictators don't enrich themselves or their family members.[45]

But no matter. For those like Thiel and others in his orbit, Yarvin has been something of a godsend: a willing enabler and excuser of fascism, someone who could provide rhetorical cover for the kind of antidemocratic coup that many from this world pine for. "Yarvin's links to élites in Silicon Valley and Washington are no longer a secret," wrote *The New Yorker* in one Yarvin profile. "In a 2021 appearance on a far-right podcast, Vice President J. D. Vance, a former employee of one of Thiel's venture-capital firms, cited Yarvin when suggesting that a future Trump administration 'fire every single mid-level bureaucrat, every civil servant in the administrative state, replace them with our people,' and ignore the courts if they objected. Marc Andreessen, one of the heads of Andreessen Horowitz and an informal adviser to the so-called Department of Government Efficiency (DOGE), has started quoting his 'good friend' Yarvin about the need for a founder-like figure to take charge of our 'out of control' bureaucracy."[46]

Few have embraced Yarvin as eagerly or as effortlessly as Thiel. The two met soon after Thiel published his antidemocratic manifesto, and struck up a "confiding correspondence" via email, with both "seem[ing] to take for granted that America was a communist country, that journalists acted like the Stasi, and that tech C.E.O.s [like Thiel] were their prey." The two formed something of a symbiotic relationship: the billionaire impresario, searching out allies and avenues for his antidemocratic efforts, and the armchair philosopher, willing to provide the rhetorical cover for why oligarchs like Thiel must rise above democracy—not only for their own sake but for the common good.[47]

It's a relationship that neither broadcasts widely, but it's one that has proved a blueprint for other oligarchs searching out similar ways to stave off any future democratic restrictions on their wealth. "Yarvin's polemics have proved useful for those on the right in search of a rationale for nerd ressentiment and plutocratic will to power," *The New Yorker* concluded. It's also one that helps illustrate just what these oligarchs want. After all, in claiming a desire for "monarchy," Yarvin joins none other than Malofeev—a man who has helped abolish democracy in Russia and launched a fascistic project under Putin that shows no signs of stopping.[48]

Yarvin is far from the only handmaiden to oligarchs in America. As we saw earlier in this book, the Wealth Defense Industry now comprises a wide swath of lawyers, accountants, family offices, and other white-collar professionals helping oligarchs amass ever-greater fortunes. And as author Katherine Stewart has discovered, parallel industries and populations have emerged to service these oligarchs in their political pursuits as well, helping them try to demolish the remaining guardrails of American democracy, all in pursuit of a kind of autocracy to mirror Russia's, or Azerbaijan's, or Turkey's, or any of the other antidemocratic regimes mushrooming around the world.

Stewart's 2025 book, *Money, Lies, and God*, is perhaps the most trenchant analysis of the illiberal movements gurgling around the U.S.—almost entirely on the right, almost entirely now in support of President Trump. Unlike other investigations into the fascistic forces in Trump's America, Stewart, using her own terms of art, provides a kind of architectural analysis of how all these antidemocratic movements in America in the 2020s fit together.[49]

On the ground, Stewart describes rank-and-file Trump voters as the "Infantry," comprising the militias, the keyboard warriors, and the other assorted flotsam who refuse to believe former President Barack Obama was born in the U.S., or that America is anything but a supposedly "Christian country." Stewart also outlines the "Power Players," the kind of middle-management types directing these movements and their talking points, as well as the "Sergeants," who are primarily far-right pastors and other related church officials, preferring not the socialistic teachings of Jesus but instead the kind of frothing vengefulness of the Old Testament. ("There is little room for the old 'Love the sinner, hate the sin' trope here," Stewart writes.) There are also the "Philosophers," who, like Yarvin, lay out the rhetorical excuses for why American democracy is a sham and must be swept away. Many of them pine for a so-called Red Caesar—a masculine leader untrammeled by anything like democratic oversight or political pushback, grabbing a society by the throat and forcing it back into a world in which men, and especially white men, are once more restored to the top of America's sociopolitical hierarchy.[50]

Many of these movements are diffuse, diverse, sometimes even at odds with one another. But they all have one common thread: access to deep, swirling eddies of as much money as they need. Specifically, they are all bankrolled by the final group Stewart outlines: "Funders." These are the members of the billionaire class funding the forces below them, using access to expanding pots of wealth to guide

American politics. Some of these American billionaires are increasingly familiar, like Leonard Leo, the benefactor who helped steer the Supreme Court picks during Trump's first term, building out Trumpist allies on the highest court of the land who could rule in favor of things like all-encompassing presidential immunity. Leo serves as the chair of CRC Advisors, which, as Stewart writes, "directs over $1 billion in right-wing funding toward reactionary causes."[51]

There is Carl Anderson, former head of the Knights of Columbus, who helps bankroll think tanks and media outlets. There are even organizations like Opus Dei, a far-right Catholic group that does not publicize its membership rolls. All of them together have access to, and help direct, a greater pile of money than anything hard-right forces in America have ever known. "The decisive development in the first decades of the twenty-first century was not the alliance between Team Money and Team God but the simple fact that, thanks to escalating inequality, the big money got a lot bigger," Stewart notes. "What was new was the number of zeroes in the checks—and the extremism of the thinking guiding the money people."[52]

More than anything else, it was the swelling pocketbooks of those billionaire illiberals, of those pro-autocrat plutocrats, that made the difference. In attempting to protect their wealth, they were willing to side with forces that could keep democracy at bay. As Stewart wrote, "When the Red Caesar arrives," he can thank the "Infantry" and the "Sergeants" and the "Power Players" for all their help along the way. But mostly, "he can thank the oligarchs for funding his rise."[53]

All of which brings us back to the WCF, and to the kind of political project that Komov, Malofeev, and the Kremlin have already helped oversee in Russia—and that some of the oligarchs on this side of the Atlantic would love to see take place in the U.S. They are all birds of a fascistic feather, eager to help one another dismantle democracy however they can.

In 2019, a year after the conference in Moldova, the WCF hosted its next annual gala in the bucolic city of Verona, Italy. I didn't have the chance to attend that conference, but Stewart did. And as she detailed, there was one American who spoke with more clarity, and certainly more conspiracy, than anyone else, recruited by the WCF to share his vision for what a post-democratic America could look like.[54]

At the time, John Eastman was not nearly as well-known as some of the other members of the religious-right circuit. A white-haired, rheumy-eyed lawyer, Eastman preferred to keep his head down, letting other fundamentalists take the spotlight. But on that summer's day in northern Italy, he agreed to give one of the keynote speeches at the WCF conference. In so doing, he gave voice to the kind of antidemocratic forces still churning within the American religious right—looking to Russia for inspiration and studying how oligarchic forces can demolish democracy around the world.[55]

Eastman spoke about "how secularism, liberalism, and gender confusion are destroying everything good in the world"—revealing him as a "committed ally of the theocrats," Stewart wrote. Eastman's views were hardly disguised; as he would later claim, Trump's political opponents, including the entire Democratic Party, are "an existential threat to the very survivability, not just of our nation, but of the example that our nation, properly understood, provides to the world." Similar to other far-right fundamentalists, Eastman had no problem framing America's political struggles in millenarian language.[56]

But there's one key element that sets Eastman apart from others in his orbit. After the 2019 WCF gathering, Eastman once more went to ground, disappearing into his legal work, all while American politics roiled. And then, about eighteen months after the WCF conference in Italy, a man in a paisley scarf and brown cowboy hat stood on a dais in front of the White House. Flanked by a number of American flags—as well as the already disgraced former New York mayor Rudy Giuliani—this man unspooled a legal strategy he'd been working on. Jabbing his finger and spitting into the microphone, he outlined a plan to block the electors in the recent presidential election, replacing them with electors who represented the supposedly true will of the voters—one that would return Donald Trump to the White House, no matter what the actual 2020 election results said. "We no longer live in a self-governing republic," he barked at the crowd. Blocking the 2020 vote "has to be done."[57]

The date was January 6, 2021. And the speaker was a man who would later be outed not only as one of the WCF's recent keynote speakers but as the author of Trump's broader strategy to overturn the 2020 election and overthrow American democracy entirely: John Eastman.[58]

Section III

Overthrow

And the empire as well is cocooned inside its own fortress of language—a language through the prism of which buildings are never destroyed but rather spontaneously combust, in which blasts come and go like Chinooks over the mountain, and people are killed as though to be killed is the only natural and rightful ordering of their existence.

—OMAR EL AKKAD[1]

9

Shadow Army

If wars are how Americans learn geography, then elections are how they learn about plutocracy.

—Jacob Silverman[1]

There was a moment, sometime back in the early 2020s, when it felt like the U.S. had finally turned a corner in its fight against a nascent oligarchy. That for the first time since the post-Watergate period, or perhaps even since the days of Teddy Roosevelt, a new era of reform was dawning.

Truth be told, there were many moments that made it seem like that new era had arrived. There was, for instance, the passage in early January 2021 of something called the Corporate Transparency Act. The text itself was a jumble of legalese, clauses and subclauses running page after page, tucked in the middle of a far more sprawling defense bill. But the core of the legislation was simple: For the first time in American history, the U.S. would finally outlaw anonymous shell companies, which had been for years the key ingredient in money laundering networks both near and far—and the key tool for oligarchs to build out their empires of secrecy, dark money, and offshore finance writ large.[2]

It was a thunderclap of a development. After serving for years as the world's greatest source of anonymous shell companies, open to any oligarch or kleptocrat or dictator who'd come calling, the U.S. was shutting down its untraceable shell corporation services once and for all. It was the single greatest anti–money laundering step the U.S.—or any other nation, given the scale of the American economy—had ever taken. Most remarkable, it was done with bipartisan support, and even overcame Trump's efforts to veto the legislation. At long last, the basic component of innumerable money laundering networks around the world was no more.[3]

It was a burst of momentum that the Biden administration, working to slough off all the breathtaking corruption and abuse of power of the Trump years, eagerly built upon. A few months into his tenure, President Joe Biden issued a formal memo "establishing the fight against corruption" as a "core [U.S.] national security interest." For the first time in American history, a U.S. president had elevated corruption alongside terrorism and great power rivalry as central threats to American security, and even American stability. "When leaders steal from their nations' citizens or oligarchs flout the rule of law, economic growth slows, inequality widens, and trust in government plummets," Biden announced. Corruption had now joined things like the Confederacy and communism among the pantheon of great anti-American threats—and it would now be treated as such.[4]

Not long later, Biden's administration published a thirty-eight-page strategy document laying out the president's vision. As the text outlined, "By effectively preventing and countering corruption and demonstrating the advantages of transparent and accountable governance, we can secure a critical advantage for the United States and other democracies." It was a wide-ranging view of all the things the administration could, and should, do: ways to launch anti-corruption programs across government, to pressure and strong-arm international offshore havens, to patch up all the rampant loopholes shredding the U.S.'s anti–money laundering efforts. It was, in many ways, the single greatest document the U.S. had ever authored about the threats of corruption, both internal and external—and a blueprint for what an administration with a competent president at the helm could accomplish.[5]

Nor did the Biden White House stop there. Almost overnight, new task forces popped up, directed by the White House to target all facets of modern oligarchy. There was a new group out of the Department of Justice, dubbed KleptoCapture, with the express writ to go after all the assets of crooked oligarchs abroad, especially Russia. All the yachts, the luxury jets, the pilfered artworks and gilded mansions and other symbols of their crass consumerism—all of it was now fair game.[6] The FBI likewise launched its own new task force, hitting many of the same oligarchs, with many of the same results.[7]

All that momentum continued in Congress, when the legislative branch picked up the anti-corruption mantle once more. After cracking down on the kinds of corporate bribery that had once been routine—the kinds that led directly to the passage of the FCPA, just after Watergate burst—Congress realized that their solutions were only half-baked. After all, while the FCPA criminalized the *paying* of bribes to foreign officials (and foreign oligarchs), it did little to actually stop the foreign officials (and foreign oligarchs) from *demanding* the bribes in the first place. The supply side may have shuttered, but the demand side remained wide open. And time and again, crooked foreign actors felt no compunction about turning the screws on American companies, seeing how far they could lean on them until they broke—until they were willing to break the law, opening the spigots of bribery once more.[8]

In 2023, though, Congress hit upon a solution. Passing a new bill called the Foreign Extortion Prevention Act (FEPA), the legislation effectively closed the circle of criminalizing bribery. Where the FCPA made it a crime for American companies and businessmen to pay off crooked foreigners, the new bill made it a crime for those foreign actors to even demand a bribe in the first place. Prosecuting would theoretically be more difficult—could the U.S. really extradite a crooked Laotian or Gabonese or Sri Lankan official trying to wheedle some extra money out of an American business?—but that wasn't necessarily the point. Suddenly, for the first time, the U.S. provided both a shield for businesses trying to do honest work and a potential sword to go after oligarchs trying to enrich themselves that much further. For the first time in American history, the entire process of bribery was treated as the criminal act it's always been.[9]

All these developments—the new shell company registry, the new task forces aimed at oligarchs' yachts and jets and other baubles, the new legislation closing the circle on criminalizing bribery—were nominally focused on threats outside the U.S.. On the Russian oligarchs acting as foot soldiers for the Kremlin, the Nicaraguan and Egyptian and Malaysian kleptocrats launching their illicit wealth directly into the U.S., the crooked officials in autocracy after autocracy looking to American corporations to fuel their own corruption. There would be, of course, knock-on effects for domestic American oligarchs, who could no longer hide behind American shell companies or construct their own networks of money laundering with foreign counterparts. But as with so much else in recent American history, these developments all crossed the finished line because they were pegged to *external* threats.[10]

There was one development, however, that directly arose from the *internal* threats of American oligarchs. And it had to do with rescuing perhaps the only body that could successfully target, investigate, and even unwind American oligarchs' financial empires: the IRS.[11]

As we saw back in chapter 5, the IRS had by the late 2010s become a ghost—an empty shell that turned phrases like "white-collar prosecution" into an oxymoron. (Is tax evasion even a crime if there's no one to actually investigate and enforce tax laws?) It hadn't died so much as it had been murdered, purposely gutted by those who wanted to give a leg up to the oligarchs now paying lower tax rates than farmers or miners or engineers—all while bankrolling their pet legislators in Congress (and elsewhere).[12]

But in 2022, that all changed. When Biden signed the Inflation Reduction Act (IRA) into law, he not only launched a range of infrastructure funding projects across the country but further allocated an additional $80 billion in IRS funding, parceled out over the following decade. It was a staggering injection, effectively doubling the agency's total budget. It was as if the White House had taken a defibrillator to the IRS, shocking it back to life.[13]

Nor was this just funding for administrative costs, or upgrading computers and call centers. As part of the new funding package, over half the allocation—nearly $50 billion total—would go toward "increased enforcement" of rules and regulations.[14] It was far and away the greatest single allotment for enforcing American tax laws in U.S. history.[15] And as both the White House and the IRS said, the focus would be on one group in particular: the oligarchs, and the white-collar tax cheats who'd spent years driving down their tax burden and wrenching American wealth inequality beyond anything ever before. As the IRS announced, the new funding would specifically be used to "restore fairness in tax compliance by shifting more attention onto high-income earners," and on all those "abusing the nation's tax laws."[16]

It didn't take long for the IRS to put the new funding to use. Almost immediately, the agency sent compliance letters to tens of thousands of Americans who hadn't even bothered to file tax returns in years. "Twenty-five thousand of these [targets] earned more than $1 million," *The New Republic*'s Timothy Noah noted, "and more than 100,000 of these scofflaws earned more than $400,000."[17] The IRS also announced it would be ramping up its audits—but only against the wealthiest Americans, who'd watched their own audit rates plummet in the previous decade alone, making tax fraud for American oligarchs "almost risk-free," as journalist David Cay Johnston said.[18] As part of its new campaign to finger wealthy tax cheats, the IRS announced it would assign nearly a thousand officers to specifically target millionaires. Thanks to this single funding allocation, the Biden administration had willed a new army of anti-oligarch investigators into being, tasked with targeting the richest Americans piling their pots of wealth higher and higher.[19]

The response from opponents—from those who wanted the IRS to continue atrophying, or even disappear outright—bordered on the ludicrous. Senator Ted Cruz whinged about a supposed "shadow army" of IRS agents coming to "hunt you down and take your money."[20] Another senator, Iowa Republican Chuck Grassley, even suggested that IRS workers would suddenly come strapped with assault rifles, as if semiautomatic weapons were somehow an effective tool to peel back shell companies and other offshore assets.[21] The rhetoric was overheated, borderline farcical, and arguably did more to make a mockery of Republicans' lust for destroying the IRS than anything else.

But not even Republican caterwauling could slow the IRS's resurgence. While Congress eventually sliced off a chunk of the funding the White House allocated to the IRS, the agency nonetheless emerged from the Biden era with a kind of robust energy it hadn't seen in decades. If the IRS had entered the Biden years looking like a scrawny, hesitant middle schooler, it emerged as a meaty, muscle-bound Barry

Bonds—one focused not on fastballs but on oligarchic tax cheats. As the Congressional Budget Office estimated, the funding increase would pay for itself multiple times over, bringing in hundreds of billions of dollars that the American people were rightly owed, in addition to slowing the rate of offshored finance flows and mitigating wealth inequality.[22]

Call it a shadow army if you'd like. But far better to call it a new push—of investigators and forensics specialists and, yes, even prosecutors—fighting to end oligarchy, and to finally enforce the tax laws that America's wealthiest had been blowing past for decades.[23]

By the early 2020s, something else—something broader, something more intangible—seemed to shift. It was an understanding that there was some kind of link between not just kleptocracy and national security, but even between wealth inequality and national cohesion more broadly. That a country couldn't have the kind of thriving, the kind of promise of an American dream, if it also had the kind of spiraling, stratospheric levels of wealth inequality the U.S. was barreling toward. That democracy could stretch to a breaking point, and rip beyond, if too much wealth pooled in the hands of too few people.

It was a reality and a realization that the U.S. hadn't truly considered in over a century, since the waning days of the Gilded Age. And it was certainly something that hadn't been directly addressed since the days of President Teddy Roosevelt, hitting the oligarchs directly where it hurt: their pocketbooks. Back then, thanks in massive part to Roosevelt's leadership, America had launched two salvos—the income tax and the inheritance tax—aimed squarely at plutocrats' pockets.

Perhaps, a few decades into the twenty-first century, the time had come for something similar. Perhaps the time had come for something new.

Enter the wealth tax. The idea itself is deceptively simple. Rather than simply try to roll back some of the oligarchs' wealth upon their receipt of income—or, God forbid, when they die, which could be decades in the future—take aim at them here and now, at the wealth they already own. After all, these oligarchs rarely have traditional income as such. (When was the last time an oligarch claimed a typical nine-to-five job?) Rather, they have a spiderweb of offshore vehicles and property investments, portfolios of stock holdings and mountains of securities, entire classes of assets that allow them to watch their net worths gallop higher and higher. All this while they hire the brightest wealth management and family office professionals—those members of the Wealth Defense Industry, acting like feeder fish on the whales they're servicing—to skirt even declining tax rates, allowing these modern American oligarchs to pay lower effective tax rates than the secretaries and bus drivers and cashiers just trying to make ends meet.[24]

But a wealth tax could be different. Instead of a tax located at a specific time or place—after a specific payment, or after a tycoon's death—a wealth tax could be a rolling, evergreen requirement. It would be an annual payment, based on an estimate of a specific oligarch's total assets. It would be a slice—relatively small for the oligarch in question, but mind-bogglingly huge for the rest of us—of their combined net worth, flattening the stark curve measuring the U.S.'s wealth inequality.

On its face, given that this would be a tax on static assets, a wealth tax might appear atypical, even anti-American. (Who wants a regular, annual tax on an asset you own, even if you don't do anything with it?) But that's only if you ignore the fact that most Americans already pay a wealth tax themselves. It's called a property tax, and it applies to any homeowner, from the smallest apartments to the largest mega-mansions. Every year, in every single state across the country, bureaucrats assess a nominal tax on every home—on what is, for most owners, the single most important asset they own. A wealth tax would simply be an annual tax on *multiple* assets.[25]

There is one further difference between America's property taxes and the proposed wealth tax ideas that began circulating around the turn of the 2020s. Whereas the property taxes are applied to every home in every state, regardless of the owners' net worths, wealth taxes would only be applied to the smallest sliver of the American body politic: the oligarchs. Only the wealthiest would face this new tax burden, forced to part with a few more percentage points of their total holdings. The vast majority of Americans would never experience or interact with a wealth tax. You could even call it, if you'd like, an oligarch tax.

That was the goal Senator Elizabeth Warren had in mind in making a new wealth tax one of the centerpieces of her 2020 presidential campaign. Spearheaded by economists like Gabriel Zucman, the wealth tax proposed by Warren would apply to "fortunes over fifty million dollars at two per cent annually, and those over one billion at three per cent."[26] Senator Bernie Sanders soon proposed his own version of a wealth tax, escalating rates on those worth $10 billion or more to 8 percent annually.[27] In a certain sense, the rates were surprisingly low, especially given that the U.S.'s (severely diminished) income and inheritance taxes were significantly higher. But even those few percentage points—a rounding error for the oligarchs involved—would reap *trillions* of dollars in new revenue in the years to come.[28]

Nor was it simply about increased tax receipts overall, or the trillions of dollars that could and should go toward patching up the mammoth fiscal hole at the center of American finances, which is set to pass an unfathomable $40 trillion in the near future. It was also about a sense of fairness, of justice, even of civic virtue. Of the reality that these oligarchs are not *apart* from America, but *a part* of America. And that with great wealth comes great responsibility. As Sanders said, "What we are trying to do is demand and implement a policy which significantly reduces income and wealth inequality in America by telling the wealthiest families in this country they cannot have so much wealth."[29]

Sanders's and Warren's campaigns, of course, eventually flamed out. But their proposals lit a fuse. In the years since, a wealth tax—an oligarch tax—has only grown in appeal. According to the Brookings Institution, some two-thirds of Americans backed the proposed wealth tax, including over half of Republicans. And oligarchs' claims that they would simply leave the U.S., taking their bloated wealth to another hideaway where they'd never have to pay American taxes, hasn't shaken support for this proposed tax. Even then, there's little evidence that wealthy Americans actually move because of tax considerations. As Cornell University professor Cristobal Young, who has studied the migratory movements of wealthy Americans, said in 2025, "The more money you make, the less likely you are to move."[30]

Certain oligarchs do move, and plenty more threaten to leave—but far more stay put, and simply stomach paying higher taxes. This goes especially for nations that institute a so-called exit tax, as in Australia, Canada, Germany, and elsewhere, which require wealthy residents trying to abscond to pay an additional fee on their unrealized capital gains—a further incentive for them to stay and comply with democratic tax policy.[31]

After all, this is far from the first time American oligarchs have threatened to uproot to avoid increased taxes. "You would think, to hear some people talk, that those good people who live at the top of our economic pyramid are being taxed into rags and tatters," said Franklin Roosevelt in 1936, highlighting the wealthiest Americans who continued to duck and dodge taxes at the height of the Great Depression. "A number of my friends who belong in these very high upper brackets have suggested to me, more in sorrow than in anger, that if I am reelected they will have to move to some other nation because of high taxes here. I shall miss them very much."[32]

In other words: Don't let the door hit you on your way out. But until then, pay your fair share—and help this country that has, time and again, given you everything.

It's a theme and a solution that has only expanded globally in recent years, including in the places most closely associated with oligarchy in the twenty-first century. And it's worth pausing on at least one other example to consider what those facing down oligarchy have tried elsewhere—and what it will cost us, and them, if we wilt against the oligarchs seeking to rule the U.S. and many other nations alongside.

When the Soviet Union cracked apart, undone by communists' economic mismanagement and anti-colonial protests finally throwing off Moscow's control, a new group of nations emerged across Eastern Europe, the Caucasus, and Central Asia.[33] And within nearly every one of these nations, a new cast of figures rose to initially dominate the post-Soviet landscape: the oligarchs. Grabbing ownership of distressed assets in these new countries—of oil fields and gas wells and mining deposits, of steel mills and manufacturing plants and other economic crown jewels—these new oligarchs quickly established themselves as the linchpins, and even the leaders, of the new states.[34]

Russia is the best-known case study of the rise of these oligarchs.[35] But the new Russian Federation—a country that never got over the loss of empire, of colonies, of standing as a great power to be feared—wasn't alone. Oligarchic forces in Kazakhstan and Azerbaijan and Belarus birthed dictatorship after dictatorship. Russia's story might be the most familiar, but it was not unique.

One of those places that trod a similar path, watching dreams of democracy be quickly supplanted by oligarchic takeover, was Ukraine. Similar to Russia, a new crop of Ukrainian oligarchs—some former plant managers, others up-and-coming entrepreneurs spying opportunities—quickly snapped up Ukraine's economic engines. Nor were they necessarily natural resource holdings. The banking and finance sector, even the telecom and television industries, quickly became the playthings of Ukrainian oligarchs, all of whom engaged in the same antidemocratic practices—paid-off militias, threats against elected officials, bankrolling whichever policy or politician they wanted—as oligarchs elsewhere.[36] Even well into the twenty-first century, one analyst wrote, "virtually all key sectors of the Ukrainian economy were under the control of the oligarchs."[37]

However, Ukraine managed a distinct path from Russia. Where those Russian oligarchs eventually subsumed into Putin's rule, transforming into little more than extensions of the Kremlin's neo-imperialist fantasies, Ukraine's politics fractured. Swings between competitive authoritarians and pro-democratic movements pushed Ukraine onto a different trajectory. Popular uprisings in 2004–5 and 2013–14 even managed something Russians had never achieved: ousting autocratic forces, backed by crooked oligarchs looking to entrench their own rule, trying to cement the kind of antidemocratic rule that had already taken root in places like Russia, Belarus, Kazakhstan, and elsewhere. Ukrainian protesters had successfully overthrown the pro-oligarch, pro-autocracy forces—many of which had direct links to Moscow.[38]

But there was a cost. After Ukrainians' second democratic overthrow in 2014, known as the EuroMaidan Revolution, Putin launched his initial invasion of southern Ukraine, claiming the Ukrainian province of Crimea as his own, and infiltrating further arms, men, and matériel into eastern Ukraine. His oligarchic proxies—folks like Malofeev, whose right-hand man I met with in Moldova—took full advantage, injecting their own resources into Ukraine to further destabilize the country. But even then, Ukrainian democracy trundled on. And democratic, pro-transparency reformers began unearthing the subterranean networks that Ukraine's own oligarchs relied on—including those Ukrainian oligarchs who'd helped open the door to Moscow's influence, and even to Russian troops themselves.[39]

For instance, there was the large-scale investigation into Ukrainian oligarch Ihor Kolomoisky. A chubby, cherubic man, Kolomoisky dominated much of Ukraine's steel, banking, and television industries. He also, as Ukrainian investigators later discovered, effectively imploded Ukraine's largest private retail bank, which he had overseen for years—and from which he pilfered billions of depositor dollars, threatening to collapse the entire Ukrainian economy as a result.[40]

There was also Dmytro Firtash, a scrub-haired oligarch who spent years dominating the Ukrainian gas trade and acting as a middleman for Russian interests in Kyiv. While long posing as a supposed Ukrainian patriot, Firtash instead plotted with Moscow and its proxies, allowing the Kremlin to further sink its teeth into Ukraine's economy while Firtash watched his own wealth swell spectacularly along the way. Eventually, though, Firtash allegedly tossed his bribery ring too wide, alerting American prosecutors, who soon opened their own case against him.[41]

There was in reality an entire constellation of oligarchs swirling Ukraine, dominating much of the country's economic landscape and trying to transform their economic heft into the kind of political power they envied in other post-Soviet kleptocracies. But because Ukrainian politics had tacked in a far more democratic direction, there was an opening for any politician willing to tackle the oligarchs head-on. And there was one figure, perhaps the savviest—certainly the bravest—politician that independent Ukraine had ever produced, who was willing to do so. His name was Volodymyr Zelenskyy.

Zelenskyy was, at first blush, hardly a candidate who seemed likely to spearhead an anti-oligarchic push in Ukraine. It wasn't just that he'd made his name as a comedian playacting as a Ukrainian politician, rather than spending years as a reformist politician railing against oligarchs. It was also that his comedy show had aired on Ukraine's 1+1 television station—which was owned by none other than the oligarch Kolomoisky.[42]

Indeed, when Zelenskyy was first elected as Ukraine's president in 2019, the assumption was that he'd simply do Kolomoisky's bidding, or at least serve as a bulwark for pro-oligarchic interests in the country. Soon, though, Zelenskyy began tacking in a different direction. Propelled by the kinds of anti-corruption activists and reformers who have long demanded more from Ukraine's top politicians, Zelenskyy pushed through a law that would tackle Ukraine's remaining oligarchs head-on. It would be the first time that any nation, post-Soviet or otherwise, would explicitly go after its oligarch class—and it would highlight one of the clearest fault lines in not only Europe but in the entire global order writ large.[43]

Dubbed the anti-oligarch law, the legislation that Zelenskyy shepherded through was unlike anything seen prior. Signed into law in November 2021, the bill created an official register of Ukrainian oligarchs—a list of all those who may have "significant economic or political influence in public life." But it wasn't just a final, formal identification of all Ukraine's oligarchs. The new legislation further required all Ukrainian officials to declare any contacts they had with oligarchs or their representatives. It also barred Ukrainian oligarchs from bankrolling any Ukrainian political parties, or even paying for any political advertisements. And it likewise banned them from bidding on any state assets that may in the future be privatized—which is how many of the oligarchs in Ukraine and elsewhere first obtained their deep wealth following the fire sale of former Soviet assets.[44]

The legislation wasn't airtight; plenty of loopholes abounded, from masking financing behind shell companies to adding an additional layer of figures who could act as cutouts between oligarchs and the politicians they may try to recruit. But it was a substantial, even debilitating blow to Ukraine's oligarchs. For the first time in Ukrainian history, a democratically elected administration had taken the country's oligarchs class on directly—and won. The oligarchs could retain their wealth, at least for the time being. But the doors of Ukrainian politics would be closed to them, to their influence, to their efforts to transform Kyiv into a stomping ground for autocratic billionaires.[45]

Even rhetorically, it was confirmation that there is no such thing as a pro-Western, or even pro-democratic, oligarch—that in the end, oligarchs of any stripe and any public standing are a threat to democracy anywhere. "In all successful European countries, there is no branch of government like the oligarchs," Zelenskyy said. "States there work in the interests of their citizens, not a handful of the richest."

As the Ukrainian president added elsewhere, "There can be no other option but to dismantle the oligarchic system."[46]

At the time, Ukraine's anti-oligarchic push generated few headlines and little attention outside the country. Years after Russia's initial 2014 invasion—and even after Ukrainian oligarchs like Firtash stood at the center of the first effort to impeach Trump—Ukraine itself was far from the center of any conversations elsewhere, whether geopolitical, geo-economic, or even in terms of wealth inequality more broadly.

But it's worth focusing for a moment on this anti-oligarchic law, both as a model and a meaning. Zelenskyy and his allies had specifically called out the oligarchs for their malign influence on Ukraine's domestic politics, domestic economy, and domestic direction. They'd correctly pinned so much of their country's ills—its rickety national defense, its sluggish economy, its cyclical swings between democratic bursts and autocratic regression—on its oligarchic class, which looked out only for itself, and which constantly allied with the revanchists in Moscow, regardless of the cost to Ukraine itself. As Zelenskyy saw it, if the country could thwart the ambitions of its oligarchs, it could finally find a stable, democratic home in the European family of nations. To his credit, this applied even to former patrons like Kolomoisky, who had by this time dropped any pretense of pro-Western leanings and become a full-throated mouthpiece for Russian interests.[47]

Yet this "de-oligarchization" push didn't simply end with this new legislation. There was one figure in particular the Ukrainian government targeted as a case study of the threats that oligarchs can pose—and what a government could do against them. Viktor Medvedchuk was a billionaire politician from eastern Ukraine who not only owned multiple Ukrainian television channels pushing pro-Russian narratives but also happened to be Putin's key contact in Ukraine. Indeed, it's difficult to overstate just how cozy Medvedchuk was with Putin. Not only were the two in regular contact, with Medvedchuk consistently feeding Putin information about domestic developments in Ukraine, but Medvedchuk had even asked Putin to be his daughter's godfather.[48] Putin obliged, bringing Medvedchuk's child a "bouquet of flowers and a teddy bear," cementing his relationship with Medvedchuk forevermore.[49]

It was a relationship that, at least for Putin, continued to pay dividends. As tensions between Moscow and Kyiv boiled more and more through the early 2020s, Medvedchuk began passing the Kremlin more and more information on domestic turbulence in Ukraine: How Ukrainians were growing increasingly fed up with Zelenskyy's leadership, how many chafed under supposed Ukrainian nationalist projects, how they all admired Russian rule—and, perhaps, even desired that rule themselves. How, in other words, they were waiting—with bated breath, with open arms—for Putin's troops to come to their aid, if only the Russian president would green-light an expanded invasion.[50]

For years, Medvedchuk had little to worry about. His political standing was never at any real risk, and as one of the dominant oligarchs in eastern Ukraine, his personal wealth was never threatened in any meaningful way.[51]

And then, in just a few short months, it all fell apart. With Medvedchuk's television channels bleating out nothing but pro-Russian propaganda, Zelenskyy finally moved against him. Backed by the swell of anti-oligarch momentum, Zelenskyy announced that his government was removing Medvedchuk's television stations from the air—and even seizing control of Medvedchuk's bank accounts as well, effectively freezing the oligarch in place. The oligarch wailed in protest, claiming to be the victim of political persecution (even as he continued handing Russia information about Ukrainian military preparedness). But it was a move that met with wide support across Ukraine. Even the Biden administration backed the action, with the U.S. embassy cheering Zelenskyy on.

In Moscow, however, it was something of a trigger—a final moment breaking the back of whatever opposition may have remained against the Kremlin's looming invasion. It's too much to say that Putin launched Europe's greatest, most devastating war since the days of Hitler because Ukraine tried to tackle its oligarchic class, or because it went after Medvedchuk specifically. The roots of Russian revanchism run far deeper than one man, stemming from Russians' inability to recognize their own history of colonialism and the lies they've told themselves for centuries that Ukraine is inseparable from Russia proper.[52]

But as Russian journalists later discovered, the starting gun for the Kremlin's invasion preparation rang out the day Ukraine went after Medvedchuk. "Three sources in the Russian president's entourage confirmed that it was this story of the destruction of Medvedchuk's [television channels] and the fact that [Ukraine] began to 'harass' him that became the last straw in Putin's decision to prepare for a military operation," Russia's *Verstka Media* reported. As one of Putin's acquaintances said, "[Putin] took it as a personal attack," viewing it as a Ukrainian escalation against him and his oligarchic proxies. "Oh, you decided to escalate?" Putin reportedly wondered. "Didn't you understand who you were dealing with?"[53]

It would, of course, be Putin who had little idea who he was dealing with. Years later, Russia is no closer to toppling Kyiv than it was in early 2022, at the cost of over a million men, a deflating economy, and a shuddering realization that Ukraine is an independent nation, never to return to the Russian bosom. And Putin is no closer to restoring the kind of oligarchic autocracy needed to ensure Russian supremacy in Kyiv. Because even while the war is, first and foremost, about Ukrainians' desire for freedom and sovereignty, it's also something that lies along another fault line: the fight for democracy against oligarchy, and the struggle to wrest control of a country's direction—of an entire nation's destiny—from the hands of a corrupt clique who are willing to ally with Moscow and sell out their homeland to protect their own wealth.[54]

It's a framing and a lesson that's been buried by all the other details of the war itself. But it's one that also, by the early 2020s, came roaring back to relevance in the U.S.—especially as oligarchic forces around America began searching out new patrons abroad, eager to help in their own campaigns to demolish American democracy.

10

Firepower

Are we investigating this? Or covering this up?
—Shehan Karunatilaka[1]

The pitch deck was one of the most laughable presentations the group of Saudi officials had ever seen. Coming in at some twenty slides, hued in stark black-and-white, the entire PowerPoint looked like something an undergraduate would have put together, or perhaps a satire of the entire investing process.[2]

The text came drenched in corporate pablum, promising things like "accelerating transformation through connectivity," pushing "aligned economic interests" that could "create previously unrealized value," pledging to be a "differentiated partner" that could "identify transformation opportunities." The specifics were laughably minimal. And the opportunities—whatever those opportunities actually were—were apparently endless.[3]

But it wasn't just the pap. It was also what the deck, which these Saudi officials were looking through in 2021, was asking for: millions, or even billions, of dollars in investments from one of the most kleptocratic regimes on the planet. The deck, organized by a new fund called Affinity Partners, centered on opening up a gargantuan funding stream from the Saudi government, and specifically cracking open some of the hundreds of billions of dollars sloshing around the Saudi regime's sovereign wealth fund—the Saudis' primary piggy bank, swelling on the back of the country's oil riches.[4]

The Saudis weren't exactly shy about throwing some of those

billions around. The golf and tennis industries, commercial real estate and luxury condos, video games and celebrity influencers, PR agencies and consultancy firms, even major companies like Boeing and Citigroup and Disney—the Saudis had bankrolled them all in recent years.[5] Much of the money had ended up in the pockets of Westerners willing to look the other way at Saudi human rights crimes.[6]

This Affinity pitch, though—it was so vapid, so vacuous, so devoid of any actual content that even the Saudi officials in charge of screening investments blanched. There weren't any "significant institutional investors from the U.S." who'd already put money into Affinity, and the Saudis certainly wouldn't be the first.[7] A due diligence report had already found Affinity's operations "unsatisfactory in all aspects."[8] And the PowerPoint didn't help matters. "They said they'd never seen such a joke of a deck," one source connected to potential investors said.[9] There was, however, one specific element the Saudis found appealing. Taking up two slides—some 10 percent of the entire presentation—was a twelve-hundred-word biography of the man now overseeing Affinity Partners: Jared Kushner.[10]

By this time, Kushner was out of the White House, and back in the private sector he'd spent years struggling through. His father-in-law, having lost the 2020 election, had returned to Florida, licking his wounds and looking for a path back to power. Kushner, though, had taken a different tack. Instead of accepting a sinecure at an Ivy League school, instead of taking some time off to enjoy with his young children, instead of simply turning back to the New York real estate scene that had chewed him up and spat him out, Kushner moved in a different direction. He would become something else—something the U.S. had never seen before from a member of a former president's family, or from someone of Kushner's stature. Something that didn't necessarily require any talent, or any particular skill.

He would become a fund manager. And Affinity—an investment fund Kushner launched immediately after he left the White House—would be his vehicle to more potential wealth than he'd ever known before.[11]

But again: This was 2021, when the post-Trump era appeared ascendant, when Trump was still viewed as little more than a twice-impeached former president who'd attempted to orchestrate a coup to remain in power. Kushner, by extension, was dead weight, a man tainted by proximity to his father-in-law, whose circle of contacts was increasingly worthless. Moreover, doing business with him carried all sorts of hazards—not least the potential blowback from a new Biden administration that was watching out for any foreign governments partnering with the Trump family.

The Saudi officials, then, had their answer. The lack of Affinity's clarity or strategy, the lack of any other major investors, the manifest "public relations risks" that came with Kushner—all of it pointed to a clear, unequivocal "no." They would not back Affinity. They would not fund Kushner.[12]

There was, however, one other vote that mattered. Crown Prince Mohammad bin Salman (MBS)—the author of Jamal Khashoggi's assassination, the lord of Saudi kleptocracy, the head of a regime dedicated to preventing women or minorities or gay Saudis from achieving anything like basic civil rights—would have his say. And as MBS saw it, Affinity wasn't some panhandling, fly-by-night investment fund looking for a handout. This was a fund overseen by a man the Saudi dictator had long ago befriended—by a man MBS claimed he'd pocketed. And as MBS knew, Kushner was a man who, if the political winds in America blew in a slightly different direction, could help take the Gulf tyrant to ever-greater heights.[13]

The Saudi panel screening investments advised against partnering with Affinity and Kushner. But MBS immediately overruled them. Kushner and Affinity would get Saudi funding—$2 billion to start, and potentially much more down the road. And MBS would once more have a partner in the U.S. whom he could steer in whichever direction he wanted.[14]

It's worth pausing on just how unprecedented this entire play from Kushner, who had just left the White House, was. It's not that he was the first family member of a former president (or other leading U.S. official) to cash in on connections. Billy Carter not only moonlighted as a lobbyist for Libya's Muammar Gaddafi but further hawked "Billy Beer" as a way to make a buck off his brother Jimmy's presidency.[15] And Hunter Biden's thirst for any way to profit off his last name—via crooked networks out of Ukraine and Romania, via overpriced artwork that raised all kinds of money-laundering concerns—helped derail his father's presidency.[16]

But what Kushner attempted—what Kushner achieved—was something else entirely. It would be as if Chelsea Clinton or Malia Obama personally cozied up to despots in Venezuela or Cuba, pitched dictatorships on their relationships with their parents, pleaded for billions of dollars for abstract investment opportunities—pledging only their personal networks, and little more, in return. (As the same source mentioned above added, Kushner and his team were "openly talking about 'networking' and 'networks' . . . They're bragging about 'networks,' they're using cliches, with no serious investment discussion.")[17] Kushner was asking foreign regimes to trust him with billions of dollars, despite the fact that he'd never managed an investment fund before. As one former Republican official told *The New York Times*, he "could recall no precedent for a government official leaving office and starting an investment firm that would immediately receive billions of dollars from foreign governments with which the official had been working while serving in government."[18]

For those inclined toward cynicism, it was one of the most breathtaking pay-to-play schemes America had ever seen. Never before had a former administration official hopped out of office, launched their own fund, and immediately watched billions stampede in. Even Republican officials who had led the charge against Hunter Biden were galled. James Comer, a Republican representative from Kentucky, said that Kushner had "crossed an ethical line," and during one phone call even told an intermediary "to tell Kushner to fuck off. I hope Kushner was listening on speaker phone."[19]

But it wasn't just Saudi Arabia that saw Kushner as a pliable source of influence—as someone they could buy off for relative peanuts, nodding along to his vacant pitch while plotting out ways to use him to their advantage. Saudi allies in the United Arab Emirates, whose own despot had first cultivated Kushner, also began tossing money at Kushner's firm around the same time.[20] So, too, did the Qatari regime—grateful to have slipped back into the U.S.'s good graces, and eager to keep pace with its geopolitical rivals. Together, the two governments poured an additional $1.5 billion into Kushner's new firm.[21]

Along with a number of smaller investors, Affinity's asset pool grew and grew throughout the early 2020s, swelling to nearly $5 billion by the end of 2024, with all that dictatorial funding providing, as Kushner said, "more firepower" for his firm.[22] And it wasn't just the capital that Affinity began managing. Thanks to multibillion-dollar pledges, Affinity raked in additional management fees that ran over $100 million—with, as the *Financial Times* pointed out, "most of any cash over its operating expenses going to Kushner, its majority owner."[23] Nearly all of it came from foreign sources, rolling in at a clip never before seen for a family member of a once-and-future American president.

Still, it wasn't just the money, or the connections, or even the model blooming before our eyes of foreign regimes plowing money into an American oligarch's wallet. It was also about *leverage*. Because of the structure of the deals, foreign investors could pull their money out after a five-year window—a deadline that, in 2026, would put it firmly within a potential Trump second term. In other words, regimes in places like Saudi Arabia or Qatar could, in the middle of Trump's second term, yank billions of dollars out of Kushner's firm, effectively imploding Affinity and decimating Kushner's standing. It was a financial sword of Damocles, dangling over one of the most influential members of Trump's first White House—and over a man who would, presumably, always have Trump's ear.[24]

Perhaps the only thing more shocking than the sudden transformation of Kushner into a billion-dollar dartboard for Gulf autocrats was that, back in the U.S., Affinity's rise barely caused a scandal.

Maybe that was understandable. At the time, Americans across the political spectrum figured that a post-Trump era had emerged. Prosecutors at both federal and state levels kept Trump himself in their sights—for campaign finance fraud, for illegally retaining (and misleading investigators about) classified documents, for attempting to overthrow the 2020 election—but the rest of the Trump orbit was largely left to the side. Democratic leaders were skittish about shining a light on presidential family members, given how scuzzy Hunter Biden's behavior had been for years and years.[25] Moreover, it wasn't clear Kushner had even committed any crimes; why bother targeting him if he didn't have any political future, anyway?

One official, however, thought differently. Ron Wyden had long cut his teeth as the senior senator from the state of Oregon. Some three decades into his tenure in the Senate, the lanky, long-limbed Wyden is arguably the most impactful, important member of Congress the Pacific Northwest has ever produced. And he's made a name for himself primarily by using his perch atop the Senate Finance Committee to specifically target white-collar cheats and criminals, trying to patch up America's shredded defenses against financial crime and foreign influence therein.[26]

When Wyden first got a whiff of Kushner's post–White House dealings, his radar went off. Not just because of who Kushner was but because of the possibilities Kushner was peddling: of using investment firms to open doors in the U.S., potentially tilting American policy for the benefit of tyrants around the world.[27]

In the middle of 2024, Wyden issued his first salvo. In a formal letter to Kushner's chief financial officer, Wyden laid out his cause for concern. "Several Middle Eastern governments are using funds managed by Affinity as a means to pay tens of millions of dollars in fees every year to . . . Kushner, creating significant conflicts of interest and potential counterintelligence risks," Wyden began. Given that Affinity was almost entirely foreign financed—and the fact that Affinity had declined to disclose all its foreign patrons—the firm "present[ed] heightened national security and other risks." As Wyden wrote:

> Mr. Kushner's limited track record as an investor, including his nonexistent experience in private equity or hedge funds, raise questions regarding the investment strategy behind the seeding investments and lucrative compensation that Affinity received from [Saudi Arabia] and other sovereign wealth funds. . . . This series of events creates an appearance that Affinity's investors are motivated not by commercial interests of seeking a return on investment, but rather by strategic considerations of foreign nationals seeking to funnel money to U.S. individuals with personal connections to former President Trump.[28]

Wyden's requests were simple. He wanted to know the identity of Affinity's funders—of those foreign regimes, oligarchs, and proxies who'd bundled billions of dollars into Kushner's firm—as well as specific communications between Affinity and regimes in places like Saudi Arabia and Qatar. It was far from a burdensome ask, nor was it a threat to indict or penalize the firm should it fail to comply. Just a bit of transparency about who was tossing billions of dollars at a fund steered by Trump's oligarchic son-in-law—and why.[29]

A month later, Affinity issued its response. The company provided "some information" related to its foreign client list, including the fact that the Saudi regime was shoveling tens of millions of dollars to Affinity and its leadership for "management fees." But it wasn't everything. There was at least one "mystery foreign investor" that Affinity "declined to identify." According to Wyden, Affinity also further "declined to provide information as to how these conflicts of interest will be addressed should former President Trump be elected to a second term in office. In fact, Affinity appears to believe this national security risk is not worthy of congressional investigation simply because Jared Kushner and Ivanka Trump have stated they have no plans to return to work in the White House."[30] The implication was laughable: that Kushner's fund was savvy enough that a regime would offer up billions of dollars, just for the chance to tap his investment know-how, rather than the glaringly obvious fact that as the son-in-law of a president, he would have far greater access to and influence on Trump than almost anyone else.[31]

Kushner himself at least admitted as such, confirming by late 2024 that he and Affinity were "able to do things on the geopolitical side, on the connections side"—things that, perhaps, a foreign regime would happily part with billions of dollars to obtain.[32] But time and again, Affinity's position was that it was a simple investment fund. And it pointed to numerous investments—into things like an Israeli car-leasing company, a Munich-based electronic fitness company, and more—that backed up that point.[33]

By the time Wyden started looking into Affinity and Kushner, there was so much smoke surrounding the firm and its foreign patrons you could choke on it. And Affinity's response—along with Kushner, who said that the requests for transparency were "not serious efforts"—didn't deter Wyden. After reissuing his request for more information, including details on how much Kushner personally made from all the dealings, Wyden upped the pressure. In late October 2024, following reports that Kushner had continued meeting with the Saudi dictator—and even begun advising the Saudi despot on U.S. foreign policy—Wyden, along with Democratic Representative Jamie Raskin, issued a letter to the Department of Justice, calling for a special counsel to investigate Kushner. Specifically, Wyden wanted to know if Kushner was "influencing U.S. foreign policy by acting as a political consultant to the Saudi government while also accepting their money."[34]

Affinity could deny any undue influence, deny that any foreign regime would ever think to use their billions of dollars to influence Kushner or any of his connections. But as Wyden said, "There is substantial reason to believe that the Saudi government's decision to engage Affinity for investment advice is a fig leaf for funneling money directly to Mr. Kushner and his wife, Ivanka Trump." Moreover, there was clear evidence that Kushner was using his perch not only to advise MBS on U.S. foreign policy, but was even "selling geopolitical advisory and political advocacy services" to foreign clients while simultaneously advising Trump's reelection campaign—a glaring conflict of interest, placing Kushner firmly in the realm of foreign lobbying.[35]

With America racing toward the 2024 election—and with memories of the 2016 foreign influence scandal fresh in the minds of many in the U.S.—it was necessary for the U.S. Department of Justice to investigate how regimes might once more be launching political influence schemes, using the oligarchs burbling to the top of the American political establishment. "While on the Saudi government's payroll, Mr. Kushner is simultaneously serving as a political consultant to former President Trump and acting as a shadow diplomat and political advisor to Saudi Crown Prince Mohammed Bin Salman and other foreign principals," Wyden added. "The scale of these undisclosed foreign payments to Mr. Kushner coupled with the national security implications of his apparent ongoing efforts to sell political influence to the highest foreign bidder are unprecedented and demand action from DOJ."[36]

As one source familiar with the back-and-forth between Wyden and Affinity told me, the core of Wyden's request rested on two unknowns: just how much Kushner personally made from these deals, and what precisely he was doing for his foreign clientele. Kushner "has some experience in real estate, but no experience running hedge funds and private equity," the source told me. If anything, it appeared little more than the same blueprint Kushner (and others in the Trump orbit) had authored earlier: selling access, selling influence, and even selling policy. The only difference was that, given the yearslong financing arrangements between Affinity and Saudi Arabia, those financial deals were going to be in place for far longer than anything ever seen before. As the source told me, "What's interesting about Jared is it's the same racket—it's just locked in for a longer time."[37]

Still, with the 2024 election just a few weeks away, there was a sense that Wyden was whistling into the wind. All eyes were on the upcoming presidential vote, which sucked up all the oxygen in Washington. Wyden's push into Kushner's finances barely cracked the news cycle. Any special counsel appointment would have to wait, at least until Kamala Harris's presidency found its legs.

Then again, perhaps it's not fair to pin the lack of interest in or coverage of Kushner's investment firm on the election alone. In an earlier generation, even as little as a decade ago, the fact that a president's son-in-law stewarded billions of dollars at the behest of numerous foreign dictators—and that those dictators could pull the plug whenever they wanted, immiserating the president's son-in-law and imploding his firm in the process—would have been an era-defining scandal. It would have dominated discourse for weeks, even months.

By the early 2020s, though, the idea of foreign despots throwing billions of dollars at American investment firms had become normalized to the point of being blasé. Little matter that these regimes built their wealth on the backs of broken bodies and bombed-out neighbors, on concentration camps and assassinated journalists, on inflaming or authoring genocides both at home and abroad. Two decades into the twenty-first century, it seemed like every major investment firm in America—run by a president's son-in-law or otherwise—had opened its doors to foreign regimes or their oligarchic foot soldiers, cracking open the American economy for as many vampiric, kleptocratic regimes as they could. Investment funds had, by the 2020s, become the perfect pass-through vehicles for foreign regimes looking to influence American policy—especially those funds run by American oligarchs themselves.[38]

In many ways, it was an unsurprising development. In the U.S., a decades-long loophole had exempted American investment firms—private equity, hedge funds, venture capital, and others—from basic anti–money laundering requirements. Similar to a decades-long loophole that allowed illicit wealth to flood America's real estate market, the lack of money laundering checks for U.S. investment firms acted as a major magnet for dirty money from around the world. As the twenty-first century trundled on, American private investment funds became a perfect tool for transnational money laundering, mixing kleptocratic wealth with other investors and scattering that money across the American economy. Small wonder that American capital markets have exploded over the past few decades, climbing into the trillions of dollars by the early 2020s, with no reason for slowdown in sight.[39]

"For years, gaps in rules for the private investment industry have led to countless cases of the corrupt stashing their illicit gains in U.S. hedge funds, private equity and venture capital," Gary Kalman, the head of Transparency International's U.S. chapter, said.[40] As a leaked FBI memo in 2020 revealed, Russian oligarchs had already laundered their cash via American investment funds. So, too, had Mexican cartel operatives, opening hedge fund accounts to cycle their drug money into the U.S. Other hedge fund representatives had specifically proposed their funds as a means of moving "prohibited items from sanctioned countries to the United States"—using American loopholes to circumvent American sanctions.[41]

Because of the lack of transparency requirements—because these firms could mask their investors, even when the chairman of the Senate Finance Committee came calling—we have incredibly little insight into which regimes have bankrolled specific American firms. We have little idea how much of the multitrillion-dollar holdings now in American capital markets originated in places like China, Russia,

Iran, Venezuela, or elsewhere. And we have almost no data on where that money ended up—let alone how much return on investment, either financial or political, those regimes received in turn.[42]

If anything, Kushner was just a microcosm, a synecdoche—a sign of how far the entire world of American private equity, hedge funds, and venture capital market funds had drifted in a pro-dictatorial direction. How oligarchic forces around the world had swamped American private investment funds, and how they wrapped themselves around American oligarchs in the process, piling their wealth on top of one another. It was almost breathtaking to behold—all the more so given how little insight we actually had into any of it.[43]

Still, every once in a while, something acted like a torchlight on the topic, highlighting just who was taking advantage and what it might mean for American politics, even beyond Kushner. Because in 2023, something slipped through all that anonymity. It wasn't a leak, and it wasn't a breach. It was, instead, a voluntary disclosure of whom one particular regime had been backing—and all the American firms, and all the American oligarchs, who'd been profiting along the way.

In 2008, at the height of the global financial crash, the Saudi regime wanted to form its own investment arm—something that could target and identify potential assets and potential partners around the world, all scouring around for much-needed capital. With an early injection of $8 billion, the new regime-controlled entity, dubbed Sanabil, claimed it wanted to "transform groundbreaking ideas into tangible realities"—and, it went without saying, create bridgeheads for the Saudi regime to further extend its interest and influence wherever it could.[44]

For years, the targets of Sanabil's investments were largely unknown. Given the dearth of transparency requirements—to say nothing of the public relations risk of taking funds from a regime as monstrous as the Saudis—that shroud of secrecy shouldn't be surprising. In the U.S. in particular, firm after firm the Saudis could theoretically target were "cagey about whether they have raised money from Saudi Arabia," unwilling to reveal whether or not they were in bed with the regime.

There were rumors, of course, and enough breadcrumbs to follow Saudi money into American investments. Silicon Valley had long had "deep connections" with Saudi Arabia, with MBS himself even visiting California in 2018 to meet directly with Apple's Tim Cook, Google's Sundar Pichai, and others. OpenAI's boyish head, Sam Altman, even spent time serving on the advisory board of Saudi Arabia's plans for the new, surreal city of Neom, set to include multiple skyscrapers and planned to run one hundred miles long. But the ultimate recipients of all that Saudi money remained a mystery.[45]

In March 2023, however, Sanabil decided to drop the veil. On its website, the Saudi investment arm publicly listed all the private investment partners it had piled into its own portfolio—all the private equity, hedge funds, and venture capital funds it had decided to pump up, transforming them into fronts for Saudi money to be firehosed around the world, and in particular in the U.S..[46] The reasons for Sanabil's disclosure remain unclear; the Saudis themselves never bothered to reveal why they had posted all the identifying information of their investment partners. Perhaps it was arrogance. Perhaps it was an oversight. Perhaps it was leverage over their partners, ending their plausible deniability and reminding them who their ultimate paymasters were—and what those paymasters were capable of.

The reasons ultimately didn't matter. For the first time, we got an insight into just which private equity heads, hedge fund managers, and venture capitalists the Saudis had been backing—and those Americans who'd bundled Saudi financing into new projects in industry after industry, plumping up not only other companies themselves but also some of the wealthiest, and increasingly antidemocratic, voices around the nation.

The total list runs to some fifty firms, listed alphabetically on Sanabil's website. There were, as *The Information* wrote, "marquee investment firms" like Craft Ventures and Insight Partners, with *Forbes* also flagging some of the "biggest names in Silicon Valley," like Iconiq Capital and Tiger Global. All told, there were dozens of firms that had taken billions of dollars from the Saudis, swelling their coffers even as the Saudi regime sank further and further into a totalitarian theocracy.[47]

Rideshare companies like Uber, meal delivery companies like

DoorDash, even messaging platforms like Slack—all of them ended up funded by private equity or venture capital funds buoyed by Saudi riches.[48] These private equity firms had effectively become pass-through vehicles for all the dirty money spewing out of Saudi Arabia—cutouts to help the Saudis back start-ups, established companies, and everything in between. The Saudi financing flowing throughout Silicon Valley was, as *The Wall Street Journal* wrote, "unprecedented."[49]

The American funds themselves have all, as of this writing, refused to comment on the Saudi connections, or on the Saudi decision to disclose their partnerships. But as one tech CEO speculated, "There's no way you could found a start-up in this [venture capital] community and not be beholden to MBS or someone one step away from him." Whatever qualms Silicon Valley may once have had about doing business with the Saudis had clearly crumbled. If there was ever any hand-wringing or moral concern, *Vox* wrote, "tech investors have clearly moved on."[50]

It was hard to disagree. There was, it appeared, no bottom—no line the Saudis could cross that would close the doors to business partners in the U.S. Murder and shred the limbs of a journalist who worked at your newspaper? No matter, at least for Jeff Bezos, with Amazon agreeing to help Saudi Arabia construct an "AI Zone" in the country.[51] Claims that you're concerned about governmental censorship, governmental overreach, and governmental tyranny? Not a problem, at least for Peter Thiel, whose Founders Fund was revealed as one of Sanabil's partners.[52] Everyone, as the Saudis figured, could be bought. Were they wrong?

But it wasn't only that these firms were taking Saudi money. To hear these tech oligarchs tell it, the Saudi regime was hardly one of the most repressive governments on the planet. It was, instead, a potential model of the future—a model of what could be achieved if a government had the right people atop it. Indeed, this infatuation with Saudi tyranny revealed perhaps more than anything else the ultimate goal of what many American oligarchs envisioned for a future in the U.S. Not the theocratic elements, necessarily. But the pairing of wealth and power—a regime that sloshes hundreds of billions of dollars at the supposed visionaries peopling Silicon Valley, without any concerns for silly things like democracy—was the ultimate end goal for these tech oligarchs.

In 2023, a Saudi Arabian think tank hosted its own conference in Miami. Some of the names in attendance were expected, such as Kushner, while others were a bit more off-the-wall, such as DJ Khaled and disgraced baseball player Alex Rodriguez. Much of the conference, however, appeared dedicated to little more than lavishing the Saudi regime with praise—to confirming, as one journalist wrote, that it was "no longer shameful to accept massive investment dollars from Saudi Arabia."[53]

It wasn't simply that it was no longer shameful; it was now, for many in Silicon Valley, a point of pride to be seen doing business with a totalitarian regime like Saudi Arabia. "The more I think about it, the more Saudi almost feels like a startup," hummed WeWork founder Adam Neumann, summing up the conference's theme.[54] Added another venture capitalist, named Ben Horowitz, "Saudi has a founder. You don't call him a founder, you call him 'His Royal Highness,' but he's creating a new culture, he's creating a new vision for the country, he's got a very exciting plan to execute, and the people in the country are fired up to do it."[55] No foreign lobbyists, paid-off PR specialists, or propaganda hacks could have said it better.

Nor did it end with those initial investments or public pleasantries. In 2024, *The New York Times* reported that Andreessen Horowitz—a venture capital firm overseen by the aforementioned Horowitz and his partner, Marc Andreessen, which itself backed everything from Airbnb to Facebook—had entered talks with Saudi Arabia to "create a $40 billion fund to invest in artificial intelligence," which "would dwarf the typical amounts raised by U.S. venture capital firms." The move would directly partner Andreessen Horowitz with the Saudi sovereign wealth fund, allowing the Americans to tap into billions more out of Riyadh—and allow the Saudi dictatorship to sink its teeth that much further into emerging AI technology in the U.S. and elsewhere.[56]

The investment could, of course, be anodyne. Maybe MBS wants to harness new AI technology to, say, help ChatGPT and its competitors provide more coherent responses to students' questions, or to create more impressive, more immersive AI-generated artwork. Or maybe, just maybe, it's for something else—for the same thing that despots for time immemorial have sought out new technology: to remain in power, in perpetuity. And to beat back any threats to their rule, wherever they may be found, using whatever tools—and whichever oligarchs—they could.

On its own, the prospect of a regime like Saudi Arabia gaining access to proprietary AI technology is harrowing—and that's even before considering the leverage the regime has over someone like a sitting president's son-in-law. Yet by the time the Saudi regime began partnering with Andreessen Horowitz, that was nowhere near the most pressing concern. Saudi Arabia, after all, was only one regime. And MBS was only one tyrant. But by the mid-2020s, American politics had burst open for all comers—for anyone who wanted to hide money behind American corporations and turn all those concerns following *Citizens United* about the safety of American elections into crashing, catastrophic reality.

11

When You're a Billionaire and Just Don't Give a Fuck

We can have democracy in this country, or we can have great wealth concentrated in the hands of a few, but we can't have both.

—*Louis Brandeis*[1]

American Ethane likes to bill itself as a "U.S.-based energy company," claiming it is the "leading provider of ethane gas" for clients in need of one of the key ingredients for both natural gas and petroleum refining.[2] Headquartered in Houston and overseen by an American named John Houghtaling, the company's political stock has risen in recent years—so much so that in 2017 American Ethane signed a key export deal with China, with Houghtaling inking the agreement while flanked by both Trump and Chinese leader Xi Jinping.[3]

On its face, there's little reason to think that American Ethane was anything besides what it claimed to be: a key link within the broader belt of American hydrocarbon producers, a rising economic player in a growing industry. In many ways, there was little to distinguish American Ethane from the other American companies peppering the Gulf shore, catalyzing America's energy export transformation. It appeared as American as baseball, apple pie, and endless fracking.[4]

Yet as investigators later discovered, the company was far from the American stalwart it publicly claimed to be. While American Ethane was registered in the U.S., it was in reality almost entirely owned by a number of Russian businessmen—including some of the most infamous Russian oligarchs who've acted as prongs for Vladimir Putin's regime in recent years. As researchers and disclosures detailed, these

Russians include figures like Alexander Voloshin, a former Kremlin chief of staff who spent multiple years by Putin's side, as well as Konstantin Nikolaev, an oligarch who had reportedly funded Maria Butina, the Russian spy who had infiltrated the National Rifle Association (NRA). Most spectacular, American Ethane's ownership group at one point even included Roman Abramovich, perhaps the most successful (and certainly most notorious) Russian oligarch of the bunch—a man who'd not only purchased the Chelsea Football Club but who slid his illicit wealth into offshore vehicles around the world, slithering into the highest ranks of Western policy and cultural circles in the process.[5]

The fact that a supposedly American firm like American Ethane was secretly controlled by a series of Russian oligarchs would have been problematic enough. Yet as with other American corporations, American Ethane had additionally tossed a raft of donations to U.S. politicians far and wide: to the most powerful Republicans in states like Louisiana, to a fund overseen by House Majority Whip Steve Scalise, and even to the reelection campaign of Mike Johnson, who would soon become the Speaker of the House. The donations themselves weren't titanic, coming in at only five figures, but they effectively illustrated how American corporations could turn into a sieve for foreign funds to drown American politics.[6]

That, at least, was the conclusion of the Federal Election Commission (FEC), the otherwise toothless organization tasked with overseeing America's tissue-thin campaign finance regulations. The FEC determined that American Ethane had specifically "made contributions using funds derived from loans from foreign entities ultimately owned by Russian nationals." As FEC investigators discovered, the company tapped a number of "offshore firms"—owned by American Ethane's Russian patrons, including Voloshin and Abramovich—for loans, and then flipped those loans directly into American elections.[7] American Ethane had become, in effect, a cutout for Russians oligarchs' offshore wealth to saturate American elections—a corporate smoke screen masking wealth from the Kremlin's proxies.[8] As the Campaign Legal Center wrote, "Put simply, American Ethane made contributions exclusively using money from foreign nationals."[9]

It's difficult to come to any other conclusion. A number of Russian oligarchs had secretly controlled a nominally American corporation, which was then used as a go-between linking these Kremlin oligarchs' offshore wealth and American politicians. It was one step removed from Putin himself directly funding American politicians and political causes—and it highlighted just how easy it was for foreign regimes to douse American elections with their wealth, and use American corporations to hide their tracks along the way.[10]

Perhaps the only thing surprising about the entire affair is that the FEC actually sniffed it out, digging into the details of the financing scheme in the first place. It was a glimpse at what an FEC properly staffed, properly funded, and properly backed could achieve—and just how essential an FEC with sufficient resources was.[11]

But even then, the FEC's findings didn't necessarily matter, at least not for American Ethane, and certainly not for any of the oligarchs involved. Instead of making an example of the company and its financing schemes, the deadlocked commission issued a slap-on-the-wrist penalty, recommending a fine of only $9,500. It was pocket change—less than that, even—for the figures involved, making a mockery of the entire process.[12]

Two of the Democratic-appointed FEC commissioners were apoplectic, issuing a blistering criticism of their colleagues who refused to punish American Ethane any more than that. "The foreign-influence problem has not gone away in the meantime, to put it mildly," they wrote. "In this case, it is beyond unfortunate that for . . . our colleagues, it was a bridge too far to penalize the use of Russian oligarchs' money to influence U.S. elections."[13]

The commissioners' fury is understandable. The FEC had somehow unearthed a case in which Russian oligarchs were actually behind a campaign financing scheme, using an American corporate entity in the process—and then allowed that company and its foreign funders to get away with it. It was like you'd been looking for a needle in a haystack, in a darkened room, with both hands tied behind your back—and then, when you in fact found it, promptly tossed it back into the pile of hay.[14]

American Ethane had, after all, crossed perhaps the reddest of red lines for American politics. Every corporate executive, every politician, every adviser and consultant and strategist involved in some form or fashion with American politics—they all know that American campaign financing remains off-limits for foreign funds. No matter how much they are bankrolled by domestic interests searching out friends and favors, no matter how much they are funded by donors looking for returns on their investments, foreign sources are verboten.[15]

Or they used to be, at least. Because by the 2020s, all those warnings from the previous decade—all those concerns about foreign actors taking full advantage of opportunities to fund American politics, using American corporations as middlemen to obscure their campaign funding—suddenly turned prescient. Warnings from then-President Obama about American elections being "bankrolled" by "foreign interests," those concerns from Justice John Paul Stevens that the *Citizens United* decision would allow "corporations controlled by foreigners" to blast apart the protections against foreign meddling—suddenly, those warnings appeared prophetic.[16]

Indeed, given just how much wealth had suddenly exploded around American politics by the 2020s, those warnings almost appeared obvious. How had more people not seen this coming? Why *wouldn't* foreign regimes take full advantage of these new corporate campaign finance opportunities—those allowances that permitted American corporations, regardless of who actually owns or controls them, to spend as much money as they could possibly want backing whichever candidates they choose? What foreign dictatorship would be obtuse enough not to take full advantage of the *Citizens United* ruling, and dip into their bottomless pockets to use and abuse this loophole that the Supreme Court laid at their feet?

What foreign regime *wouldn't* use corporate campaign financing to try to buy American politics?

It's not as if others didn't see this coming, or didn't realize what was happening in real time. In 2019, a former congressional staffer named Michael Sozan authored a white paper with the Center for American Progress trying to wrangle the issue, trying to get a handle on the actual scope and scale of foreign interests using these corporate loopholes for their own benefit. American Ethane had been only one company among the millions more scattered across the U.S.—a single grain of sand in a far larger American corporate desert. How many other American companies might have flipped into fronts for foreign interests? How many others had opened the gateways to foreign funding of American politics?[17]

The answer, as Sozan found, was simple: No one knows. No one has any idea just how much foreign financing, bundled through corporate pass-throughs and post–*Citizens United* networks, is now drenching American politics. No one knows at the federal level. No one knows at the state level. No one knows at any level of American government.

"Because foreign entities can invest in U.S. corporations—and those corporations can in turn spend unlimited amounts of money on U.S. elections—foreign entities can now exert influence on the nation's domestic political process," Sozan wrote. Indeed, foreign entities—dictatorships, cartel heads, fentanyl dealers, you name it—could choose from a whole suite of options to inject their funds into American elections. For instance, they could take a controlling stake in an American corporation, and then cycle their money into things like a PAC (political action committee), without any limit in sight. They could take those corporate funds and plow them into multiple political nonprofits, trading them back and forth until no one had any idea where the money had initially come from. They could, if they wanted, use those funds to bankroll ballot measures directly, in whichever state they want.[18]

Or they could do all of the above, using corporation after corporation to obscure their money, pouring funds from one corporate entity into another without ever disclosing the origins of those funds—Russian nesting dolls of dark money groups, untraceable to its ultimate foreign origins, without any Americans ever aware how much international funding had taken over American elections.

"Over the past several years, we have begun to understand the full extent of the threat posed by foreign authoritarian governments funneling illicit cash through shell companies and opaque nonprofit entities into American politics and elections," Debra Perlin, a policy director at Citizens for Responsibility and Ethics in Washington (CREW), said. Despite all the prohibitions on foreign actors donating directly to American campaigns, "foreign investors skirt this requirement by funneling cash into our elections through U.S. corporations"—corporations that have no limit on how much they can give to support candidates, and never need to identify who is ultimately controlling them.[19]

But it's not just the unknowability of the ultimate source of the funds that makes it impossible to get a firm grasp on how much of American politics has been auctioned off to foreign regimes. It's also that we have no idea whatsoever how many U.S. corporations are controlled by foreign actors. Millions of corporations now exist across the country, with extraordinarily few disclosure and identity requirements. (One of the many reasons the U.S. transformed by the early twenty-first century into the world's greatest font of shell companies.)[20] That combination—of dark money groups feasting on corporate financing, and the lack of any kind of sense of the scope of foreign control of American corporations—makes the true scale of foreign funding in U.S. politics unknowable. It "is virtually impossible to discern the extent of foreign-influenced corporate spending in U.S. elections," Sozan wrote, since "regulators and the public are not able to discern whether a corporation is foreign-influenced or whether a foreign-influenced corporation has spent from its treasury to sway U.S. elections."[21] It's become, if anything, a bit like the search for dark matter in the cosmos: something you could see stretching and distorting things in real time, but that you still couldn't detect, let alone measure.

There are at least *some* figures we know. For instance, OpenSecrets tabulated that total spending in the 2024 election cycle exceeded $20 billion, with some three-quarters of that going toward federal elections.[22] Likewise, the 2024 election cycle broke the record for "outside spending," which rose to about $4.5 billion total, some fifteen times more than it was less than two decades prior.[23] And contributions from dark money groups—those groups specifically designed to mask their donors' identities—surpassed a staggering $1 billion. It wasn't just the first time in American history that we'd reached that number, but it was nearly *one hundred and fifty times more* than similar dark money groups contributed in 2010, around the same time as the *Citizens United* ruling. And that's not even including the groups that only partially disclose their donors, which would approximately double that amount.[24]

And again: How much of this is foreign financed? Given that foreign investors now own some 30 percent of all U.S. stock, worth somewhere around $20 trillion—and given that the regulators at the FEC are hemmed in, overworked, strapped for resources, and purposely deadlocked—it's a question with an impossible answer.[25] "At the moment, we do not know how much foreign dark money makes its way into our political campaigns, but we do know that the doors are wide open for political money to be weaponized by well-funded hostile powers," former FEC Commissioner Ellen Weintraub, one of the few who has raised the alarm about foreign funding in U.S. elections, said.[26]

As Weintraub further pointed out, none of this is hypothetical. After all, as the 2020s opened, the number of cases before the FEC involving foreign contributions to U.S. elections has already nearly tripled. The endless spiral of dark money groups, the increasing swell of foreign funds, the growing pile of foreign dictatorships, all of whom are searching for American policies that will help keep them in power—it's a recipe for not just disaster but for the end of American sovereignty as we know it.[27]

Even worse: Thanks to the *Citizens United* ruling, voters themselves are powerless to stop foreign funds from coursing through American corporations and directly into American elections, even at a local level. In 2023, nearly 90 percent of voters in Maine elected to prohibit foreign regimes from bankrolling the state's elections.[28] But in the summer of 2025, an appeals court blocked that prohibition, claiming that the measure "silences U.S. corporations that have their own First Amendment rights"—regardless of who actually controls those corporations. One Maine senator, Rick Bennett, summed up the ruling: "It means that foreign government–controlled entities, even with 100 percent foreign government control, can still spend millions of dollars in Maine elections."[29] And it meant that similar laws in other states are almost certainly doomed to failure—regardless of voters' desires, and regardless of the impact on American democracy.

If it were simply the rise of American corporations as vehicles for foreign funding to saturate American elections, that would be one thing. But all this was concomitant with the rise of a modern American oligarchy—all those men (and the occasional woman) who had their own designs on and desires for American politics. All of whom knew precisely how to take advantage of the loopholes granted by the Supreme Court. And all of whom had, by the early 2020s, sought out partnerships abroad, locating those same dictatorships who were eager to take advantage of any American ally—corporate, oligarchic, or otherwise—they could find.

But while figures like Zuckerberg, Pichai, Kushner, and (as we'll see in the next chapter) Musk all opened up their services to dictatorships around the world, scholars in the U.S. continued to find new ways to highlight just how much America had sunk into an oligarchy itself.

As the 2020s dawned, the numbers on economic inequality in the U.S. grew more and more bleak. In 2020, the RAND Corporation issued a new study focused on income (rather than just wealth) inequality. As authors Kathryn Edwards and Carter Price wrote, starting in 1975, incomes for the bottom 90 percent of Americans began stagnating, largely unchanged for the half century since. But incomes for the top 1 percent had more than *quadrupled*. Had things instead remained steady—had incomes continued growing at similar rates to the decades prior to 1975—the bottom 90 percent of Americans would have "collectively taken home $2.5 trillion more in income." Instead, that wealth had been sucked upward, pocketed by fewer and fewer Americans as the years wound on.[30]

These forces deflated America's middle class, making life nastier, more brutish, and even shorter for many Americans. And now, for the first time, political scientists finally began studying the links between economic inequality and democracy—and finding that the links between inequality and democratic decline were more obvious than any had ever assumed.

It's not like folks couldn't see a correlation; anyone following the news, watching dictatorships spread like a fungus as the world grew more and more unequal, could see those two forces proceeding simultaneously. But did one necessarily compel the other? Was there an actual relationship there? Or was it all simply coincidence?

One of the first to tackle the question head-on was Robert Andersen, a sociology professor at the University of Toronto. Surveying dozens of countries, Andersen tried to answer one question: Did economic inequality really have a detrimental effect on democracy? Measuring both democratic support and spiraling inequality, the answer was unequivocal. Not only was there a direct linkage—but it was clearer, and much worse, than anyone ever thought.

Whereas most scholars had linked support for democracy with the *overall* wealth of a country—finding that the wealthier the nation, the greater the likelihood of backing democracy—Andersen discovered that "income inequality matters much more." Overall wealth was still important, but the economic disparity *within* a country was far more pertinent to that nation's support for democracy. Democracy, he wrote, has "less support in countries with high income inequality." The more unequal a nation, the less the support for democracy, full stop.[31]

Andersen's findings didn't stop there. "There is increasing evidence that economic inequality plays a role in a whole array of attitudes and behaviors considered important to the health of democracy, including attitudes toward income inequality, social trust and tolerance, and participation in voluntary associations," he continued. "The general finding is that the more unequal a society, the less likely people are to be socially tolerant, to trust one another, to favor equality, and to participate in voluntary associations." In other words: As economic inequality takes off, nations will fray further and further, with cohesion collapsing and societies atomizing. As inequality grows, democracy implodes—and often slips into something far worse.[32]

Other scholars have confirmed as much in the years since. In 2024, South Korean scholar Sang Kyung Lee determined that "where inequality is more severe, citizens in liberal democracies are more attracted to authoritarian leaders."[33] Around the same time, a pair of other researchers, the University of Chicago's Susan Stokes and Tecnológico de Monterrey's Eli Rau, backed up those findings. Publishing their analysis in *Proceedings of the National Academy of Sciences*, Stokes and Rau tried to ascertain just how strong that relationship between democratic erosion and economic inequality truly was. And as they determined, the link between the two is "stunningly robust."[34]

"The more unequal income distribution is in a democracy, the more at risk it is of electing a power-aggrandizing and norm-shredding head of government," the two researchers wrote. That is, as a society's inequality balloons, the likelihood of electing a strongman—a figure who will seize the levers of power, demolishing his country's democracy in the process—only grows. As the researchers confirmed, there was a direct relationship between economic inequality and the rise of modern autocracy. Few other things, like how long the democracy had actually been around, mattered. "Even wealthy and longstanding democracies, like the United States, are vulnerable if they are highly unequal," the authors wrote. "The larger the share of national income and wealth going to the top 1 percent and top 10 percent of the population, the more likely the democracy is to erode."[35]

Still, one question remained: Precisely *why* did such soaring inequality make residents of a specific nation less and less supportive of democracy? Unlike other researchers, Stokes and Rau tried to answer that question—or at least provide a range of likely theories for future researchers to tackle. As they noted, increased inequality contributes directly to increased polarization, which has been linked time and again to democratic decline and national fracture. Those on the wrong side of income inequality—those losing more and more, all while watching a country's upper crust sprint away with a nation's wealth—tend to gravitate toward the fringes on both ends of the political spectrum, searching out answers and proposing solutions that the more moderate center is incapable of providing. This "pernicious polarization," as political scientists have described it, is an endless spiral outward, until one party or political movement resorts to antidemocratic actions—coups, political persecution, exile, or worse—to cement their grip on power. Economic inequality, in other words, is the lubricant for the forces demolishing democracy.[36]

And that's only among the politically engaged. As Rau and Stokes also found, "Public perceptions of unfairness in economic distributions and opportunities contribute to cynicism about the broader system, weakening people's commitment to political norms and institutions." The kind of unseen, unspoken forces gluing democratic societies together—respecting election outcomes, disapproving of political violence, a willingness to work together across the political aisle—hold only as long as voters believe in the ultimate fairness of their political and economic systems. But once that perception of fairness goes, so does the belief that democracy is worth saving.[37]

Is that any surprise? If a democratic system resulted only in an elite who dominated a nation's economic wealth, all while selling themselves to foreign patrons in the process, what appeal would democracy still have? Working longer hours, sacrificing time with family and friends, forgoing vacations or recreation or any kind of relaxation, all just to tread water—even as the richest in a given nation grow ever richer, lifting their wealth beyond any kind of democratic checks, squirreling it away for themselves and their children and their grandchildren, forevermore—why wouldn't that lead to grievance? Why wouldn't that lead to retribution? Why wouldn't that lead to a desire to toss democracy to the side and replace it with something else, damn the consequences?

Why wouldn't a democracy with this kind of crescendoing economic inequality lead—invariably, time and time again—directly to the *collapse* of that democracy? Is that where we've always been headed, ever since inequality first began taking off decades ago, and ever since the oligarchs reemerged once more, crawling back to the top of America's economic pyramid and suffocating the chances and the democratic desires of the rest of us?

Why would Americans continue to abide a government that allowed so few to profit at the expense of so many? The examples of the sheer egregiousness of American oligarchy are increasingly easy to find, especially in the 2020s. There's Amazon's Jeff Bezos, spending tens of millions of dollars on the construction of a ten-thousand-year clock in West Texas, a testament to, if nothing else, the depth of one man's disposable income.[38] (Does he think humans millennia from now won't have watches?) There's Mark Zuckerberg's recent purchase of a $300 million mega-yacht, a boat multiple times longer than a blue whale, which not only boasts a helipad and a decompression chamber but even comes with a separate, $30 million "support vessel" just for kicks.[39] There are all the things the rest of teeming, toiling humanity will never know, or can only dream of: the multiple mega-mansions, the cavalcades of luxury cars, the private jets with private hangars to fly to private enclaves and private compounds.

Or, perhaps, even private islands—including those where, just over a century ago, American oligarchs saw their first great triumph, overthrowing a sovereign government and now potentially considering an overthrow once more.

The Hawaiian island of Lanai is relatively small, tucked like a hinge between the larger outposts of Molokai and Maui. Shaped a bit like a squatting frog peering out toward the Pacific, the island has rarely caught the attention of those outside Hawaii. During the late nineteenth century, as a group of American oligarchs toppled Hawaii's government, instituted a police state, and steered the island chain toward the U.S., Lanai was an afterthought, peopled by just a few hundred laborers.[40]

But as the decades passed, communities on the island coalesced. Workers on the plantations formed families, which grew into neighborhoods, which led to the creations of schools and churches and the kinds of sinews that make a place worth living. Lanai was no tourist destination. Instead, for thousands of locals, it was something else: home.

And then, in 2012, something changed. An American named Larry Ellison arrived on Lanai—and said he wanted to buy the entire island.[41]

The fact that Ellison offered to purchase the island isn't necessarily surprising, at least to those who know him. "Ellison's love of Hawaii dates to his childhood, when he flew over the islands and found himself enthralled by their beauty," wrote Bloomberg's Sophie Alexander.[42] As the cofounder of Oracle, the multinational computer technology company, Ellison's net worth had grown to nearly $400 billion, with *Forbes* placing him as the second-richest American, just behind Musk.[43] A man with "a penchant for six-figure cars and eight-figure mansions," the octogenarian, who recently married a woman nearly fifty years his junior, at one point considered purchasing the Los Angeles Lakers, before moving on to more tropical climes.[44]

As Ellison quickly learned, all that money could open more doors in Hawaii than anything ever seen before. In 2012, for only $300 million, Ellison purchased some 98 percent of the island's territory. Lanai was, for all intents and purposes, his. Suddenly, all those communities in Lanai were staring up at an American oligarch, once more swooping in, once more hoovering up their land—once more steering things, regardless of what the locals wanted.[45]

In public, Ellison talked about his plans to turn Lanai into a "model for sustainable enterprise." Chattering about supporting the local economy and local business, Ellison spoke of using his wealth to reinvigorate local livelihoods, turning Lanai into a thriving pearl on the necklace of Hawaii. It would become a haven for travelers and tourists, but also a place in which local communities—families who'd called the island home long before it ever caught the billionaire's eye—could, perhaps for the first time, thrive.[46]

On one score, Ellison was right. In the years since his purchase, the "once-sleepy island" has become "a common destination for yachts and private jets," with figures like Musk and even Tom Cruise paying visits. (Years before he was wanted for war crimes, Netanyahu also visited Lanai, where he reportedly "took a Pilates class.")[47] With the island's main hotel kitted out with $75 million in renovations, visitors could now enjoy oceanside suites at a "five-star, five-diamond resort," with botanical gardens, lagoon-style pools, and even a cliff-side Nobu restaurant, all a stone's throw away.[48] Much of the island has become an exercise in ultra-luxury that seems swiped from a season of HBO's *White Lotus*—a comparison that makes sense, given that the show's first season, set in Hawaii, featured panoramic views of Lanai itself.[49]

But when it came to Ellison's claims that he'd also look out for local Lanai livelihoods, he couldn't have been more misleading. As Alexander tells it:

> [On] Lanai, Ellison is a modern American king—incomprehensibly wealthy and powerful. Many residents both rent from him and work for him, and a provision in his residential leases states that if you're terminated from a job with any of his companies, you can be kicked out of your home, too. . . . [B]ecause there are no real alternatives to Ellison's control, his decisions carry the force of law, with a minimum of discussion and hardly any due process.[50]

When a retired journalist on Lanai was asked about Ellison's initial promises—those pledges to restore the local economy, sprinkling and spreading the island with his wealth for the betterment of all Lanai—he responded, "Hawaiians have a word: It's called *waha*—bullshit."[51]

Surveying the island, it's hard to disagree. Whatever communities once existed in Lanai have quickly rotted. Restaurants have shuttered. Poorer Lanaians have been pushed out, into the sea, the lucky ones landing on other islands, others priced out of paradise completely. Ellison has acted less as a patron and more as a one-man typhoon, upending the island completely, ending entire livelihoods in the process, all without any means of recourse. Trying to stop Ellison is like spitting into a hurricane.[52]

Still, locals are pushing back, where and how they can. A few years ago, an anonymous Instagram account began peppering feeds with memes about Ellison's oligarchic stranglehold on the island. One post mocked Ellison's pledges of a new "housing project" for struggling islanders, including a photo of Mao with the claim that an "anonymous source close to the project said all homes come with a 'photo' of the project's benefactor so locals can say 'mahalo' ['thank you'] as they come home each day." Another featured a photo of Ellison, his hand thrust toward the camera, with the caption, "Talk to the hand that feeds you." And after Ellison's company tore down a beloved local church, the account shared a photo of the building's remains, along with the text, "When you're a billionaire and just don't give a f—."[53]

It's a story that Hawaii has seen before, though perhaps not at this magnitude. What's old is—suddenly, suffocatingly—new again. Wealthy mainland Americans swoop in, snatching up pristine lands, ousting Hawaiians, obliterating local economies, jump-starting yet another cycle in which the riches of these Hawaiian islands course straight into the pockets of wealthy interlopers, leaving little to the locals. And Ellison is only one billionaire, someone who'd spent less than a percentage point of his total net worth to take over Lanai. How many more oligarchs are plotting the same? How many others are simply trying to keep up with Ellison, effectively seizing Hawaiian—and American—sovereignty once more?

Because the parallels between Ellison's Lanai purchase and the oligarchs of the Gilded Age don't stop with simply turning Hawaii into a personal fiefdom. In 2022, *The Washington Post* reported that Ellison, who'd long bankrolled Republican politicians and causes, was directly involved with something else: conversations about how Donald Trump and his allies could overturn the 2020 election. It's unclear what Ellison said regarding Trump's attempted coup on January 6, 2021. But as the *Post* reported, Ellison's participation was "the first known example of a technology industry titan joining powerful figures in conservative politics, media and law to strategize about Trump's post-loss options."[54]

It was all an odd, unsettling echo. Just as in the 1890s, here was an American oligarch, lording over his Hawaiian empire, once more involved in conversations about plots to overturn democracy. Somewhere, just out of sight, Sanford Dole and the other American oligarchs of his era were nodding along in understanding, watching as Ellison became the first American oligarch caught out trying to return Trump to the White House—a push that another oligarch, with dreams of far greater empires of his own, would soon join.

12
Circus Monkeys

No society can surely be flourishing and happy, of which the far greater part of the members are poor and miserable.

—Adam Smith[1]

In the farthermost reaches of western China, in an arid, sprawling land known as East Turkestan, one of the greatest human rights crimes of the era continues to unfurl. The traditional home of the Uyghur nation—a predominantly Muslim people closely related to ethnic Kazakhs and Kyrgyz in neighboring Central Asia—East Turkestan has long been subject to the kinds of colonial policies that tip from land theft and ethnic cleansing directly into genocide, highlighting the entire range of ruthless, racist crimes the Chinese Communist Party is capable of.[2]

Detailing developments in East Turkestan is like descending into the furthest reaches of dystopia. In recent years, Beijing has transformed the entirety of East Turkestan—a nation nearly the size of Alaska, even bigger than neighboring Mongolia—into a "virtual prison," as *The New York Times* described, in order to control and destroy the Uyghurs' identity.[3] Unleashing everything from racial facial recognition tools to the tracking of DNA samples and iris scans of ethnic Uyghurs, Beijing's policies have become "as race-based as apartheid in South Africa was," added *The Economist*.[4] The entire region is now saturated in surveillance—so much so that, as *Der Spiegel* pointed out, "Nowhere in the world, not even in North Korea, is the population monitored as strictly as it is in" East Turkestan.[5] All this while the CCP oversees a program of forced sterilization and abortions on hundreds of thousands of Uyghur women—all as an attempt to destroy not only current Uyghur lives but to annul the next generation of Uyghurs before they're even born.[6]

And then there are the camps. Constructing thousands of so-called reeducation facilities across the region, China has created the largest, most sprawling series of concentration camps the world has seen since the days of the Holocaust, scarring the entirety of East Turkestan.[7] These camps have disappeared millions of Uyghurs, who were sucked into the maw of the CCP's dictatorship, subjecting them to everything from involuntary organ harvesting to rampant torture to outright execution.[8] Those lucky enough to survive are forced to sing songs with lyrics like "Xi Jinping is great! The Communist Party is great! I deserve punishment for not understanding that only President Xi Jinping and the Communist Party can help me."[9]

This is all official policy out of Beijing. The creation of the CCP's gulag stems directly from the man whose name bounces off the camps' walls: Xi. As *The New York Times* reported, a series of leaked documents placed the blame for all this inhumanity, all this colonialism, all these policies that Adolf Hitler or Slobodan Milošević would recognize directly at Xi's feet. The Chinese despot told his colleagues that, when it comes to East Turkestan, his regime would implement the "organs of dictatorship" to show "absolutely no mercy" to the Uyghurs. That Beijing would, in effect, stop at nothing to erase the Uyghurs from this earth.[10]

For years, Xi's mission in East Turkestan was largely kept secret. The region's remoteness, the lack of a substantial Uyghur diaspora elsewhere, the paucity of information floating out of East Turkestan—all masked the sheer scale of Beijing's criminality, as well as the CCP's ultimate goals of erasing the Uyghurs entirely. By the end of the 2010s, though, that mask began to slip. Stories of escaped Uyghurs began spilling out, and satellite footage began rolling in that captured the full scope of the camps.[11] As the 2020s dawned, China's denials became increasingly empty, with evidence piling atop evidence. Comparisons between what China was doing and earlier, World War II–era genocides became increasingly inescapable. By early 2021, the U.S. declared that China's efforts amounted to genocide.[12] Canada soon followed suit, as did France, the Netherlands, and more. A tide, at least rhetorically, had turned.[13]

But so did it turn commercially, too. Soon, Volkswagen announced it was leaving East Turkestan, selling off its remaining facilities in the region.[14] Companies and brands like H&M, Calvin Klein, and Tommy Hilfiger declared that they would no longer purchase goods from East Turkestan.[15] Over and again, company after company found that launching commercial projects in the middle of a genocide was a bridge too far, both for themselves and for their consumers. The bar may have been exceptionally low—should it really have taken an outright genocide to exit China?—but it nonetheless existed. A corporate trickle had turned into a flood. Investments, manufacturing, sales in East Turkestan—all of it was, in relatively short order, ended.

Or almost all of it. Because on December 31, 2021, one company announced that it was not only staying in China but that it was expanding directly *into* East Turkestan. "On the last day of 2021," the company posted on the Chinese messaging site Weibo, "we meet in Xinjiang," using the Chinese colonial name for East Turkestan. Featuring images of "traditional Chinese lion dances" and photos of people holding placards claiming that they "(heart) Xinjiang," the company announced that it was bucking the exodus, opening a new showroom to hawk its wares in East Turkestan. Rather than joining the stampede out of the region, the company declared that it was running headlong toward the scene of genocide—sprinting directly into the middle of perhaps the greatest crime of the twenty-first century.[16]

The post was authored by a company that, in public, claimed a progressive identity, known widely as an inspired, even revolutionary firm, charting a cleaner, clearer path for humanity.[17] A company that, in its press releases and testimonials, yoked itself to the reputation of its founder, a man widely viewed as a one-of-a-kind visionary.[18] A company that had, in recent years, also increasingly tethered itself to the regime in Beijing—finding itself increasingly reliant on remaining in the Chinese Communist Party's embrace, and on providing the regime with more and more leverage with each passing year.[19]

The company was, as you may have guessed, Tesla.[20] For those who only knew the company as a progressive lodestar of the electric vehicle revolution, the move was head-spinning. But for those who'd followed Musk's trajectory, it was only the latest step in the oligarch's lurch toward pro-Beijing positions and pro-Beijing rhetoric. It wasn't just that, for Musk, the Chinese Communist Party was "very responsive to the people," and "possibly more responsive to the happiness of people than in the U.S."[21] It was that, as he added around the same time, "China rocks, in my opinion."[22] As the oligarch saw it, the "economic prosperity that China has achieved is truly amazing, especially in infrastructure!"[23] Nor was it just rhetoric. While continuing to speak out in favor of the regime, Musk even became the first American—the first person who wasn't Chinese, in fact—to write for *China Wangxin*, the official magazine of the Chinese censorship agency, outlining his views on everything from Mars colonization to the relationship between "technology and humanity."[24]

It was all very strange, abnormal stuff. Musk was by no means the first American corporate head to express rhetorical fealty toward the Chinese regime. But wasn't this a man who was supposed to be some kind of "free speech warrior," standing at the vanguard against censorship and governmental pressures?[25] Did he not realize that China was the global leader in, among other things, the number of journalists jailed and total people executed?[26] Or was something else steering his comments, his conversations, his convictions that China was a model suddenly worth emulating?

After all, by this point, all the news of the regime's camps and crimes in East Turkestan was becoming public. Just how far would Musk go to talk up, or even aid, a dictatorship like this?

On its face, Tesla's relationship with China appeared as just one more cog in the Sino-American commercial relationship. But as 2021 bled into 2022, there were clear signs that Tesla, with Musk at the helm, was charting a different path in China from other corporations. Not only had the company raced headlong toward its Chinese partnership even after the regime made its revisionist, revanchist aims clear, from destroying Hong Kong democracy to clearing the path for Xi to serve as dictator for life, but as the new year dawned the company announced it was now—opening a showroom directly in the heart of a genocide.[27] It was as if Chevrolet had opened up a new production plant in Berlin in the late 1930s, or Ford had announced a new facility in Rwanda in the early 1990s. Who expands *into* a rippling, well-documented genocide?

The announcement sent shock waves not only through Uyghur and Muslim rights groups, but throughout the U.S. as well. Tesla, said the Council on American Islamic Relations, was "supporting genocide."[28] The Alliance for American Manufacturing agreed, with Scott Paul, the labor group's president, saying, "Anyone still doing business in the region is complicit" in China's genocide.[29]

Musk himself never commented on Tesla's expansion into East Turkestan. But in Walter Isaacson's monumental biography of the Tesla chief, one small nugget stands out. In a conversation with journalist Bari Weiss (who is now the editor in chief of CBS News), Musk admitted that Twitter—a company he had recently purchased, and was in the process of rechristening as X—would have to tiptoe around China. The company, Musk admitted, "would indeed have to be careful about the words it used regarding China, because Tesla's business could be threatened." It was the closest Musk had ever come to admitting what was patently obvious: that his substantial holdings in China provided the regime with significant, even crippling, leverage over him.[30]

Yet Musk didn't stop there, and quickly slid into outright genocidal apologia. "China's repression of the Uyghurs," Musk claimed, "had two sides." Musk didn't bother to describe what those "sides" were, or if, for instance, there were also "two sides" to previous genocides like the Holocaust. China may be committing horrific crimes, yes—but, as Musk saw it, perhaps the Uyghurs deserved it? Who were we to judge?[31]

Again, Musk wasn't simply some bored billionaire, pontificating from his couch. He was someone who—through his own decisions, of his own making—had turned to China for his financial future. By 2022, Tesla was obviously reliant on China for the mass production of its vehicles, with the majority of the company's cars now rolling off Chinese factory floors. Moreover, Musk's own economic fortunes were intimately tied up in Tesla's corporate value, with Musk himself personally owning hundreds of millions of shares in the company, representing tens of billions of dollars in value.[32] In other words, as one analysis read, "Musk's wealth is largely dependent on Tesla shares"—and on the corporate health of a company forced to remain in the favor of the Chinese Communist Party.[33]

It all added up to arguably the most glaring example of leverage between Beijing and an American oligarch seen yet. "China is the linchpin to Tesla's overall long-term strategy," one analyst said.[34] Musk has "often been a dependable ally to Beijing," *The Wall Street Journal* wrote, with *The New York Times* pointing out that he "cannot easily extricate himself [from China], should he even want to. Because the billionaire's wealth is tied up in Tesla stock, his personal fortune now hinges on what happens in China."[35] Or as Vivek Ramaswamy, a former Republican presidential primary candidate, said, "I have no reason to think Elon won't jump like a circus monkey when Xi Jinping calls in the hour of need."[36]

Taken together, it all meant that Musk was, if not quite Beijing's puppet, then someone who knew who was paying his bills. And it meant he would never speak out against what the regime was doing in East Turkestan. "Tesla and Musk have huge business with China, and he has never condemned the CCP, even though there's the ongoing genocide against the Uyghurs," one leading Uyghur rights activist, who has closely followed Tesla's involvement, told me. "Musk cooperates with Xi, with the CCP. . . . They don't criticize [the regime's] system because of the money."[37] It was a simple formula: Musk and his oligarchic allies would apparently choose profit over positions against genocide—even profit over patriotism—every time. As then-Senator Marco Rubio said, "Nationless corporations are helping the Chinese Communist Party cover up genocide and slave labor" in East Turkestan—and they include Tesla.[38]

At the time, Musk's accelerating reliance on Beijing gained few headlines, coming as it did amidst his bungled takeover of Twitter and his increasingly bizarre, reportedly ketamine-addled behavior.[39] But in hindsight, it's clear that Musk's willingness to whitewash Beijing was simply a precursor to his willingness to peddle whatever kind of conspiratorial, pro-autocratic messaging was necessary to help Trump get back to the White House. Musk's transformation into a mouthpiece for all the authoritarian policies curdling around Trumpism may have been shocking to some, but not to those who'd already watched his transformation into a bullhorn for a dictatorship dominating China.[40]

Yet even then, China wasn't the only foreign dictatorship—and not even the only American adversary—whose messaging and propaganda Musk was helping launder. Soon, another American enemy spied an opportunity with Musk—and figured out how to turn him, his ego, and his standing into something they could use for themselves.

Shortly after Russia launched its expanded invasion of Ukraine in early 2022, Musk immediately swooped in to aid Kyiv's efforts against Russian troops. Both Musk and Ukrainian officials realized that Starlink—the Musk-led company arranging satellite coverage in far-flung reaches of the world—was perfectly placed to help Ukrainian troops converse across the battlefield. Musk even directly oversaw Starlink's Ukrainian strategy, convening with company engineers for days on end, outlining ways the company could help circumvent Russian jamming. Soon, thousands of Starlink terminals flooded into Ukraine, with Musk transforming into the most impactful nongovernmental official of the early phases of the war. As one Ukrainian commander said, "Without Starlink, we would have been losing the war."[41]

A few months later, however, something shifted. As Ukrainians regained ground—as they launched counteroffensives that scattered Russian troops, threatening to corral and capture tens of thousands of Moscow's forces in the process—Musk grew skittish. A defense of the territory Ukraine still held was one thing. But pushing the Russians back wholesale? Slipping a noose around entire Russian brigades? Questions of war—questions of escalation—nipped at the back of Musk's mind. As he texted Isaacson following another of Ukraine's successful pushes to regain ground, "This could be a giant disaster."[42]

For most observers, Ukrainians had every right to evict Russian neo-imperialists from their territory. Part of this was moral; given the rampant evidence of Russian war crimes, torture, and even abduction of Ukrainian children in occupied regions, any continued Russian hold on Ukrainian lands threatened only more of the same. But part of it was also strategic; given that Moscow was primarily propelled by revanchism, the sort of imperialism that had previously motivated figures like Hitler or Milošević, rolling back Russian troops and proving the futility of such colonial expansion was clearly necessary. Ukraine was on the front line of the fight for not only tangible topics like territory but things far loftier and far more important, like freedom, democracy, and anti-imperialism writ large.[43]

For Musk, though, there was something more important yet: Armageddon. At least, that's what later reporting revealed, trying to parse Musk's thoughts during late 2022, when his views on the war—and on the rightness of Ukraine's fight—flipped on their heads. In Musk's mind, Ukraine's successful parries against Russia were less signs of strategic success, and more risks that could lead directly to nuclear annihilation. As Ukraine's pushback continued throughout 2022, Musk went into "crisis-drama mode," with the oligarch suddenly starting to worry that Ukrainian success—and Starlink's key role therein—could "lead to a nuclear war."[44]

Musk's concerns didn't arise in a vacuum. With his troops smothered and scattered, Putin had also begun rattling a nuclear saber, claiming that further Ukrainian advances would result in Moscow unleashing nuclear warfare on Kyiv, and potentially far beyond. Any nuclear threats, of course, must be taken seriously, and Putin blundering into nuclear warfare in the midst of his military collapse was perfectly imaginable.

But where other strategists and policymakers, in the U.S. and far beyond, immediately dove into analysis and adaptation, Musk did something else entirely: He buckled. Cowed by a foreign dictator's nuclear threat, Musk immediately crumbled, becoming the first—and arguably most notorious—major figure to waffle in the face of nuclear threats. And he did so while giving in, hook, line, and sinker, to Russian propaganda—and setting a precedent that nuclear bluffing, out of Moscow or anywhere else, could actually work.[45]

Musk's buckling took place as Ukrainian troops were set to launch an amphibious assault on a chunk of southern Ukraine claimed by Moscow: Crimea. As Kyiv plotted out a plan to send a half-dozen drone submarines, packed with ordnance, to target Russian military holdings in Crimea—all while using Starlink to navigate—Musk declined Ukraine's request to use Starlink in the operation. To Musk, Russia's claims to Crimea were sound. In Musk's mind, if anything threatened Moscow's grip on the peninsula, Putin would make good on his nuclear threats.[46]

To be fair to Musk, the belief that Crimea maintains a sacrosanct place in Russia's eyes—that it is, as Putin has dubbed it, Russia's "Temple Mount"—remains widespread among gullible Westerners, all of whom have little familiarity with the region.[47] No matter that Crimea, which Russia annexed in 1783, wasn't majority Russian until the Second World War (and only then as a result of Stalin's massive ethnic cleansing campaigns).[48] No matter that Crimeans themselves voted for independence from Moscow in 1991, alongside the rest of Ukraine.[49] No matter that support for Russian annexation was a clearly declining, minority opinion before Russia's initial invasion in 2014—and that Crimeans never once voted to rejoin Russia.[50]

These facts, this history—it was all immaterial, at least for Musk. All that mattered were Moscow's lines about Russia's and Crimea's "eternal unity."[51] Which was why, as Ukraine's submarines reached the peninsula, Ukrainian officials realized they were blind—that Musk had specifically refused to allow Ukrainians to use Starlink's guidance system in Crimea, condemning the entire operation to failure and confirming Putin's belief that he could use nuclear threats to expand his empire. As Musk himself later claimed, attacks on Crimea that could sink the Russian fleet "would have been like a mini–Pearl Harbor and led to major escalation."[52]

Little matter that, in the years since, Ukraine has unleashed fusillade after fusillade against Russian holdings in Crimea, not only eliminating Moscow's fleet from the peninsula but further destroying Russia's entire headquarters there.[53] Crimea has become, just like the rest of Russia-occupied Ukraine, yet another theater of battle, with Russians fleeing the peninsula en masse.[54] While Kyiv has still not regained Crimea itself (at least as of this writing), any thought that attacking Crimea presented some kind of "red line" for Moscow has long dissolved.[55] Any notion that assaulting Crimea would lead to nuclear war has proven laughable—as many at the time understood.[56]

Still, Musk's pull toward Moscow didn't end simply with decisions not to allow Ukrainian counteroffensives to reclaim Ukrainian territory in Crimea. Shortly after interceding to aid the Russians, Musk "took it upon himself to help find an end to the Ukrainian war"—but only on terms that the Russians had long peddled.[57] As Musk proposed, Ukraine should declare itself a "neutral" country.[58] (Left unsaid was the fact that Ukraine had been an officially neutral country when Russia first launched its invasion.)[59] Musk also called for referenda in Russian-occupied territories to decide the future of those Ukrainian provinces.[60] There should be no reparations, no war crimes tribunals, no future for Kyiv aside from a status as a Russian vassal. There would be only, in other words, appeasement. There would be only what Moscow wanted—which the Ukrainians well recognized. As Ukraine's ambassador to Germany posted in response to Musk's proposals, "Fuck off is my very diplomatic reply to you."[61]

Hanging over Musk's sudden public move in favor of Russia's interests was a whole range of unknowns. What had caused this wholesale shift? These bizarre minutiae that Musk was suddenly posting about—things like Soviet-era policies or Crimean water rights—where was Musk getting this from? What had drawn him, in such a short period of time, out of Kyiv's camp and directly toward the Kremlin?[62]

For those who'd followed Moscow's messaging for years, long before Russia first invaded Ukraine in 2014, the answer was obvious: These talking points all came from the Kremlin itself. Maybe not from Putin in particular, but it was clear that Moscow had sicced interlocutors on Musk, seeing him—and especially his ego—as someone and something to manipulate. Surely, though, Musk wouldn't actually transmit messages from Putin directly, right? Surely he wouldn't actually become a mouthpiece for a Russian despot, a European imperialist, a man launching the most devastating war Europe had seen since the days of Hitler and Mussolini?

If only. As *The Wall Street Journal* reported in October 2024, Musk had been having a number of "secret conversations" with Putin himself. Since late 2022, Musk and the Russian tyrant spoke on everything from "personal topics, business and geopolitical tensions," and more. Moreover, those conversations had coincided with "public and private pressure from the Kremlin" regarding Musk's efforts in Ukraine—pressure that itself coincided with Musk flipping from a Ukrainian ally to someone who helped prevent Kyiv from retaking Ukrainian territory. And all while the Biden administration was reportedly unaware that the conversations were even taking place.[63]

It was all boggling. The world's wealthiest man—this American oligarch—had been having secret back-channel conversations with the man attempting to upend the American-led global order. It was all without any precedent. Nor were these conversations only about Ukraine. There was one specific request from Putin, whose own failures had flipped Russia into being a junior partner to China: Could Musk prevent Starlink from operating over Taiwan? Could he, in other words, help keep Taiwan in the dark should Beijing launch its long-awaited invasion of the island? And could he do this "as a favor to China"?[64]

Putin must have realized he was pushing on an open door. Just as Musk had begun peddling Russian propaganda points about neighboring nations (most especially Ukraine), so, too, had he begun pushing Chinese propaganda about places like Taiwan. In 2023, Musk claimed that the relationship between Taiwan and China is analogous to the U.S. and Hawaii, and that Taiwan was an "integral part of China."[65] Taiwan should become, as Musk saw it, a "special administrative zone" under China's control.[66]

Never mind the fact that Taiwan has never been ruled by the Chinese Communist Party, or that it is an island with its own distinct history as a separate polity.[67] And never mind the fact that a strong majority of the island's inhabitants now consider themselves Taiwanese, rather than Chinese—or that Taiwan now represents one of East Asia's most vibrant, most open, and most equitable democracies.[68] None of that, for Musk, mattered. All that mattered were the dictatorial talking points he'd picked up—and the fact that his personal and professional wealth remained linked directly to Beijing. "We can't tell whether or not Musk's free will is for sale," the Taiwanese foreign minister deadpanned. "But Taiwan is not for sale, that's for sure."[69]

Musk's transformation into a mouthpiece for Beijing "is a problem—it's a huge problem," Michael Sobolik, a leading China analyst at the Hudson Institute, told me. "What we know publicly is that he's already become a 'useful idiot,'" a term first popularized to describe ignorant Westerners whitewashing the Soviet Union. When it comes to this pro-Beijing rhetoric, Sobolik continued, "It offends me morally, but it doesn't really surprise me at all—whether it's Elon, or pick your billionaire tycoon."[70] All that mattered was building out their own wealth, and finding allies in dictatorships around the world in the process—even those, maybe *especially* those, whose interests stood as anathema to America's.

As Musk admitted in 2023, "I'm kind of pro-China."[71] At that point, no one would disagree.

Thankfully, by 2024, this pro-dictatorial politicking appeared to finally catch up with Musk. Officials and analysts had cottoned on to the fact that Musk was, as one *New York Times* headline blared, a "national security risk."[72] Aiding Moscow's occupation in Ukraine, pushing pro-Beijing talking points to help the regime, rising to the point where he could singlehandedly throw a kill switch that directly undercut American—and, it almost went without saying, democratic—interests: All of it added up to a level of public pressure against the billionaire that he'd never seen prior. Coupled with Musk's collapse into a sewer of disinformation and conspiracy, the walls suddenly seemed to be closing in.[73]

Nor was it just the American public souring on the billionaire. In Congress, at least one senator, New Hampshire's Jeanne Shaheen, requested a formal investigation into Musk's foreign ties, tasking both the Air Force and the Department of Defense's Office of Inspector General with digging into Musk's conversations with Putin, among others. Further investigations revealed that both Musk and SpaceX had "repeatedly failed to comply with federal reporting protocols aimed at protecting state secrets"—a massive red flag, given both Musk's access to certain classified information and SpaceX's key contracts with the federal government. Concerns had escalated to such a point that, by 2024, Musk had specifically been denied high-level security access—a direct result of the "potential security risks" he now posed, as one Pentagon official said.[74]

It was a striking shift. A onetime savant, a onetime savior of American industry had transformed in just a few short years into a man many in the federal government could no longer trust—a situation that was entirely of Musk's own making. After all, no one had forced Musk to open himself up to overwhelming Chinese leverage, placing his professional future in the palms of the Chinese Communist Party. No one had made him open up clandestine links with Russia's dictatorship, keeping the highest ranks of the American government in the dark while he parroted Russian propaganda points for the rest of us. No one had forced him to do any of this.

Then again, no one had forced Jared Kushner to open himself up to billions and billions of dollars of dirty money spewing out of Middle Eastern dictatorships. No one had forced figures like Bezos, Zuckerberg, and Pichai to build out their own links with tyrants around the world, gutting their pretenses about supporting liberal democracy, or even supporting American interests. And, of course, no one had forced Donald Trump to ink his own financial arrangements—all his real estate investments, all his anonymous shell companies, all his crypto dealings—with despot after despot.[75]

No one had forced them to do any of this. But as all these oligarchs increasingly understood, it was Trump, more than anyone else, who stood as the most important figure for their prospects moving forward. It was Trump, and Trump alone, who could guarantee they could get away with this. And they all realized that in order to create a world safe for oligarchy, there was only one path available:

They had to reelect Donald Trump.

Section IV

Empire

They were careless people . . . they smashed up things and creatures and then retreated back into their money or their vast carelessness, or whatever it was that kept them together, and let other people clean up the mess they had made.

—F. SCOTT FITZGERALD[1]

13

The Corruption Is the Point

It's all about business and money. That's what it's all about. America is a business. It's a corporation.

—Tyrell Davis[1]

If there was a single moment when Americans recognized that an oligarchy was no longer simply ascendant but was now towering over and touching upon the entirety of American politics, it was January 20, 2025.

That day, in the Capitol rotunda, amidst dignitaries and diplomats, a quartet of men stood off to the side. There was Zuckerberg, in his boyish mop, staring off into the distance. There was Bezos, parked just to his left, with his bald pate reminiscent of a cueball, or perhaps Lex Luthor. There was Pichai, wrapped in an overcoat, shaking hands with those around him. And there was Musk, peering across the crowd, chin tilting forward, hand resting on the chair in front of him.[2]

Americans knew who each of them were, separately. But standing together that day, with a combined net worth pushing toward $1 trillion, they looked a bit like a Mount Rushmore of robber barons—a testament to the melding of American billionaires and American politics, without any precedent whatsoever.[3]

And Americans realized it. It wasn't just the numbers, or the fact that figures like Musk had blown past all previous campaign finance tallies, shoveling nearly $300 million to pro-Republican and pro-Trump causes, breaking every record in the process.[4] It wasn't just the fact that these billionaires, and many others in their class of oligarchs, had massed toward Trump in the final stretch of the election, with more of their wealth backing the once-and-future president than in any election cycle in American history.[5] All told, nearly 20 percent of all funding in the 2024 election came from billionaires—a gobsmacking share for a group that barely topped one hundred individuals total.[6]

It's not that other wealthy Americans hadn't gravitated toward Trump's opponent, Kamala Harris; many of them clearly preferred things like political stability, an independent central bank, minimizing deficit spending, and other policies Harris promised. But for most of the wealthiest donors in the 2024 election, that wasn't enough. For the billionaires who barreled the most money into America's election, Trump—the only billionaire who'd ever become president—was their candidate.[7]

Some three-quarters of the top twenty-five donors splurged on Trump. Following Musk's lead, oligarchs like Timothy Mellon ($172 million donated), Miriam Adelson ($148 million), Ken Griffin ($108 million), Paul Singer ($65 million), and many more poured everything they could into getting Trump reelected.[8] As the *Financial Times* reported, Trump was "particularly dependent" on these oligarchs, "with about a third of the money raised by [Trump's] campaign and allied groups coming from billionaires." Trump would ride the billionaires and their riches directly into the White House.[9]

It was a marriage of wealth and power without any comparison in American history. And it stemmed from the Supreme Court's ruling, some fifteen years ago, in *Citizens United.* All the threats, all the openings, all the malignant promise of the *Citizens United* decision—all the ways that American oligarchs could now take over American politics—all of it had come crashing to fruition. Small wonder that, in the immediate aftermath of the inauguration, Google searches for "oligarchy" spiked.[10]

Then again, perhaps it wasn't simply that snapshot—of those oligarchs cozying together, watching the president they'd bankrolled sworn in once more—that convinced many Americans that an oligarchy had arrived. Perhaps it came just a few days earlier, when outgoing President Joe Biden sat in the Oval Office, issuing a closing speech that circled that very topic. As George Washington had warned about "foreign entanglements," as Dwight Eisenhower had warned about a "military-industrial complex," Biden wanted to use his farewell address to warn about something else he saw swirling in American politics, threatening to strangle America's democratic experiment entirely.[11] As he said:

> In my farewell address tonight, I want to warn the country of some things that give me great concern. And that's the dangerous concentration of power in the hands of very few ultra-wealthy people, and the dangerous consequences if their abuse of power is left unchecked. Today, an oligarchy is taking shape in America of extreme wealth, power, and influence that literally threatens our entire democracy, our basic rights and freedoms, and a fair shot for everyone to get ahead.[12]

It was one of Biden's more lucid, most insightful comments. Despite all his personal tribulations and trip-ups, Biden had led a surprisingly anti-oligarchic administration. From the rise of the White House's new counter-kleptocracy policies—the task forces, the anti–money laundering regulations, the leadership and rhetoric highlighting the spiraling threats of dirty money—to the push to turn the IRS into a beefed-up tool to tackle wealthy tax cheats, Biden had made significant progress on multiple fronts. He'd elevated these kinds of anti-corruption efforts into a core national security focus. And he'd overseen an administration that helped make things like the U.S.'s new shell company registry a reality.[13]

The progress wasn't nearly complete; *Citizens United* still stood there, whisking any oligarch who wanted into the heart of American politics. But if you squinted, you could see a new era forming—a liminal look at what a post-oligarchic America could actually resemble. An era without American oligarchy, peeking just over the horizon.

And then Trump was inaugurated. And all that progress—indeed, nearly a century's worth of work to beat back corruption, both domestic and foreign—crumbled in the blink of an eye.

The first evidence of the sledgehammer the new Trump administration would take to America's anti-corruption policies came just two weeks into his second term. The new attorney general, Pam Bondi, unveiled a series of memos outlining the Department of Justice's new priorities. Unsurprisingly, in a White House overseen by the first white-collar criminal ever elected to the presidency, Bondi's department revealed that it was decimating many of the key planks of the anti-bribery, anti-kleptocracy regime it had built out over the years—some of which were on the books since before Trump was even born.[14]

The first on Bondi's chopping block was a statute known as the Foreign Agents Registration Act (FARA). First enacted in the late 1930s (and the subject of my previous book), FARA was a relatively simple piece of regulation, requiring transparency for Americans lobbying on behalf of foreign regimes. FARA didn't block the practice; thanks to First Amendment protections, Americans had wide leeway when it came to who they could lobby for—who they could spin, who they could whitewash, who they could open doors in Washington and around the country for.[15]

For decades, FARA was itself a backwater, largely unenforced and almost entirely overlooked. That disuse allowed the foreign lobbying industry—which now comprised not just traditional lobbying shops but also PR professionals, consultancies, white-shoe law firms, think tanks, and many more—to blossom into a multibillion-dollar behemoth, flipping into the go-to tool for foreign dictatorships looking to tilt American policy however they wanted.[16] Following Trump's first election, which elevated foreign lobbyists to more political power than they'd ever seen prior, FARA saw new life. Prosecutors went after foreign lobbyists, from Trump's campaign director to his national security adviser to many more, landing guilty pleas or outright convictions, and forcing much of the industry into the light for the first time.[17]

Nor was this a partisan pursuit; in 2024, then-Senator Bob Menendez was found guilty for, among other things, secretly moonlighting as an agent of the military dictatorship in Egypt—for "conspiring to act as a foreign agent" on behalf of Cairo, lobbying his congressional colleagues and ghost-writing for his dictator clients, all in return for gold bars that Menendez hid around his house.[18]

By the early 2020s, FARA was finally relevant, arguably for the first time ever. And then Bondi came in, and announced those days were done. FARA would still remain on the books, but Bondi—who herself had once worked as a foreign lobbyist for the theocratic dictatorship in Qatar—announced that it would focus solely on lobbying crimes that were "similar to more traditional espionage." It's unclear what Bondi was talking about; not only does the U.S. already have separate legislation targeting espionage, but FARA has nothing to do with spying. It is instead meant to specifically shine light on the subterranean lobbying networks operating in the shadows around Washington—how foreign regimes, foreign oligarchs, and many others push for their preferred policies, from lifting sanctions to ending corruption investigations to even launching wars.[19]

But now, thanks to Trump, it was a nonstarter. Where FARA had once been the lodestar for foreign lobbying legislation around the world, Bondi announced that it was now effectively dead—and all that information and transparency that Americans once had access to would be no more.[20]

In another memo, Bondi declared that the Trump administration was also dissolving another prong of the U.S.'s fight against kleptocracy: the FBI's Foreign Influence Task Force. First created in 2017—during Trump's first term, ironically—the group had quickly transformed into the U.S.'s leading tool for tracking and tracing foreign influence campaigns around the country, dedicated to dismantling infiltration campaigns out of Russia, China, Iran, Venezuela, and more. Given the explosion in interference campaigns in recent years, the FBI's task force had only grown in import since its inception. But Bondi announced its elimination, killing off the U.S.'s only body dedicated to investigating foreign influence.[21]

Next on the chopping block was the Kleptocracy Asset Recovery Initiative. Inaugurated in 2010, this was a body dedicated to freezing, seizing, and repatriating assets linked to dirty money networks around the world, who often plowed their illicit wealth directly into the U.S. While this task force was always fighting an uphill battle—the millions it returned hardly compared with the billions (or more) pilfered—it nonetheless stood as a testament to the U.S.'s public willingness to go after these networks. In Nigeria, in Malaysia, in Uzbekistan—in country after country, this body helped return some of the looted wealth, and helped restore some of the U.S.'s mangled credibility in the fight against dirty money. And now, with the stroke of a pen, it was gone.[22]

Bondi's scythe continued on. She announced the U.S. was also eliminating another task force dedicated specifically to oligarchs' assets. Known as KleptoCapture, the relatively new initiative grew out of Russia's expanded invasion of Ukraine in 2022, and out of the realization that oligarchs in Russia and elsewhere were simply prongs of kleptocratic governments across the globe. Yachts, mansions, luxury jets, priceless artwork, armadas of high-end automobiles—it was all fair game for KleptoCapture. If they could identify the proceeds of illicit wealth—especially linked to those closest to the Kremlin—they could swipe it, and help close off the American economy to Russian influence that much further. That was the case, at least, until early 2025, when the Trump administration destroyed it outright.[23]

These are all a jumble of names and acronyms, neologisms unfamiliar to those outside Washington. But pulling back, one thing from Bondi's memos was clear: In a single day, just a few weeks into Trump's new administration, the U.S. had eliminated or kneecapped its most successful and most prominent counter-kleptocracy tools. Years of progress had been undone. Decades of legislation had been left for dead. The American economy was suddenly opening itself up for illicit wealth, for foreign influence, for kleptocratic regimes writ large in a way it never had prior. Oligarchs around the world watched how their counterparts in America had pried open a White House, and suddenly realized that they could do the same. That they could join in the fun—join in this feast of making white-collar crime great again.

And the best was yet to come.

As the dust settled on Bondi's memos, Trump himself took up his pen—quite literally. Busy shaking down American media outfits, strong-arming American universities, and unleashing the most authoritarian administration the country had seen at least since the days of Richard Nixon, Trump turned to dismantling America's remaining anti-corruption credentials. Where he'd previously danced around and badmouthed America's anti-kleptocracy toolkit, now he would destroy it wholesale.

His first target was the Foreign Corrupt Practices Act (FCPA), which had itself been a direct outgrowth of Nixon's rank corruption. Trump openly described the FCPA, the very bedrock of America's anti-corruption efforts, as a "horrible law."[24] To Trump, the FCPA wrongly blocked American companies from engaging in the kind of routine, high-level bribery that firms elsewhere practiced. Rather than a shield that protected American corporations from being themselves targeted by rapacious regimes, and rather than a tool that helped starve dictatorships of much-needed cash, Trump thought the FCPA was a "horror show" for the U.S.[25]

In an executive order, Trump garroted the FCPA entirely. He announced that all enforcement of the legislation was effectively dead, restoring "American economic competitiveness" and allowing American companies to once more engage in "routine business practices in other nations"—a handy euphemism for bribery. Foreign corruption, in other words, was once more back on the table. Kleptocratic regimes and crooked American businessmen around the world rejoiced, knowing they wouldn't have to worry about pesky prosecutions anymore. One of the greatest post-Watergate reforms was now dead, for all to see.[26]

But Trump also had something more recent in his sights. In 2021, the U.S. passed the country's first shell company registry. It was the single most important tool in ending the U.S.'s role as a global leader in creating anonymous shell companies. Without anonymous shell companies in the U.S., oligarchs and dictators would have far more difficult times building out their own kleptocratic networks, hiding their ill-gotten gains in American real estate, American private equity, American investments, and more.[27]

In 2024, the registry—a private database, accessible only to American officials—finally came online. It was a remarkable moment. For the first time in decades, America's best days as a titan of the offshore world were behind it.[28]

And then, in early March 2025, Trump destroyed all that progress. Describing the shell company legislation as a "Biden rule"—and ignoring the fact that it was a bipartisan bill, passed over Trump's veto—Trump claimed the new regulations had "been an absolute disaster" for small businesses. "The economic menace of [shell company] reporting will soon be no more," he wrote.[29]

Trump himself was, of course, no stranger to anonymous shell companies. His own real estate portfolio was drenched in them, hiding all manner of international financing networks long before he ever ascended to the presidency. Given that Trump, with his background as a luxury real estate magnate, was the first American leader to emerge from an industry reliant on anonymous shell company financing, it was perhaps unsurprising that he raced to the rescue of shell corporations.[30] Still, the announcement was a shock; not only did fentanyl dealers, cartel heads, Chinese laundering networks, Iranian arms exporters, and more—the kinds of groups Trump was nominally opposed to—rely on these kinds of shells, but law enforcement bodies around the country were broadly supportive of shell company transparency.

Trump, though, couldn't have cared less. As his Treasury Department said, it would no longer "enforce any penalties or fines" for American shell companies that didn't comply with the regulations. The legislation would still remain, at least on paper. But in the real world, it would be like America's greatest counter-kleptocracy tool had never existed.[31] Even worse: Trump's White House announced it would torch all the shell company data the federal government had already gathered—a collective bonfire, destroying all the corporate records shining light on American shell companies.[32] (For good measure, the Trump White House shortly afterward announced it would also gut proposed anti–money laundering rules for things like private equity and hedge funds, meaning they, too, could continue accepting as much dirty money from around the world as they wanted.)[33]

Trump's actions were, in a certain sense, breathtaking. Rather than trying to repeal all these pieces of legislation outright, Trump had discovered a workaround—a legislative loophole that allowed him to decide which laws his administration would enforce, and which ones they could effectively demolish. Rather than uphold his constitutional duty to make sure that all laws passed by Congress were "faithfully executed," Trump simply announced that there was a whole suite of legislation that folks no longer needed to worry about.[34] He had created a new legal architecture by fiat, providing a public road map for as much white-collar crime as crooked regimes and corrupt oligarchs could want.

And still he wasn't done. While he was busy dismantling legislation, he was also busy creating new ways to attract illicit wealth into the U.S. One of his new tools was the creation of a "gold card" visa scheme. Sitting in the Oval Office, Trump hawked a "path to citizenship" for anyone who could pay $5 million. Anyone—any drug lord, any human rights abuser, any oligarch—who could meet that fee could visit the U.S., setting them on a path to American citizenship. "They'll be wealthy and they'll be successful, and they'll be spending a lot of money and paying a lot of taxes and employing a lot of people, and we think it's going to be extremely successful," Trump said. For good measure, he held up a physical gold card for reporters to see—complete with his face, his scrawl, and THE TRUMP CARD emblazoned on its front.[35]

These kinds of "golden visa" schemes aren't novel. They've been a favorite tool of kleptocrats around the world, looking to purchase citizenship in offshore havens like Dominica, Malta, and Cyprus for years. They're the perfect tools for figures looking for an escape hatch, dodging investigations or arrest.[36] The U.S. had its own related version of this years ago, but in 2022 legislators passed much-needed reforms to patch up those money-laundering loopholes.[37] Trump, though, simply ignored those regulations. He wasn't even coy about who he was trying to entice back into the U.S.; when asked specifically about whether Russian oligarchs could obtain this "gold card" visa, Trump responded, "Yeah, possible. Hey, I know some Russian oligarchs that are very nice people."[38]

A few months later, this new Trump gold card scheme launched. The price had dropped: now, for only $1 million, anyone could "unlock life in America." American residency—and eventual citizenship—was now for sale, to anyone who could scrounge up the cash. Kleptocrats couldn't have asked for more.[39]

Many of Trump's moves were aimed at lifting whatever barricades or obstacles remained for foreign oligarchs. Domestically, though, things were just as favorable to plutocrats—and American oligarchs could join their foreign counterparts in feasting on a whole new range of opportunities.

We could spend the rest of this book detailing all the ways Trump has made the lives of the wealthiest Americans easier, aiding the other members of the billionaire class who'd helped him rise. But highlighting just a few examples will suffice. Take Trump's signature piece of legislation, the One Big Beautiful Bill, which was little more than a gift-wrapped outlay for America's billionaires. Arguably the most economically regressive piece of legislation the country had ever seen, the bill gashed things like Medicare, Medicaid, and many more services that poorer Americans relied on, all while adding trillions upon trillions of dollars to America's exploding national debt—a burden that would fall far more on working- and middle-class Americans rather than the wealthy Americans who'd helped place Trump in office.[40]

Buried in the bill were multiple gifts to American billionaires. Where figures like Teddy Roosevelt had once pledged higher taxes targeting America's plutocrats, Trump made a complete mockery of Roosevelt's legacy. The bill not only increased the already substantial exemption for wealthy Americans who'd previously had to pay an estate tax but made this new exemption permanent. Trump even indexed the estate tax to inflation, meaning that this new, perpetual exemption is only going to rise, more and more, in the years to come, letting almost all wealthy Americans slip by without having to pay any estate tax whatsoever. Where this tax had once been one of the key tools for breaking up American oligarchs' estates, preventing the rise of a new feudal class of wealthy Americans, suddenly it was an empty shell, helping assure the rise of an American aristocracy.[41]

Likewise, Trump's bill not only blocked efforts to raise income tax rates on the wealthiest Americans, but further provided them larger tax breaks than any other class of Americans. American oligarchs would be able to keep far more of their wealth, at every turn, guaranteeing that the ever-upward surge of American wealth inequality would continue. Trump had shredded whatever legacy remained of Roosevelt's efforts—and, thanks to his One Big Beautiful Bill, made all these pro-oligarch benefits permanent.[42]

Yet it wasn't only the collapsing tax rates for wealthy Americans. The Trump administration took special aim at the IRS—not only to undo all the agency's gains in the past few years, especially as it pertained to targeting oligarchs, but to neuter the agency to the point of uselessness. In June 2025, the administration proposed slashing the IRS's overall funding by more than half. These cuts would not only roll back all the progress made under Biden, but would gut the IRS's budgets to their lowest point in decades.[43] And the cuts would focus on one specific area: enforcement, especially against the wealthiest Americans.[44] As the Tax Law Center said, the cuts will "further erode high-end tax enforcement"—and will make the agency even more shorthanded, short-staffed, and unable to go after the wealthy Americans evading taxes through their spiderwebs of offshore vehicles and anonymous shell companies.[45] Where the IRS had once been the main agency making sure American oligarchs complied with basic tax laws, the Trump administration promised to dismember it almost entirely. You could almost picture American oligarchs dancing on the IRS's grave.

Thanks to the cuts, the federal government will miss out on hundreds of billions of dollars in revenue—and potentially more.[46] Coupled with the administration announcing it would also shutter its teams dedicated to prosecuting tax evasion, the signal was blindingly obvious: Wealthy Americans would no longer need to worry about things like paying their fair share—or even paying anything at all. They could keep as much as they wanted.[47] With Trump in the White House, American oligarchy would be safe and secure, in ways never seen before.

At a certain point, tracking all Trump's moves began to feel simply like an exercise in futility—a list without an end, coming from an administration without a bottom. All the reforms, all the efforts, all the generations taking their shoulder to the wheel, trying to drive the ship of the American state toward a better, or at least less corrupt, future—all of it was undone. Now back in the White House, Trump stood triumphant. And so, too, did all the networks, regimes, and oligarchs who wanted to pry apart the remaining barricades to using their wealth to gain whatever they needed from a White House now open for business, to all comers.

And what business it was. As with his other pro-oligarch moves, we could spend the remainder of this book running through all the ways that Trump, his family members, and his inner circle have profited from his return to the White House. All the ways Trump's second term made the concerns about corruption in his first term appear like child's play. All the ways Trump has blasted past any previous precedents of presidential scandals—and how he has single-handedly replaced things like "Teapot Dome" as shorthand for political corruption.[48]

America had seen previous corrupt administrations, sure. But they'd never seen anything like this.

Where to begin? Perhaps with the most traditional forms of Trumpian corruption: real estate investments. Where concerns in Trump's first term centered on foreign regimes and oligarchs covertly slipping their wealth into Trump properties via shell companies, the Trump Organization in the second term has tossed any guardrails out the window, bosoming up to regime after regime around the world, profiting wherever and however they can. New Trump resorts in Oman, Trump towers in Saudi Arabia, Trump golf courses in Vietnam—over and over, the Trump Organization has launched projects with abandon, predicated almost entirely on the fact that the company is connected directly to the American president.[49] Why wouldn't a foreign regime trying to curry favor with the U.S. open its doors to a brand-new Trump building, opening up a direct line to the White House? As Eric Trump said, illustrating this point, "We're the hottest brand in the world right now."[50]

Or what about an emergent industry that was saturated in more corruption and more money laundering threats than perhaps anything else—crypto? Where the Biden administration had previously tried to prosecute crypto magnates accused of gross financial crimes, the Trump administration threw its doors open to the industry in ways few ever thought possible.[51] There were things like Trump's own "memecoin," which instantly became a beacon for wealth from around the world to stampede into the president's pocket.[52] Creating this "Trump coin" was like publicly "issuing the account number for a Swiss bank account," one critic said, pointing out how anyone, anywhere could directly enrich a sitting president.[53] Little surprise that we soon saw pay-to-play dinners for those who invested most in Trump's crypto project, letting them bid directly for Trump's attention—and that we saw prosecutions of crypto oligarchs dropped as soon as they started lining the president's pockets.[54]

And little surprise that foreign dictatorships quickly recognized the opportunity. In the most egregious example, the United Arab Emirates spearheaded a multibillion-dollar investment involving World Liberty Financial, a crypto firm cofounded by the Trumps. The funding itself was the "single largest investment in a crypto company ever," providing the Trumps' company with funds they "could invest to generate returns in the tens of millions annually." All this while Trump himself green-lit the shipment of high-end computer chips to the Emiratis—directly overriding national security concerns from cabinet officials that those chips would then be "shared with China," and directly threaten American national security.[55]

Or what about something we'd truly never seen before? What about a regime using a $400 million luxury jet to bribe a sitting American president? A supposed "gift" from the Qatari dictatorship, this airliner bribe was so brazen, so inescapable, that it even momentarily pierced the bubble of Trump's die-hard supporters, many of whom were themselves taken aback at the sheer egregiousness of the entire transaction.[56] But that moment was unfortunately fleeting. Even worse, there's no reason to think this jet—a deluxe airliner, given without any kind of compensation whatsoever—is the end of foreign regimes trying to buy Trump's affections. Think of it instead as a starting gun: as the bar over which other regimes will now have to leap, if they want to out-bribe Qatar. Any regime now knows the price. And any regime—every dictatorship, every oligarch, everywhere—now knows how easy it is to pay off a sitting American president.

The question of how much Trump and his family have personally profited off his second term is almost beside the point. *The New Yorker* estimated in 2025 that they'd already pocketed approximately $3.4 billion, with *Forbes* also estimating multibillion-dollar growth.[57] But even if that final number is somewhat nebulous, one thing was clear. If, as was said about his first administration, "the cruelty was the point," things had changed by the second term. With Trump back in the White House, the corruption was now the point.[58]

But perhaps the most egregious evidence of corruption—and, from where I sit, perhaps the most concerning—had nothing to do with how Trump personally profited in the White House. It had instead to do with a decision Trump took early on, in a single prosecution against the sitting mayor of Trump's hometown of New York City.

In the waning days of the Biden administration, the Department of Justice had launched an unprecedented prosecution of New York City Mayor Eric Adams, a fellow Democrat. As prosecutors outlined, Adams had not only abused his office, trying to interfere with investigators while entrenching one of the most corrupt administrations New York had ever seen. He'd also crossed that reddest of red lines for an American politician: soliciting funding from foreign sources.[59]

Given the broader collapse of American campaign finance regulations, the idea that some kind of "red line" even exists might seem like a bit of an anachronism. But as every American politician knows, there's one thing you cannot do. You can solicit and accept as much money from domestic sources as you could possibly want; you can ignore all the tissue-thin campaign finance laws that remain regarding these kinds of domestic donations. But stepping past American borders—going directly to foreign sources for funding—is a step no major politician before Adams had been charged with taking.

It's not like there hadn't been evidence of foreign funding in previous American elections. Multiple prosecutions had already revealed as much—and as we saw in the previous section, American corporations had already transformed into the perfect cutouts to mask this kind of foreign funding in American politics. Trump himself stood accused of accepting millions of dollars in Egyptian financing during the 2016 race, helping offset a $10 million injection in the waning days of that presidential campaign.[60] But those networks all at least made a pretense of subterfuge, of throwing up a front to obscure the foreign funding—of using all the loopholes available to tap into the bottomless swills of money floating just beyond America's borders, looking for a way to flood American politics.

Adams, though, waved away all that. A man never known for his subtlety, prosecutors alleged that Adams went to foreign sources directly, traveling to Turkey to meet one-on-one with potential funders, including at least one Turkish billionaire. Adams "welcomed the offer of foreign contributions," at one point even directing staff members to help organize these foreign funding networks. He allegedly did whatever he could to open the spigots of foreign financing for his reelection efforts.[61]

It was an appalling, historic case. For the first time in U.S. history, a prominent American politician had been formally indicted for this kind of foreign fundraising. Even in an era of rising foreign influence efforts, Adams's case stood out—not only because a fellow Democratic administration had gone after him, but because of the signal the prosecution sent other American politicians thinking of potentially turning to foreign funding themselves. The Biden administration had thrown down the gauntlet. Come whatever else, accepting foreign money in American elections was still a bridge too far.

Or, at least, it was. Because shortly after Trump reentered the White House, he killed the investigation and prosecution of Adams. Not for any legitimate reasons; his administration initially tried to claim that the prosecution had been bungled, and then claimed the case interfered with Adams's ability to carry out the White House's immigration policies.[62] At a certain point, though—as prosecutor after prosecutor resigned, going public with how the Trump administration was killing the investigation for purely political reasons—the White House stopped even bothering to defend its move.[63] It was Trump's Department of Justice—and it would prosecute, or not, whoever it pleased.

Much of the coverage of the Adams case focused on trivial details, highlighting things like the free airline upgrades Adams received, or the pro-Trump comments Adams was suddenly spewing. But buried amidst the fallout from the administration racing to Adams's rescue lay a starker, darker reality. In dropping Adams's prosecution, the Trump administration had suddenly given the go-ahead to every other American politician looking to access foreign funding for their own elections. That last remaining "red line" had crumbled. As long as a politician remained on Trump's good side, and as long as that politician did Trump's bidding, they could tap into as much foreign funding for their own elections as they could possibly want. Turkey, Azerbaijan, China, Russia, Iran, Venezuela—it didn't matter where the money came from. American politicians could now take funding from wherever, and whoever, they wanted. They could even get caught, if they were as sloppy as Adams. But if they did what Trump wanted, they wouldn't need to worry about prosecution.

It was a decision that, in years to come, may well be seen as momentous as *Citizens United.* It was the final demolishing of any sanctity, any safety, any sovereignty of American elections. As Adams himself said, "You win the race by raising money. . . . Have to raise money. Everything else is fluff." He wasn't wrong. But now, thanks to both Trump and Adams, the potential pool of money to be raised had just exploded in size. American elections could be funded by anyone who wanted in, from any country around the world.[64]

It was a new era for American oligarchy, and for all the foreign regimes watching American politics open up before them. Only one question remained: What comes next?

14

Age of Empires

We are only termites on a planet and maybe when we bore too deeply into the planet there'll [be] a reckoning—who knows?

—*Harry Truman*[1]

In March 2024, months before his father-in-law stampeded to re-election, Jared Kushner sat in a small, crowded conference room at Harvard University. Clad in a charcoal sweater and blue button-down, Kushner was there as a featured guest in the school's Middle East Dialogues series.[2]

Yet Kushner wasn't there that day to discuss the deals he'd inked with a range of Middle Eastern despots, or all the revelations about how dictators in places like Saudi Arabia had reportedly bragged about his naivete. Neither was he there to talk about his relationship with Israel's Benjamin Netanyahu, who would shortly be indicted for war crimes, stemming in large part from Israel's crimes against humanity in Palestine. Nor was he there to discuss, a few months after the October 7 massacre, the fact that the Abraham Accords—a previous series of governmental agreements, stewarded by Kushner, that were supposed to bring peace to the Middle East—were now in tatters, perhaps the most obvious diplomatic failure the U.S. had seen in decades.[3]

Instead, Kushner was there to share his thoughts on the next steps in Israel's ongoing campaign against Gaza. Specifically, Kushner wanted to float a scenario that all but the most far-right members of the Israeli leadership would find reprehensible.[4]

As Kushner laid it out, the best step forward for Israel was simple:

ethnic cleansing. Describing the threat Palestinian civilians faced from daily bombings, Kushner suggested that Israeli forces round up Palestinians and force them out of Gaza entirely—perhaps to somewhere in the arid, desolate deserts of southern Israel. "I would just bulldoze something in the Negev [Desert]," Kushner said. "I would try to move people in there. I know that won't be the popular thing to do, but I think that that's a better option to do, so you can go in and finish the job."[5]

As later clips from the conversation illustrate, Kushner's interlocutor, Harvard professor Tarek Masoud, is momentarily taken aback. "Is that something they're talking about in Israel?" Masoud asks. "I mean, that's the first I've really heard of somebody, aside from [Egyptian] President Sisi, suggesting that the Gazans who are trying to flee the fighting could take refuge in the Negev. Are people in Israel seriously talking about that possibility, about hosting Gazan refugees in what is considered Israel proper?" In other words: Are voices in Israel seriously considering depleting Gaza of all civilians—of clearing Palestinians out of Gaza wholesale?[6]

Kushner looks on, mute, inscrutable. He tosses his hands up. "I don't know. I'm sitting in Miami Beach right now, and I'm looking at this situation and I'm just thinking, what would I do if I was there?"[7]

Masoud jumps in, pointing out the blaringly obvious: that once the Palestinians leave, the likelihood of Israel granting their return to Palestine evaporates. "There are real fears on the part of the Arabs . . . [that] once Gazans leave Gaza, Netanyahu's never going to let them back in," he says.[8]

Kushner shrugs, offering a one-word response: "Maybe." In a sense, he's not wrong; the future is, technically, unknowable. But given Netanyahu's administration—with its messianic claims of Israel's right to all of Palestine (and beyond), and with Israelis' overall opposition to a Palestinian state—Kushner's response borders on the imbecilic.[9] Of course the Israeli government would prevent Palestinians' return. Of course this kind of ethnic cleansing, with Gazans barred from returning to Gaza, would be permanent.

But Kushner didn't stop there. "I'm not sure there's much left of Gaza at this point," he mused, leaving unsaid the fact that it is Israel that is responsible for turning Gaza into little more than a strip of rubble and ruin. As Kushner saw it, perhaps that wasn't the worst thing, anyway. He continued: "So if you think about even the construct like Gaza—Gaza was not really a historical precedent. It was the result of a war. You had tribes that were in different places, but then Gaza became a thing. So you have another war. Usually when wars happen, borders are changed historically over time."[10]

Kushner goes on from there, but the gist of his comments is simple. For Kushner, and for the Israeli expansionists aligned with him, borders are mutable. Malleable. Subject to change, based on the whims of the victor. Moreover, Gaza—Palestine, even—isn't legitimate. It was a hodgepodge creation of different peoples, different clans, without any true historical claims to the region. Of course, the identical argument could be made about the United States: that the U.S. was simply an agglomeration of different peoples in different states, without any long-standing claims to North America. This is the same logic imperialists elsewhere use, whether Russians describing Ukraine, or Chinese describing Taiwan, and more. To the imperialists' eyes, these constructs are false, faulty, and deserving of whatever happens to them—even if they disappear from the global map wholesale.

And what would remain of Palestine? On that, Kushner is coy. But he does let slip one comment pointing a direction forward—for himself, for his Israeli allies, for an administration overseen by his father-in-law. "Gaza's waterfront property—it could be very valuable," he smirked. "I think, from Israel's perspective, I would do my best to move the people out and then clean it up."[11] Empty Gaza, and then rebuild it on your own terms, for your own people. Consign Palestine to the ash heap of history—and then bring the tourists in, fattening your wallet along the way.

Kushner's suggestions in 2024 were thankfully met with sweeping criticism, at least in the media. But for those who'd followed Kushner's work, there was nothing surprising about his views.

After all, this was a man who not only helped spearhead the most pro-Israel administration the U.S. had ever seen but who had directly aided Israeli expansionists for years in the West Bank.[12] For nearly a decade, Kushner acted as codirector of his parents' foundation, funding an Israeli settlement known as Bet El, sending tens of thousands of dollars to back construction on stolen Palestinian land.[13] Even amid the raft of Israeli imperialist projects, Bet El stands apart. It is "considered one of the most politically radical settlements," founded by Israelis "who believed they were fulfilling God's promise by settling the West Bank."[14] As one Israeli colonizer said, "Bet El is very important because it establishes our claim that God gave us this land."[15] The Kushners' foundation has been so integral to Bet El's success that it achieved the donor level of "Master Builders," transforming into one of the most prominent financiers of Israel's overall imperialist mission.[16]

Yet Kushner wasn't just financing this colonial expansion. In recent years, he also began profiting from Israeli imperialism itself. In 2024, the Israeli government approved Kushner's purchase of nearly 10 percent of an insurance and financing firm called Phoenix Financial Ltd, making Kushner the company's largest shareholder. On its face, the transaction isn't necessarily problematic; promising to generate Kushner a tidy profit, the deal appears generally straightforward. But Phoenix isn't simply some small-scale, mom-and-pop shop; it is instead one of Israel's leading insurance firms—and has been one of the key bulwarks of Israel's expansion in both Palestine and Syria for years, acting as financial lubricant for more building, more construction, and more Israeli imperialism than ever before.[17]

As one investigation discovered, Phoenix is the central node for an entire range of investments in Israeli entities operating across occupied Palestinian land, from sewage and water treatment facilities to concrete factories to gas stations and beyond. The company has even "provided financial services to the local councils" steering these imperialist outposts.[18] A spiderweb of different projects, Phoenix acts as the financial lifeblood for much of Israel's theft of Palestinian lands, so much so that its investments in companies expanding across Palestine now run into the billions of dollars—a substantial source of revenue for a company in which Kushner now sits as the primary shareholder.[19]

Then again, maybe we never had to look at Kushner's investments to get a sense of how he feels about Palestine, and how willing he is to bend over backward for Israel's far-right expansionism. In 2019, while still in his father-in-law's first administration, Kushner laid out something he called the Middle East Economic Plan, a multibillion-dollar program that would supposedly present a "peace to prosperity" for the entire region. Bundling together infrastructure and business projects, the program came with a 136-page document outlining all the details of Kushner's "brainchild."[20]

The program itself is a tepid, lackluster affair, with the accompanying document detailing the plan reading "like a glossy magazine," full of "photos of children walking to school and smiling farmers." But there is one thing that is conspicuously missing from the vision. As Deutsche Welle found, there wasn't a single mention of "Palestinian state," "Palestine," or "occupation" in this entire document detailing Kushner's vision for the region's future.[21] Nothing about the expansion of Israel's land theft in the West Bank. Nothing about how Israel propped up groups like Hamas for years.[22] And certainly nothing about how Kushner had specifically aided the funding of Israel's imperialism, strangling the prospects of regional peace that much further.[23]

All of this—the investments, the donations, the rhetoric, the excuses—paints a damning, disturbing picture. Plenty of other Americans have backed Israel's expansion in Palestine, either for purely geopolitical moves or out of a sense of millenarian religious beliefs. But few have done so with the proximity to power that Kushner enjoyed—with the official position, with the megaphone, and with the financial backing that he brought to bear.

It's too much to say that Kushner was the cause of America's continued alliance with Israel, regardless of the death and destruction in Gaza. But he is clearly one of the primary faces of the alliance—a man profiting not only from its continuation, but also putting a public spin on what is perhaps the clearest, most galling attempt at ethnic cleansing in the twenty-first century. Moreover, it's Kushner—not Netanyahu, and not any of the other far-right conservatives laundering Israel's crimes—who has already seen his seeds beginning to bear fruit in Gaza. Shortly after his comments about Gaza's "valuable" waterfront property spilled out, such views trickled up to Trump himself. Gaza "could be better than Monaco," Trump said later in 2024, openly musing about turning the scene of such regular horrors into a simple real estate transaction. "It has the best location in the Middle East, the best water, the best everything."[24] The people—they can be moved, carted, forced on cattle trains, and dumped in distant lands. But the land? That's there for the taking.

And should that day come, Kushner will almost certainly be there, standing to profit. It should be no surprise that, in September 2025, *The Washington Post* reported that Kushner pitched a multibillion-dollar strategy that would enact a "voluntary" move for Palestinians. The proposal, laid out in a thirty-eight-page document, would have the U.S. place Gaza in a "trusteeship," organizing the "relocation" of every Palestinian in Gaza. The proposal even lays out the cost benefits of such removal, down to the cent, claiming each Palestinian leaving Gaza would save authorities approximately $23,000. (It even proposes building an "Elon Musk Smart Manufacturing Zone," as if this is something Gazans would ever want.) Worse yet: Investors in the plan get more money if more Gazans flee—incentive, as if investors and Israel's government needed more of it, to force every Palestinian out of Gaza completely.[25]

Kushner hasn't yet commented publicly on the leaked plans. But one former American official summed up the vision as little more than a "massive ethnic cleansing campaign," aimed at emptying Gaza of Palestinians—and making those overseeing the operation even richer along the way.[26]

The fact that Kushner has been perhaps the most prominent pro-Israeli figure in the American political firmament is execrable, and a testament to how much damage a single oligarch can do. But there's a further element that makes Kushner's central role steering America's Middle East policy remarkable. During Trump's second term—and unlike in his first—Kushner doesn't actually have any official position in the White House. He is instead nominally independent, someone who doesn't have to even go through a charade of vetting, of confirmation, of disclosure about which regimes may be paying him, or how much, or why. He is an oligarch without any official constraints—and one still able to maintain such a grip on American strategy and American policy.[27]

In public, Kushner's detachment from the current White House is attributed to Trump's attempted coup on January 6, 2021. Even after his father-in-law won the election in 2024, Kushner initially managed to keep a public distance, playing down any links to or influence on the White House.[28] He'd pop his head up from time to time—he was at Trump's 2025 inauguration, for instance, lost amidst a sea of other oligarchs—but he has a far less public profile in the 2020s than he did in the 2010s.

In reality, though, these claims of supposed distance and lack of influence are a feint. Why would Kushner have ever pulled himself away from the man now steering American politics? If he had actually distanced himself from the White House, why would all those foreign regimes continue to blast billions of dollars at him and his firm? If he's not a player in the Trump era, why do foreign despots, such as Saudi Arabia's Mohammad bin Salman, continue to plug him for both advice and strategy?[29]

Kushner's influence has not only continued during Trump's second term, but is arguably more impactful than ever. As Reuters reported in early 2025, Kushner "remains involved behind the scenes," including by "advising on Trump's Middle Eastern strategy, helping select appointees and guiding certain cabinet members through the transition."[30] Specifically, Kushner is "very, very close" to Trump's chief of staff, Susie Wiles, speaking to her "regularly."[31] All told, according to Trump biographer Michael Wolff, Kushner has a "hidden hand" in Trump's second administration—one you can see shadows and hints of, but one that hasn't received nearly enough attention, or nearly enough investigation.[32]

Perhaps most pertinent, Kushner has been a direct adviser to the man who replaced him as the head of the Middle Eastern portfolio: Steve Witkoff. A former player in New York real estate, Witkoff is perhaps even less qualified than Kushner when it comes to steering regional policy, with his only credentials being a lifelong friendship with Trump.[33] Thankfully for Witkoff, though, he has Kushner there to help guide him. Even without an official title in the White House, Kushner has "been focusing on getting Steve up to speed . . . and helping Steve with strategy," one source told Reuters. The relationship culminated in late 2025, when the two of them helped convince Hamas to release remaining Israeli hostages—a welcome development, but one that did nothing to address the underlying causes of the conflict, nor Israel's ultimate designs on Palestine.[34]

It's unclear if Witkoff knows, or even cares, that Kushner has taken in billions from foreign patrons in the region, or that he's specifically invested in the success of Israeli expansionism. But that's almost beside the point. Suddenly, in the middle of one of the U.S.'s most debilitating relationships—with a regime in Israel bent not just on destroying any semblance of Palestinian statehood but potentially carving up neighbors in Syria, Jordan, and beyond—stands Kushner, acting like a conductor, passing along connections, pushing preferred policies. A man whose only qualification is that he is related to the sitting U.S. president. A man who's only ever aided Israeli brutality however he can—and watched his own net worth rise, and rise again.

And it's certainly paid off. In September 2025, *Forbes* announced that Kushner had himself finally become a billionaire—an announcement that came on the same day a United Nations report found Israel guilty of committing genocide against Palestinians in Gaza.[35]

While Kushner's involvement in diplomacy may begin with relentless Israeli expansionism, it doesn't end there. Alongside Saudi Arabia, the UAE, and Israel, the other prominent link between Kushner and a foreign dictatorship remains a partner we saw earlier: Russia.

The Kremlin has spent years engineering methods to influence and interfere in democracies around the world—and has often used its own oligarchs to do so. Certain Russian oligarchs launched think tanks, while others helped fund some of the far-right fundamentalist networks we met earlier in this book.[36] Others targeted a range of organizations in the U.S., including groups like the National Rifle Association, with promises of new markets in Russia if only these groups could help restore U.S.–Russian ties.[37] Oligarchy has always been a means to an end for Moscow: for launching the Kremlin to the "great power" status it craves, and for entrenching and emboldening autocratic forces wherever it can.[38]

And as we've seen throughout this book, the Kremlin wasn't shy about trying to tap into the emerging oligarchic class in the U.S. Figures like Musk provided not only platforms but also ways to influence policy, even going so far as to withhold aid from Ukraine on the battlefield. But even with Musk's involvement in the 2024 election, there was one other oligarch whom Moscow saw as its entry point to reset relations with the U.S.: Kushner.

Kushner's links with Moscow reach back to the 2016 interference efforts, when Kirill Dmitriev—the head of Russia's sovereign wealth fund, himself a "smooth-talking oligarch" widely viewed as Putin's "shadow foreign minister"—tried to use Kushner as a launchpad to infiltrate the first Trump administration.[39] When that fizzled, Kushner's ties with Dmitriev went into hibernation. Dmitriev "maintained a connection" with Kushner, wrote the Russian outlet *Meduza*, but it appeared perfunctory at best.[40] As the *Daily Beast* added, the two continued to communicate "about ways the U.S. and Russia could work together," but the conversations never amounted to much.[41] Unlike the Saudis or the Emiratis, there's no evidence that Moscow plowed billions of dollars into Kushner's fund, or that it even viewed him as anything more than an empty suit with declining political influence.

And then Trump won the election. And almost immediately, the old links tethering Dmitriev and Kushner reignited. "The Kremlin tried to start communicating with Trump almost as soon as he won the 2024 presidential election," one analysis in *Foreign Affairs* read. "It reached out to [Trump] through formal Russian and U.S. intelligence channels. But it also reactivated links to various figures in Trump's orbit. Most notably, Kirill Dmitriev . . . used his ties to Trump's son-in-law, Jared Kushner," to reopen conversations between Moscow and Washington wholesale.[42] The link between the two was so important that Kushner and Dmitriev even arranged the initial phone call between Trump and Putin, effectively bringing the Russian dictator back in from the geopolitical cold.[43]

As with the other Middle Eastern tyrants, Kushner emerged as part facilitator and part adviser. After reopening channels with Moscow, Kushner then steered Witkoff—whom Trump has also assigned as the official head of the Russia portfolio—to Dmitriev, who helped whisk Witkoff around Moscow, even as the Kremlin continued to decimate chunks of Ukraine.[44]

In a vacuum, there's nothing necessarily untoward about Kushner's actions. Linking connections, opening doors, mediating between

Moscow and Washington and helping restore links between geopolitical forces like the U.S. and Russia—it could, from one angle, be viewed as a worthwhile endeavor. In another world, with a Russia that wasn't busy carving up neighbor after neighbor, launching the world closer to nuclear war than anything we've seen in decades, Kushner's efforts could almost be commendable.

Yet that's not the world in which we live. Instead, we have Kushner acting as the primary contact for Dmitriev, emerging as the key figure connecting Trump and the Kremlin.[45] Nor is Dmitriev simply some bagman. He has himself been directly sanctioned by the U.S. government, specifically for his role in financing and facilitating Russia's criminal invasion of Ukraine. As the Biden administration said when announcing sanctions against Dmitriev in 2022, the Russian official was a key tool for Putin to "raise funds abroad, including in the United States." In other words, Dmitriev was specifically pinpointed by the U.S. as a linchpin in Russia's war machine—and one of the key figures aiding and abetting the most devastating, debilitating war Europe has seen in nearly a century.[46]

Kushner, naturally, has never publicly commented on the sanctions, or on the fact that his Russian interlocutor, a man with whom he has a "personal relationship," is a point person for Russia's imperial project.[47] He's never commented on the fact that Dmitriev reportedly sees himself as Russia's "counterpart to Kushner." Nor did he ever comment on the fact that, as Russian journalist Mikhail Zygar has described, Kushner's relationship with Dmitriev "was the primary link between Trump's camp and the Kremlin," and that Kushner and Dmitriev were "connecting [Moscow and Washington] across the ocean."[48]

Kushner has, in fact, stayed mum on the entire relationship. But the fruits of those links are there for the rest of us to see. Summits between Trump and Putin. A Ukrainian war effort suddenly slowing, watching its American support dry into nothing.[49] A previously isolated, flagging Russia suddenly thrown a lifeline—suddenly able to snatch victory from the jaws of defeat. And a Russian empire with wind in its sails once more.

Not all of it was caused by Kushner, of course. But all of it is downstream from a relationship restored—and from a pair of oligarchs, in Kushner and Dmitriev, who helped make it possible.

It was quickly clear that even if the Kremlin didn't initially get all it wanted—even if, as the time of this writing, Ukraine is still mostly free and mostly sovereign—Russia is well on its way to marching back to a relationship reset with the U.S. But there is still one domino Moscow wants to see fall, perhaps more than anything else: sanctions. Specifically, the Kremlin wants an end to all the piling sanctions the U.S. has launched for years—and for the return of a world where Russian oligarchs and Russian officials can travel, and can move their money, wherever they want.[50]

The Russian sanctions themselves date back to 2012, when the U.S. created a new sanctions program that targeted not industrial sectors, but specific officials. Named after Sergei Magnitsky—a Russian accountant who discovered a sprawling tax fraud scheme among Russian higher-ups, and was promptly murdered by Russian security forces for his efforts—these sanctions have been easily the most remarkable sanctions-related innovation not just in years, but in decades.[51]

Rather than block entire Russian industries, they instead targeted the oligarchs atop the Russian regime itself. Blocking these oligarchs from accessing the American economy, preventing them from traveling to the U.S., freezing any American assets they may have—the advantages of these sanctions run on and on. Most of all, they publicly highlight just how corrupt these figures are—a boon not only for Russia's democratic opposition but for other nations seeking out evidence for similar sanctions and similar ways to disrupt oligarchic networks elsewhere. Putin himself is one of the few global leaders now placed under these kinds of direct sanctions—a remarkable achievement, and a global stain on his reputation.[52]

In the years since their introduction, these Magnitsky sanctions have proven wildly popular. Not only have they been expanded globally, now targeting officials and oligarchs from Uzbekistan, Venezuela, Nicaragua, and more, but they are widely regarded as perhaps the most important tool to target, upend, and dissolve networks of kleptocrats, oligarchs, and organized crime syndicates around the world. Preventing these individuals from accessing American finance, American investments, and American influence networks—all while publicly highlighting the corruption at the root of their wealth—these targeted sanctions are one of the most effective anti-oligarch tools ever invented. Indeed, with the collapse of the U.S.'s anti-bribery legislation and policies elsewhere, the Magnitsky sanctions are perhaps the most prominent pillar of the U.S.'s anti-corruption regime remaining.[53]

Which is why it's little surprise that lifting these sanctions has been at the center of Russia's influence and interference efforts for over a decade. It was one of the prime motivating factors behind Moscow's 2016 interference campaign in the U.S., when the Kremlin sought to cultivate Trump and his allies with the express purpose of lifting these Magnitsky-style blockades. It was at the core of the Russian and pro-Kremlin networks involved in Trump's first impeachment scandal in 2019, when a series of oligarchs tried to peddle so-called dirt on Trump's political opponents in return for lifting sanctions and investigations.[54] And it is, even years later, still at the heart of Moscow's current pitch to Trump: that in return for restoring relations—and in return for opening up Russia to American investors once more—the White House should lift these sanctions, eliminating the key tool still keeping Russian oligarchs, and oligarchs around the world, at bay. And this has been the primary plank of Dmitriev's pitch to Kushner as well: that the U.S. should lift the sanctions still weighing down Russia, its economy, and its kleptocratic leadership—Dmitriev included.[55]

Thus far, Dmitriev hasn't gotten his way. Yet as he sees it—and as Putin continues to believe—it's just a matter of time before these sanctions crack and crumble, swept away like so much of the U.S.'s anti-corruption program elsewhere. And they have every reason to be confident. With Trump back in power, the efficacy of these Magnitsky sanctions has already begun imploding. And the last, best means of targeting and upending oligarchs elsewhere is turning to dust, with only the kleptocrats, the despots, and the tyrants cheering on its demise.[56]

All of which leads us back to Kushner, and the kind of pro-imperialist, pro-oligarch impact he's already had, even without an official position in Trump's new administration.

In 2024, after years of Israeli colonizers launching pogroms and terrorist acts against Palestinians in the West Bank, the Biden administration finally broke against them, launching a series of targeted sanctions against the most extremist, most vitriolic Israeli "settlers" occupying Palestinian lands.[57] One of the newly sanctioned entities was a "settlement development organization," which was a "key part of the Israeli extremist settlement movement."[58] Another series of sanctions targeted Israelis who had "engaged in threats and acts of violence against Palestinians, including in their homes."[59] As the White House said, the "high levels of extremist settler violence" had reached such "intolerable levels" that these sanctions were the only possible remedy—that, for the first time, the U.S. would start using its key tool targeting oligarchs and crime bosses elsewhere to now target Israel's imperialists.[60]

Given the hundreds of thousands of Israelis now living on stolen Palestinian land—and the fact that the primary Israeli backers of this violence, including in the Israeli government, are still unsanctioned—these sanctions were a drop in the bucket.[61] But they were, if nothing else, a symbol: a sign that even the stalwart pro-Israeli support in the Biden wing of the party was fracturing. And that could be seen in the response from those Israelis on the ground, authoring the pogroms and the arson attacks shattering Palestinian families.[62] The sanctions, which dried up much of the funding of these Israeli efforts, "infuriated" those leading Israel's settler movement, with some claiming they were shocked that Washington would ever turn on them like this.[63] The sanctions were also a salvo against those Americans like Kushner who'd long helped buttress these Israeli settlements—and a sign that, out of power, there was only so much Kushner and his allies could do to aid the erosion and elimination of a Palestinian state.

On their own, the sanctions were a relatively small move. But if Democrats remained in power—and as Israel continued barreling further and further toward its status as a rogue state, viewing the borders of its neighbors as mere suggestions—they would almost certainly expand, blanketing Israel with more and more sanctions moving forward.

But, of course, that's not what happened. Trump won the election in 2024, and entered office in January 2025. And less than a week into his second term, the Trump administration lifted all the sanctions the U.S. had placed on these Israeli colonizers.[64] Almost overnight, these Israeli imperialists watched all their American assets become unfrozen, and were suddenly free to tap as much American financing as they wanted. They were once more free to expand their efforts—their vandalizing, their armed assaults, their efforts at ethnic cleansing—knowing they would face no American punishment as a result. As Brad Brooks-Rubin, a former U.S. sanctions official, wrote, lifting these sanctions not only makes the settlers' "economic activity" easier but it "provides a psychological and rhetorical victory for the movement and its allies, especially in the United States."[65]

Israeli expansionists could not have asked for more. They'd gotten everything they wanted from the Trump administration—and from a man whose son-in-law has been their biggest stalwart, their biggest benefactor, and their biggest cheerleader in an administration willing to grant Israel a blank check in Palestine, and far beyond.

For those who'd long advocated the use of these targeted sanctions, the Trump administration's move to lift sanctions on Israeli settlers was heartbreaking. Not only because of what the move meant on the ground—and for the Palestinian lives now being devastated as a result—but because of what it portended. Trump revealed that these sanctions could be used not just to target the crooked or the corrupt but as a means of strengthening the kind of right-wing, autocratic regimes swelling around the world. Suddenly, sanctions were simply a tool in Trump's hands to craft the kinds of geopolitical outcomes he wanted—and to aid his allies elsewhere in the project of authoritarian kleptocracy.

Palestinians were the first casualties of this shift. But they would not be the last.

It wasn't long before Trump expanded the use of these kinds of targeted sanctions for his own ends. Before his inauguration, political scientists Dan Nexon and Alex Cooley warned that Trump would use these kinds of sanctions "to persecute foreign officials who offend Trump"—which was now precisely what was taking place.[66] He lifted sanctions against figures in Hungary who'd already ensconced their own authoritarian, antidemocratic regime.[67] He specifically sanctioned a judge overseeing the prosecution of disgraced former Brazilian leader Jair Bolsonaro—a man who'd previously attempted his own coup to retain power in Brazil, and whose own supporters had already tried to assassinate the judge Trump now sanctioned.[68] Over and over, Trump used these targeted sanctions to slap down democratizing forces, to elevate like-minded authoritarians, and to make a complete mockery of the legacy of Sergei Magnitsky, who was murdered for his efforts to expose corruption.

It was, in many ways, the end of an era. America's targeted sanctions had long been one of the most remarkable anti-corruption, anti-oligarch tools extant—a sign of America's potent financial power and America's anti-corruption credentials. Now, though, that period was coming to a rapid close. Trump had officially flipped these sanctions inside out, turning them into pro-corruption, pro-oligarch tools. Tools that any regime could now use for their own ends. Tools that Moscow could now pry apart even further—and that oligarchs around the world would no longer have to worry about.

It was the final victory for international oligarchy looking to take advantage of Trump's new administration. And it was a signal victory for imperialists—in Israel, in Russia, and elsewhere—looking to usher in a new age of conquest. It was an age of oligarchy now giving way to a new age of empires.

And back in the U.S., there was one man—one oligarch—looking to take advantage of it all.

15

Turnkey Totalitarianism

Righteousness without power is just an opinion.
—*Valentina Allegra de Fontaine*[1]

On election night 2024, Elon Musk sat in Trump's gilded Florida palace, known as Mar-a-Lago. He was one of a few select invitees to Trump's election watch party—part of a core group of advisers, strategists, and hangers-on huddling with the hopeful candidate, there to find out whether or not Americans would return the billionaire to the White House.[2]

In one photo of the evening, Trump can be seen leaning in to an expectant Musk.[3] It's unclear what they're talking about. Perhaps it was Musk's record-setting, jaw-dropping donations propelling Trump back to the precipice of power—the hundreds of millions of dollars Musk splurged on Trump's reelection, totaling over a quarter of a billion dollars. The funding didn't go directly to Trump himself; because of the scant campaign finance regulations still remaining in the U.S., Musk was still prevented from making this kind of direct donation. Musk instead funneled the funds to a series of super PACs—including one, America PAC, which he himself created. Drenched in nearly $300 million from Musk, these groups could then spend the funds however they wished, pushing pro-Trump messaging across the finish line.[4]

The funding was magnitudes more than anything seen previously. Even in recent elections dominated by billionaire donors, no one had ever approached Musk's largesse. In 2020, Michael Bloomberg offloaded approximately $150 million to Democratic causes (besides his own campaign)—a gargantuan sum, but still barely more than half of Musk's 2024 total.[5] In 2016, Democratic backer Tom Steyer donated over $90 million—far more money than almost every American will ever know, but still a far cry from Musk's donations.[6] And back in 2012, in the first presidential contest following the *Citizens United* ruling, Sheldon and Miriam Adelson donated just a little less than $100 million total to GOP causes.[7]

At every turn, media, civil society, and even politicians decried the rise of this kind of billionaire donor class. As one *Politico* headline from 2012 described, that year's election was the "year of the big donor"—a claim that was surely accurate, but appears almost laughable in hindsight, given how these "big donors" have dominated all elections since.[8]

Indeed, all those previous election cycles were mere warm-ups to the 2024 campaign. In addition to Musk, there was Timothy Mellon, bundling nearly $200 million to Republican causes. There was Miriam Adelson once again, donating nearly $150 million on her own. Richard and Elizabeth Uihlein, Ken Griffin, Jeffrey and Janine Yass—all of them pushed nine-figure donations to Republican causes. Billionaire after billionaire barreled as much of their money into American politics as they wanted, breaking no laws, cementing an oligarchy in real time.[9]

But it was Musk who sat with Trump on election night in Mar-a-Lago. Who, among all the billionaire backers of this billionaire president, was set to see the most gain. It was Musk whom everyone would watch rise, rule, and then detonate in spectacular fashion. And it was Musk who, in the process, illustrated just how close an American oligarch, even outside official power, could come to the center of American policymaking, all for the betterment of his own interests—even if that ended up helping America's adversaries along the way.

Musk began enjoying the fruits of Trump's victory almost immediately. Even before Trump himself returned to the White House, Musk started outlining the contours of his new, so-called Department of

Government Efficiency (DOGE). A mix of both reactionary and revolutionary elements, DOGE resembled less a traditional federal department and more the kind of political operation—with handlers, with ideological requirements, with unfettered access—seen in dictatorial regimes elsewhere.[10] Sicced across the federal government, DOGE employees tracked political fealty, infiltrated federal functions, and gained access to the kinds of financial systems that few outside the highest realms of American politics had ever known.[11]

Mostly, though, DOGE slashed and burned, simply for the sake of slashing and burning. In program after program, department after department, DOGE took a flamethrower to services across the government. Foreign aid programs? Decimated. Park rangers? Canned. Nuclear security personnel? Axed.[12] There was no rhyme, no reason, no rationale. The only thing that mattered was disemboweling as much of the federal government as possible. If a program had the term "diversity" or "equity" in it, it was specifically targeted—even if that meant funding for things like financial equity were eliminated.[13]

All this was overseen by Musk—an oligarch unelected, a billionaire unleashed. Distracted by the trappings of office, as well as all the opportunities for self-enrichment suddenly spilling open, Trump appeared largely apathetic about DOGE's destruction.

Musk, though, couldn't have been happier. And why wouldn't he be? While he was publicly deferential, in reality the center of political gravity had shifted. Musk's presence, and DOGE's successes, meant that for the first time since Woodrow Wilson—who suffered a series of strokes in office and ceded much of his presidential powers to his wife—the U.S. had someone who could properly be considered a co-president. In Wilson's case, the redelegation had been under wraps, kept out of the public eye. Not so with Musk, who exerted his power openly. It was as if Musk had chartered a fourth branch of the government—one above the legislative, out of reach of the judicial, and on par with the executive. An oligarchic branch of government: unaccountable, unassailable, in existence only because of the hundreds of billions of dollars that Musk and his co-oligarchs controlled.[14]

No one benefited more from this arrangement than Musk—especially when it came to the oligarch's personal finances. DOGE "gutted multiple regulatory agencies, including those that oversee [Musk's] businesses," wrote the *Financial Times.* "Among these, the FDA, which monitors Neuralink, Musk's brain chip company; the Federal Aviation Administration, which regulates SpaceX; and USAID, which investigated Starlink."[15] All those concerns about oversight, all those questions about compliance, all those worries about potential investigations—all that disappeared, almost overnight. Musk now regulated the regulators.

He also watched all his other projects and investments boom. Thanks to his role by Trump's side, Musk's X (formerly Twitter) rose to far greater heights than ever before. Companies that once boycotted the platform—a site that had transformed into a sieve for frothing conspiracies since Musk's takeover—were pressured into returning.[16] The company's financial free fall, which began when Musk bought the platform, finally ended.[17]

Additionally, with his access to Trump, and to as much federal data as he could digest, Musk had a leg up on any competitor in any area his companies operated. Already embedded in America's space and defense contracting industries, Musk now had a wide-open field in front of him.[18]

Take, for instance, one of the most preposterous—and potentially lucrative—projects under Trump's new administration: the so-called Golden Dome missile shield.[19] As envisioned by Trump, this kind of missile defense program would not only protect the American homeland from any inbound enemy launches, but could directly reward the man who'd helped return him to the White House. In early 2025, SpaceX and its partners "emerged as frontrunners to win a crucial part" of the new program, estimating preliminary costs at upward of $10 billion—a tidy turnaround for a single project. Yet that wasn't all. As sources disclosed, SpaceX "proposed setting up its role in Golden Dome as a 'subscription service' in which the government would pay for access to the technology, rather than own the system outright." In other words, the proposed missile system shielding the United States would not be owned by the U.S. itself but would instead remain in the hands of the country's wealthiest man.[20]

From Musk's end, it was an obvious pitch. (Why wouldn't he push for as much as he could get, including personally controlling the missile umbrella protecting the U.S.?) And it was a testament to how much one man, and one oligarch, could get from the federal government. As one of the sources familiar with the proposal said, "There's an attitude that the national security and defense community has to be sensitive and deferential to Elon Musk because of his role in the government."[21] When it came to American national security, there were no longer any checks or balances. There was only what this oligarch wanted—even if that meant having his fingers, and not the president's, on the button that could protect the U.S. from a hellfire of incoming missiles.

At the time, it was difficult to see any through line threading Musk's and DOGE's arson. It all seemed so haphazard, so hamfisted—especially when DOGE had to undo some of its cuts, as it did with the nuclear weapons personnel it tried to fire.[22]

But pulling back, certain trend lines emerge. In addition to targeting anything deemed even remotely "woke," there was a series of curious decisions made whose outcomes seemed to align, clearly and consistently, with the interests of certain American adversaries. In an administration supposedly dedicated to staring down America's enemies—especially those in China, Iran, Venezuela, and more—Musk's and DOGE's actions just so happened to aid many of those same adversaries, time and again.

Take China, for instance. In addition to all the cuts to things like the FBI's Foreign Influence Task Force and foreign lobbying regulations—which will only aid Beijing's influence and interference efforts in the U.S.—Musk's DOGE specifically kneecapped organizations that did more than arguably anything else in the U.S. to highlight the cruelty of the Chinese Communist Party.[23] Rather than enhance the U.S.'s fights against Beijing's reach, DOGE actively aided the CCP's efforts to strengthen itself domestically, and to expand its influence far further than ever before.[24]

For years, it was easy to find those in the U.S. who supported the freedom of Tibet. The mountainous nation—slightly smaller than Mongolia, slightly larger than South Africa, enjoying the highest elevation of any country around the world—had more friends than it could count. And it needed all the support it could find. Conquered by the Chinese Communist Party in the late 1940s and 1950s, Tibetans spent decades on the front lines of China's party-state dictatorship. Jailed and harassed, stripped of independence and identity, Tibetans' experiences served as a precursor for how Beijing would treat Uyghurs, and any other group dreaming of any kind of autonomy from the CCP.[25]

Thankfully, the Tibetan diaspora—which includes figures like the Dalai Lama, exiled from Tibet—found success after success in stirring support for Tibet's cause. Indeed, throughout much of the latter half of the twentieth century, FREE TIBET shirts were so ubiquitous as to be commonplace, even in the U.S.[26]

But as the years bled by, pressure from the CCP expanded, even into American industries like Hollywood, strangling any outward support for Tibetan independence.[27] Even as China's choke hold on Tibet continued—resulting in ethnic cleansing, cultural erasure, and all the trappings that come with horrific colonialism—public backing for Tibet's cause waned.[28]

But it didn't disappear entirely. The Tibetan diaspora has remained active, agitating for a cause that the CCP tries to snuff out wherever it can. And while it may not be as public as it once was, U.S. support for the nation—now occupied by Chinese forces for over seventy-five years—continued on.

Then Musk arrived, siccing DOGE on federally funded media outlets—the kinds that reach into corners of the world that no other outlet can cover, including regions like Tibet. One of those outlets, Radio Free Asia (RFA), was a case in point. Founded in 1996, RFA was not only the first media organization to break the news of China's concentration camp system in East Turkestan—a revelation only possible because RFA published Uyghur-language news, with Uyghur-speaking reporters—but for years, it was the key source for getting news out of Tibet.[29] Those in Tibet and the rest of China came to rely on RFA, as well as other U.S.-funded sources, like Voice of America (VOA), for an idea of what was actually happening in the country. Even more impressive, RFA wasn't just an online publication; as its name indicates, it also broadcast over radio, which remains a key tool for accessing news in both China and Tibet. "Both RFA and VOA do something that basically no one else does, which is reach audiences inside China through non-internet means," Bethany Allen, who runs China investigations and analysis at the Australian Strategic Policy Institute, said in 2025. "RFA radio reach[es] people who otherwise would not have access to independent information."[30]

Given the censorship and surveillance swamping Tibet, RFA was often the only information lifeblood for the entire Tibetan nation. The coverage ran the gamut: stories on self-immolation of Tibetan monks, revelations on environmental destruction and environmental protests in Tibet, investigations into how the CCP was stripping Tibet of both resources and people, all while trying to obliterate any sense of Tibetan identity wholesale. Unsurprisingly, Beijing loathed the outlet; as one Chinese propaganda source said in 2023, since its inception "RFA has never ceased its fabrication, attack, and smear campaign against China."[31]

And then, in one of its first actions after Trump's reentry into the White House, Musk murdered the outlet. DOGE announced it was gutting the agency overseeing RFA, starving RFA of its congressionally mandated funding. Within weeks, RFA was a husk, with some 90 percent of staff laid off—and with the outlet announcing that it would be suspending all Tibetan radio broadcasts.[32] VOA, likewise, announced it was laying off nearly all its personnel, leaving it little more than an empty shell, and leaving all its readers without an alternative for news.[33]

The cuts were devastating across the board, and around the globe. But it was in Tibet that the outcome was most destructive. Within just a few weeks, Musk and DOGE had effectively cut Tibet off from the rest of the world—and turned Tibet into little more than a black hole, with the CCP finally in complete control.

Chemi Lhamo is typically an ebullient, cheery advocate for the rights of Tibetans. Born to Tibetan refugees, Lhamo now lives in Canada, where she has transformed into arguably the most charismatic, effective speaker for Tibetan rights in the twenty-first century. Her love of Tibet, and for the future of Tibet, spills out when she speaks, wrapping audiences in stories of Chinese occupation, of populations unbowed, of a nation still surviving. In an otherwise dreary world of Chinese expansionism, Lhamo is a rare bit of light that manages to educate and uplift at the same time.[34]

Yet when I spoke with her in early 2025, shortly after Musk's cuts went through, even Lhamo sounded deflated. "Some of the cuts are going to be a huge blow to the Tibetan diaspora at large," she told me. "The info we are reliant on are the news sources that have private channels of communications that can get information out—and that for us has been RFA and VOA. With the cuts, whether it was aimed specifically at the Tibetan community or not, it has had a huge impact, so much so that we now no longer have detailed information from Tibetans inside Tibet—and vice versa."[35]

It was as if Musk and DOGE had thrown up blinders around a nation the size of Angola or Peru, excising Tibet from the rest of the world. RFA was by no means massive, but it was the keyhole through which information slipped about China's rank crimes in Tibet. And almost overnight, it was gone. Lhamo continued, "Now, we're looking at almost no exchange."[36]

Nor did Musk and DOGE stop there. Around the same time, DOGE also announced it was gutting the U.S.'s National Endowment for Democracy (NED). Created in the 1980s, the group had spent years becoming a home for exiled democracy and anti-corruption activists.[37] Like RFA, the endowment's success could be found in its enemies; routinely pilloried by authoritarian regimes around the world, countries like Beijing accused it of "evil deeds," claiming it was "colluding with anti-China destabilizing forces" in places like Tibet.[38]

But now, thanks to DOGE, it was heading to the scrap heap—as were any resources for democracy activists and pro-transparency organizations reliant on the endowment for organization, for funding, and for success. Pro-democracy groups across China—in Tibet, as well as Hong Kong and East Turkestan, and even as far as Taiwan—watched one of their main bastions of support blink out, disappearing almost entirely.[39]

For these groups, there was no heads-up, no opportunities for appeal, no chance to find funding elsewhere. For the first time in decades, American support had vanished, all because of Musk and DOGE.

Pro-CCP and Chinese propaganda voices couldn't believe their victories—and couldn't celebrate enough. "The so-called beacon of freedom, VOA, has now been discarded by its own government like a dirty rag," said one Chinese propaganda outlet, celebrating the demise of Voice of America.[40] "China welcomes this, of course, and so do other countries," said one pro-China voice.[41] Tenzin Pema, who'd worked as director of RFA's Tibetan service, said, "Our sources inside Tibet have told us that all channels and Chinese state-run media outlets in Tibet are covering and celebrating this news."[42]

"What DOGE under [Musk's] leadership has done has directly gone not just to China's benefit but to things the party has been begging the U.S. to do for decades," Michael Sobolik, one of the few voices in Washington highlighting Musk's pro-CCP moves, told me. "Closing down RFA is a gift to Xi Jinping on a silver platter, with zero reason to do so. Going after NED—that's also a gift to Xi Jinping."[43]

Lost amid the swirl of other cuts—of layoffs and buyouts, and of an unchecked oligarch rampaging across Washington—the demise of all these bodies helping to elevate pro-democracy voices in China barely cracked the broader news cycle. But in sifting through the detritus left by DOGE, it's easy to spot a pattern. China may not have directed Musk to do any of this, and may not have even known these cuts were coming. But it gained, time and again, from all of DOGE's work. Reporters lost their jobs, and Tibetans—and Uyghurs, and Hong Kongers, and even anti-CCP Chinese—lost their lifelines.

Thanks to Musk, Beijing stood triumphant. "The impact of what he's done is a gift" to Beijing, said Sobolik, ". . . and even beyond that."[44]

Hanging over it all are unanswered questions: Why? Why would Musk and his underlings specifically target these groups, all of which are mere rounding errors in terms of the federal budget? Why would they specifically snuff out the sole means of getting information about Tibet—and East Turkestan, Hong Kong, North Korea, Myanmar, and many other places where ruling dictators want no information slipping out—to readers and listeners and viewers? Why go after these programs that so few Americans had ever even heard of, let alone experienced?

As with most things, clues can be found in reading through Musk's cascading social media feed on X. As he posted in early 2025, outlets like Voice of America are full of "radical left crazy people talking to themselves," all on the American taxpayers' dime.[45] It's unclear what Musk is talking about; VOA's coverage, just like RFA's journalism, is simple news, with little (if any) editorialization along the way. The outlets' work often bordered on the stuffy, even stilted, fitting the trappings of traditional journalism. Indeed, the outlets' reputation for hard-hitting, evidence-based coverage—writing about things like the crimes at China's colonial boarding schools, or the political prisoners disappeared across Tibet—was one of the primary reasons Beijing loathed them.[46]

Then again, perhaps the answer isn't complicated. As we saw in the previous section of the book, Musk had spent much of the 2020s growing more and more reliant on Tesla's success in China, both as a source of his personal wealth and his professional standing. To swipe an overused analogy, it was a bit of domino theory in effect: Musk's political standing relied predominantly on his personal wealth, which relied predominantly on the health of the Tesla shares populating Musk's portfolio, which relied predominantly on scaling up sales and production in China—all of which relied entirely on remaining in the good graces of Beijing itself.

It's not as if any of this was a secret, necessarily. As a *Wall Street Journal* headline blared after Trump's election, China specifically saw Musk as a "conduit" to Trump. Given the outflow from China of other American investors and corporate heads, Musk was "one of the few options left" for Beijing. And given that China was "crucial" for Tesla's success, Beijing clearly enjoyed "leverage" over Musk himself—leverage that it would be only too happy to exercise with Musk now in the White House.[47]

If anything, that leverage only accelerated as 2025 took off. Paradoxically, even as he was burrowing further and further into the

American political firmament, Musk's overreliance on China only expanded that much more. Part of this was out of Musk's control. Given China's own domestic electric vehicle technology, native Chinese companies had begun eating into more and more of the industry's market share that Tesla had once enjoyed.[48] It wasn't long until Chinese consumers, nearly half of Tesla's consumers, began snapping up Chinese electric vehicles instead of Teslas—and until markets elsewhere realized they also had non-Tesla options. By mid-2025, Tesla's sales decline had begun to nose-dive, recording negative sales growth month after month after month.[49]

But part of it, as anyone who followed either the news or Musk's X feed could see, was the oligarch's increasingly unhinged behavior, his increasingly shaky grasp on reality, even as he continued grasping at more and more levers within the White House itself. Completely alienating much of the previous Tesla market—made up largely of center-left liberals interested in eliminating their carbon footprint—Musk watched Tesla sales dry up across the board. The first quarter of 2025 recorded Tesla's largest drop in sales ever, a staggering 71 percent collapse in profits.[50]

All of it added up to, as one analyst said, a "nightmare for Tesla." Dreams of selling tens of millions of cars by the end of the 2020s had transformed into a fantasy, as did dreams of ever making things like Tesla's Cybertruck popular.[51]

And all this—the collapsing sales, the decreasing market share, the flatlining innovation—meant that Tesla was now further reliant on the success of the company's existing infrastructure, most especially its plant in Shanghai, which still produced about half of Tesla's overall stock.[52] And as the success of this plant was still reliant on the largesse and go-ahead of the Chinese Communist Party, it meant that Musk was himself growing more and more reliant on remaining on good terms with the party—and that the leverage Beijing already held was, somehow, continuing to swell.

All of which led to one question: If China had all this leverage over America's leading oligarch—over a man who was, in effect, America's co-president—what would it do with it?

It will be up to future historians and archival researchers in both Beijing and Washington to get a firm answer to that question. But here, in the middle of the 2020s, the answer appears clear: China would do whatever it could with it—and Musk would take a whole sweep of steps that, from the outside, certainly make it seem like he was willing to help along the way.[53]

As we saw above, he would gut all the U.S.'s best means of highlighting the ongoing criminality of the Chinese Communist Party, snapping off any way for Tibetans or Uyghurs or anyone else to get their stories out. He would help silence all those anti-Beijing activists who'd relied for so long on the U.S. to give them a voice.

He would also open his own business empire that much further to Chinese funding elsewhere, beyond even just Tesla. As the *Financial Times* reported in March 2025, "wealthy Chinese investors" had been secretly funneling "tens of millions of dollars into private companies controlled by Elon Musk," all "using an arrangement that shields their identities from public view."[54] As court documents revealed, Musk's SpaceX had "allow[ed] investors from China to buy stakes in the company as long as the funds are routed through the Cayman Islands or other offshore secrecy hubs."[55] It was a bizarre formula, one only adopted "as a way to hide foreign investment."[56] But why would they need to hide this kind of corporate investment in the first place? And why would SpaceX think this was a good idea? The company—and its secretive Chinese investors—offered little more than crickets in response. But when the news about these clandestine investments spilled out, one think tanker asked, "How can someone in Musk's position have so many connections to China but still be a good person to reform the U.S. government?"[57]

These concerns were heightened when Musk nearly accessed the U.S.'s most secretive war plans for fighting China in a future war—without the president's knowledge. Which is precisely what happened in April 2025, when Musk came within a hair's breadth of receiving the most intimate, most tightly guarded national security secrets the U.S. maintains—and which Beijing would undoubtedly go to any lengths to obtain.[58]

The documents Musk nearly obtained were known as "special access programs," *The Wall Street Journal* reported, running through the

U.S. military's "most sensitive secrets." Typically, they are off-limits to all but the highest rungs of the American political establishment. But Musk apparently had little trouble tracking them down. Compiling dozens of these documents into a memo, Department of Defense higher-ups reportedly planned to divulge these details to Musk at a meeting at the Pentagon. It's unclear how exactly the memo containing such classified information came together, with some sources pinning it on Secretary of Defense Pete Hegseth and others pointing to a subordinate misunderstanding a Hegseth directive.[59]

Two things, however, are clear. First, there was no reason for Musk to access the "most technical and closely guarded secrets about U.S. weapons development," especially regarding potential war with China. He had no official public position; he was not a member of the American military establishment; and he was, despite his swaggering around the White House, not in any position to order the American military to do anything whatsoever. Yet the innermost vault of American military secrets was suddenly there, in the offing, waiting for Musk to peruse.[60]

Second, and far more concerning, the sitting U.S. president apparently had no idea this was happening—that the country's leading oligarch was set to obtain the U.S.'s most perilous national security secrets, including about China. When Trump first heard about the planned meeting, detailed by journalists at *The Wall Street Journal*, he claimed it was "fake news."[61] But in private—and to his credit, however limited that may be—Trump directly intervened to thwart Musk. "Certainly you wouldn't show that [information] to a businessman," Trump said, pointing out that "Elon has businesses in China, and he would be susceptible perhaps to that."[62]

The whole affair had a whiff of the pot calling the kettle black; given all the regimes that have leverage over Trump and his family, or who have plowed investments into Trump's family business outright, Trump's comments rang hollow.[63] Plus, after all, Trump was the one who opened the door to Musk in the first place. He was the one who placed that top-secret information—as well as all the levers of other power available in the White House—at Musk's fingertips.

Much of this relationship between Musk and the Chinese Communist Party is purely transactional. (As the *Financial Times*'s Joe Leahy said, "Undoubtedly, Beijing sees him as an important lever in the White House.")[64] But there's an additional element swirling around it that points in a complementary direction, and which circles back to the kind of political underpinnings apparently motivating Musk, Zuckerberg, Thiel, and many others in this oligarchic orbit: authoritarianism, mass surveillance, and the end of any kind of democratic oversight or control whatsoever.

It's not that Musk was acting on antidemocratic orders out of Beijing per se. But Musk was also behaving as if he wanted to *be* the CCP. More specifically, he and his underlings have acted as if they want to create the kind of unprecedented, all-encompassing surveillance state Beijing has perfected in recent years—and that Musk and his oligarchic cronies could use to now target Americans.

This might sound fanciful, bordering on histrionic. But as *The New York Times* reported in early 2025, when it was not eliminating anti-corruption and pro-transparency programs, DOGE was busy "assembling a sprawling domestic surveillance system for the Trump administration—the likes of which we have never seen in the United States." Reporting on these subterranean DOGE efforts is scant, but what information remains available quickly tips into the dystopian. As the *Times* continued, Musk and Trump "have knocked down the barriers that were intended to prevent them from creating dossiers on every U.S. resident. Now, they seem to be building a defining feature of many authoritarian regimes: comprehensive files on everyone so they can punish those who protest."[65]

It's unclear what form these files would ultimately take, or what specific information they might even contain. But it's not difficult to see what the outcome would be, resembling what one Georgetown law professor called a "database of ruin," providing material for "blackmail, discrimination, harassment, or financial or identity theft."[66] "This is what we were always scared of," added Kevin Bankston, currently the senior adviser on AI governance at the Center for Democracy and Technology, a civil rights group. "The infrastructure for turnkey totalitarianism is there for an administration willing to break the law."[67]

This kind of database would precisely mirror the kinds of surveillance pervasive in China, producing all manner of information to the Chinese Communist Party. Information on financial decisions, on physical movement, on intimate attractions and political preferences and even political thoughts. Information that has helped the party remain in power for decades, and that has served as a model for other dictatorships around the world.[68] And information that has apparently become the envy of a figure like Musk. "There is more to Musk's China admiration than Tesla's bottom line," the *Financial Times* noted. "China's surveillance capitalism shows Musk what is possible."[69]

It's easy to imagine this kind of doom loop playing out: of an oligarch using his governmental perch to pilfer and organize as much information on every American as he can, and then to collate that information into a database that could track and trace all the most pertinent, and even most private, movements and decisions from all those Americans. To create the kind of tool that, to swipe an Orwell quote, would lead to a governmental boot stamping on humans'—or at least Americans'—faces, forever.[70]

At the same time, it's easy to hand-wave away much of this concern. Musk, after all, had a wildly public falling-out with Trump during the summer of 2025, leaving his role in the White House and ending the co-presidential model, at least for the time being.[71] Musk has, presumably, lost access to much of the information he once handled. And in the process, those efforts to create this kind of database have presumably dried up as well. Then again, we don't know how much information Musk and DOGE managed to exfiltrate before his departure, so who's to say the efforts have dried up at all?

Whichever direction this plays out, though, one thing is clear: Musk, and many of the other oligarchs threading this book, do suffer an envy. And it's not just of China. It's an envy of the kind of authoritarian, kleptocratic model rampant in other nations. It's an envy of all those who have slaughtered democracy in other countries—or even snuffed out those countries entirely.

And it's an envy—of what Russia is trying to do to Ukraine, of what Israel is now doing to Palestine, of what China has already done to Tibet and East Turkestan and may well do to Taiwan—that has also led to the return of something we long thought dead, but which was, in reality, only slumbering: Manifest Destiny. That is, the dream of conquering and seizing new lands entirely—this time, with the oligarchs at the wheel.

16

We Own Everything

Our cause is noble. It is the cause of mankind, and the danger to it springs from ourselves.

—George Washington[1]

Much of what we saw upon Trump's return to the White House was unsurprising. The efforts to target universities and media.[2] The tax breaks for billionaires and pardons for those insurrectionists jailed after January 6, 2021.[3] The appointment of lackeys or conspiracy theorists to run America's security services, from the FBI to Homeland Security to the Department of Defense.[4] Even Trump's flirtation with running for a third term—and the rising fact that, should he remain in power, America's 2028 election is unlikely to be either free or fair—was far from shocking.

There was, however, at least one clear surprise, including a goal few could have predicted: territorial expansion. The topic wasn't just taboo in the U.S., but was so underdiscussed that it was almost pointless to bring it up. It had been decades since an administration had gestured at American expansion, or even sparked a national conversation on the topic, let alone centered it as part of its policy playbook.[5]

But then Trump reentered the White House, and that taboo shattered. Mere days into his second term, Trump began floating the idea of expanding America's borders once more. He openly mused about annexing Canada, transforming the entire nation into a fifty-first state.[6] He spoke about reseizing the Panama Canal, returning it to American sovereignty.[7] And he floated bizarre calls to claim Gaza, turning the obliterated Palestinian homeland into a "Riviera of the Middle East."[8]

Most of these plots could be dismissed; the appetite for an American Gaza was negligible, as was the likelihood of a successful thrust into Canada. But there was one expansionist dream that stood apart from the others. "We have to have Greenland," Trump said in March 2025. "It's not a question of: Do you think we can do without it? We can't."[9] As he said elsewhere, "One way or the other, we're going to get it."[10]

Trump's calls to steal Greenland, which remains as of this writing an autonomous territory of Denmark, were enough to cause whiplash. While he'd mused about pushing into Greenland during his first term, he'd dropped the idea entirely during the 2020s, not mentioning it once during his 2024 campaign.[11]

But it wasn't just that Trump plucked the idea seemingly out of nowhere. While America has seen plenty of expansionism in its history, this new, Trumpian chapter—and Greenland in particular—was unlike anything we'd ever seen before. There were no streams of American settlers preceding American sovereignty, demanding that the U.S. expand its borders for their protection, as we previously saw in places like Texas or Oregon.[12] There was no national security crisis or all-out war necessitating a border change, as previously led to the U.S. grabbing places like Puerto Rico or New Mexico or California.[13] Nor was there a battered, beleaguered European empire trying to convince the U.S. to take over a distant chunk of their territory, as with Louisiana and Alaska.[14]

Trump's sudden thrust toward Greenland was without any kind of historical model.[15] And yet, just out of sight, reason enough lurked. Trump's abrupt interest in Greenland had nothing to do with national security concerns, and certainly nothing to do with any endogenous demands from Greenlanders for American rule. It had, instead, everything to do with the oligarchs corralling in Trump's corner now driving American foreign policy decisions—and dreaming of a post-democratic and even post-American future, both for themselves and for the rest of us.

It's not especially difficult to see how American oligarchs view Greenland, and all the resources the island holds. Zinc, copper, gold, oil, even uranium and platinum: Greenland, as the world's largest island, is a trove of minerals. Thanks to the nation's frozen climes, that natural wealth remains largely untapped. But that doesn't mean that wealth hasn't been mapped, and that excavation plans haven't been plotted. And it doesn't mean American oligarchs haven't spent years dreaming of the day when that wealth could be mined, stripped, and exported—and when they could turn Greenland into their own personal treasure chest.[16]

Actually accessing the materials, however, is only half the battle. Greenland's native Inuit population has not only enacted a raft of environmental protections and mining restrictions, but given their continued sovereignty over the island, they will continue to have final say on all contracts, payment disbursements, and even how much of that profit will go to non-Greenlanders themselves. All that buried wealth, in other words, belongs to the Inuit who've called Greenland home for centuries. That sovereignty is sacrosanct—and remains the biggest hurdle to the biggest profits for American oligarchs.[17]

But what if something could be done about that sovereignty? What if something—or someone—could eliminate that last, best hurdle for American oligarchs trying to carve up Greenland?

Enter Trump, and the oligarchs propelling him to power. "Some of Donald Trump's biggest campaign donors and investors . . . are positioned to potentially profit from any American takeover of Greenland," *The Guardian* reported in April 2025. These funders range from tech moguls to fossil fuel company heads, all invested in mining companies scattered across Greenland. They had launched Trump back to the White House, and they now had "their own set of plans" for Greenland.[18]

Combing through financial and donation disclosures, a clear picture emerges. It is a "closed loop" of "investors, billionaires, [and] Trump," all of whom stand to see spectacular financial gains should America claim Greenland.[19]

Take KoBold Metals, for instance. The mining outfit is helping lead Greenland's "modern gold rush"—and enjoys investments from a range of American oligarchs, including Zuckerberg and Bezos, as well as the hedge fund Andreessen Horowitz, which we last saw kowtowing to Saudi Arabia. Another company, Critical Metals Corp, is backed by a hedge fund that Trump's commerce secretary spent years running, as well as by a range of other investors who've already plowed hundreds of millions of dollars into Trump's personal piggy bank, Trump Media. It's a "circle of grift," Robert Weissman, who helps run the pro-transparency group Public Citizen, said. "Put money into the Trump family bank and the money comes back to you in the form of some government policy." As Weissman pointed out, this "even includes the deployment of the [American] empire"—all the state power, all the illiberal might that comes with a country bent on thieving yet another neighboring nation, as it's done through much of its history already.[20]

In many ways, this American imperialism is a logical culmination of the infiltration of the U.S. government by the country's ruling oligarchs. Of course they would try to begin pushing American foreign policy—even American empire itself—for their own ends. Of course they would begin steering American power and expanding American sovereignty in order to expand their own pocketbooks.

It's not as if financial considerations hadn't motivated American expansionism in the past. Americans' lust for gold propelled the U.S.'s expansionism and ethnic cleansing efforts into Georgia, the Dakotas, and California, while the desire for arable lands and new trade routes pushed Americans to steal lands in Minnesota, the Pacific Northwest, Florida, and elsewhere.[21]

But again, those bursts of expansion had a bottom-up component, with American settlers on the ground demanding American protections and American imperialism. And all too often, the federal government was skittish about potential expansion; hesitation about formally annexing places like Texas or Hawaii, as we saw earlier in this book, nearly prevented America from actually claiming those nations.[22] (Indeed, such hesitation poleaxed other efforts to annex Cuba, the Dominican Republic, or even Canada itself—all of which remain independent.)[23] This time, though, it is a purely top-down, oligarch-driven affair. There is only a president "flanked by wealthy investors who have eyed [Greenland] as a potentially lucrative venue for mining metals and minerals," wrote *The New York Times*.[24] There are no streams of American settlers demanding American support. There are no wars or national security crises demanding American expansion. There is only a small group of oligarchs who want to see a return on their investments, in both the White House and Greenland—and who are willing to end Greenlanders' sovereignty, and to destroy yet another Indigenous nation, to get it.

And yet, even that story—of the president's wealthiest backers aiming him at Greenland, trying to steal the world's biggest island outright—is a bit too pat. It's not that it's untrue; all the financial documents and mineral maps are there, free to peruse, showing how much some of these American figures have to gain if they could end Greenland's sovereignty. But in the twenty-first century, there's another angle—one simultaneously odd and oddly apt—highlighting the kinds of corruption and cronyism pushing a new industry to the fore of American expansionism, and far beyond democracy itself: crypto.

The broader world of crypto has seen its sails swell under Trump, whose administration has gone all in on backing the industry, gutting regulations and streamlining federal support.[25] Despite years of scandal besetting the industry—and despite a general sense of pointlessness still pervading much of the world of crypto—the industry's pioneers have glommed onto the Trump White House in ways never seen previously, donating millions of dollars to boost Trump's return to office.[26] And they've been repaid handsomely. It's not just that Trump and his family have tethered their own wealth to crypto, buoyed by Trump's own memecoin and his stewardship of World Liberty Financial; it's also that the world of crypto has produced America's newest crops of billionaire-oligarchs, all of whom realize how much profit there is to be had at the feet of the Trump administration.[27]

Nor is this partnership simply about profit for profit's sake. Undergirding it all is a sense—an ideology, really—that democratic oversight and democratic checks on the finance pooling around this industry is anathema to the entire idea of crypto in the first place. That any restrictions on projects or profit are to be avoided. That anything trammeling the pursuit of wealth is to be opposed. And that, if they cannot achieve their goals in the United States of America, then perhaps it is best to leave the U.S. itself behind—or even implode the U.S. outright, so that a new libertarian, crypto-saturated utopia can arise, assuring a reign for these oligarchs forevermore.

Dryden Brown is a slender, sandy-haired twentysomething with a California lilt and a dream of a future far beyond America. He is small, unassuming even, someone you'd never mistake for a globe-striding force of either territorial expansion or historical mission. But he is, perhaps more than anyone else, the face of America's sudden designs on Greenland—a topic he was only too happy to discuss with me when we spoke in early 2025.[28]

"We think Greenland is a very interesting place," Brown told me. "We view it as one of the last frontiers of Earth."[29] He's not wrong; the sparse, sere tundra, the moonlike outcroppings, the frothing sea—Greenland has never been a typical vacation destination. Yet that didn't stop Brown from traveling to the island in 2024—not simply to visit but to try to purchase the island outright. Touching down in a twin-propeller plane, Brown set up meetings at Greenland's parliament, broaching the idea. How much would it take? How much would Greenlanders need to sell their sovereignty?[30]

The Greenlanders quickly disabused Brown of any idea that they're for sale. "We own this country," one Greenlander said about his birthright. "We own the resources. We own everything."[31] So Brown pivoted: If he couldn't purchase their loyalty or their land, could they find a different financial arrangement? Greenland currently receives approximately $500 million annually in subsidies from Denmark—what if he could find a way to supplant that funding? And if he could do that, what would Greenland be willing to offer him in return?[32]

Brown himself is not an oligarch, nor is he a mining magnate. He is something else: an organizer pushing for a future in which Greenland no longer belongs to the Inuit and other native Greenlanders, but is the home of something he and the other crypto-libertarians in his milieu refer to as a "network state."[33]

It's a term that's percolated for years. A "network state," says crypto backer Balaji Srinivasan, is a "highly aligned online community with a capacity for collective action" that "crowdfunds territory around the world and eventually gains diplomatic recognition from preexisting states."[34] Scraping past the technobabble, the idea for a network state is relatively simple: It is a new nation, both online and on land, that can provide an escape hatch for all the crypto enthusiasts and antidemocrats who want to do away with regulatory oversight or financial checks. Who envision a world in which they can expand both their wealth and their influence as wide as they want. Who believe that nation-states—including places like the U.S.—are passé, outmoded ways of organizing societies, and that the next iteration of humanity must belong to these self-appointed visionaries, authoring a revolutionary future wherever they can.[35]

Which is where figures like Brown come in. Overseeing an organization called Praxis, Brown has sketched out both a blueprint and a manifesto for what this network state could look like. "As local communities dissolve and Nation States stumble, Network States will ascend," Praxis claims. "The next global superpower will be a Network State." And as Brown sees it, Praxis will be the first to usher in this network state, and author the newest chapter in humanity's political evolution.[36]

Reading through Praxis's manifesto is like slipping down a rabbit hole, forced to trek through the muck of meaningless terms and outlandish political philosophies. "In this world, the primary contested space is not land, but the mind," the text begins. "Today, we are at an inflection point where power is increasingly determined by the ability to capture mindshare of globally dispersed communities." As Praxis sees it, these network states, also referred to as "Sovereign Networks," are the only solution—and are destined to overtake nation-states like the U.S. "Sovereign Networks will represent Citizens controlling trillions of dollars of assets, represented on their native asset registries," the manifesto continues. "We'll watch the flippening of Sovereign Networks over Nation States in real time." (In late 2024, Praxis updated its manifesto to change "Sovereign Networks" to "Digital Nations.")[37]

Wading through the gobs of gibberish, Praxis is effectively promising a new sociopolitical model: a community that offers the chance to leave your own nation behind and build something anew. Much of the infrastructure would be dispersed, online, available and trackable via things like blockchain. But it's one thing for this kind of community to exist in the online ether. In order to convince future populations to come aboard—in order to recruit new members to their new "nation," effecting the kind of geopolitical shift that Praxis promises—they will need actual, physical territory. Land upon which to build this crypto citadel. Land that is unused and unclaimed, at least by major powers. Land that should be available—and that should be theirs.[38]

Brown's allies have already made efforts at building out this vision elsewhere. In Honduras, network state enthusiasts tried constructing a "private tech city" called Próspera, envisioning a world of "low taxes and pro-Bitcoin policies."[39] But local Hondurans—who don't need to look far into their history to discover other wealthy Westerners trampling their lands—pushed back, thwarting the supposedly libertarian utopia before it could take off.[40] Similar ventures in places like Nigeria have also fallen flat.[41] Greenland, though, still beckons—and still provides an opportunity for Brown to bring his crypto-city to fruition. "With Greenland, we have the opportunity to ring in a new age of expansion," Brown said, "this time peaceful and mutually beneficial, but no less invigorating."[42]

If Brown and Praxis were merely writing overheated political treatises, the kinds best left to freshman-year term papers, that would be one thing. But Brown—who does not have a college degree, and who has no substantial professional accomplishments to his name—has managed to pull together significant investment from across America, including from some of the country's most prominent oligarchs.[43]

The leading figure linked to Praxis is none other than Peter Thiel, who we last saw authoring his own treatise on how and why he and his oligarchic fellow travelers must "escape" democratic oversight. The Thiel-backed organization Pronomos Capital invested in Praxis's seed round, which itself brought in millions of dollars, and helped launch Praxis and Brown toward Greenland.[44] Overseen by Patri Friedman, the grandson of libertarian economist Milton Friedman—and a person who once surgically implanted a Tesla key into his hand—Pronomos has poured significant funding into these kinds of post-nation-state ventures.[45] Nor is Thiel the only major backer of Pronomos; joining him is Marc Andreessen, an oligarch who himself has no problem genuflecting before nation-states like Saudi Arabia. Jon Lonsdale, yet another oligarchic venture capitalist, has also backed Praxis, as have self-described "futurist" Shervin Pishevar and even the Winklevoss twins, formerly of Facebook.[46]

Perhaps the most conspicuous oligarch linked to Praxis emerged in the 2020s as arguably the most radical figure of the bunch: Sam Altman. Currently overseeing OpenAI and steering much of the world's artificial intelligence revolution, Altman has maintained a low profile as it pertains to his investment in Praxis, so much so that, according to *The New York Times*, he's not listed on Praxis's formal membership roster. Still, his interest is hardly a secret, with Altman's Apollo Ventures firm funding Praxis directly.[47]

Leaving aside all the raging concerns about the world Altman's ChatGPT has helped create—the rampant copyright violations, the environmental damage, the collapse in students' abilities to craft their own essays, and more—Altman's willingness to back Praxis's vision of a post-nation future raises questions about not only his own political leanings, but about his vision for the future of the United States itself. "Altman has strange politics," Gil Duran, who has tracked the network state movement perhaps more than anyone else, wrote in 2024. "His investment in Praxis makes it clear that, despite platitudes about creating a better future, he's betting on some kind of dramatic collapse."[48]

It didn't take long for this constellation of forces—oligarchic donors and techno-authoritarian investors congealing around Trump, pushing Brown's vision of a network state in a place like Greenland—to bear fruit. While Trump barreled forward, barking about nabbing Greenland without any apparent rationale (and without any consent from Greenlanders themselves), details soon began leaking out about what this kind of crypto-slash-oligarchic takeover of Greenland could look like.

According to a number of sources, a range of "Silicon Valley tech investors" have begun "promoting the frozen island as a site for a so-called freedom city, a libertarian utopia with minimal corporate regulation." Aligning with Praxis's vision for a network state in Greenland, these oligarchic investors envisioned transforming Greenland into a paradise of scientific, even utopian, invention, building the island into a "hub for artificial intelligence, autonomous vehicles, space launches, micro nuclear reactors and high-speed rail," Reuters reported.[49]

Some of the names mentioned were those already connected with Praxis. Both Thiel and Andreessen were reportedly propelling the idea, as was Lonsdale, who called outright for "expanding our country to Greenland." (Thiel has denied interest or involvement, while Andreessen declined to comment.) But there was one additional name mentioned: Ken Howery, himself a former venture capitalist who cofounded PayPal alongside Thiel and Musk. Yet Howery wasn't simply another hyper-capitalist floating out of Silicon Valley; he was appointed by Trump himself as the U.S.'s newest ambassador to Denmark—and was specifically "expected to . . . lead Greenland-acquisition negotiations," those familiar with his appointment said.[50]

Or as Praxis's social media feed posted in response to Howery's appointment: "According to plan."[51]

Support for American annexation is minimal among Greenland's native population, with some 85 percent of the nation's residents specifically saying that they never want their land to become American. Given that this polling was done before Trump's neo-imperialistic comments—and well before Danish intelligence uncovered an American interference operation aimed at stealing Greenland, as we learned in the summer of 2025—that opposition has almost certainly escalated.[52]

For those on the American side, though, Greenlanders' desires are beside the point. Just as with the native Alaskans, the native Hawaiians, and hundreds upon hundreds of other Indigenous nations across North America, the thoughts and perspectives of the Greenlanders are immaterial. Brown may claim a desire to hear out Greenlanders, and even to respect their wishes. But the framing and the language Brown and his backers routinely use taps into a far longer American legacy, far beyond just Greenland itself: Manifest Destiny.

The nineteenth-century ideology—a messianic belief that America, by both might and religious right, was destined to conquer much of North America and beyond—was one of the most malignant, odious political philosophies of the era, anywhere in the world. Excusing and whitewashing all manner of horrific crimes, from ethnic cleansing and death marches to streams of concentration camps and even outright genocide, Manifest Destiny pervaded every stratum of American governance during the era, helping unify an otherwise fractious country. It's impossible to overstate the depth of the violence attached to Manifest Destiny.[53] Mass hangings, government-led massacres, the obliteration of entire nations, all in pursuit of American expansion and American power: the entire era is a testament to the different variations of colonial violence that Americans could create, all for the benefit of the U.S.[54] Given its continent-wide geographic scope and scale—as well as the fact that the ideology itself extended into the twentieth century—there is every reason to consider such ideology as America's original sin.

Thankfully, for much of the twenty-first century, it appeared such ideology was dead, a crusted-over relic of eras past. While legacies of Manifest Destiny continued to flare, especially when it came to debates about memorializing American history, a general sense now grew that Manifest Destiny was little more than grotesque imperialism, a chapter of American history condemned, a period never to be repeated—and certainly not celebrated.

And then this new crop of oligarchs rose, and began calling for Manifest Destiny to return once more. The push for Greenland "reflects a fascination with settling new American frontiers, rooted in nostalgia for the nation's 1800s western expansion," Reuters noted. Pishevar, one of Praxis's backers, agrees. As he said, American expansion into Greenland "can be the dawn of a new Manifest Destiny."[55]

It's an idea that Brown parrots as well. When I asked him how his views and his vision aligned with the calls for a renewed Manifest Destiny, he didn't dispute the connection. But instead of leaving it there, he flipped the framing of Manifest Destiny into a kind of excuse for revanchism. As Brown told me, it was actually the Greenlanders, almost all of whom are Inuit, who are the interlopers on the island—and that Greenland rightfully belongs not to them but to those descended from European explorers. To those, in other words, like Brown.[56]

"Manifest Destiny is an idea and reference to specific European peoples that came to North America," Brown told me. "You go to the museum in [Greenland's capital of] Nuuk, and there's a big display of the history of Greenland, and it says in the museum that the Vikings were there before . . . the Inuit. So I don't know—there's a totally valid historical argument to be made that the Nordic peoples have a . . . deeper historical claim to Greenland than the Inuit."[57]

Little matter that the U.S. is, of course, not a Nordic nation. Those details aren't important. All that matters is that these "Nordic peoples"—and other descendants of European settlers, in North America and elsewhere—have a destiny to reconquer Greenland itself. And it's time for that destiny to be made manifest.

In speaking to Brown, his monologue on "Nordic peoples" and their claims to Greenland felt like an unusual tangent. It's unclear if his oligarchic backers felt the same; figures like Pishevar, who is originally from Tehran, would never be considered "Nordic." Then again, these views are far from the most problematic ideas attached to Brown. Far worse is already in the public record—material that Brown's backers have apparently ignored, or potentially even support.

As former Praxis employees have revealed, Brown himself has no use for niceties like democracy. He "believes that monarchy is superior to democracy," said one former employee. Another added that his "worldview and ideal governance is authoritarian fascism." He is "fascinated" in particular by petty tyrants like Napoleon, apparently overlooking the French despot's staggering failures in both the Americas and Europe.[58] And while a man shouldn't necessarily be judged on his bookshelf alone, it is telling that Brown's shelves include works by Oswald Spengler, a German philosopher who influenced the Nazis, as well as Russian fascist writer Alexander Dugin. Former employees claimed that Brown also encouraged them to read the work of Italian fascist Julius Evola, even going so far as to cite Evola's philosophies as a means to "guide the company's recruitment of new members."[59]

The list of Brown's linkages to far-right figures continues. He hired a Holocaust denier named Mike Mahoney, who was a "central figure among some online white power accelerationist communities," which encourage racial violence as a means of cementing white rule. Under Brown, Praxis also recommended that employees read works by another modern fascist writer, Costin Vlad Alamariu (better known by his nom de plume, Bronze Age Pervert).[60]

Some of this infatuation slips into Brown's public rhetoric. For instance, Praxis publicly states that it is aiming to "restore Western Civilization," claiming it will help humanity "pursue heroism and exploration, sun and steel."[61] In its so-called Declaration of Ascent, Praxis writes, "As the warrior-kings once sought the sacred Grail, so too shall we build an empire where true power flows from heroic courage and alignment with the divine order."[62] Praxis will create a world with a "neo-Gilded Age" aesthetic, all while striving for "the cultivation of . . . beauty" wherever it operates.[63] It's unclear what kind of "beauty" Brown has in mind, but an internal Praxis branding guide specifically praised "traditional, European/Western beauty standards on which the civilized world, at its best points, has always found success."[64]

In Brown's office sits a photo of himself alongside perhaps the most influential monarchist-cum-fascist providing ideas and policies to the modern far right: Curtis Yarvin.[65] As we saw in the second section of this book, Yarvin has envisioned a world in which America descends into outright dictatorship—and that this is to be welcomed. Calling for a new age of American autocracy, Yarvin has grown close to Thiel, with Andreessen and others describing him as a "good friend."[66] Yarvin has even watched his ideas percolate in the White House, with Vice President J. D. Vance specifically citing Yarvin's recommendations to gut the "administrative state."[67]

And along the way, he has apparently built out a relationship with Brown. Yarvin, who has called for similar network state projects in the past, not only "attended Praxis events" but even "stayed in Brown's house for a week at least once."[68]

The miasma of racist readings, figures, and comments attached to Brown—he "genuinely believed that Black people are not as smart as white people," one former employee said—are available to anyone willing to look for them.[69] Yet this hasn't stopped any of these oligarchic figures from bankrolling Brown, and it hasn't stopped Praxis from raising over a half-billion dollars in funding already.

Then again, should we be surprised that these oligarchs continue to back Brown, given all the allegations stacked against him? After all, not only is Brown proposing to build a world in which all the fascistic proclivities of many of these oligarchs could become real. He's also proposing something they all thirst for: exit. Exit from oversight. Exit from regulation. Exit from democracy.

They have "long pushed for 'exit projects' free from the constraints of the modern Western state," noted *The New York Times* in an article profiling Praxis. Labor rights, environmental protections, paying any taxes whatsoever—these are all hindrances to the only thing that matters: enrichment, purely for enrichment's sake.[70]

Some of these oligarchs are explicit in this focus on "exit." There was Thiel, who as we saw earlier specifically called for "find[ing] an escape from politics in all its forms."[71] Others, like crypto billionaire Brian Armstrong, in speaking at a network state conference in 2024, have since jumped aboard the idea. "I also believe in exit," said Armstrong, adding elsewhere that all those in the world of crypto need to "think about how we actually go create physical places in the world to preserve freedom over the long term. I think that's ultimately crypto's destiny."[72]

For Armstrong, who has splashed significant funds around Washington to propel pro-crypto regulations, the need for this new nation is clear. The U.S. is in "slow decline," with him and his ilk "losing freedoms."[73] Given that his net worth is now estimated at some $13 billion—and the fact that the tax rate for those in his bracket is nearly as low as it's ever been—it's unclear what "freedoms" Armstrong believes he's losing.[74] In a sense, it doesn't matter. Any threat to his wealth is a threat too much. The time has come—in Greenland, or anywhere else—to form this network state. To form a new nation.

To start their own country. To bring together a group of oligarchic "Founding Fathers" who can jump-start, as Brown called it, a new "superpower."[75]

The idea that they are a new crop of "Founding Fathers" is one these Praxis figures and funders readily embrace. Brown himself says as much. "I find the [U.S.'s] founding story to be deeply inspiring to me," he told me. "And like America in the early days, we're doing a political experiment in new polity development, a new form and so on."[76]

It's all heady, high-minded stuff, placing these figures in the same pantheon as Washington, Jefferson, and Madison. But Praxis is clear that its success will not be America's—that it will instead only be predicated on "American collapse and defeat."[77] As they see it, America is slowly sinking into a morass of tangled regulation and wokeness run amok, of the Lilliputian masses of American democracy tying down the country's true visionaries—the country's true heroes. And the only way for them to succeed is to dispense with democracy—and dispense with America—entirely.

From a certain perspective, the parallels to America's Founding Fathers make a kind of cramped sense. After all, America's Founders launched a new nation on new shores, authoring an untried, untested vision of a future far from the reach of their previous governmental masters.

But the parallels end there. Those early figures brought an unparalleled combination of political, military, and financial genius—and a promise, however hollow and hypocritical it may have been, for a birth of freedom within a new land. Moreover, the Founding Fathers' new creation specifically sought to leave the utter dominance of Europe's moneyed classes behind—and to slice apart the sprawling, oligarchic, generation-spanning estates suffocating nations elsewhere.

Brown and his backers pledge no such thing. Instead, they want to usher in a world that those Founding Fathers specifically tried, at least rhetorically, to leave behind: a world of oligarchic dominance, in which notions of republican virtue, liberal freedoms, and democratic expansion are all oxymorons.

And it's not just that these modern oligarchs' efforts are a repudiation of the American Founders' views. For many Americans, Washington, Jefferson, Madison, and others are, if nothing else, at least considered a patriotic bunch—a group that, all their faults otherwise, at least served and sacrificed for a belief in the United States of America. For Brown and his oligarchic backers, however, that idea is turned on its head. Their fortunes, their future, and their fealty are dedicated not to America but to another nation completely: a nascent "superpower" dedicated to overtaking the United States, to challenging the U.S. wherever and however it can, and to immiserating the Americans Brown and his allies want to leave behind. To serving, in all that they can, another country entirely.

In that sense, there's another group of self-styled "Founding Fathers" that is a more apt comparison to what Brown, his oligarchic backers, and the other billionaires supporting him are trying to accomplish.[78] Another group that sought to toss off the shackles of democracy and entrench an antidemocratic oligarchy. Another group of secessionists, willing to sacrifice anything and everything to "exit" the United States, and to specifically create one of the greatest geopolitical rivals the U.S. has ever known. Another group of wealthy figures, owing their rise and their riches to America—but who, when threatened with even the barest restrictions on such wealth, sought to crack apart the United States, slaughtering American troops and American citizens alike, all in the pursuit of no longer being Americans themselves.

They were known as the Confederacy. And while they claimed that they wanted to create a world free for their wealth, for their views, and for their antidemocratic reign, today they are remembered as something else:

Traitors.

17

Your Government Is on Trial

You don't decree a Republic—you make it.

—Juliette Adam[1]

In late August 1910, Teddy Roosevelt stood under a beating Kansas sun, sweat beading on his forehead and curdling around his neck, and unleashed a vision for an America that was, as one historian later dubbed it, "nothing short of revolutionary."[2]

Roosevelt's entire speech that day was an exercise in the unexpected. First, there was Roosevelt himself. A year and a half after his presidency had ended, Roosevelt could look back at a legacy that was already, in many ways, revolutionary. He'd shattered trusts and corporate conglomerates, ushered in brand-new regulatory agencies that cleaned up entire industries, and broken the backs of crooked political rings around the country, not least in Washington. Most especially, he'd launched an unprecedented crusade against corporate wealth in American politics—and laid the groundwork for a new pair of tax programs that would dissolve much of the wealth hoarded by the country's richest oligarchs. It was a raft of democratic reforms the likes of which the country hadn't seen from a White House since at least the days of Abraham Lincoln, and arguably the biggest burst of peacetime reform the country had ever known.

But out of the White House, Roosevelt grew restive. His handpicked successor, William Taft, proved far more amenable to corporate interests than expected, rolling back much of his predecessor's progress. His relationship with Taft had fractured so much, and so quickly, that by mid-1910 Roosevelt was already toying with running for the presidency once more—this time as a third-party candidate.[3]

Yet it wasn't just his falling-out with Taft that brought Roosevelt to Kansas that day. Stopping off in the village of Osawatomie—a flyspeck of a town tucked along the Missouri border—Roosevelt saw the trip as an opportunity. A chance to lay out a new vision for both American politics and the American economy. An occasion where he could outline a burly, bold platform for a future America that was far fairer, and far freer, than the America he now saw.[4]

Walking to the town center, clambering aboard a kitchen table—the best the tiny town could do for a stage—Roosevelt looked out across the rippling crowd. Tens of thousands had turned out to hear him: men in three-piece suits, women with parasols popped open, guardsmen in flat-brim campaign hats, all there to listen to the former president. The entire day felt less like a campaign stop and more like a festival—"much like a country fair, with booths where sandwiches and drinks were being sold," said one write-up.[5]

Roosevelt scanned the audience. He paused, and the crowd hushed. And then he started—and he didn't stop for nearly ninety minutes. He waved his arms. He thumped his chest. He glared, and he grinned, and he gleamed his teeth in the sweltering Kansas heat.[6]

The entire speech, at least visually, was vintage Roosevelt. But the text of the talk—that was unlike anything anyone had seen before. Certainly not from any major political figures in America at the time. And certainly not from a former president. As UCLA's George Mowry described it, Roosevelt's speech that day was "the most radical speech ever given by an ex-President."[7]

That's almost certainly true. Roosevelt's oration on that muggy, buggy day wasn't simply an exercise in platitudes or boring policy prescriptions. It was instead a blueprint for an America free of oligarchs once and for all. A vision for an America that would finally toss the plutocrats out of the temples of American democracy, restoring American politics and American economic opportunity to the broad masses of Americans themselves.[8]

Roosevelt dubbed his vision a "new nationalism." And it is, over a century later, a vision whose time has come—and a vision that must be realized, if the U.S. is ever to be saved from the oligarchs trying to suffocate American democracy once and for all.[9]

Fanning himself, roaring to the crowd, Roosevelt laid out what this new nationalism would look like. "At many stages in the advance of humanity, this conflict between the men who possess more than they have earned and the men who have earned more than they possess is the central condition of progress," Roosevelt boomed. "In our day it appears as the struggle of freemen to gain and hold the right of self-government as against the special interests, who twist the methods of free government into machinery for defeating the popular will. At every stage, and under all circumstances, the essence of the struggle is to equalize opportunity, destroy privilege, and give to the life and citizenship of every individual the highest possible value both to himself and to the commonwealth."[10]

It was, in other words, those monied classes—those plutocrats, those barons of industry, those oligarchs clawing back their power across America—that were the primary obstacle to progress. These "special interests" that Roosevelt had targeted as president enjoyed all manner of privileges, rights, and immunities that the rest of America had no access to. These oligarchs and their allies were not "job-creators," or bastions of free enterprise and free markets; they were simply people willing to use their power for their own purse, twisting American politics for their own financial ends—to the detriment of the rest of the country.[11]

"The absence of effective State, and, especially, national, restraint upon unfair money-getting has tended to create a small class of enormously wealthy and economically powerful men, whose chief object is to hold and increase their power," Roosevelt said. "The prime need is to change the conditions which enable these men to accumulate power which it is not for the general welfare that they should hold or exercise." It was as if capital had a gravitational pull of its own, Roosevelt continued, something that expanded exponentially as fortunes swelled. At a certain point, almost inevitably, that capital became political—and began to poison democracy itself, all for the benefit of its oligarchic owners. "The really big fortune, the swollen fortune, by the mere fact of its size, acquires qualities which differentiate it in kind as well as in degree from what is possessed by men of relatively small means," Roosevelt observed.[12]

As Roosevelt saw it, this was a condition that stretched far before his presidency, at least all the way back to the Civil War itself. "Exactly as the special interests of cotton and slavery threatened our political integrity before the Civil War, so now the great special business interests too often control and corrupt the men and methods of government for their own profit," he continued. "We must drive the special interests out of politics. That is one of our tasks today."[13]

The playbook Roosevelt described, fleshing out this new nationalism, was sprawling. But there was one fulcrum on which success hinged: preventing corporations from injecting their money into American politics. "There can be no effective control of corporations while their political activity remains," the former president said, with the audience cheering back. It wasn't just that corporate funds in American politics should be regulated, or should at least have a patina of transparency. Corporate money in American politics should be banned, full stop: "Laws should be passed to prohibit the use of corporate funds directly or indirectly for political purposes; it is still more necessary that such laws should be thoroughly enforced."[14]

It was that second clause—the fact that laws and regulations must be *enforced*, rather than just passed—that Roosevelt paused on. The former president had seen how the oligarchs of his day could defend their capital, setting up tax shelters and hidden finance networks, bankrolling and bribing and backing politicians who would protect them, all while dodging even basic tax laws. He'd seen how these oligarchs and their allies had eliminated any differences between tax *minimization* and tax *evasion*, all for their own benefit. "There must remain no neutral ground to serve as a refuge for lawbreakers," he bellowed, "and especially for lawbreakers of great wealth, who can hire the vulpine legal cunning which will teach them how to avoid both jurisdictions."[15]

Roosevelt didn't want to be misconstrued; he wasn't calling for expropriation, or nationalization, or any of the other outright property seizures that protesters and proletarians both before and after had turned to, seizing the assets and the wealth of the oligarchs when all else fails.

Roosevelt wanted nothing to do with this "mob violence"; even these "special interests" were "entitled to justice—full, fair, and complete."[16]

But they were not entitled to the sheer unfairness, the rank inequality, and the destabilizing dominance they'd achieved, in both American politics and the American economy. Their good times could not continue. And unless that changed—unless their fortunes were shrunk, and the towering wealth inequality of America in the early twentieth century deflated—they would find out, in the worst kinds of ways, that such unfairness simply could not last. The swell of oligarchic capital into American politics may have been inevitable—but so, too, was the backlash.

"Those who oppose reform will do well to remember that ruin in its worst form is inevitable," the former president said, "if our national life brings us nothing better than swollen fortunes for the few—and the triumph in both politics and business of a sordid and selfish materialism."[17]

Over a century later, Roosevelt's vision rings with a kind of clarity long missing from American leadership. And it's perhaps even further from reality now than it was then. Given that everything from wealth inequality to the total fortunes of modern American oligarchs is more pronounced in the twenty-first century than it ever was in Roosevelt's time, there's every reason to think that we're currently living through the greatest, most devastating era of plutocracy the U.S. has ever seen. Toss in the fact that American corporations maintain far more rights in the 2020s than they did in the 1910s, and it's almost indisputable that American democracy, such as it is, is dominated to a far greater degree by a nexus of unconstrained wealth than anything the country has seen before, and far beyond anything Roosevelt—or Lincoln, or even the Founders—could have ever imagined.[18]

But even with all those changes, the differences between modern America and Roosevelt's era are, in many ways, simply of scale. It's not as if modern oligarchs and their corporate counterparts have unlocked some new ways of decimating democracy, of turning American politics to their own ends. It's not as if they've invented some new playbook, perverting politics for their pocketbooks alone. The technology may have evolved, and the geopolitical arena may have shifted. But the core of the tension—a tension that Roosevelt, Lincoln, Jefferson, and many more Americans past have identified throughout different American eras—remains. It is the tension between those with massed, growing capital, and those without. It is the tension between those who control the biggest property portfolios, and those who do not. It is the tension between those who sit atop the largest fortunes, Smaug-like, using that wealth to fiddle with the machinery of politics, and those who squat far below, looking up, wondering at the sheer unfairness of it.

It is a tension that reaches far back within, and even far beyond, America. It is a tension that is at this point almost a cliché: of the haves and the have-nots, of the 1 percent and the rest of us, of the mega-wealthy and the plebes and the political structures and strictures under which they both live.[19]

It is a tension that has two resolutions only, which Roosevelt correctly identified. There is reform—or there is revolution.

Roosevelt knew which one he'd prefer, both as president and afterward. Reform remains the path of least resistance—and, perhaps ironically, the path that allows the oligarchic class to retain the greatest amount of their assets. It is a path spearheaded not only by Roosevelt, helping shepherd things like the income and inheritance taxes, but by progressive successors like his distant cousin, Franklin, overseeing the growth of the kinds of regulations and enforcement actions that keep fortunes in check.

But it was also a path chosen by far more moderate—even, if you will, conservative—forces of the mid-twentieth century. Like Harry Truman, who kept the income tax regime targeting the wealthiest Americans steady after FDR's demise, holding a lid on a new generation of oligarchs emerging after the Second World War. Like Dwight Eisenhower, who held America's inheritance tax requirements steady through the 1950s, making sure America's most fortunate families couldn't reign in perpetuity, passing down their wealth for generations to come—and ensuring that the initial policies spearheaded by figures like Jefferson, which broke up these kinds of landed estates, continued well into the twentieth century.

It was a series of leaders who saw the direct link between America's economic equality and its national security. Who realized that the status and stature of America on the global stage was directly connected to the health of its democracy. And who realized that American prowess and leadership were directly linked to the fairness, both real and perceived, of the American economy—and to preventing a small caste of American oligarchs from rising to dominate both.

It was a realization that, as time wore on, crumbled. It began in the 1960s, when successive administrations began eroding the tax regimes keeping American oligarchs in check. By the end of the twentieth century, those efforts had collapsed almost entirely. And now, a quarter of the way into the twenty-first century, Roosevelt's vision of a new nationalism appears more distant than ever—a faded outline of a past proposal, long forgotten, long buried by the rise of modern oligarchs themselves.

But it's still there. And it's worth scraping away the dust and detritus that have accumulated over Roosevelt's vision to see what will be useful moving forward. Amidst this era of towering American authoritarianism—ushered in by the oligarchs, who stand to benefit most—it's time to start planning out what a new era must look like.

Call it, in a nod to Roosevelt, the era of New Patriotism. Here's what it should contain.

First things first: Start with the low-hanging fruit. In his role as chief arsonist, Trump has done more to burn America's anti-corruption credentials to the ground than anyone else in modern American history. But in all his havoc, Trump has consistently chosen the path of least resistance. Instead of actually uprooting all of America's anti-corruption policies, which would require formally repealing many of these bills in Congress, Trump has simply announced that they would no longer be enforced. Things like the Foreign Corrupt Practices Act, which bans Americans from engaging in foreign corruption; the Foreign Agents Registration Act, which brings transparency to the foreign lobbying sector; the U.S.'s shell company registry, which was supposed to end the U.S.'s central role as a titan of offshore finance—all of them are, under Trump, effectively dead. In announcing they are no longer going to be enforced, Trump has personally opened the door to corrupt networks from around the world to flood the U.S. with as much looted wealth as they can carry.

But those laws are still on the books. Rather than rebuilding entirely, a future administration would simply announce that, starting on day one, those laws will once more be enforced. No need for the kind of historic legislative pushes that resulted in these bills' creations; since they're still technically the law of the land, all a future White House has to do is say that these laws and regulations will be active once more—and that noncompliance will be met with prosecution, time and again.

The same goes for all the anti-corruption task forces that Trump has torched. The bodies dedicated to uncovering foreign interference, to investigating how dirty money networks hide their wealth in the U.S., to tracking how oligarchs around the world transform their illicit finance into yachts and mega-mansions and priceless artwork—the blueprints for them are still there. A new administration can immediately resuscitate all these task forces—and can make sure they're properly staffed, resourced, and expanded.

On the regulatory side, a future White House must finally implement the rules the Biden administration first proposed to close anti–money laundering loopholes in the real estate, hedge fund, private equity, and venture capital industries. For decades, these industries have all sucked up billions, and potentially trillions, of dollars in illicit wealth from around the world. With relatively little lift, a future administration can end these loopholes for good. These industries have feasted at the trough of kleptocracy for long enough, ballooning into dirty-money monstrosities in the process. That time must now come to an end.

On the punitive side, a future White House must also restore the U.S.'s targeted sanctions programs—the kinds that freeze and block any assets linked to corrupt networks—to what they were actually created for. Trump has flipped these tools on their heads, slapping sanctions on those who *oppose* corruption and abuse of power (such as those investigating Brazilian coup plotter Jair Bolsonaro), and lifting them against those previously revealed as crooked expansionists (such as Israeli colonizers in the West Bank). Trump's entire tenure has made a mockery of these sanctions, which had previously been phenomenal tools for disrupting corrupt networks around the world. It's time for them to return to form—and to be expanded far and wide against far more kleptocratic forces, including in nominal American allies like Saudi Arabia, the United Arab Emirates, Hungary, Turkey, and many more.

These are all easy prerogatives, led by the executive. All of them would go a significant way toward restoring the U.S.'s anti-corruption credentials, if not actual leadership. But a future White House can't stop there—and can't work alone. In tandem with congressional allies, a New Patriotism front must work in lockstep to flesh out other anti-corruption, and specifically anti-oligarch, programs.

Again, they should start with the easiest things they can find. They should, for instance, reform the U.S.'s federal lobbying regulations, including by issuing outright bans on former politicians and members of congressional and executive staff from working as foreign lobbyists. Their time serving in Washington is a public trust; there's no reason they should be allowed to monetize that trust while acting as lobbyists and mouthpieces for non-American regimes, especially dictatorships and kleptocracies around the world, after they leave office.

Likewise, the White House and congressional allies should expand the bans on not only what members of Congress or the presidency can do but, more specifically, what *family members* of those politicians and officials can do. Whether it's Hunter Biden or the entire brood of Trump children—and, perhaps most notoriously, Jared Kushner—America has seen a deluge of family members in recent years profit from proximity to power, peddling their last names to the highest bidders abroad. With little expertise, figures like Biden or Kushner have raked in millions from crooked foreign networks. The former's foreign dealings helped implode his father's presidency; the latter has done even more, and even worse—much of which has somehow escaped notice during Trump's second term, which this book will hopefully help rectify. But both of them have worked in tandem to normalize a practice that, for years, was anathema to Washington—and helped normalize a figure like Trump, who has turned the White House into his own personal piggy bank.

No more. Congress must pass legislation placing outright bans on any new foreign deals, anywhere in the world, for family members while their relatives are in office. This timeframe could also be expanded, extending from the point their relative even *declares* their candidacy for office, to years—five? ten? more?—after their relative leaves either Congress or the White House. Might this deter some candidates from running? Maybe. Might this lead to fallings-out among politicians and their children and siblings and cousins who want to flip their last names into an easy profit? Possibly. Then again, is that necessarily a bad thing?

Both of these—barring former officials from foreign lobbying and banning family members from foreign profiteering—are bipartisan issues. Most especially, they have wide support across America; if these bans go through, no one will march in protest. ("First they came for Jared Kushner, and I said nothing!" is a sentence no one would ever utter.) They are easy ways to build momentum for a future administration, and a perfect launchpad for a New Patriotism movement.

And that momentum will be needed, because from there the path gets rockier. Slightly more difficult, but by no means impossible, will be the kind of funding decisions that a future administration and its congressional allies will need to chart. As Trump has made amply clear, the U.S. can have as many laws as it wants, but without enforcement and funding those regulations are worthless.

Which is why a future White House must demand—and must receive—as much funding for the bodies spearheading these new anti-corruption, anti-oligarchic efforts as it can. Like the Financial Crimes Enforcement Network (FinCEN), tasked with upholding anti–money laundering regulations. And the task forces mentioned above, following their resuscitation. And, perhaps most especially, the Internal Revenue Service—the single body that can do more to rein in oligarchs' tax evasion than anything else, all by simply enforcing the law.

As we've seen throughout this book, American oligarchs have enjoyed a range of realities that allow them to drive down their tax rate even lower than all other Americans. The rise of financial secrecy and offshore vehicles; the expansion of the so-called Wealth Defense Industry; the collapse of tax rates more broadly—all of it has added up to a perfect cocktail for oligarchy in America. But those tools are only part of the story. A significant part of this transformation is the success of Republican-led efforts to strangle the IRS, all but killing off the lone body tasked with gathering America's tax receipts—and with trying to actually track down those oligarchs sitting atop an ever-greater pile of wealth.

The solution, then, is simple: fund the IRS. Give the IRS everything it needs to go after these tax cheats—these oligarchs who'd prefer to starve other Americans, sometimes quite literally, instead of paying what America is owed. Give them as much funding as they could possibly handle, and then some more. And aim it all at the wealthiest Americans, all of whom have offshored and squirreled away the most wealth. Investigate, uncover, and prosecute—and do it all over and over again, until the effective tax rate for America's wealthiest finally starts pushing upward again, back to where it belongs.

If the administration wants to create a new, elite body within the IRS to specifically target these figures, all the better. Call it, say, the Anti-Oligarch Task Force, and sic it on the wealthiest American tax dodgers it can find. And let it be the spear tip in the fight against modern oligarchy, and against all the hangers-on in the Wealth Defense Industry who have devoted their one life on this earth to helping the rich get richer.

Much of this is perfectly feasible. And indeed, the Biden administration already created an outline for what the potential funding and restructuring of the IRS could look like, which a future administration should build upon.

There are two areas, however, that will require far more political capital and far more political muscle to force through. Given their importance, they may well become the centerpiece of any future administration—and would do far more to further the fight against oligarchy than anything else.

The first is something that's been nipping around the edges of political discourse in recent years: instituting a new wealth tax. As we saw earlier in this book, this idea is not novel. Not only have American governments routinely instituted new forms of taxation throughout history, but many Americans, even within the working and middle classes, already pay a form of wealth tax, known as the property tax. The idea that a wealth tax is some kind of injurious, even anti-American, step is hogwash. Pitched as a means of mitigating America's wealth inequality, a new wealth tax is simply an extension of previous measures meant to corral American oligarchy. A wealth tax would be as American as apple pie or baseball—or, for that matter, the income and inheritance taxes before it.

Many Americans, long inured to the idea of new or more taxes, would disagree. But if it's pegged directly to oligarchy, and if it is purely progressive in nature, it would be far more salable. Legislators should apply it only to those whose wealth is estimated to run to, say, nine figures—or even ten figures, if you're being charitable. It should be applied uniformly to the monied classes, without fear or favor, based on estimates of total net worth—including how much international wealth these oligarchs may maintain. If they want to enjoy the privileges of American citizenship, this is the price they must be willing to pay.

Opponents and sycophants will claim that you're "soaking the rich." To this charge, you can nod along: This is, indeed, a measure aimed not just at the "rich" but at the richest who have ever existed. At the end of the day, it is taxes—and taxes alone—that will do the most to lessen America's wrenching wealth inequality. It is taxes that will cleave off the peaks of the towering fortunes these oligarchs now control. It is taxes that will force those fortunes downward—or will, at the very least, give the rest of us some time to catch up.[20]

And it is the wealth tax whose time has come. Combined with a push to raise income and inheritance tax rates for America's wealthiest—back to the rates that existed under Truman and Eisenhower, ideally—it is this new tax regime that can restore America to the kinds of equitable opportunity that Teddy Roosevelt first called for over a century ago.

There is one other idea that Roosevelt focused on as president, and revisited on that steamy day in Kansas, whose time has also come: eliminating corporate money from American politics. And the best place to start would be by overturning *Citizens United*.

Eliminating the ruling will not be a silver bullet when it comes to running corporate financing out of American politics, but it's still a phenomenal place to begin. Which is why the future anti-oligarchic push must focus on reversing *Citizens United*, however we can. Perhaps it's by finding a way to cap what campaigns and candidates can *spend*, rather than what they can take in, making the mounting piles of corporate and oligarch donations effectively worthless. Perhaps it's passing new transparency requirements that are so extensive, and so widely enforced by a reformed FEC, they make this kind of secretive corporate funding prohibitively difficult, or even pointless. Perhaps it's stacking the Supreme Court with justices outspoken in opposition to the ruling—or even expanding the Supreme Court itself, such that a majority of justices can strike down *Citizens United*.

Or perhaps there's another mechanism: a constitutional amendment, eliminating the *Citizens United* ruling entirely.[21] The constitutional amendment process is at this point nearly an anachronism; whatever muscle memory Americans once had about passing amendments has long faded. Given that any successful constitutional amendment requires supermajorities in both Congress and among the states, the path looks so steep as to seem impossible.

But that's a mirage. Already, nearly half the states across the U.S. have formally backed an amendment to overturn *Citizens United*. Nor is this necessarily a partisan issue; not only have nominally Republican states like Alaska, Utah, and Montana joined the push to toss out *Citizens United*, but some two-thirds of Republicans themselves back the move.[22] That hasn't yet translated to any kind of political progress; Republicans, by and large, continue to back a man who is oligarchy made flesh, and whose family has ransacked the country more than any previous family in American history. But with the right messaging, and with the right political winds, this can easily become a bipartisan issue that can cross the finish line.

And it's only getting timelier. Because it's no longer simply American oligarchs prying apart America's elections, seizing and steering the outcomes for themselves. It's now foreign regimes using those loopholes—all that corporate secrecy, all that corporate financing—to inject their own money and their own interests into American politics. Thanks to all these corporate financing allowances, American elections remain American in name only. There's no telling how wide the phenomenon of foreign regimes plowing money into American politics is, but given the case studies already uncovered—and the fact that the Trump administration has tossed the doors open for foreign regimes looking to fund American politicians at all levels of government—the rot runs far wider than just the New York mayor's office, or even the White House itself.

Ending these loopholes, ending all this corporate financing of American politics—it's no longer about wresting American democracy from those with the deepest pockets. Now it's about American national security writ large. And about making sure that American democracy remains in the hands of Americans themselves.

There's one additional charge that those backing this New Patriotism messaging will have to face: that all this will simply push American oligarchs to other nations, forcing them to uproot for more tax-friendly climates, depriving the U.S. of its wealth entirely. That you'll be both strangling the goose and smashing the golden egg simultaneously.

This is a canard. As we've seen elsewhere, the wealthiest castes of society tend to stomach higher tax rates. They may moan, they may whine, they may bleat about the supposed unfairness of it all—but by and large they tend to swallow increased rates when they come. The data bears this out; rarely do the wealthiest members of society become economic migrants.

Sure, some do. There is a sufficient number of anecdotes to make this seem like a plausible result of higher taxes for the oligarchs. Odds are, you can think of at least a few wealthy businessmen or actors or playboys who moved elsewhere in order to escape increased taxes. It does happen, from time to time.

But for those few willing to toss aside all the privileges and protections that come with American citizenship, all because they don't want to pay higher taxes, we should welcome their departure. These are people who would rather shift their entire lives and change their entire national identities, all because they don't want to comply with the new rules and regulations of a democratically elected government—a government that is now demanding that these oligarchs pay a fairer share.

The oligarchs who leave are the ones who would rather slough off American citizenship than comply with Americans' wishes. Higher taxes, increased investigations and prosecutions, new barricades to prevent oligarchs from manipulating American politics for their own ends—let these all flush out those billionaires who never wanted to pay the price and bear the burden of American citizenship. Who only wanted to be American when it meant making and hiding as much money as they possibly could. Who only believed in America as far as their pocketbooks would let them, and no further. Who will, in leaving, reveal how loyal they are—or are not—to America.

Because this is the other element of this New Patriotism push. It's not simply about the financial realities, the kind of economic equanimity that allows a nation to actually thrive. It's also about the term contained in the program name itself: *patriotism*.

As we've seen throughout this book, these oligarchs, almost to a man, playact as patriots. Posing as figures who keep American (and not just corporate) interests at heart, they have claimed they're simply furthering American power and American influence wherever they go. But at a certain point those American and corporate interests diverge—and at that point, these oligarchs will always follow the path that leads to the greatest corporate, and greatest personal, gains. At that point, American interests are left behind. And at that point, a dictator will come calling, spotting that cleavage—and knowing that, at the end of the day, these figures will always choose oligarchy over America.

It's a pattern as old as oligarchy itself; as we saw back in the first chapter, even the oligarchs of Athens would turn to blood enemies in Sparta if it meant they didn't have to comply with pressure from Athenian voters. So is it with those oligarchs of the twenty-first century, and all the American adversaries—in Beijing, Moscow, and elsewhere—who realize the openings these figures provide.

Nor is it just abetting bloodied regimes and American enemies, all for their own financial gain. Now, some modern American oligarchs even dream of something else: a new nation, expansive and expanding, in which they can reign unhindered, unshackled from any notions of democracy or oversight or regulation whatsoever. Where they can, with all their wealth and utopian visions, create a new "superpower" to rival and eventually supplant the U.S. entirely. The fact that this hasn't been viewed more widely as treason is a failure of both messaging and understanding. But it's difficult to describe it any other way.

All of which means these oligarchs have become—like the Confederate oligarchy before them—a national security concern, threatening to tip into a national security crisis. It's no longer simply about wealth equality, or even democracy itself, but the future of the U.S. as a nation unto itself—stable, sound, and still shining as a city on the hill, a haven for so many people strangled by their own oligarchies around the world.

None of this will be easy. The slings and slurs against those advocating for all this are almost laughably predictable. Teddy Roosevelt—a man who, perhaps more than anyone else, single-handedly embodied the American ethos, for both good and ill—realized as much. In the middle of his talk in Kansas, after citing a line from Abraham Lincoln expounding on the importance of labor over capital, Roosevelt said that his speech would see him "even more strongly denounced as a Communist agitator than I shall be anyhow."[23] Roosevelt's prediction quickly came true; following his speech, as the University of North Texas's Robert La Forte wrote, "In general, the Eastern United States denounced him as [a] 'communist agitator.'"[24]

So it goes. But the fact remains: Roosevelt was right then, just as those calling to cull the oligarchs' wealth—and to prevent them from spiraling into an even greater national security threat than they already are—are right now.

Unfortunately, many of those anti-oligarchy calls are coming only from one part of one political party. With much of the GOP in thrall to their own oligarch—a man who has seen his own personal fortune explode since ascending to the presidency, monetizing his rule however he can—many of these solutions must come from the Democratic Party alone. And given just how chummy many Democratic leaders remain with America's oligarchic class, the solutions must come specifically from the party's economic left wing.

Thankfully, that's where much of the political energy of the 2020s is now found. While Democratic initiatives stall out elsewhere, it is the messaging around economic fairness, and especially anti-oligarchic efforts, that has recently injected life into the waffling Democratic Party.

You can see it in the turnout. Hundreds of thousands, potentially millions at this point, have flocked to join Senator Bernie Sanders on his Fighting Oligarchy tour. Nor are these blue bastions. People in places like Shreveport, Louisiana; Bakersfield, California; Butte, Montana; and many more have cheered on Sanders's tour, enthralled by the rhetoric that places oligarchs and wealth inequality at the center of America's woes.[25]

You can also see it in terms of early returns. In New York City, Zohran Mamdani burst past an entrenched Democratic machine, itself reliant on deep-pocketed donors across the city and state. Mamdani's victory centered on much the same messaging: forcing the wealthiest New Yorkers to pay more. It's a message suddenly surging around the country. It's a message whose time has finally come.[26]

And it's a message that, in many ways, is the last, best chance to rescue a nation tilting into autocracy, replacing an era of democratic stability with an era of illiberal empire once more. It's an era whose contours are already becoming clear: in Palestine, savaged by Israeli imperialists; in Ukraine, still sacrificing everything it can to beat back Russian revanchism; in Tibet and East Turkestan and Taiwan, watching a despotic regime in Beijing break the backs of any and all opposed to the Chinese Communist Party's hegemony. It's also an era you can see taking shape in places like Greenland, caught in the crosshairs of the American oligarchs dreaming of ways to escape democratic shackles, regardless of what Greenlanders may actually want. (All the more reason Democrats must pledge, here and now, to undo any of Trump's claims to Greenland; to do everything they can to support Ukraine's efforts to push Russia back; to recognize Palestine's statehood; and, if the moment comes, to be ready to recognize the independence of Tibet, East Turkestan, and Taiwan.)

It's an era that risks seeing these nations disappear entirely. And it's an era that, given these oligarchs' designs on creating a new superpower to surpass America, may well usher in the eventual disappearance of the U.S., as well. An American oligarchy could become a post-American oligarchy. An American-led world could become an America-less world. It's hardly out of the realm of possibility.

Mostly, though, this oligarchic, imperial era bearing down on us is one that resembles one centuries past, when other nations, caught in the maw of ravaging empires, blinked out of existence, never to be seen again. When entire countries could be overturned, devoured outright, disappeared entirely. All in the name of oligarchy. All in the name of empire.

Which is why it's perhaps fitting that we close this book on American oligarchy, and on American empire, with a quote from Liliʻuokalani, the last sovereign of Hawaii, who watched her nation be dismembered by a number of American oligarchs, swallowed entirely by a nation marching from sea to shining sea, and far beyond.

Speaking to Americans both then and now, Liliʻuokalani wrote, "I would ask you to consider that your government is on trial before the whole civilized world, and that in accordance with your actions and decisions will you yourselves be judged."[27]

So it goes for our oligarchs. So it goes for our empire. And so it goes for the rest of us. May we—for the sake of our nation, and of so many other nations both before and ahead of us—make the right decision.

Afterword

November 2025

I can detect the near approach of the storm, I can hear the moaning of the hurricane, but I can't say how, when, or where it will break forth.

—E. M. Martineau[1]

On November 16, 2025, Ukrainian President Volodymyr Zelenskyy listened on speakerphone to an unfamiliar voice. This new interlocutor, speaking with a reedy American accent, had a plan for Zelenskyy: a series of bullet points, all approved by the American president, for what Zelenskyy would have to do to end Ukraine's war with Russia.

The list of demands ran on and on. There were new limits Ukraine would have to place on its military, preventing Ukraine from ever matching Russia's battlefield advantages. There was the reality that Ukraine would have to give up any dreams of ever joining NATO. There were the revelations that, even as Ukraine's ability to defend itself shrank, Russia would see sanctions soon lifted, and that Moscow would once more be welcomed into the geopolitical fold, as if the war had never happened.[2]

But that wasn't all. As this new voice instructed Zelenskyy, Ukraine would have to finally, formally give up not just Crimea but all of the Donbas—including territory that Russia hadn't even occupied. After years of fighting, and after millions of casualties, Ukraine would have to cede territory—and abandon Ukrainian populations—that Russia never conquered.

The proposals were beyond anything Zelenskyy or his administration had ever heard. They went beyond anything anyone outside Moscow had ever proposed. The demands effectively gelded Ukraine, ensuring that Kyiv would remain forever prone before Russia. Indeed, they read less as a list of negotiated points, and more as a wish list of outcomes straight from the Kremlin.

Which is exactly what they were. Zelenskyy didn't know it at the time, but the list of demands had originated not in any Western capital but in Moscow. And the man unspooling these new demands—Jared Kushner, now emerging from the shadows, taking center stage in the ongoing war between Russia and Ukraine—was there to tell Zelenskyy that the plan was now Washington's, and that Kushner was there to make sure the plan was now implemented.[3]

The entire, sordid saga of Kushner's supposed "peace plan" in late 2025 generated immediate headlines and swift backlash. But while much of the attention focused on the bungled, haphazard nature of the plan itself—and of how little anyone outside of Kushner and his partner, Steve Witkoff, actually knew about the details ahead of time—less attention was focused on the implications of the proposal, or on what it meant for the oligarchic takeover of American foreign policy. Because even while Kushner sat there, demanding that Ukraine cede territory Russia had never gained on the battlefield, his surge to the center of the greatest war Europe had seen in nearly a century spoke far more about not just his own future, but about the future of oligarchy in America—and what that rise would mean for global stability writ large.[4]

Take Kushner first. After months of operating largely out of sight, orchestrating hiring and steering policy from the background, the latter half of 2025 saw Kushner step once more back into the limelight. There were the financial dealings, only growing in scope and import, such as when he partnered with Saudi backers to launch the biggest leveraged buyout the world had ever seen, snapping up the video game company Electronic Arts.[5] There was the autocratic regime in Serbia setting up at least one secret deal with Kushner, even as Serbian protesters successfully thwarted another Kushner real estate project in Belgrade.[6] Most memorably, there was Kushner's involvement in crafting a so-called ceasefire in Gaza, which granted Israel the right to occupy the majority of southern Palestine—and expedited Israel's goal of preventing a Palestinian state forevermore.[7]

But all that was a warm-up for Kushner's sudden thrust into leading the U.S.'s efforts to end fighting in Ukraine. In late October, Kushner and Witkoff huddled in Miami for a multiday meeting with the man Putin first sicced on Kushner years ago: Kirill Dmitriev, the sanctioned Kremlin insider, tasked with recruiting Kushner to Moscow's side. Over a series of "intensive discussions," Kushner and Witkoff cobbled a series of supposedly original points that could purportedly solve the contretemps between Russia and Ukraine.[8]

But as journalists Christo Grozev and Michael Weiss later revealed, Kushner's supposed "peace plan" was anything but original. Instead, "many of its most controversial conditions were contained in a document" that circulated out of the Kremlin months earlier. Rather than Kushner's creative handiwork, his plan was "at its core a recycled Russian document." Kushner's plan, listing all the ways Ukraine would capitulate to Moscow, "contains specific language that appeared almost exactly word-for-word in an earlier text—one drafted solely by Dmitriev," the journalists continued.[9]

The two documents in question weren't precisely identical. Certain clauses were tweaked, while others were expanded or eliminated. But on the whole, as Grozev and Weiss continued, many of the "key concepts" of Kushner's plan—capping the Ukrainian military, granting Russia massive swaths of Ukrainian territory, and lifting sanctions on Moscow—originated not with Kushner but with the Kremlin. Remarkably, Dmitriev even admitted as much. In a leaked call with another Russian official, Dmitriev confirmed that he would "informally pass [Moscow's document] on directly, saying that all this is informal. And they"—that is, Kushner and Witkoff—"can present it as their own." Which is precisely what happened.[10]

If Kushner was merely caught out laundering Russian talking points, that would be one thing. But it's worth pausing on the implications, not just for Ukraine or Russia but for the rest of us around the world. Kushner was not only the consummation of the rise of oligarchy in America; he was now pushing a plan that threatened to destabilize the world more broadly, and ignite a new nuclear age—and a race toward nuclear proliferation unlike anything seen in decades.

It wasn't merely that Kushner, with his father-in-law behind him, was pushing a policy of appeasement, granting an imperialist power the opportunity to garrote a smaller neighbor. It was that, suddenly, there was a new principle of geopolitics staring all of us in the face. With Kushner's plan, the U.S. was pledging to recognize a nuclear power's right to carve up a non-nuclear neighbor. Russia wouldn't get all of Ukraine, at least not yet. But Moscow would at least get some—some Ukrainian land, some Ukrainian populations—all while leaving Russia primed to continue its invasion at a later date.

Russia's nuclear bluffing, in other words, had worked. It was a lesson that wouldn't be lost on all those non-nuclear powers—Japan and South Korea, Canada and Poland, Kazakhstan and Australia and Germany and many more—staring down nuclear-armed imperialists near their borders. It was a lesson that came straight from the mouth of an American oligarch: an unelected billionaire, subject to no oversight or disclosure requirements, there solely because of his relationship with his father-in-law. There now dominating American policymaking, and much more besides.[11]

There are dozens of other factors that have led to this forthcoming age of nuclear proliferation, from Russia's imperialism to China's irredentism to America's strategic myopia and inability to successfully manage alliances. But when the story of this new surge of nuclear powers is written, there will be the rise of an American oligarchy at the center, operating for its own benefit, with little thought for the rest of us, or for what their reign may mean for the world—or what remains of it.

Those implications are still to be sorted out, in the months and years to come. But instead of dwelling on them, perhaps it's worth closing on a different sort of harbinger, which took place just a few days after Kushner demanded that Zelenskyy sacrifice both Ukrainian land and Ukrainian people at the altar of Russian revanchism.

Thousands of miles away from Kyiv, on a cloudy evening in Washington, America's leading executives gathered at the White House. Clad in coats and tails, they weren't there to bend the knee to Trump, as many had already done for months. They were there instead to fete another man, finally gliding back into Washington once more as one of the U.S.'s closest partners: Saudi Arabia's Mohammad bin Salman.[12]

None of the corporate heads applauding MBS that day had any doubts about who the Saudi head was, or what he'd already done in his years dominating Saudi Arabia. They all knew the details of how MBS had ordered his henchmen to assassinate and saw apart *Washington Post* journalist Jamal Khashoggi. (His initials, wrote one journalist, could also be short for "Mr. Bone Saw.")[13] They'd all heard the news about the mass executions continuing apace in Saudi Arabia, and all the ways women remained relegated to second-class citizenship under MBS's reign. They all knew that MBS remained a towering tyrant: an absolute monarch, anathema to all that American democracy supposedly represented.

But none of that mattered. Because they also knew that, as Saudi's chief despot, MBS oversaw a treasure chest worth hundreds of billions of dollars, which he'd already begun splashing at all comers. They'd watched Saudi Arabia inject its capital into all the primary pillars of the American economy: real estate and commercial properties, hedge funds and artificial intelligence, consultancies and public relations firms and universities and much, much more. They'd witnessed Saudi Arabia effectively cripple, and then take over, the American golf industry, just as it had already done to the worlds of tennis, boxing, and other sports fields. They'd seen how Saudi Arabia pocketed American politician after politician—and how Saudi funding had first buoyed Kushner, and then the rest of the Trump clan.

And all these corporate heads wanted their piece. Which is why, on that overcast evening in Washington, they filed into the White House, cheering their support for MBS, hoping some of the Saudis' financial crumbs might fall into their laps. There were dozens of them there that day, all of them there in their tuxedos, marching in like a troop of clapping penguins. Apple's Tim Cook, Nvidia's Jensen Huang, Coinbase's Brian Armstrong, heads of OpenAI and Citigroup and GM and Ford—dozens upon dozens of America's oligarchic class shuffled in, crowding amidst the golden drapes and gilded plates, bleating their support for MBS. All of them sat, smiled, and listened to Trump announce that Saudi Arabia would now become a formal American ally, and that MBS's regime would increase its total investment in the U.S. to some $1 trillion. And all of them realized that part of that investment, and potentially much more, could be theirs, if only they were willing to join a man best known for dismembering a critical journalist.[14]

In total, the White House guest list that day featured nearly fifty executives. In the long annals of American oligarchs and corporate heads kowtowing to foreign dictators, it was unlike anything ever seen before. The sheer number of CEOs, the amounts of attendant wealth, the related corporate power—never before in American history had so many, with so much, gathered to cheer on a foreign tyrant.[15]

Yet even amidst this flotsam of American business leaders, one oligarch stood out—one oligarch who had once served as an effective co-president, but who hadn't been seen in Washington since his public falling-out with Trump months earlier. One man who chose this evening to make his return to the White House, slipping once more into the innermost sanctum of American power. Once more illustrating just how high American oligarchy could rise.

It was Elon Musk. He was there that evening, hailing Trump and MBS alike. There once more in the halls of the White House.

As if he'd never left.

Acknowledgments

Books are strange things. You may write them on your own, but they nonetheless require a village to actually come to fruition, both before and during the actual process of drafting. This book was no different, and I'm deeply indebted to all the family, friends, and even the occasional adversary for helping me see this thing through.

First, I'd like to once more thank my editor, Hannah O'Grady, and the entire ever-stellar team at St. Martin's Press. Without Hannah's vision, this book never would have come together, and not nearly as quickly as it did. She believed in this book from its inception, and helped pull all the right points to the fore, allowing me space to explore all the history I wanted while never losing sight of the book's ultimate message. Kathryn Hough, Sara Beth Haring, and Maddie Alsup have each helped bring this book to life as well, leaving me endlessly grateful for their support.

The same can be said about my agent, Samantha Shea. Like Hannah, Samantha believed in this book when it was barely an idea on the page. As ever, none of this would exist without Samantha, who remains the best agent a writer could ask for.

In a book as sweeping as this one, hopscotching around history and policy and everything in between, there were plenty of experts I relied on to make sense of it all. I am deeply indebted to Jeffrey Winters for his work and his willingness to speak with me about all things oligarchy. I'm also grateful to Lorenz Gonschor and John Rosa for their aid on Hawaiian history. I'd also like to thank Chemi Llamo for her unstinting support for Tibet, and Uyghur activists for keeping the world aware of what the Chinese regime is still doing to Uyghurs. I'm also deeply grateful to many of the figures at the Citizens for Responsibility and Ethics in Washington (CREW), especially Stuart McPhail, Robert Maguire, and Debra Perlin, as well as Joe Westby,

Courtney Radsch, Kathryn Brightbill, and Michael Sobolik. There are many more who will remain unnamed, in both Washington and elsewhere, who I am deeply grateful to. I'd also like to thank Sue Warga for formatting the endnotes for this book, as well as Angely Mercado for fact-checking.

Parts of this book would not have been possible without a series of editors at a number of American media outlets. I'd like to particularly thank *The New Republic*'s Jason Linkins and *Mother Jones*'s Daniel Schulman, who have not only allowed writers (like me) to explore many of these topics, but who never lost sight of the threats of oligarchy at home and abroad. I'd also like to thank Katherine Stewart and Gabriel Zucman, whose pioneering work on some of these topics is featured throughout this book, and who deserve as wide an audience as possible.

Beyond the experts helping make this book readable, there was a series of friends who made this book—and a life spent writing books like this—possible. First, I want to thank David Smith, not only for providing me a couch to crash on during my visit to Moldova to report on the World Congress of Families, but for remaining the best advocate Moldovan democracy could find. I'd also like to thank Matt Fleskes, whose years of tireless advocacy convinced me that Teddy Roosevelt deserved much greater attention than I initially thought. I'd like to thank Kyle Holmes and Joe Dwyer for providing a much-needed respite in Cooperstown, joining me in watching Ichiro's Hall of Fame induction, and Jeremy Blomberg for joining me in witnessing the Seattle Mariners win a playoff game—an event I never thought I'd live long enough to actually see. I'm also deeply grateful to John Sapienza and Chris Tzeng for not only allowing me to officiate at their wedding but for providing me (and everyone else) with bottomless picklebacks. Many other friends are worth singling out for all the joy and rapport they've brought into my life: Clement Uduk, Nick Rischiotto, Stan Antonio, Natalie Clericuzio, Amy Feran and Max Feil, Robert and Marjolein de Veer, Ella Hall and Eric Doctor, Akshay Dayal, Jasdeep Singh, Matt Lawyue, Sam Woodard, Justin Young, Nick Farris, Ryan Walsh, Maggie Sermont, Crystal Vitagliano, Ian Fischer, Peter Steffensen, Kevin Schell, Arthur Wang,

Nia Roberts, Chris Chen, Emily Bowers, Daniel Mollengarden, and Liang Liu.

I'd like to particularly thank Matt Sermont and Matt Youn, not only for all their years of camaraderie but also for leading the best fantasy football leagues you can find. I only ask that, in return for seeing their names committed to immortality on these pages, they let me finally win a championship.

Nothing—not this book, not this life—is possible without the family I have. Babu Ji and Ama Ji, Jaya and Jacob and Ari, Pu and Mashall, Nitu and Raina, Chote Mama and Nisha Mami, Pranathi, the entire community in Central Louisiana—thank you for welcoming me as family, year after year. Nettie and Grant, I can't wait to spend more time (and watch more Mariners games) with you in the near future, as well as with Aunt Mary, Uncle Tim, Aunt Kate, Uncle John, Aunt Barbara, Aunt Carol, Aunt Patty, Aunt Jeanne, and Tess Korth. I'd also like to thank everyone in Portland, including the Cavenaughs, the Dos, Bonnie Hossack, and Sharon Beckman, for the best neighbors a kid could have grown up with. I'd also like to particularly thank Mercedes Krcma for helping plan my mom's surprise seventy-fifth birthday party (which will, by the time she reads this, no longer be a surprise!). And I'd like to thank Nelly Stevenson, who has helped us raise a child in Brooklyn, and Jackie Goldzweig Panitz, for providing us with much-needed breaks (and Devi with much-needed donuts).

I'd also like to thank the Squaxin nation, whose continued existence is not only a testament to resilience but a reminder that, if you want to see American empire, all you have to do is look.

As always, I'm endlessly lucky to have the parents I do. Mom, Dad—thank you, for this and for everything. (And thank you for all the unpaid babysitting hours.) I'd also like to thank my brother Norwood, who remains an example of all that is good in this world. And I am endlessly grateful to my wife, Versha Sharma, who somehow combines breathtaking beauty with unparalleled brilliance, and with a bottomless font of patience for a husband constantly buried in his work (or watching a combination of baseball and old Lego videos).

This book is dedicated to someone who has brought more light, more laughter, and more exhaustion into my life than anyone ever before: Devi Rose, our Gudiya. For those lucky enough to have met Devi, you know she is part toddler, part tornado. (If you wish for a child with more energy than any other, don't be surprised when your wish comes true.) Your endless curiosity is a gift, a flame that I hope never goes out. Watching you learn, navigate, and understand the world—and watching you realize that answers can often lead to more questions—has been more rewarding than anything I could have ever asked for. Building Legos, tossing the ball back and forth, and playing "peekaboo pillows" with you—all while speaking gibberish or singing "Frosty the Snowman," far louder than our neighbors probably appreciate—is worth more than any amount of money could ever buy. I'm already in awe of you—and I can't wait to see what you do next.

But first: Go give your mother a hug, and tell her you love her!

Notes

Epigraphs

1. Enrique Zorrilla, quoted in David Maraniss, *Clemente: The Passion and Grace of Baseball's Last Hero* (New York: Simon & Schuster, 2007), 137.
2. Batman, in *Batman: The Animated Series*, season 1, episode 34, "I Am the Night," written by Michael Reaves, Bob Kane, and Eric Radomski, directed by Boyd Kirkland, aired November 9, 1992, on Fox Kids.

Oligarchs by the Numbers

1. Juliet Chung, "$1 Trillion of Wealth Was Created for the 19 Richest U.S. Households Last Year," *The Wall Street Journal*, April 23, 2025.
2. Emmanuel Saez and Gabriel Zucman, *The Triumph of Injustice: How the Rich Dodge Taxes and How to Make Them Pay* (New York: W. W. Norton, 2020), 98.
3. Saez and Zucman, *The Triumph of Injustice*, 23.
4. Saez and Zucman, *The Triumph of Injustice*, 145.
5. Saez and Zucman, *The Triumph of Injustice*, 145.
6. Laura Doan, "Rockefeller Became the First Billionaire over a Century Ago. Here's What to Know About America's Wealthiest Today," CBS News, September 29, 2025.
7. "Elon Musk" (profile), *Forbes*, September 9, 2025, https://www.forbes.com/profile/elon-musk/, accessed November 28, 2025.
8. Anna Massoglia, "Dark Money Hit a Record High of $1.9 Billion in 2024 Federal Races," Brennan Center for Justice, May 7, 2025.
9. Massoglia, "Dark Money Hit a Record High."
10. "Israel Has Committed Genocide in the Gaza Strip, UN Commission Finds," press release, Office of the High Commissioner for Human Rights, United Nations, September 16, 2025.
11. Monica Hunter-Hart and Giacomo Tognini, "How Jared Kushner's Bold Bets in the Middle East Made Him a Billionaire," *Forbes*, September 16, 2025.
12. David D. Kirkpatrick, "The Number: How Much Is Trump Pocketing off the Presidency?," *The New Yorker*, August 11, 2025.

Prologue

1. John Steinbeck, quoted in Carl Freedman, "From Nixon to Trump: Metastases of Cultural Power," *Los Angeles Review of Books*, June 4, 2018.
2. Dexter Filkins, "A Saudi Prince's Quest to Remake the Middle East," *The New Yorker*, April 2, 2018.
3. Filkins, "A Saudi Prince's Quest."
4. "Infiltrating America: How the United Arab Emirates Launched an Unprecedented Political Interference Campaign in the United States," Human Rights Foundation, February 2024.
5. David D. Kirkpatrick, "The Most Powerful Arab Ruler Isn't M.B.S. It's M.B.Z.," *The New York Times*, June 2, 2019.
6. Andrea Bernstein, *American Oligarchs: The Kushners, the Trumps, and the Marriage of Money and Power* (New York: W. W. Norton, 2020), 354.
7. David D. Kirkpatrick, Ben Hubbard, Mark Landler, and Mark Mazzetti, "The Wooing of Jared Kushner: How the Saudis Got a Friend in the White House," *The New York Times*, December 8, 2018.
8. Bernstein, *American Oligarchs*.
9. Thomas Grove, Warren P. Strobel, Aruna Viswanatha, Gordon Lubold, and Sam Schechner, "Elon Musk's Secret Conversations with Vladimir Putin," *The Wall Street Journal*, October 25, 2024.
10. Seb Starcevic, "Musk Backs Criticism of Zelenskyy That Says He 'Doesn't Want Peace,'" *Politico*, February 18, 2025.
11. Associated Press, "Elon Musk's Peace Plan for Ukraine Draws Condemnation from Zelenskyy," NPR, October 4, 2022.
12. Maura Reynolds, "Fiona Hill: 'Elon Musk Is Transmitting a Message for Putin,'" *Politico*, October 17, 2022.
13. Akanksha Sharma and Michelle Toh, "Taiwan Hits Back at Elon Musk's Claim That It Is 'Part of China,'" CNN, September 14, 2023; Noah Kirsch, "Musk's Views on Uyghurs Even Creeped Out Bari Weiss: New Book," *Daily Beast*, September 13, 2023.
14. Bloomberg, "Apple CEO Tim Cook Praises Tesla-Beating BYD on China Visit, Pushes AI-Infused Environmental Theme as Geopolitical Tensions Loom," *Fortune*, March 24, 2024.
15. Katie Razzall and Sarah Bell, "Facebook Was 'Hand in Glove' with China, BBC Told," BBC, March 10, 2025; Loulla-Mae Eleftheriou-Smith, "China's President Xi Jinping 'Turns Down Mark Zuckerberg's Request to Name His Unborn Child' at White House Dinner," *Independent*, October 5, 2015.
16. Andrew Kaczynski, "Before DOGE, Ramaswamy Spent Years Attacking Musk for Ties to China," CNN, December 4, 2024.
17. Miranda Nazzaro, "Chinese Leader Xi Gets Standing Ovation at Banquet with U.S. Executives," *The Hill*, November 16, 2023.
18. Ruth Marcus, "Big Tech's Power Surge," *The Washington Post*, January 20, 2025.

Section I: Capital

1. Benjamin Franklin, in Max Farrand, ed., *The Records of the Federal Convention of 1787* (New Haven, CT: Yale University Press, 1937), 1:81.

Chapter 1: A Terrible Word

1. "Desmond Shum on How Xi Jinping Beat Down China's Red Aristocrats," *The Economist*, April 22, 2024.
2. "Oligarchy," *Britannica Kids*, https://kids.britannica.com/students/article/oligarchy/631900, accessed November 28, 2025.
3. Peter Lattman, "The Origins of Justice Stewart's 'I Know It When I See It,'" *The Wall Street Journal*, September 27, 2007.
4. Jeffrey A. Winters, *Oligarchy* (Cambridge: Cambridge University Press, 2011.
5. "Aristotle, from *The Politics*, c. 340 BCE," in Paul Halsall, ed., *Ancient History Sourcebook* (online), https://sourcebooks.web.fordham.edu/ancient/aristotle-politics1.asp.
6. Aristotle, *The Politics and the Constitution of Athens*, ed. Stephen Everson (Cambridge: Cambridge University Press, 1996), 72.
7. In a sense, Aristotle was simply reasoning backward to a definition that Plato had laid out decades before, defining oligarchy in his *Republic* as a system in which "the rich rule and the poor man has no share." Winters, *Oligarchy*, 27n35.
8. Aristotle, *The Politics*, 72.
9. Liv McConnell, "What Is an Oligarchy, and Why Are People Worried the U.S. Is Becoming One?," *Teen Vogue*, March 26, 2025.
10. George Orwell, *1984* (1949; New York: Plume, 2022).
11. Scott Snyder and Greg Capullo, *Batman Vol. 1: The Court of Owls* (New York: DC Comics, 2013).
12. Winters, *Oligarchy*.
13. Jeffrey A. Winters, interview with author.
14. Winters, *Oligarchy*, 2. It's worth noting that even the oligarchs themselves are wedded to this incorrect view about what "oligarchy" means. In late December 2024, billionaire Marc Andreessen claimed that since "you always end up with a small minority in charge of a large majority in basically every society," he believed that "every society in history has been an oligarchy." If that's the case, of course, there's nothing to actually distinguish "society" and "oligarchy"—and the study of the latter becomes pointless. Bari Weiss, "Marc Andreessen on AI, Tech, Censorship, and Dining with Trump," *Free Press*, December 10, 2024.
15. Winters, *Oligarchy*, 3.
16. Winters, *Oligarchy*, 3.
17. Winters, *Oligarchy*, 5.
18. Jeffrey A. Winters, interview with author.

19. Charles Barsotti, "Two Large Men Wearing Suits" (cartoon), *The New Yorker*, April 25, 2011.
20. Jeffrey A. Winters, interview with author.
21. Winters, *Oligarchy*, 208.
22. Winters, *Oligarchy*, 208.
23. Winters, *Oligarchy*, 210.
24. Winters, *Oligarchy*, 87–88.
25. John P. McCormick, *Machiavellian Democracy* (Cambridge: Cambridge University Press, 2011), 1.
26. James Madison, "The Same Subject Continued: The Union as a Safeguard Against Domestic Faction and Insurrection" (Federalist #10), *New York Packet*, November 23, 1787.
27. George Thomas, "The Other Fear of the Founders," *The Atlantic*, February 12, 2025.
28. Gouverneur Morris, July 2 and 19, 1787, in James Madison, *Journal of the Federal Convention*, ed. E. H. Scott (Chicago: Albert, Scott, 1893), 1:288, 383.
29. Thomas, "The Other Fear of the Founders."
30. Thomas Jefferson to James Madison, October 28, 1785, in *The Papers of Thomas Jefferson*, ed. Julian P. Boyd et al. (Princeton, NJ: Princeton University Press, 1950), 8:681–682.
31. Thomas Jefferson to John Adams, October 28, 1813, in *The Adams-Jefferson Letters: The Complete Correspondence Between Thomas Jefferson and Abigail and John Adams*, ed. Lester J. Cappon (Chapel Hill: University of North Carolina Press, 1959), 2:387–392.
32. Winters, *Oligarchy*, 6.
33. Alexis de Tocqueville, *Democracy in America*, trans. and ed. Harvey C. Mansfield and Debra Winthrop (Chicago: University of Chicago Press, 2002).
34. Manisha Sinha, "The Oligarchs' Revenge," *The Nation*, October 6, 2020.
35. Matthew Karp, *This Vast Southern Empire: Slaveholders at the Helm of American Foreign Policy* (Cambridge, MA: Harvard University Press, 2016), 157.
36. "The Presidency. Republican Mass Meeting at the Cooper Institute. Speech of Hon. Charles Sumner. The Republican Party—Its Origin, Its Necessity, and Its Permanence," *The New York Times*, July 12, 1860.
37. "The Presidency. Republican Mass Meeting."
38. "The Presidency. Republican Mass Meeting."
39. Dominic Sandbrook, "What New Oligarchs Can Learn from the Old," *The Times* (London), January 17, 2025.
40. Richard White, *The Republic for Which It Stands: The United States During Reconstruction and the Gilded Age, 1865–1896*, Oxford History of the United States (New York: Oxford University Press, 2017).
41. H. W. Brands, *American Colossus: The Triumph of Capitalism, 1865–1900*

(New York: Doubleday, 2010), 8; Alice Cattley, "What the Richest People in History Would Be Worth Today," Yahoo Finance, September 24, 2024.

42. "The Strike at Homestead Mill," *American Experience*, PBS, https://www.pbs.org/wgbh/americanexperience/features/carnegie-strike-homestead-mill/, accessed November 28, 2025; "Andrew Carnegie: The Richest American of All Time," Blenheim Partners, January 2019, https://blenheimpartners.com/wp-content/uploads/2019/01/Andrew-Carnegie-The-Richest-American-of-All-Time.pdf.
43. Andrew Lisa, "How the World's Richest Person in Every Decade Made Their Fortune," Yahoo Finance, November 29, 2024.
44. James Bruno, "The Lessons of Theodore Roosevelt," *Washington Monthly*, September 6, 2019.
45. Juliet Chung, "$1 Trillion of Wealth Was Created for the 19 Richest U.S. Households Last Year," *The Wall Street Journal*, April 23, 2025.
46. Lily Rothman, "How American Inequality in the Gilded Age Compares to Today," *Time*, February 5, 2018.
47. Andrew Carnegie, *The Gospel of Wealth* (New York: Carnegie Corporation, 2017), 8.
48. Virginia Montanez, "Andrew Carnegie: Respected Genius or Selfish Industrialist?," *Pittsburgh Magazine*, February 14, 2025.

Chapter 2: Reign of Terror

1. David Malo, quoted in Ralph S. Kuykendall, *The Hawaiian Kingdom, vol. 1, 1778–1854, Foundation and Transformation* (1938; Honolulu: University of Hawaii Press, 1980), 155.
2. Helena G. Allen, *Sanford Ballard Dole: Hawaii's Only President, 1844–1926* (Glendale, CA: A. H. Clark, 1988).
3. Allen, *Sanford Ballard Dole*, 19.
4. Steven Hahn, *A Nation Without Borders: The United States and Its World in an Age of Civil Wars, 1830–1910* (New York: Viking, 2016).
5. Claudio Saunt, *West of the Revolution: An Uncommon History of 1776* (New York: W. W. Norton, 2015), 210.
6. Julia Flynn Siler, *Lost Kingdom: Hawaii's Last Queen, the Sugar Kings, and America's First Imperial Venture* (New York: Grove, 2013).
7. Warren Zimmermann, *First Great Triumph: How Five Americans Made Their Country a World Power* (New York: Farrar, Straus and Giroux, 2004), 285.
8. Zimmermann, *First Great Triumph*, 285.
9. Lorenz Gonschor, interview with author. It's worth noting that Hawaiian independence was recognized by far, far more countries than the Republic of Texas, the only other American state that ever enjoyed its own period of recognized independence.
10. Siler, *Lost Kingdom*, 142.

11. Kealani Cook, "Defining the Empire: American Political Rhetoric in the Early Territory, 1898–1903," *Social Process in Hawai'i* 46 (2020): 21–35, quote at 31.
12. Zimmermann, *First Great Triumph*, 286.
13. "1887: 'Bayonet Constitution' Strips the Hawaiian Monarchy of Much of Its Power," Native Voices: Native Peoples' Concepts of Health and Illness, National Library of Medicine, accessed November 28, 2025, https://www.nlm.nih.gov/nativevoices/timeline/372.html.
14. Zimmermann, *First Great Triumph*, 287, 292.
15. Cook, "Defining the Empire," 22.
16. Lili'uokalani, *Hawaii's Story by Hawaii's Queen* (Boston: Lee and Shepherd, 1898).
17. Lili'uokalani, *Hawaii's Story*, 201.
18. Lili'uokalani, *Hawaii's Story*, 56.
19. Lili'uokalani, *Hawaii's Story*, 177–184.
20. Zimmermann, *First Great Triumph*, 288.
21. Lili'uokalani, *Hawaii's Story*, 226–236.
22. Allen, *Sanford Ballard Dole*, 117.
23. Siler, *Lost Kingdom*, 219.
24. "A Shameful Conspiracy in Which the United States Was Made to Play a Part," *The New York Times*, November 20, 1893.
25. Quoted in Siler, *Lost Kingdom*, 228, 229.
26. Lili'uokalani, *Hawaii's Story*, 177–178.
27. Lili'uokalani, *Hawaii's Story*, 303.
28. Zimmermann, *First Great Triumph*, 289.
29. "Grover Cleveland on the Overthrow of Hawaii's Royal Government," 1893, Digital History, item 1283, https://www.digitalhistory.uh.edu/disp_textbook.cfm?smtID=3&psid=1283.
30. "Grover Cleveland on the Overthrow of Hawaii's Royal Government"; Grover Cleveland, "Annual Message to Congress," December 4, 1893, Teaching American History, https://teachingamericanhistory.org/document/state-of-the-union-address-94/.
31. Ralph Thomas Kam, "The Private Sorrows of the Overthrow," *Hawaiian Journal of History* 50 (2016): 96–97.
32. Allen, *Sanford Ballard Dole*, 194.
33. "Joint Resolution to Provide for Annexing the Hawaiian Islands to the United States," July 7, 1898, Enrolled Acts and Resolutions of Congress, General Records of the United States Government, 1778–1992, RG 11, National Archives.
34. Siler, *Lost Kingdom*, 243.
35. Lili'uokalani, *Hawaii's Story*, 247–248.
36. Siler, *Lost Kingdom*, 252.
37. Allen, *Sanford Ballard Dole*, 210.

38. Allen, *Sanford Ballard Dole*, 215.
39. *San Francisco Chronicle*, September 5, 1887, in Lili'uokalani, *Hawaii's Story*, 375.
40. Siler, *Lost Kingdom*, 257.
41. Siler, *Lost Kingdom*, 269.
42. Zimmermann, *First Great Triumph*, 291.
43. Siler, *Lost Kingdom*, 285 ("vast majority"); Adrienne LaFrance, "Remembering the Nation of Hawaii," *The Atlantic*, September 30, 2015 ("wept audibly"); Bernice Piilani Irwin, quoted in Michael Tighe, "A Look at a Century of Annexation," part 1, *Hawai'i Tribune Herald*, August 9, 1998 ("Those who were present"); Siler, *Lost Kingdom*, 285 ("I am ashamed").
44. Cook, "Defining the Empire," 21.
45. Allen, *Sanford Ballard Dole*, 273.
46. Lili'uokalani, *Hawaii's Story*, 370, 372.
47. David Starr, "William McKinley and Theodore Roosevelt: White Supremacists and Imperialists," *Daily Kos*, June 21, 2021.
48. *Congressional Record*, June 11, 1898, 5792. See also Ashley Marie Gjovik, "The Hawai'i Affair: American Imperialism and the Engineering of Territorial Expansion," Santa Clara University School of Law, December 27, 2020, https://gjovik.co/wp-content/uploads/2023/10/Gjovik-Hawaii-Affair-2020-12-25-Draft.pdf.
49. *Congressional Record*, June 11, 1898, 5792.

Chapter 3: Eaten Away

1. This quote is attributed to Republican industrialist and U.S. senator from Ohio Mark Hanna (1837–1904).
2. "The Childhood Home of a Renowned President," National Park Service, https://www.nps.gov/thrb/index.htm, accessed November 28, 2025.
3. Christopher Klein, "Inside Theodore Roosevelt's Gilded Age Upbringing," History.com, May 3, 2022.
4. Edmund Morris, *Theodore Rex* (New York: Random House, 2002).
5. "The Square Deal," *TR Encyclopedia*, Theodore Roosevelt Center, https://www.theodorerooseveltcenter.org/encyclopedia/politics-and-government/square-deal/, accessed November 28, 2025.
6. Sidney Milkis, "Theodore Roosevelt: Life Before the Presidency," Miller Center, University of Virginia, https://millercenter.org/president/roosevelt/life-before-the-presidency, accessed November 28, 2025.
7. Morris, *Theodore Rex*.
8. Daniel Immerwahr, *How to Hide an Empire: A History of the Greater United States* (New York: Farrar, Straus and Giroux, 2019), 80.
9. Morris, *Theodore Rex*.
10. Paul Krugman, "Elizabeth Warren Does Teddy Roosevelt," *The New York Times*, January 28, 2019.

11. Jesse Eisinger, "No, President Trump, the Income Tax Wasn't a Mistake. But It Was an Accident," *ProPublica*, April 8, 2025.
12. Eisinger, "No, President Trump."
13. Eisinger, "No, President Trump."
14. Theodore Roosevelt, "Message of the President," December 5, 1905.
15. "Money-in-Politics Timeline," Open Secrets, https://www.opensecrets.org/resources/learn/timeline, accessed November 28, 2025.
16. "Roosevelt Says Nation Must Curb Plutocracy," *The New York Times*, October 5, 1906.
17. "Roosevelt Says Nation Must Curb Plutocracy."
18. As far as anyone can tell, Roosevelt never used the term "oligarch" himself. His preferred term of art when discussing the spectacularly wealthy Americans distorting the country's economy and politics was "plutocrat," a word whose Greek roots mean "rule of wealth" or "rule of the wealthy"—and a term that has unfortunately fallen out of popular use in the twenty-first century.
19. Theodore Roosevelt, "Sixth Annual Message," December 3, 1906.
20. Roosevelt, "Sixth Annual Message."
21. Roosevelt, "Sixth Annual Message."
22. "A Brief History of Estate Taxes," Sparrow Capital, https://www.sparrowcapital.com/resource-center/estate/a-brief-history-of-estate-taxes, accessed November 28, 2025.
23. Roosevelt, "Sixth Annual Message."
24. Theodore Roosevelt, "Seventh Annual Message," December 3, 1907.
25. "From the Archives: President Teddy Roosevelt's New Nationalism Speech," The White House, December 6, 2011, https://obamawhitehouse.archives.gov/blog/2011/12/06/archives-president-teddy-roosevelts-new-nationalism-speech.
26. Theodore Roosevelt, *An Autobiography* (New York: Charles Scribner's Sons, 1913), 425.
27. Quoted in Tom Wheeler, "Who Makes the Rules in the New Gilded Age?," Brookings Institution, December 12, 2018.
28. Darien B. Jacobson, Brian G. Raub, and Barry W. Johnson, "The Estate Tax: Ninety Years and Counting," Internal Revenue Service, *Statistics of Income Bulletin*, summer 2007, 118–128.
29. Eisinger, "No, President Trump."
30. Emmanuel Saez and Gabriel Zucman, *The Triumph of Injustice: How the Rich Dodge Taxes and How to Make Them Pay* (New York: W. W. Norton, 2020), xvi.
31. Sam Pizzigati, "Tax the Rich? We Did That Once," Inequality.org, December 2, 2022; Mark Luscombe, "Historical Look at Estate and Gift Tax Rates," Wolters Kluwer, March 9, 2022.
32. Anthony Summers, *The Arrogance of Power: The Secret World of Richard Nixon* (New York: Penguin, 2000).

33. "Senate Select Committee to Study Governmental Operations with Respect to Intelligence Activities (The Church Committee)," U.S. Senate, https://www.senate.gov/about/powers-procedures/investigations/church-committee.htm, accessed November 28, 2025.
34. Mike Koehler, "The Story of the Foreign Corrupt Practices Act," *Ohio State Law Journal* 73, no. 5 (2012): 930–1013.
35. David Montero, *Kickback: Exposing the Global Corporate Bribery Network* (New York: Viking, 2018), 24.
36. Montero, *Kickback*, 26.
37. Montero, *Kickback*, 26.
38. Montero, *Kickback*, 23, 26.
39. John Thomas Noonan, *Bribes: The Intellectual History of a Moral Idea* (New York: Macmillan, 1984).
40. Montero, *Kickback*, 25.
41. Koehler, "The Story of the Foreign Corrupt Practices Act," 941.
42. Koehler, "The Story of the Foreign Corrupt Practices Act," 940; Frank Church, quoted in Casey Michel, Trevor Sutton, and Matthew Duss, "The Anticorruption Angle," *Foreign Affairs*, August 8, 2025.
43. The law additionally required that all publicly traded companies keep accurate books, preventing the use of shell companies for bribery and "falsified financial accounting," while also making it illegal to hide any bribes behind other middlemen or subsidiary agents. Montero, *Kickback*, 31.
44. Remarkably, this all took place at a time in which many nations encouraged and incentivized this kind of bribery. "It was no small feat the United States took it upon itself to prohibit bribery, at a time when other governments essentially looked the other way regarding kickbacks and their impact," the journalist David Montero writes. "The United States had effectively granted itself the power to police foreign corporations, even though the home countries of those entities did not outlaw bribery themselves, and in some cases tacitly encouraged it." Montero, *Kickback*, 31.
45. Eileen Shanahan, "3 More Corporations Tell About Illegal Aid to Nixon," *The New York Times*, November 16, 1973.
46. "Suitcases, Secret Lists, and Citizens United," *Planet Money*, NPR, July 1, 2022. These suitcases should not be confused with the envelopes of cash Nixon's vice president, Spiro Agnew, accepted as bribes while in office. Clearly, the Nixon administration was flexible when it came to the means with which bribes were transported. Rachel Maddow and Michael Yarvitz, *Bag Man: The Wild Crimes, Audacious Cover-Up, and Spectacular Downfall of a Brazen Crook in the White House* (New York: Crown Books, 2020).
47. Shanahan, "3 More Corporations Tell About Illegal Aid to Nixon."
48. "Suitcases, Secret Lists, and Citizens United."
49. "Money-in-Politics Timeline," Open Secrets, https://www.opensecrets.org

/resources/learn/timeline, accessed November 28, 2025; Pawel Laider and Maciej Turek, "The Tillman Act: 34 Stat. 864 (1907)," *Basic Documents in Federal Campaign Finance Law* (Krakow: Jagiellonian University Press, 2015).

50. The legislation was so worthless that Nixon didn't even bother with a public bill-signing ceremony. "Money-in-Politics Timeline."
51. John P. Hollihan, "The Federal Election Campaign Act Amendments of 1974: The Constitutionality of Limiting Political Advertising by the Non-Candidate," *Florida State University Law Review* 3, no. 2 (1975): art. 3.
52. "Fact Sheet: Federal Election Campaign Act Amendments of 1974," October 15, 1974, box 14, folder "Federal Election Campaign Act Amendments—1974," Philip Buchen Files, Gerald R. Ford Presidential Library.
53. Federal Election Commission, "The First Ten Years," April 14, 1985, https://www.fec.gov/resources/cms-content/documents/firsttenyearsreport.pdf.
54. "River of Money" (editorial), *The New York Times*, January 8, 1975.
55. "Statement by the President" [upon signing the Federal Campaign Act Amendments of 1974], October 15, 1974, box 14, folder "Federal Election Campaign Act Amendments—1974," Philip Buchen Files, Gerald R. Ford Presidential Library.

Chapter 4: Worse Than Useless

1. Quoted in Chris Lehmann, "The Constitution Was Meant to Guard Against Oligarchy," *The New Republic*, February 10, 2022.
2. Buckley v. Valeo, 424 U.S. 1 (1976).
3. Buckley is not as well remembered as his brother, conservative firebrand William F. Buckley, who helped pave the way for right-wing despots around the world to target and access American policymakers. In the 1960s and 1970s, the primary vehicle for whitewashing right-wing despots was *National Review*, a magazine founded by William F. Buckley, where he and his stable of writers apparently never found a hard-right despot they couldn't support. Those the publication lauded included Spain's Francisco Franco, whom Buckley dubbed an "authentic national hero"; Portugal's António Salazar, who claimed in *National Review* that he was "fighting for Western civilization and Christian values"; and Chile's Augusto Pinochet, whom Buckley viewed as a "bona fide leader who knew how to exercise power." After Pinochet used a car bomb to assassinate a political opponent in Washington, DC, Chilean officials turned directly to Buckley for advice on how to "sanitize Pinochet's reputation," and Buckley happily obliged. Jacob Heilbrunn, *America Last: The Right's Century-Long Romance with Foreign Dictators* (New York: Liveright, 2024), 137–165.
4. Federal Election Commission, "*Buckley v. Valeo*: Summary," https://www.fec.gov/legal-resources/court-cases/buckley-v-valeo/, accessed November 28, 2025.
5. Ralph K. Winter, "The History and Theory of *Buckley v. Valeo*," *Journal of Law and Policy* 6, no. 1 (1997): art. 7.

6. Bradley A. Smith, "*Buckley v. Valeo*: Jim Buckley's Finest Hour," Federalist Society, August 28, 2023.
7. Winter, "The History and Theory of *Buckley v. Valeo*."
8. Buckley v. Valeo, 424 U.S. 1 (1976).
9. Federal Election Commission, "*Buckley v. Valeo*: Summary."
10. Burt Neuborne, "Campaign Finance Reform & the Constitution: A Critical Look at Buckley v. Valeo," Brennan Center for Justice, January 1, 1998.
11. Federal Election Commission, "*Buckley v. Valeo*: Summary."
12. Federal Election Commission, "*Buckley v. Valeo*: Summary."
13. Jeffrey Rosen, "Passing the Buckley," *The New Republic*, October 27, 1997.
14. The law limits each of the number of FEC commissioners to only three per party, so that one party could never have a majority of commissioners. However, it also requires agreement from at least four commissioners to launch an investigation—meaning that the president, if he or she appoints commissioners who will rule as the president wants, can easily block any new FEC investigations. I'd like to thank CREW's Stuart McPhail for highlighting this point.
15. Rosen, "Passing the Buckley."
16. "Editorial: The Federal Election Commission Is Worse Than Useless," *Los Angeles Times*, March 31, 2016.
17. Adam Winkler, *We the Corporations: How American Businesses Won Their Civil Rights* (New York: Liveright, 2018).
18. Winkler, *We the Corporations*, 35–70.
19. Kim Phillips-Fein, "Company Men," *The New Republic*, March 29, 2018.
20. Winkler, *We the Corporations*, xii–xv.
21. Winkler, *We the Corporations*, 129–136.
22. Phillips-Fein, "Company Men."
23. Winkler, *We the Corporations*, 290–300.
24. "Consumer Victory" (editorial), *The New York Times*, May 28, 1976.
25. Winkler, *We the Corporations*, 305–323.
26. Winkler, *We the Corporations*, 305–323.
27. First National Bank of Boston v. Bellotti, 435 U.S. 765 (1978).
28. As Phillips-Fein noted in "Company Men," the decision was in hindsight unsurprising, given that it "was authored by Lewis Powell, who had famously written a secret memo to the Chamber of Commerce prior to his confirmation to the Court, urging business to take a strong stance against a rising 'attack on free enterprise,' and so helping to spark a new era of conservative activism."
29. Phillips-Fein, "Company Men."
30. Daniel I. Weiner, "*Citizens United*, Explained," Brennan Center for Justice, December 12, 2019.
31. Weiner, "*Citizens United*, Explained."
32. *Citizens United v. FEC*, 558 U.S. 310 (2010).

33. Winkler, *We the Corporations*, 309.
34. *Citizens United v. FEC*, 558 U.S. 310 (2010).
35. *Citizens United v. FEC*, 558 U.S. 310 (2010).
36. Matt Ford, "Elon Musk Is Demolishing the Rationale for *Citizens United*," *The New Republic*, March 24, 2025.
37. *Citizens United v. FEC*, 558 U.S. 310 (2010).
38. *Citizens United v. FEC*, 558 U.S. 310 (2010).
39. Weiner, "*Citizens United*, Explained."
40. "*Citizens United* and the 'Effective Disclosure' System That Wasn't," Campaign Legal Center, January 23, 2011.
41. Weiner, "*Citizens United*, Explained."
42. Jeffrey A. Winters, interview with author.
43. Mark Roe, "*Dodge v. Ford*: What Happened and Why?," Harvard Law School Forum on Corporate Governance, December 1, 2021.
44. Weiner, "*Citizens United*, Explained."
45. *Citizens United v. FEC*, 558 U.S. 310 (2010).
46. Ford, "Elon Musk Is Demolishing the Rationale for *Citizens United*."
47. Barack Obama, "Remarks by the President in State of the Union Address," January 27, 2010.
48. Obama, "Remarks by the President in State of the Union Address."
49. *Citizens United v. FEC*, 558 U.S. 310 (2010).
50. "Justice Alito Mouths 'Not True' During 2010 State of the Union," *Des Moines Register*, January 20, 2015.

Section II: Alliance

1. Quoted in Matthew Restall, *When Montezuma Met Cortés: The True Story of the Meeting That Changed History* (New York: Ecco, 2018), 237.

Chapter 5: How Greedy Can You Get?

1. *Seize the Moment* (podcast), November 10, 2024, https://www.instagram.com/reel/DCMkiyIpMKS/.
2. Martin Gilens and Benjamin I. Page, "Testing Theories of American Politics: Elites, Interest Groups, and Average Citizens," *Perspectives on Politics* 12, no. 3 (2014): 564–581.
3. Gilens and Page, "Testing Theories of American Politics."
4. Gilens and Page, "Testing Theories of American Politics."
5. "Study: U.S. Is an Oligarchy, Not a Democracy," BBC, April 17, 2014.
6. Jeffrey A. Winters, *Oligarchy* (Cambridge: Cambridge University Press, 2011), 25.
7. Gilens and Page, "Testing Theories of American Politics."
8. Thomas Piketty, *Capital in the Twenty-First Century*, trans. Arthur Goldhammer (Cambridge, MA: Belknap Press of Harvard University Press, 2014).
9. Thomas Piketty, Emmanuel Saez, and Gabriel Zucman, "Distributional Na-

tional Accounts: Methods and Estimates for the United States," Working Paper 22945, National Bureau of Economic Research, 2016.

10. Noah Kirsch, "The 3 Richest Americans Hold More Wealth Than Bottom 50% of the Country, Study Finds," *Forbes*, November 9, 2017.
11. "The Top 1% in the United States Makes over 26 Times More Than the Bottom 99%," Economic Policy Institute, https://www.epi.org/multimedia/the-top-1-in-the-united-states-makes-over-26-times-more-than-the-bottom-99/, accessed November 28, 2025.
12. Emmanuel Saez and Gabriel Zucman, *The Triumph of Injustice: How the Rich Dodge Taxes and How to Make Them Pay* (New York: W. W. Norton, 2020), 7.
13. Juliet Chung, "$1 Trillion of Wealth Was Created for the 19 Richest U.S. Households Last Year," *The Wall Street Journal*, April 23, 2025.
14. "Nine Charts About Wealth Inequality in the United States," Urban Institute, April 25, 2024.
15. Chung, "$1 Trillion of Wealth Was Created."
16. Chung, "$1 Trillion of Wealth Was Created."
17. Harriet Marsden and Richard Windsor, "Vladimir Putin: How Much Is Russian President's Net Worth?," *The Week*, April 4, 2025; Tania Branigan, "China Blocks Bloomberg for Exposing Financial Affairs of Xi Jinping's Family," *The Guardian*, June 29, 2012; "This World's Richest Family Surpasses Net Worth of Billionaires Including Elon Musk, Mukesh Ambani, Gautam Adani, and More," *Times of India*, October 4, 2024.
18. Chung, "$1 Trillion of Wealth Was Created."
19. Oliver Bullough, *Moneyland: The Inside Story of the Crooks and Kleptocrats Who Rule the World* (New York: St. Martin's, 2019); Nicholas Shaxson, *Treasure Islands: Uncovering the Damage of Offshore Banking and Tax Havens* (New York: Palgrave Macmillan, 2011); Atossa Araxia Abrahamian, *The Hidden Globe: How Wealth Hacks the World* (New York: Riverhead Books, 2024).
20. Brooke Harrington, *Offshore: Stealth Wealth and the New Colonialism* (New York: W. W. Norton, 2024), 16.
21. Nick Shaxson, "More Than $12 Trillion Stuffed Offshore, from Developing Countries Alone," Tax Justice Network, May 9, 2016.
22. Franklin Roosevelt himself at one point wanted an income tax of 100 percent, effectively confiscating any further income the wealthiest Americans themselves made, though his advisers later talked him out of such a move. Franklin D. Roosevelt, "Letter to the House Ways and Means Committee on Salary Limitation," February 15, 1943, American Presidency Project, University of California, Santa Barbara.
23. John F. Kennedy, "Address and Question and Answer Period at the Economic Club of New York," December 14, 1962, American Presidency Project, University of California, Santa Barbara.
24. John Wahl, "Tax Cuts and Tragedy: JFK Wanted to Lower Income Tax and

LBJ's Political Maneuverings to Get It Do[ne]," One Bridge Wealth Management, April 8, 2024.

25. Niall McCarthy, "Taxing the Rich: The Evolution of America's Marginal Income Tax Rate (Infographic)," *Forbes*, April 26, 2021.
26. Larry Kudlow and Brian Domitrovic, "Recalling the Days When Democrats Cut Taxes," CNBC, March 5, 2014.
27. Mark Luscombe, "Historical Look at Estate and Gift Tax Rates," Wolters Kluwer, March 9, 2022.
28. Luscombe, "Historical Look at Estate and Gift Tax Rates."
29. Associated Press, "U.S. National Debt Reaches a Record $37 Trillion, the Treasury Department Reports," NBC News, August 12, 2025.
30. Casey Michel, "How the U.S. Became the World's Refuge for Dirty Money," *Mother Jones*, January–February 2024.
31. Brenda Medina, "How the World's Richest Defend Their Wealth, with Help from a Dedicated Industry," International Consortium of Investigative Journalists, June 1, 2021.
32. Kate Barron-Alicante and Astrid Scholz, "Tackling the Wealth Defense Industry," *Stanford Social Innovation Review*, winter 2025. It's worth noting as well that much of this is perfectly legal—and one of the primary reasons that the federal tax code has grown from just a few hundred pages a century ago to a staggering 70,000 pages now. Andrew Lundeed and Scott Hodge, "The Income Tax Code Spans More Than 70,000 Pages," Tax Foundation, October 23, 2013.
33. D. T. Cochrane and Dennis Howlett, "Explainer: What's the Difference Between Tax Avoidance and Tax Evasion?," Canadians for Tax Fairness, August 10, 2021.
34. "Peter Thiel," *Encyclopedia Britannica*, accessed November 29, 2025.
35. Justin Elliott, Patricia Callahan, and James Bandler, "Lord of the Roths: How Tech Mogul Peter Thiel Turned a Retirement Account for the Middle Class into a $5 Billion Tax-Free Piggy Bank," *ProPublica*, June 24, 2021.
36. Alicia Adamczyk, "The Rise of the Roth IRA: Gen Z and Millennials Have a New Favorite Investment Account," *Fortune*, June 14, 2024.
37. Internal Revenue Service, "Roth IRAs," pub. no. AT-2001-54, accessed November 29, 2025.
38. Elliott, Callahan, and Bandler, "Lord of the Roths."
39. Elliott, Callahan, and Bandler, "Lord of the Roths."
40. Elliott, Callahan, and Bandler, "Lord of the Roths."
41. Elliott, Callahan, and Bandler, "Lord of the Roths."
42. Elliott, Callahan, and Bandler, "Lord of the Roths."
43. Elliott, Callahan, and Bandler, "Lord of the Roths."
44. Sarah C. G. Christopherson, "IRS Enforcement Boost Was Supposed to Last 10 Years. Congress Killed It in Under Three," Institute for Taxation and Economic Policy, September 16, 2025.

45. Clea Simon, "Turns Out IRS Audits of Wealthy Offer Terrific Return on Investment for Taxpayers," *Harvard Gazette*, July 19, 2023.
46. Phil Swagel, "The Effects of Increased Funding for the IRS," Congressional Budget Office, publication 57444, September 2, 2021.
47. "Justice Department Settles with Conservative Groups over IRS Scrutiny," Reuters, October 26, 2017; Vanessa Williamson, "Cutting IRS Funding Is a Gift to America's Wealthiest Tax Evaders," Brookings Institution, January 26, 2023.
48. "Gutting the IRS" (series), *ProPublica*, https://www.propublica.org/series/gutting-the-irs, accessed November 29, 2025.
49. Paul Kiel and Jesse Eisinger, "How the IRS Was Gutted," *ProPublica*, December 11, 2018.
50. Saez and Zucman, *The Triumph of Injustice*, 61.
51. Saez and Zucman, *The Triumph of Injustice*, 14.
52. Winters, *Oligarchy*.

Chapter 6: Liberty Means Order

1. Quoted in Adam Winkler, *We the Corporations: How American Businesses Won Their Civil Rights* (New York: Liveright, 2018), xvii.
2. Gerry Shih, "Chinese Internet Regulator Welcomed at Facebook Campus," Reuters, December 8, 2014.
3. Paul Mozur, "Warm West Coast Reception for China's Web Czar (Chillier in Washington)," *The New York Times*, December 8, 2014.
4. Wayne Ma, "Star Player in China Internet Chief's Visit to Facebook: A Book," *The Wall Street Journal*, December 8, 2014.
5. Ma, "Star Player in China Internet Chief's Visit to Facebook."
6. James Griffiths and Steven Jiang, "Former Chinese Internet Czar Lu Wei Sentenced to 14 Years in Prison for Bribery," CNN, March 26, 2019.
7. Fang Xiao, "Lu Wei Inspects Several U.S. Internet Giants; Zuckerberg's Desk Displays Xi Jinping's Works" [in Chinese], ThePaper.cn, December 8, 2014, https://web.archive.org/web/20150102155022/https://www.thepaper.cn/newsDetail_forward_1283974; Mozur, "Warm West Coast Reception."
8. Mozur, "Warm West Coast Reception."
9. Xi Jinping, *The Governance of China*, vol. 2 (Beijing: Foreign Languages Press, 2017).
10. Heather Timmons, "Facebook Is Making Employees Read Chinese Propaganda to Impress Beijing," *Quartz*, July 21, 2022.
11. Elizabeth C. Economy, "Zuckerberg's Love Affair with Xi Jinping," Council on Foreign Relations, December 9, 2014.
12. Economy, "Zuckerberg's Love Affair with Xi Jinping."
13. John H. Cushman Jr., "Nike Pledges to End Child Labor and Apply U.S. Rules Abroad," *The New York Times*, May 14, 1998.
14. Brian Merchant, "Life and Death in Apple's Forbidden City," *The Guardian*, June 18, 2017.

15. Bethany Allen, *Beijing Rules: How China Weaponized Its Economy to Confront the World* (New York: Harper, 2023).
16. Economy, "Zuckerberg's Love Affair with Xi Jinping."
17. Sarah Wynn-Williams, *Careless People: A Cautionary Tale of Power, Greed, and Lost Idealism* (New York: Flatiron Books, 2025), 144–145.
18. Ma, "Star Player in China Internet Chief's Visit to Facebook."
19. Timmons, "Facebook Is Making Employees Read Chinese Propaganda"; Parmy Olson, "Watch Mark Zuckerberg Give a 20-Minute Speech in Chinese," *Forbes*, October 26, 2015; Paul Mozur, "With 'Smog Jog' Through Beijing, Zuckerberg Stirs Debate on Air Pollution, *The New York Times*, March 19, 2016.
20. Jane Perlez, "A Chat in Chinese with Mark Zuckerberg, as Tech Giants Jostle for Face Time," *The New York Times*, September 24, 2015.
21. Loulla-Mae Eleftheriou-Smith, "China's President Xi Jinping 'Turns Down Mark Zuckerberg's Request to Name His Unborn Child' at White House Dinner," *Independent*, October 5, 2015.
22. Tom Phillips, "Mark Zuckerberg Accused of 'Kowtowing' to China for Handing Out Copies of Xi Jinping's Speeches," *The Telegraph*, December 8, 2014.
23. Economy, "Zuckerberg's Love Affair with Xi Jinping"; Timmons, "Facebook Is Making Employees Read Chinese Propaganda."
24. Wynn-Williams, *Careless People*, 145.
25. Wynn-Williams, *Careless People*, 149.
26. Wynn-Williams, *Careless People*, 152.
27. Wynn-Williams, *Careless People*, 304.
28. Wynn-Williams, *Careless People*, 305.
29. In Wynn-Williams's phrasing, Facebook provided "white-glove service" to the Chinese Communist Party. Wynn-Williams, *Careless People*, 313.
30. Matt Sheehan, "How Google Took On China—and Lost," *MIT Technology Review*, December 19, 2018; "A New Approach to China: An Update," *Google Official Blog*, March 22, 2010.
31. Ernesto Dal Bó and Guo Xu, "Google's Dragonfly: The Ethics of Providing a Censored Search Engine in China," Case Series, Haas School of Business, University of California, Berkeley, October 24, 2020.
32. Ryan Gallagher, "Google Plans to Launch Censored Search Engine in China, Leaked Documents Reveal," *The Intercept*, August 1, 2018.
33. Noah Smith, "Google's Prototype Chinese Search Engine Links Searches to Phone Numbers," *The Guardian*, September 18, 2018.
34. Joe Westby, interview with author.
35. "Project Dragonfly: Google, Human Rights, and Censorship in China," *North Carolina Journal of Law and Technology* (blog), https://journals.law.unc.edu/ncjolt/blogs/project-dragonfly-google-human-rights-censorship-china/, accessed November 29, 2025.
36. Jack Poulson, "I Quit Google over Its Censored Chinese Search Engine. The

Company Needs to Clarify Its Position on Human Rights," *The Intercept*, December 1, 2018; Ryan Gallagher, "Google Shut Out Privacy and Security Teams from Secret China Project," *The Intercept*, November 29, 2018.
37. Ryan Gallagher and Lee Fang, "Google Suppresses Memo Revealing Plans to Closely Track Search Users in China," *The Intercept*, September 21, 2018.
38. "Letter from Google Employees Regarding 'Dragonfly' Project" (n.d.), uploaded by *ThinkProgress*, https://www.scribd.com/document/394572047/Letter-from-Google-employees-regarding-Dragonfly-project, accessed November 29, 2025.
39. Casey Michel, "Google's Secret 'Dragonfly' Project Is a Major Threat to Human Rights," *ThinkProgress*, December 11, 2018.
40. Ryan Gallagher, "Senior Google Scientist Resigns over 'Forfeiture of Our Values' in China," *The Intercept*, September 13, 2018.
41. "Letter from U.S. Senators to Google CEO Sundar Pichai on 'Dragonfly,'" August 3, 2018, uploaded by *ThinkProgress*, https://www.scribd.com/document/394571780/Letter-from-U-S-Senators-to-Google-CEO-Sundar-Pichai-on-Dragonfly.
42. Gerrit De Vynck, "Google's China Search Engine Project Was 'Experiment,' CEO Says," Bloomberg, November 1, 2018.
43. Nick Bastone, "Google's Dragonfly Execs Didn't Take Written Notes and Isolated Internal Teams to Hide China Search Plans from Other Employees," *Business Insider*, November 29, 2018.
44. Courtney Radsch, interview with author.
45. Joe Westby, interview with author.
46. "Has Elon Musk Damaged His Business Empire," *Money Talks* (podcast), hosted by Ethan Wu and Tom Standage, April 24, 2025.
47. Rebekah Barton, "Marvel Fans Irate, 'Nothing More Annoying' Than Comparing Tony Stark to Elon Musk," InsideTheMagic.com, April 14, 2022.
48. Michael Kan, "Neuralink's First Brain Implant Patient Now Beats Friends in Video Games," *PCMag*, May 8, 2024.
49. "Has Elon Musk Damaged His Business Empire"; Joe McDonald, "Tesla Delivers First Cars in China, Plans Expansion," *USA Today*, April 22, 2014.
50. Walter Isaacson, *Elon Musk* (New York: Simon & Schuster, 2023), 313; "China Overtakes U.S. as World's Biggest Car Market," *The Guardian*, January 8, 2010.
51. Yoko Kubota and Raffaele Huang, "China Looks to Musk as Conduit to Trump, Seeking to Ward Off Harsh Policies," *The Wall Street Journal*, November 24, 2024.
52. Trefor Moss and Tim Higgins, "Tesla to Build Auto Factory in Shanghai," *The Wall Street Journal*, July 10, 2018.
53. Isaacson, *Elon Musk*, 314.
54. Isaacson, *Elon Musk*, 314.

55. Laura He, "Elon Musk Says His Shanghai Factory Makes the 'Highest Quality' Teslas," CNN, June 2, 2023.
56. Mara Hvistendahl, "How Elon Musk Became 'Kind of Pro-China,'" *The New York Times*, March 27, 2024.
57. Kubota and Huang, "China Looks to Musk as Conduit."
58. Mark Kane, "Half of All Teslas Are Made in China," Inside EVs, April 10, 2024.
59. Isaacson, *Elon Musk*, 246.
60. Selina Cheng and Raffaele Huang, "Why Musk Now Needs China More Than It Needs Him," *The Wall Street Journal*, April 30, 2024.
61. Tom Carter, "Tesla Is Stalling in China Just as Its Rivals Pick Up Speed," *Business Insider*, September 3, 2025; Zeyi Yang, "How Did China Come to Dominate the World of Electric Cars?," *MIT Technology Review*, February 21, 2023.
62. Keith Bradsher, "What Elon Musk Needs from China," *The New York Times*, November 22, 2024.
63. Arwa Mahdawi, "What a Surprise! Free Speech Absolutist Elon Musk Doesn't Really Love Free Speech," *The Guardian*, April 6, 2024.
64. Mathias Döpfner, "Elon Musk Reveals Tesla's Plan to Be at the Forefront of a Self-Driving Car Revolution—and Why He Wants to Be Buried on Mars," *Business Insider*, December 5, 2020.

Chapter 7: Hit Job

1. Spoken by the character Billy Costigan in *The Departed* (2006), directed by Martin Scorsese.
2. Andrea Bernstein, *American Oligarchs: The Kushners, the Trumps, and the Marriage of Money and Power* (New York: W. W. Norton, 2020), 121.
3. Kelsey Keith, "Charles Kushner Unloading New Jersey Manse for [$2 Million]," *Curbed New York*, October 24, 2011; Jodi Kantor, "For Kushner, Israel Policy May Be Shaped by the Personal," *The New York Times*, February 11, 2017.
4. Bernstein, *American Oligarchs*, 162.
5. "ICC Issues Arrest Warrants for Netanyahu, Gallant and Hamas Commander," *UN News*, November 21, 2024.
6. Bernstein, *American Oligarchs*, 162.
7. Bernstein, *American Oligarchs*.
8. Andrew Prokop, "As Trump Takes Aim at Affirmative Action, Let's Remember How Jared Kushner Got into Harvard," *Vox*, July 6, 2018.
9. Bernstein, *American Oligarchs*, 161.
10. Daniel Golden, "The Story Behind Jared Kushner's Curious Acceptance into Harvard," *ProPublica*, November 18, 2016.
11. Bernstein, *American Oligarchs*, 163.
12. Bernstein, *American Oligarchs*, 274.

13. Leon Neyfakh, "I Loved the *New York Observer*. Now It's Complicit in the Trump Campaign," *Slate*, November 7, 2016.
14. Andrea Bernstein, "Who Is Jared Kushner?," *The New Yorker*, January 6, 2020.
15. Kyle Pope, "The Jared Bubble," *Columbia Journalism Review*, October 6, 2017.
16. Michael M. Grynbaum, "New York Observer Ending Print Edition," *The New York Times*, November 12, 2016.
17. Neyfakh, "I Loved the *New York Observer*"; Rich Cohen, "The Potemkin Prince," *Vanity Fair*, November 2017.
18. "What You Need to Know About 666 Fifth Avenue," CBS News, June 19, 2017.
19. "News of Realty: Xerox Move Due," *The New York Times*, February 6, 1969; David W. Dunlap, "Citigroup Sign Replacing Those 3 Sixes at the Top," *The New York Times*, January 3, 2002.
20. "The Wolf of Wall Street: A Walking Tour," *The Telegraph*, https://www.telegraph.co.uk/travel/arts-and-culture/The-Wolf-of-Wall-Street-a-walking-tour/, accessed November 29, 2025.
21. Ryan Goodman and Julia Brooks, "Timeline on Jared Kushner, Qatar, 666 Fifth Avenue, and White House Policy," Just Security, March 11, 2020; Charles V. Bagli, "A Big Deal, Even in Manhattan: A Tower Goes for $1.8 Billion," *The New York Times*, December 7, 2006.
22. Bernstein, *American Oligarchs*, 255.
23. Bernstein, *American Oligarchs*, 255.
24. Goodman and Brooks, "Timeline on Jared Kushner."
25. David D. Kirkpatrick and Kate Kelly, "Before Giving Billions to Jared Kushner, Saudi Investment Fund Had Big Doubts," *The New York Times*, April 10, 2022.
26. Talia Lakritz, "A Timeline of Ivanka Trump and Jared Kushner's Relationship," *Business Insider*, June 1, 2025.
27. Michael R. Sisak, Jake Offenhartz, and Jennifer Peltz, "Judge Imposes $364 Million Penalty in Trump's New York Civil Fraud Case," *PBS NewsHour*, February 16, 2024.
28. Lakritz, "A Timeline of Ivanka Trump and Jared Kushner's Relationship."
29. Michael Barbaro, "Donald Trump Clung to 'Birther' Lie for Years, and Still Isn't Apologetic," *The New York Times*, September 17, 2016.
30. "Report of the Select Committee on Intelligence, United States Senate, on Russian Active Measures Campaigns and Interference in the 2016 U.S. Election, Volume 5: Counterintelligence Threats and Vulnerabilities," August 2024.
31. Bernstein, *American Oligarchs*, 328.
32. Ben Aris, "Who Is Russian Sovereign Wealth Fund Boss Kirill Dmitriev, Whose Middle East Connections Helped Broker the Release of U.S. Prisoner Marc Fogel?," *IntelliNews*, February 15, 2025.

33. "Putin's Man from Stanford: Who Is Kirill Dmitriev, the Key Russian Negotiator with the U.S.?," *Important Stories*, February 18, 2025; Guy Faulconbridge, "Who Is Putin's Investment Envoy Kirill Dmitriev and What Will He Discuss in Washington?," Reuters, April 2, 2025; Andrew Ryvkin, "Harvard Henchman: Putin's Point Person for Brokering a Ukraine Peace Agreement with Trump Is a Rich, Ivy League Smoothie," *Air Mail News*, March 22, 2025.
34. "Report on the Investigation into Russian Interference in the 2016 Presidential Election" (Mueller Report), Vol. 1, March 2019.
35. Elizabeth Chuck, "What the Mueller Report Says About Jared Kushner, Ivanka Trump, and Donald Trump Jr.," NBC News, April 18, 2019.
36. Eric Lichtblau, "Questions Remain About Putin's Request for a Back Channel to the Trump Transition," *Time*, May 21, 2019.
37. David Filipov, Amy Brittain, Rosalind S. Helderman, and Tom Hamburger, "Explanations for Kushner's Meeting with Head of Kremlin-Linked Bank Don't Match Up," *The Washington Post*, June 1, 2017; "Read Jared Kushner's Prepared Remarks [to Congressional Investigators]," *The New York Times*, July 24, 2017; Julia Ioffe, "What Jared Kushner's Statement Reveals About Russian Methods," *The Atlantic*, July 24, 2017.
38. Elena Panfilova, "Who Is Mr. Dmitriev?" (in Russian), *Novaya Gazeta*, April 7, 2025.
39. Maggie Michael, "In Yemen's Secret Prisons, UAE Tortures and U.S. Interrogates," Associated Press, June 22, 2017; Matt Spivey, "Sudan Takes UAE to World Court over 'Complicity in Genocide,'" BBC, March 6, 2025.
40. Michael Schaffer, "'Dark Money' Is Tainting Washington Think Tanks. A New Report Shows It's Worse Than You Think," *Politico*, January 3, 2025; Ben Freeman, "The Emirati Lobby in America," Quincy Institute for Responsible Statecraft, December 5, 2022.
41. "Interview of: Jared Kushner," Executive Session, Permanent Select Committee on Intelligence, U.S. House of Representatives, July 25, 2017.
42. Bernstein, *American Oligarchs*, 354.
43. "Interview of: Jared Kushner."
44. Dexter Filkins, "A Saudi Prince's Quest to Remake the Middle East," *The New Yorker*, April 2, 2018.
45. David D. Kirkpatrick, "The Most Powerful Arab Ruler Isn't M.B.S. It's M.B.Z.," *The New York Times*, June 2, 2019.
46. Kirkpatrick, "The Most Powerful Arab Ruler."
47. David D. Kirkpatrick and Carlotta Gall, "Audio Offers Gruesome Details of Jamal Khashoggi Killing, Turkish Official Says," *The New York Times*, October 17, 2018.
48. Bradley Hope and Justin Scheck, *Blood and Oil: Mohammed bin Salman's Ruthless Quest for Global Power* (New York: Grand Central Publishing, 2020).
49. David D. Kirkpatrick, Ben Hubbard, Mark Landler, and Mark Mazzetti,

"The Wooing of Jared Kushner: How the Saudis Got a Friend in the White House," *The New York Times*, December 8, 2018.

50. Kirkpatrick et al., "The Wooing of Jared Kushner."
51. Filkins, "A Saudi Prince's Quest."
52. Filkins, "A Saudi Prince's Quest."
53. Kirkpatrick et al., "The Wooing of Jared Kushner"; David Ignatius, "The Saudi Crown Prince Just Made a Very Risky Power Play," *The Washington Post*, November 5, 2017.
54. Kirkpatrick et al., "The Wooing of Jared Kushner."
55. Kirkpatrick et al., "The Wooing of Jared Kushner."
56. Kirkpatrick et al., "The Wooing of Jared Kushner."
57. Alex Emmons, Ryan Grim, and Clayton Swisher, "Saudi Crown Prince Boasted That Jared Kushner Was 'In His Pocket,'" *The Intercept*, March 21, 2018.
58. Kirkpatrick et al., "The Wooing of Jared Kushner."
59. Laura Strickler, Ken Dilanian, and Peter Alexander, "Officials Rejected Jared Kushner for Top Secret Security Clearance, but Were Overruled," NBC News, January 24, 2019.
60. Maggie Haberman, Michael S. Schmidt, Adam Goldman, and Annie Karni, "Trump Ordered Officials to Give Jared Kushner a Security Clearance," *The New York Times*, February 28, 2019; Strickler, Dilanian, and Alexander, "Officials Rejected Jared Kushner."
61. Shane Harris, Carol D. Leonnig, Greg Jaffe, and Josh Dawsey, "Kushner's Overseas Contacts Raise Concerns as Foreign Officials Seek Leverage," *The Washington Post*, February 27, 2018.
62. These concerns trickled all the way up to H. R. McMaster, Trump's national security adviser at the time, who realized that Kushner had been effectively freelancing American foreign policy, failing not only to coordinate with the U.S. National Security Council but also to report the visits and conversations with foreign officials in the first place. Harris et al., "Kushner's Overseas Contacts Raise Concerns."
63. Harris et al., "Kushner's Overseas Contacts Raise Concerns."
64. Nahal Toosi, "'It Makes Me Angry': Tillerson Vents Frustrations with Kushner," *Politico*, June 27, 2019.
65. Toosi, "'It Makes Me Angry.'"
66. Benjamin Siegel and Katherine Faulders, "Tillerson: Trump Faced 'Steep Learning Curve' on U.S.-Russia Policy, Immigration," ABC News, June 27, 2019; Dan De Luce, "Kushner Cut Me, Other Top Diplomats Out of the Loop in Talks with Saudis, Tillerson Says," NBC News, June 27, 2019.
67. Emmons, Grim, and Swisher, "Saudi Crown Prince Boasted."
68. Youssef M. Ibrahim, "Qaddafi Terms the $220,000 Given Billy Carter a Loan Tied to Business," *The New York Times*, June 27, 1981; Sam Cabral, "Hunter Biden: The Struggles and Scandals of the U.S. President's Son," BBC, June

11, 2024; Christopher Hitchens, "More Than a Good Feeling," *Slate*, January 12, 2009.

69. Blair Guild, "Report: Kushner Sought Deal for $500M Bailout from Ex-Qatari Prime Minister," CBS News, July 11, 2017.
70. Goodman and Brooks, "Timeline on Jared Kushner."
71. Patrick Wintour, "Qatar Given 10 Days to Meet 13 Sweeping Demands by Saudi Arabia," *The Guardian*, June 23, 2017.
72. Goodman and Brooks, "Timeline on Jared Kushner."
73. Goodman and Brooks, "Timeline on Jared Kushner."
74. Goodman and Brooks, "Timeline on Jared Kushner."
75. Charles V. Bagli and Jesse Drucker, "Kushners Near Deal with Qatar-Linked Company for Troubled Tower," *The New York Times*, May 17, 2018.
76. Goodman and Brooks, "Timeline on Jared Kushner."
77. Charles V. Bagli and Kate Kelly, "Deal Gives Kushners Cash Infusion on 666 Fifth Avenue," *The New York Times*, August 3, 2018.
78. Jesse Drucker and Emily Flitter, "Jared Kushner Paid No Federal Income Tax for Years, Documents Suggest," *The New York Times*, October 13, 2018.
79. Bernstein, *American Oligarchs*.

Chapter 8: Homophobic Fascists

1. Paul Lynch, *Prophet Song* (London: Faber and Faber, 2023).
2. Madalin Necsutu, "Moldova Hosts the World Congress of Families," Balkan Insight, September 14, 2018.
3. Jim Dobson, "Inside Vladimir Putin's Outrageous Underground Wine Cellar in Moldova," *Forbes*, February 26, 2029.
4. Kristina Stoeckl, "The Rise of the Russian Christian Right: The Case of the World Congress of Families," *Religion, States, and Society* 48, no. 4 (2020): 223–228.
5. Eugen Străuțiu, Steven D. Roper, William E. Crowther, Dareg Zabarah-Chulak, Victor Juc, and Robert E. Hamilton, eds., *The Armed Conflict of the Dniester: Three Decades Later* (Lausanne: Peter Lang, 2023).
6. Conversation with author.
7. "Account of WCF Founder Allan Carlson in Russia," uploaded by Casey Michel, https://www.scribd.com/document/381183064/Account-of-WCF-Founder-Allan-Carlson-in-Russia, accessed November 29, 2025.
8. Allan Carlson, interview with author; "Account of WCF Founder Allan Carlson in Russia."
9. "Account of WCF Founder Allan Carlson in Russia."
10. "Account of WCF Founder Allan Carlson in Russia."
11. "Account of WCF Founder Allan Carlson in Russia."
12. "Account of WCF Founder Allan Carlson in Russia."
13. "French Businessman Defends Plans to Build Crimea Theme Park," France24, August 16, 2014.

14. Matt Maldonado, "Russia's Hardest Working Oligarch Takes Talents to Africa," PONARS Eurasia, September 28, 2020.
15. Courtney Weave, "Malofeev: The Russian Billionaire Linking Moscow to the Rebels," *Financial Times*, July 24, 2014.
16. Human Rights Campaign Foundation, "Exposed: The World Congress of Families," June 2015.
17. Human Rights Campaign Foundation, "Exposed."
18. Casey Michel, "Christian Fundamentalists Gathering in Moldova Want You to Know They're Not Extremists," *ThinkProgress*, September 17, 2018.
19. Hannah Levintova, "How U.S. Evangelicals Helped Create Russia's Anti-Gay Movement," *Mother Jones*, February 21, 2014.
20. Dessie Zagorcheva, "Putin and the Weaponization of Family Values," Center for European Policy Analysis, March 18, 2024.
21. There was nothing illegal about accepting Malofeev's funding, given that the Russian oligarch had not yet been sanctioned by the United States. "Russian Oligarch Charged with Violating U.S. Sanction," press release, U.S. Department of Justice, April 6, 2022; Peter Montgomery, "Tom Cotton Bill to Ban 'Malign Foreign Influence' on Nonprofit Boards Exempts Some Religious-Right Groups," People For, September 19, 2025.
22. Levintova, "How U.S. Evangelicals Helped Create."
23. Levintova, "How U.S. Evangelicals Helped Create."
24. Sam Sweet, "The Christian Oscars," *The New Yorker*, February 7, 2014.
25. Casey Michel, "How Russia Infiltrated the World of American Religious-Right Filmmaking," *ThinkProgress*, February 8, 2019.
26. Casey Michel, "Newly Emerged Photo Shows Ben Carson with Key Employee of Sanctioned Russian Oligarch," *ThinkProgress*, January 31, 2019.
27. Casey Michel, "The Latest Front in Russian Infiltration: America's Right-Wing Homeschooling Movement," *ThinkProgress*, January 17, 2019.
28. Michel, "The Latest Front in Russian Infiltration."
29. Michel, "The Latest Front in Russian Infiltration."
30. Michel, "The Latest Front in Russian Infiltration."
31. Alexey Komov, interview with author.
32. Alexey Komov, interview with author.
33. Alexey Komov, interview with author.
34. John Ganz, "Trump's Petty-Tyrant Brand of Fascism," *The Nation*, September 17, 2025.
35. Jonathan Mahler, Ryan Mac, and Theodore Schleifer, "How Tech Billionaires Became the G.O.P.'s New Donor Class," *The New York Times Magazine*, October 18, 2024.
36. Ava Kofman, "Curtis Yarvin's Plot Against America," *The New Yorker*, June 2, 2025.
37. Ross Douthat, "Peter Thiel and the Antichrist," *The New York Times*, June 26, 2025.

38. Peter Thiel, "The Education of a Libertarian," *Cato Unbound*, April 13, 2009.
39. Thiel, "The Education of a Libertarian."
40. Sarah Churchwell, "How Gatsby Foretold Trump's America," *Financial Times*, April 4, 2025.
41. Brooke Harrington, "The Broligarchs Are Trying to Have It Their Way," *The Atlantic*, August 4, 2024; Agatha Bordonaro, "Peering Through the Clouds: The Murky World of Offshore Finance," Faculty of Arts and Sciences, Dartmouth College, September 25, 2024.
42. Nicolas Truong, "The Reactionary International: How Three Ideological Families Are United in Hating Progressivism," *Le Monde*, April 13, 2025.
43. Joshua Chaffin and Zusha Elinson, "The Ideological Gurus Battling for the Soul of Trump World," *The Wall Street Journal*, May 9, 2025; Kofman, "Curtis Yarvin's Plot Against America."
44. David Marchese, "Curtis Yarvin Says Democracy Is Done. Powerful Conservatives Are Listening," *The New York Times Magazine*, January 18, 2025; Ray Gamache, *Gareth Jones: Eyewitness to the Holodomor* (Cardiff: Welsh Academic Press, 2016); Adam Hochschild, *King Leopold's Ghost: A Story of Greed, Terror, and Heroism in Colonial Africa* (New York: Houghton Mifflin, 1999); Fintan O'Toole, "What Made the Irish Famine So Deadly," *The New Yorker*, March 10, 2025.
45. Kofman, "Curtis Yarvin's Plot Against America."
46. Kofman, "Curtis Yarvin's Plot Against America."
47. Kofman, "Curtis Yarvin's Plot Against America."
48. Kofman, "Curtis Yarvin's Plot Against America."
49. Katherine Stewart, *Money, Lies, and God: Inside the Movement to Destroy American Democracy* (New York: Bloomsbury, 2024).
50. Jason Wilson, "'Red Caesarism' Is Rightwing Code—and Some Republicans Are Listening," *The Guardian*, October 1, 2023.
51. Stewart, *Money, Lies, and God*, 42.
52. Stewart, *Money, Lies, and God*, 87.
53. Stewart, *Money, Lies, and God*, 143.
54. Angela Giuffrida, "City of Love? Christian Right Congress in Verona Divides Italy," *The Guardian*, March 29, 2019.
55. "John Eastman," World Congress of Families XIII, https://wcfverona.org/en/eastman-1/, February 27, 2019.
56. Stewart, *Money, Lies, and God*, 98, 117.
57. Michael S. Schmidt and Maggie Haberman, "The Lawyer Behind the Memo on How Trump Could Stay in Office," *The New York Times*, October 2, 2021; Hannah Grabenstein, "Who Is John Eastman and Why Is He Important to the Jan. 6 Hearings?," *PBS NewsHour*, June 16, 2022.
58. Schmidt and Haberman, "The Lawyer Behind the Memo."

Section III: Overthrow

1. Omar El Akkad, *One Day, Everyone Will Have Been Against This* (New York: Knopf, 2025), 5.

Chapter 9: Shadow Army

1. Jacob Silverman, *Gilded Rage: Elon Musk and the Radicalization of Silicon Valley* (New York: Bloomsbury, 2025), 176.
2. "Are You Ready? The Corporate Transparency Act Becomes Effective Jan 1, 2024," Thomson Reuters Tax and Accounting, October 19, 2023.
3. Leigh-Alexandra Basha, Daniel J. Bell, and Sebastian Orozco Segrera, "Congress Passes the Corporate Transparency Act—Overriding Presidential Veto," McDermott Will & Schulte, December 15, 2020.
4. "Memorandum on Establishing the Fight Against Corruption as a Core United States Security Interest," The White House, June 3, 2021.
5. "Fact Sheet: U.S. Strategy on Countering Corruption," The White House, December 6, 2021.
6. "Attorney General Merrick B. Garland Announces Launch of Task Force KleptoCapture," press release, U.S. Department of Justice, March 2, 2022.
7. "Securing America's Elections: Oversight of Government Agencies," statement of Nikki Floris, FBI, before the House Judiciary Committee, October 22, 2019.
8. "DOJ and SEC Enforcement Actions per Year," Foreign Corrupt Practices Act Clearinghouse, Stanford Law School, https://fcpa.stanford.edu/statistics-analytics.html, accessed November 29, 2025.
9. "Congress Passes Landmark Law to Criminally Prosecute Corrupt Foreign Leaders," Transparency International U.S., December 14, 2023.
10. "Countering Russia's Kleptocrats," Transparency International, https://www.transparency.org/en/campaigns/countering-russia-kleptocrats-after-ukraine, accessed November 29, 2025; "USA PATRIOT Act," Financial Crimes Enforcement Network, https://www.fincen.gov/resources/statutes-and-regulations/usa-patriot-act, accessed November 29, 2025.
11. "U.S. Department of the Treasury, IRS Announce $1.3 Billion Recovered from High-Income, High-Wealth Individuals Under Biden-Harris Inflation Reduction Act Initiatives," press release, Department of the Treasury, September 6, 2024.
12. "Trends in the Internal Revenue Service's Funding and Enforcement," Congressional Budget Office, publication 56467, July 2020.
13. "The IRS Is Getting $80 Billion. For What?," *1A*, NPR, September 7, 2022.
14. Phil Swagel, "The Effects of Increased Funding for the IRS," Congressional Budget Office, publication 57444, September 2, 2021.
15. Howard Gleckman, "The War on the IRS," Tax Policy Center, Urban Institute and Brookings Institution, December 16, 2014.

16. "IRS Announces Sweeping Effort to Restore Fairness to Tax System with Inflation Reduction Act Funding," news release, Internal Revenue Service, September 8, 2023.
17. Timothy Noah, "How Joe Biden Made the IRS Great Again," *The New Republic*, March 6, 2024.
18. David Cay Johnston, "The IRS Finally Takes the Gloves Off," *The Nation*, March 1, 2024.
19. Fatima Hussein, "IRS Collects Milestone $1 Billion in Back Taxes from High-Wealth Taxpayers," Associated Press, July 11, 2024.
20. German Lopez, "Conspiracy Theories: How More Funding for the I.R.S. Became a Political Firestorm," *The New York Times*, August 26, 2022.
21. Joan E. Greve, "Armed . . . Auditors? The IRS Becomes the Latest Target of GOP Misinformation," *The Guardian*, August 19, 2022.
22. "The Revenue and Distributional Effects of IRS Funding," The Budget Lab, Yale University, March 13, 2025.
23. "Empowering the IRS: Understanding the Full Potential of the Inflation Reduction Act's Historic Investment in the Internal Revenue Service," The White House, February 8, 2024.
24. "What Is a Wealth Tax?," Tax Policy Center, Urban Institute and Brookings Institution, January 2024.
25. Benjamin Wallace-Wells, "The French Economist Who Helped Invent Elizabeth Warren's Wealth Tax," *The New Yorker*, October 9, 2019.
26. Wallace-Wells, "The French Economist."
27. "Senator Bernie Sanders' Wealth Tax: Budgetary and Economic Effects," Penn Wharton Budget Model, Wharton School, University of Pennsylvania, January 23, 2020.
28. Huaqun Li and Karl Smith, "Analysis of Sen. Warren and Sen. Sanders' Wealth Tax Plans," Tax Foundation, January 28, 2020.
29. Thomas Kaplan, "Bernie Sanders Proposes a Wealth Tax: 'I Don't Think That Billionaires Should Exist,'" *The New York Times*, September 24, 2019.
30. Anthony Effinger, "County Commissioner Brings Expert on Millionaire Migration into Preschool Debate," *Willamette Week*, August 6, 2025.
31. Emma Agyemang, "The Problem with Taxing the Rich," *Financial Times*, September 16, 2025.
32. Franklin D. Roosevelt, "Address at Worcester, Mass.," October 21, 1936, American Presidency Project, University of California, Santa Barbara.
33. Vladislav M. Zubok, *Collapse: The Fall of the Soviet Union* (New Haven, CT: Yale University Press, 2021).
34. Aleksandr V. Gevorkyan, *Transition Economies: Transformation, Development, and Society in Eastern Europe and the Former Soviet Union* (New York: Routledge, 2018).

35. David E. Hoffman, *The Oligarchs: Wealth and Power in the New Russia* (New York: PublicAffairs, 2011).
36. Mykhailo Minakov, "The War and the Future of Ukraine's Oligarchy," Kennan Institute, Wilson Center, August 3, 2022.
37. Kira Rudik, "Ukraine's Anti-Oligarch Law: President Zelenskyy's Populist Power Grab?," Atlantic Council, November 15, 2021.
38. Anders Aslund, "The Maidan and Beyond: Oligarchs, Corruption, and European Integration," *Journal of Democracy*, July 2014.
39. Etienne Bouche, "Another Ukraine: A Disinformation Platform Run by an Exiled Ukrainian Oligarch in Russia," France24, February 29, 2024.
40. "Kolomoyskiy, Once Powerful Ukraine Tycoon, Loses $1.9 Billion Fraud Case," Radio Free Europe/Radio Liberty, July 30, 2025.
41. "Ukrainian Businessman Arrested in Austria on U.S. International Corruption Conspiracy Charges," press release, United States Attorney's Office, Northern District of Illinois, March 14, 2015.
42. Matthias Williams and Natalia Zinets, "Comedian Faces Scrutiny over Oligarch Ties in Ukraine Presidential Race," Reuters, April 1, 2019.
43. Mykola Stetsenko, "Corruption in Ukraine: Myths and Reality," Just Security, June 13, 2024.
44. "Ukrainian President Signs 'Anti-Oligarch Law,'" Radio Free Europe/Radio Liberty, November 5, 2021.
45. Mykhailo Minakov, "The Paradox of De-Oligarchization," Kennan Institute, Wilson Center, June 27, 2023.
46. "President Immediately Signed the Anti-Oligarchic Law Passed by the Verkhovna Rada," Office of the President of Ukraine, November 5, 2021.
47. Andriy Yermak, "De-Oligarchization of Ukraine Is President Zelenskyy's Top Priority," Atlantic Council, November 8, 2021.
48. Andrew Roth, "Who Is Viktor Medvedchuk and Why Does His Arrest Matter to the Kremlin?," *The Guardian*, April 13, 2022.
49. Simon Shuster, "The Untold Story of the Ukraine Crisis," *Time*, February 2, 2022.
50. Bogdan Kochubey, "Zelenskiy Strips Putin Ally Medvedchuk, Three Others of Ukrainian Citizenship," Reuters, January 11, 2023.
51. Igor Burdyga, "The Rise and Fall of Putin's Man in Ukraine," Open Democracy, July 26, 2022.
52. Eugene Finkel, *Intent to Destroy: Russia's Two-Hundred-Year Quest to Dominate Ukraine* (New York: Basic Books, 2024).
53. "How Putin Came to Hate Ukraine: An Investigation into How the Russian President Came to the Idea of War with Ukraine" (in Russian), *Verstka Media*, April 25, 2023.
54. Alessandra Lewis, "Russia's Kleptocracy: Domestic Consequences of Corruption," The Borgen Project, August 17, 2025.

Chapter 10: Firepower

1. Shehan Karunatilaka, *The Seven Moons of Maali Almeida* (New York: W. W. Norton, 2022), 70.
2. Bess Levin, "Further Evidence Emerges the Saudis Did Not Pay Jared Kushner Billions Because They Thought He Was an Investing Genius," *Vanity Fair*, April 2022.
3. Ken Klippenstein, "Jared Kushner Flaunted His Influence with Saudi Arabia, Russia in Pitch to Investors," *The Intercept*, April 18, 2022.
4. Klippenstein, "Jared Kushner Flaunted His Influence."
5. "Report: PIF's LIV Golf Investment Nearing $5 Billion," Reuters, May 5, 2025; Matthew Futterman, "Saudi Arabia's New $1 Billion Proposal and the Battle to Control Tennis," *The Athletic*, March 13, 2024; Peter Grant and Eliot Brown, "Saudi Fund Invests Hundreds of Millions in Proposed NYC Skyscraper," *The Wall Street Journal*, July 7, 2025; Adam Lowenstein, "The American PR Firm Helping Saudi Arabia Clean Up Its Act," *The Guardian*, December 22, 2022; Sheelah Kolhatkar, "McKinsey's Work for Saudi Arabia Highlights Its History of Unsavory Entanglements," *The New Yorker*, November 1, 2018; Eli Tan, "Saudi Money Makes a Big Splash in Video Games," *The New York Times*, July 12, 2024; Adam Coogle, "Saudi Arabia Uses Celebrities to Whitewash Abuses," Human Rights Watch, December 19, 2020; Nirmal Narayanan, "Saudi Arabia, Boeing Agree Deal on Advanced Air Mobility," Arab News, September 22, 2025; Hadeel Al Sayegh, "Saudi's Kingdom Holding Buys $450 Mln Stake in Citigroup from Alwaleed," Reuters, November 29, 2023; Alex Weprin, "Saudi Arabia's Investment Fund Adds Disney and Facebook to Holdings," *Hollywood Reporter*, May 15, 2020.
6. "What Can You Be Flogged For in Saudi Arabia?," BBC, January 16, 2015; "Saudi Woman Imprisoned for Tweeting in Support of Women's Rights Released After Four-Year Ordeal," Amnesty International, February 10, 2025. Not that everyone was necessarily happy with their decisions; as golfer Phil Mickelson said, the Saudis are "scary motherfuckers to get involved with"—but that didn't stop Mickelson from helping spearhead the Saudi investments in the golf industry. Ewan Murray, "Phil Mickelson's Spectacular Fall and Golf's Infighting over Saudi Riches," *The Guardian*, February 26, 2022.
7. David D. Kirkpatrick and Kate Kelly, "Before Giving Billions to Jared Kushner, Saudi Investment Fund Had Big Doubts," *The New York Times*, April 10, 2022.
8. Kirkpatrick and Kelly, "Before Giving Billions to Jared Kushner."
9. Klippenstein, "Jared Kushner Flaunted His Influence."
10. Klippenstein, "Jared Kushner Flaunted His Influence."
11. Mary Papenfuss, "Saudis Give $2 Billion to Jared Kushner's Fund After Cozy Trump Ties: Report," Yahoo, April 11, 2022.
12. Ryan Bort, "Gee, Wonder Why Mohammed Bin Salman Personally Intervened to Give Jared Kushner $2 Billion," *Rolling Stone*, April 11, 2022.

13. Kirkpatrick and Kelly, "Before Giving Billions to Jared Kushner."
14. Kirkpatrick and Kelly, "Before Giving Billions to Jared Kushner."
15. Youssef M. Ibrahim, "Qaddafi Terms the $220,000 Given Billy Carter a Loan Tied to Business," *The New York Times*, June 27, 1981; Ethan Trex, "A Brief History of Billy Beer," *Mental Floss*, October 24, 2010.
16. Jake Tapper and Alex Thompson, *Original Sin: President Biden's Decline, Its Cover-Up, and His Disastrous Choice to Run Again* (New York: Penguin, 2025); Kenneth P. Vogel, *Devils' Advocates: The Hidden Story of Rudy Giuliani, Hunter Biden, and the Washington Insiders on the Payrolls of Corrupt Foreign Interests* (New York: William Morrow, 2025); Casey Michel, "The Emerging Artistry of Hunter Biden," *The Atlantic*, September 22, 2021.
17. Levin, "Further Evidence Emerges."
18. Eric Lipton, Jonathan Swan, and Maggie Haberman, "As Kushner's Investment Firm Steps Out, the Potential Conflicts Are Growing," *The New York Times*, April 9, 2024.
19. David Catanese, "In His New Book, Kentucky Rep. James Comer Says He Had Choice Words for Trump Relative," McClatchy DC, January 23, 2025.
20. Mandy Taheri, "Jared Kushner Says $1.5Bn from Qatar, UAE Came 'Irrespective' of Trump Win," *Newsweek*, December 22, 2024.
21. Gillian Tan, "Kushner's Affinity Gets Additional $1.5 Billion from Qatar, Abu Dhabi's Lunate," Bloomberg, December 20, 2024.
22. "Kushner's Affinity's Assets Jump to $4.8 Billion After Gulf Cash Injection," Reuters, March 28, 2025.
23. Antoine Gara, James Fontanella-Khan, Marton Dunai, and David Sheppard, "What Jared Kushner Did Next," *Financial Times*, February 3, 2025. As one SEC filing declared, only 1 percent of the funds placed with Kushner came from domestic sources—all other funding came from non-American sources; Lipton, Swan, and Haberman, "As Kushner's Investment Firm Steps Out"; SEC Form ADV for A Fin Management LLC, March 28, 2024, https://static01.nyt.com/newsgraphics/documenttools/5e7a823cdb42ea30/13b10bcc-full.pdf#page=8.
24. "Wyden Investigation of Kushner Firm Continues; New Letter Outlines Affinity Partners' Fee Structure, Lack of Return to Investors, Questionable Deals with Foreign Governments," news release, United States Senate Committee on Finance, September 25, 2024.
25. Jon Levine, "Hunter Biden Almost Certainly Broke Foreign Lobbying Laws: Experts," *New York Post*, July 23, 2022.
26. "Membership," United States Senate Committee on Finance, https://www.finance.senate.gov/about/membership, accessed November 29, 2025.
27. "Wyden, Raskin Call for Department of Justice to Appoint a Special Counsel to Investigate Jared Kushner for Acting as an Unregistered Foreign Agent," press release, House Committee on Oversight and Government Reform: Democrats, October 24, 2024.

28. Ron Wyden, letter to Lauren Key, A Fin Management LLC, June 12, 2024, https://www.finance.senate.gov/imo/media/doc/chairman_wyden_to_fin_management_on_kushner_firm_paymentspdf.pdf.
29. "Wyden Probes Kushner Firm Payments from Gulf States, Potential FARA Loophole," news release, United States Senate Committee on Finance, June 12, 2024.
30. Ron Wyden, letter to Chad Mizelle, Affinity Partners, September 24, 2024, https://www.finance.senate.gov/imo/media/doc/chairman_wyden_to_affinity_partnerspdf.pdf.
31. Ron Wyden, letter to Chad Mizelle.
32. Eliot Brown, Vivian Salama, and Deborah Acosta, "Jared and Ivanka's Excellent Adventure," *The Wall Street Journal*, October 4, 2024.
33. Sharon Wrobel, "Jared Kushner's Saudi-Backed Private Equity Fund Clinches First Investment in Israel," *Times of Israel*, September 6, 2023; Ingrid Lunden, "EGYM, the Munich-Based Smart Fitness Startup, Raises $225M from Jared Kushner's Affinity Partners," *TechCrunch*, July 5, 2023.
34. Aram Roston and Alexandra Ulmer, "Exclusive: Democratic Lawmakers Request Probe into Kushner After Reuters Saudi Report," Reuters, October 24, 2024.
35. "Wyden, Raskin Call."
36. "Wyden, Raskin Call."
37. Interview with author.
38. "Private Investment Funds Are a High Risk for Money Laundering: Advisers Should Know Who's Investing," Transparency International U.S., May 2021.
39. "Treasury Exposes U.S. to Increased Risks of Dirty Money by Delaying, Reopening Private Investment Anti–Money Laundering Rule," FACT Coalition, July 21, 2025.
40. "U.S. Treasury Proposes Anti–Money Laundering Rule for Investment Advisers," Transparency International U.S., February 13, 2024.
41. Timothy Lloyd, "FBI Concerned over Laundering Risks in Private Equity, Hedge Funds—Leaked Document," Reuters, July 14, 2020.
42. "New GFI Report Finds Private Investment Funds Vulnerable to Money Laundering in Latin America," press release, Global Financial Integrity, December 22, 2022.
43. "The Potential Vulnerability of Alternative Investments in Hiding Assets: Hedge Funds," Rapid Response Brief, ACAMS, 2022.
44. "World Class Program," Sanabil Investments, https://www.sanabil.com/en/program/1, accessed November 29, 2025; Akela Lacy, "Saudi Arabia Owns Stake in Firm That Bought Democratic Party's Campaign Tech," *The Intercept*, April 23, 2023.
45. Becky Peterson and Kate Clark, "Saudi Arabia Discloses Ties to Andreessen Horowitz, Dozens of Other Venture Funds," *The Information*, April 3, 2023.

46. Sanabil Investments, "Our Portfolio," https://web.archive.org/web/20230404010252/https://www.sanabil.com/en/our-partners/, accessed November 29, 2025.
47. Peterson and Clark, "Saudi Arabia Discloses Ties."
48. Jonathan Guyer, "How Saudi Money Returned to Silicon Valley," *Vox*, May 1, 2023.
49. Eliot Brown and Greg Bensinger, "Saudi Money Flows into Silicon Valley—and with It, Qualms," *The Wall Street Journal*, October 16, 2018.
50. Guyer, "How Saudi Money Returned."
51. Elizabeth Lopatto, "Jeff Bezos Makes His Most Ghoulish Deal Yet," *The Verge*, May 15, 2025.
52. Biz Carson, "Saudi Arabia Wealth Fund Reveals Investments in Founders Fund, Tiger Global," Bloomberg, April 20, 2023.
53. Guyer, "How Saudi Money Returned."
54. Guyer, "How Saudi Money Returned."
55. Connie Loizos, "Andreessen Horowitz Is Now Openly Courting Capital from Saudi Arabia, Despite U.S. Strains," *TechCrunch*, April 1, 2023.
56. Maureen Farrell and Rob Copeland, "Saudi Arabia Plans $40 Billion Push into Artificial Intelligence," *The New York Times*, March 19, 2024.

Chapter 11: When You're a Billionaire and Just Don't Give a Fuck

1. Quoted in Robert B. Reich, *Reason: Why Liberals Will Win the Battle for America* (New York: Knopf, 2004), 11.
2. American Ethane website, https://www.americanethane.com, accessed November 29, 2025.
3. "CEO John Houghtaling," https://www.americanethane.com/ceo-john-houghtaling/, accessed November 29, 2025; "American Ethane CEO John Houghtaling at Signing Ceremony Witnessed by President Donald Trump and President Xi Jinping in Beijing," American Ethane, April 17, 2017.
4. "Supplementary Statement of Reasons of Commissioner Ellen L. Weintraub," in the Matter of American Ethane Co., LLC, et al., MUR 7491, Federal Election Commission, October 28, 2022, https://www.fec.gov/files/legal/murs/7491/7491_34.pdf.
5. "Second General Counsel's Report," in the Matter of American Ethane Co., LLC, et al., MUR 7401, Federal Election Commission, https://www.fec.gov/files/legal/murs/7491/7491_20.pdf, accessed November 29, 2025; Luke Harding, "Former Putin Adviser Has Secret Investment in U.S. Energy Firm Praised by Trump," *The Guardian*, July 10, 2018; Mike McIntire, "Billionaire Backer of Maria Butina Had Russian Security Ties," *The New York Times*, September 21, 2018; Mike Soraghan, "U.S. Ethane Exporter Linked to Russian Owners and Spy Case," E&E News by Politico, August 1, 2018; Paul MacInnes, "UK 'Fully Prepared' to Take Roman Abramovich to Court over

Frozen £2.5bn," *The Guardian*, June 2, 2025; "Abramovich and Deripaska Among 7 Oligarchs Targeted in Estimated £15 Billion Sanction Hit," press release, UK Foreign, Commonwealth and Development Office, March 10, 2022.

6. "Supplementary Statement of Reasons of Commissioner Ellen L. Weintraub."
7. Dan Friedman, "Russians Used a U.S. Firm to Funnel Funds to GOP in 2018. Dems Say the FEC Let Them Get Away with It," *Mother Jones*, October 30, 2022.
8. "Supplementary Statement of Reasons of Commissioner Ellen L. Weintraub."
9. Saurav Ghosh, "The FEC Is Allowing Foreign Money to Influence Our Elections," Campaign Legal Center, November 10, 2022.
10. Friedman, "Russians Used a U.S. Firm to Funnel Funds."
11. Ewan Palmer, "Mike Johnson's Campaign Contributions from Company Tied to Russia," *Newsweek*, October 27, 2023.
12. Friedman, "Russians Used a U.S. Firm to Funnel Funds."
13. Friedman, "Russians Used a U.S. Firm to Funnel Funds."
14. "Statement of Reasons of Chairman Allen Dickerson and Commissioners Sean J. Cooksey and James E. 'Trey' Trainor, III," in the Matter of American Ethane Co., LLC, et al., MUR 7491, Federal Election Commission, October 27, 2022.
15. U.S. Congress, "Foreign Money and U.S. Campaign Finance Policy," IF10697, March 25, 2019, https://www.congress.gov/crs_external_products/IF/HTML/IF10697.web.html#:~:text=FECA%20bars%20foreign%20nationals%20from,30121(a)(1)).
16. U.S. Congress, "Foreign Money and U.S. Campaign Finance Policy"; Krista Gesaman, "Should Foreign Corporations Spend Money on U.S. Political Candidates?," *Newsweek*, January 22, 2010.
17. Michael Sozan, "Ending Foreign-Influenced Corporate Spending in U.S. Elections," Harvard Law School Forum on Corporate Governance, December 6, 2019.
18. Sozan, "Ending Foreign-Influenced Corporate Spending in U.S. Elections."
19. "What Supporters Are Saying About the *Get Foreign Money Out of U.S. Elections Act*," Office of Rep. Jamie Raskin, https://raskin.house.gov/_cache/files/a/5/a5ab3124-2583-497f-881b-1da35ed5f019/ACC69975E7AE41E21C53B60CAFC00A0F.get-foreign-money-out-of-u.s.-elections-act-stakeholder-quotes.pdf, accessed November 29, 2025.
20. "The World's Biggest Enablers of Financial Secrecy," Financial Secrecy Index by the Tax Justice Network, last updated June 3, 2025, https://fsi.taxjustice.net.
21. Sozan, "Ending Foreign-Influenced Corporate Spending in U.S. Elections."
22. Albert Serna Jr. and Anna Massoglia, "Big Money, Big Stakes: 5 Things

Everyone Should Know About Money in 2024 Elections," Open Secrets, November 6, 2024.

23. Anna Massoglia, "Outside Spending on 2024 Elections Shatters Records, Fueled by Billion-Dollar 'Dark Money' Infusion," Open Secrets, November 5, 2024.
24. Serna and Massoglia, "Big Money, Big Stakes."
25. Geoffrey Morgan, "Foreigners Are Buying U.S. Stocks at Record Pace Despite Trade War," Bloomberg, September 26, 2025.
26. "Written Testimony of Chair Ellen L. Weintraub, Before the Subcommittee on National Security, Committee on Oversight and Reform, U.S. House of Representatives. May 22, 2019. Unclassified," National Security Archive, https://nsarchive.gwu.edu/media/20074/ocr.
27. "Written Testimony of Chair Ellen L. Weintraub."
28. Emma Davis, "Maine Votes to Ban Foreign Spending in Elections," *Maine Morning Star*, November 7, 2023.
29. Emma Davis, "First Circuit Rules Maine Ban on Foreign Government Election Spending Likely Unconstitutional," *Maine Morning Star*, July 14, 2025.
30. Kathryn A. Edwards and Carter C. Price, "A $2.5 Trillion Question: What If Incomes Grew Like GDP Did?," RAND, October 6, 2020.
31. Robert Anderson, "Support for Democracy in Cross-National Perspective: The Detrimental Effect of Economic Inequality," *Research in Social Stratification and Mobility* 30, no. 4 (2012): 389–402.
32. Anderson, "Support for Democracy in Cross-National Perspective."
33. Sang Kyung Lee, "Inequality and the Eroding Base of Liberal Democracy," *Social Science Research* 124 (2024): 103087.
34. Eli G. Rau and Susan Stokes, "Income Inequality and the Erosion of Democracy in the Twenty-First Century," *Proceedings of the National Academy of Sciences* 122, no. 1 (2024): e2422543121.
35. Rau and Stokes, "Income Inequality and the Erosion of Democracy."
36. Jennifer McCoy, Benjamin Press, Murat Somer, and Ozlem Tuncel, "Reducing Pernicious Polarization: A Comparative Historical Analysis of Depolarization," Carnegie Endowment for International Peace, May 5, 2022.
37. Rau and Stokes, "Income Inequality and the Erosion of Democracy."
38. Jeannine Mancini, "Jeff Bezos Spent $42 Million to Build a Massive Clock That Ticks Just Once a Year for the Next 10,000 Years—But Why?," Yahoo Finance, December 20, 2023.
39. Ryan McVinney, "Zuckerberg's Yacht: A $300 Million LAUNCHPAD for Controversy," Yachtworld, July 11, 2024.
40. Madeline Stone, "9 Crazy Facts About Larry Ellison's Hawaiian Island," *Business Insider*, September 24, 2014.
41. Russell Subiono, Savannah Harriman-Pote, Emily Tom, and Krista Rados, "A Look Inside Life on an Island Owned by Larry Ellison, the 4th Richest Person in the World," Hawaii Public Radio, July 28, 2023.

42. Sophie Alexander, "Larry Ellison's Lanai Isn't for You—or the People Who Live There," Bloomberg, June 9, 2022.
43. "Larry Ellison" (profile), *Forbes*, https://www.forbes.com/profile/larry-ellison/, accessed November 29, 2025; Melina Khan, "Forbes Releases the Richest People in America List: See Billionaires," *USA Today*, September 9, 2025.
44. Alexander, "Larry Ellison's Lanai Isn't for You."
45. Meredith Galante, "Larry Ellison Just Bought 98% of This Pristine Island in Hawaii," *Business Insider*, June 20, 2012; Alexander, "Larry Ellison's Lanai Isn't for You."
46. Malia Mattoch McManus, "Oracle CEO Ellison Dreams of Making Hawaii Island Model of Sustainability," Reuters, October 4, 2012.
47. Alexander, "Larry Ellison's Lanai Isn't for You."
48. Four Seasons Resort Lanai website, https://www.fourseasons.com/lanai/, accessed November 29, 2025.
49. Beth Gillette, "Sensei Lanai Is Basically the White Lotus—I Checked In to See If It Lives Up to the Hype," *Cosmopolitan*, April 10, 2025.
50. Alexander, "Larry Ellison's Lanai Isn't for You."
51. Alexander, "Larry Ellison's Lanai Isn't for You."
52. Alexander, "Larry Ellison's Lanai Isn't for You."
53. "Lanai Comedy," Instagram, https://www.instagram.com/lanaicomedy/.
54. Isaac Stanley-Becker and Shawn Boburg, "Oracle's Larry Ellison Joined Nov. 2020 Call About Contesting Trump's Loss," *The Washington Post*, May 20, 2022.

Chapter 12: Circus Monkeys

1. Adam Smith, *The Wealth of Nations*, ed. Edwin Cannan (New York: Modern Library, 2000), 90.
2. Eva Dou, Jeremy Page, and Josh Chin, "China's Uighur Camps Swell as Beijing Widens the Dragnet," *The Wall Street Journal*, August 17, 2018.
3. Akeda Pulati, Kamalturk Yalqun, and Adili Yilihamu, "China: Free Our Parents from Concentration Camps," *The New York Times*, August 19, 2019.
4. "China: Minority Region Collects DNA from Millions," news release, Human Rights Watch, December 13, 2017; "China Has Turned Xinjiang into a Police State Like No Other," *The Economist*, May 31, 2018.
5. Bernhard Zand, "A Surveillance State Unlike Any the World Has Seen," *Der Spiegel*, July 26, 2018.
6. Associated Press, "AP Report: China Stifling Uighur Births with IUDs, Abortion, Sterilization," PBS, June 29, 2020; "Male Chinese 'Relatives' Assigned to Uyghur Homes Co-Sleep with Female 'Hosts,'" Radio Free Asia, October 31, 2019.
7. "China Must Dismantle Its Grotesque Network of Brainwashing Factories"

(editorial), *The Washington Post*, October 20, 2018; Fred Hiatt, "In China, Every Day Is Kristallnacht," *The Washington Post*, November 3, 2019.

8. "China's Genocide Against Uyghurs," Institute for European, Russian, and Eurasian Studies, George Washington University, https://ieres.elliott.gwu.edu/project/chinas-genocide-against-uyghurs/, accessed November 29, 2025; Will Martin, "China Is Harvesting Thousands of Human Organs from Its Uighur Muslim Minority, UN Human-Rights Body Hears," *Business Insider*, September 25, 2019; "China: Draconian Repression of Muslims in Xinjiang Amounts to Crimes Against Humanity," Amnesty International, June 10, 2021; "'Break Their Lineage, Break Their Roots': China's Crimes Against Humanity Targeting Uyghurs and Other Turkic Muslims," Human Rights Watch, April 19, 2021.
9. Nathan Vanderklippe, "'It Is About Xi as the Leader of the World': Former Detainees Recount Abuse in Chinese Re-education Centres," *Globe and Mail*, July 3, 2018.
10. Austin Ramzy and Chris Buckley, "'Absolutely No Mercy': Leaked Files Expose How China Organized Mass Detention of Muslims," *The New York Times*, November 16, 2019.
11. "Mapping Xinjiang's 'Re-education' Camps," Australian Strategic Policy Institute, November 1, 2018; "Satellite Images Show China's Expansion of Muslim Detention Centers," *Weekend Edition Saturday*, NPR, August 29, 2020.
12. "Determination of the Secretary of State on Atrocities in Xinjiang," U.S. Department of State, January 19, 2021.
13. Leyland Cecco, "Canada Votes to Recognize China's Treatment of Uighur Population as Genocide," *The Guardian*, February 22, 2021; Reuters, "Dutch Parliament Becomes Second in a Week to Accuse China of Genocide in Xinjiang," CNN, February 26, 2021; "French Lawmakers Officially Recognise China's Treatment of Uyghurs as 'Genocide,'" France24, January 20, 2022.
14. "Exclusive: VW Buckles After Years of Pressure to Sell Up in Xinjiang," Reuters, November 27, 2024.
15. "China Canceled H&M. Every Other Brand Needs to Understand Why," Bloomberg, March 14, 2022; Natalie Sherman, "China Probes Calvin Klein over Xinjiang Cotton," BBC, September 25, 2024; Keith Bradsher, "China to Investigate U.S. Retailer, Sending a Message over Xinjiang," *The New York Times*, September 24, 2024.
16. "Tesla Showroom in China's Xinjiang Region Blasted by Rights Groups," Reuters, January 4, 2022.
17. Curtis Bunn, "Teslas Were a Symbol of Progressive Values. Now Some Progressives Are Ditching the Cars," NBC News, March 17, 2025.
18. Louise Perry, "How History Will Remember Elon Musk," *The New York Times*, June 3, 2025.

19. Danielle Chemtob, "Tesla's China Reliance Poses a Major Conflict for Musk," *Forbes*, February 7, 2025.
20. Mara Hvistendahl, Jack Ewing, and John Liu, "A Pivot to China Saved Musk. It Also Binds Him to Beijing," *The New York Times*, March 27, 2024.
21. Mathias Döpfner, "Elon Musk Reveals Tesla's Plan to Be at the Forefront of a Self-Driving Car Revolution—and Why He Wants to Be Buried on Mars," *Business Insider*, December 5, 2020.
22. Shawn Langlois, "'China Rocks!'—The U.S., Not So Much, According to Elon Musk," MarketWatch, August 2, 2020.
23. Michelle Toh, "Elon Musk Praises China's 'Economic Prosperity' on 100th Anniversary of Chinese Communist Party," CNN, July 1, 2021.
24. Theo Wayt, "Elon Musk Writes Column for Chinese Censorship Agency's Magazine," *New York Post*, August 15, 2022; Yang Liu, "Elon Musk's Article in China Cyberspace, Exclusive Digital Version and Translation," Beijing Channel, August 13, 2022.
25. Alex Kirshner, "Heartbreaking: Elon Musk Just Made a Great Point About Free Speech," *Slate*, April 25, 2025.
26. Arlene Getz, "Special Report: In Record Year, China, Israel, and Myanmar Are World's Leading Jailers of Journalists," Committee to Protect Journalists, January 16, 2025; "Global: Executions Soar to Highest Number in Almost a Decade," Amnesty International, May 29, 2024.
27. Joe Walsh, "Tesla Criticized for Opening Showroom in China's Controversial Xinjiang Region," *Forbes*, January 3, 2022.
28. CAIR National (@CAIRNational), "By doing business in China's Xinjiang Province, where millions of #Uyghur Muslims are being held in concentration camps and forced labor facilities, Tesla is supporting genocide. Elon Musk must close Tesla's Xinjiang showroom," X, posted January 3, 2022, https://x.com/CAIRNational/status/1478184977535844353.
29. Walsh, "Tesla Criticized for Opening Showroom."
30. Walter Isaacson, *Elon Musk* (New York: Simon & Schuster, 2023), 570.
31. Isaacson, *Elon Musk*, 570.
32. Theron Mohamed, "Elon Musk Just Spent $1 Billion on Tesla Shares. He'll Have to Spend a Lot More to Ramp Up His Control," *Business Insider*, September 15, 2025; Michelle Chapman, "Musk Is Getting Millions of Tesla Shares Worth About $29 Billion After Judge Ordered His Pay Package Revoked," PBS, August 4, 2025.
33. Grace Dean, "What Is Elon Musk's Net Worth? Find Out the Astonishing Wealth of the Tech CEO," *Business Insider*, July 25, 2023; Robert Frank, "Most of Elon Musk's Fortune Now Comes from His Private Companies," CNBC, September 11, 2025.
34. Joshua Keating, "Are Elon Musk's China Ties a National Security Risk?," *Vox*, March 21, 2025.

35. Selina Cheng and Raffaele Huang, "Why Musk Now Needs China More Than It Needs Him," *The Wall Street Journal*, April 30, 2024; Mara Hvistendahl, "How Elon Musk Became 'Kind of Pro-China,'" *The New York Times*, March 27, 2024.
36. Andrew Kaczynski, "Before DOGE, Ramaswamy Spent Years Attacking Musk for Ties to China," CNN, December 4, 2024.
37. Dolkun Isa, interview with author.
38. "Elon Musk: Tesla Criticised After Opening Xianjiang Showroom," BBC, January 3, 2022.
39. Kirsten Grind and Megan Twohey, "On the Campaign Trail, Musk Juggled Drugs and Family Drama," *The New York Times*, May 30, 2025.
40. Ali Swenson and Chris Megerian, "Elon Musk Uses His X Ownership to Be a Mouthpiece for Trump Narratives and His White House Position to Push His Priorities," PBS, February 6, 2025.
41. Yaroslav Trofimov, Micah Maidenberg, and Drew FitzGerald, "Ukraine Leans on Elon Musk's Starlink in Fight Against Russia," *The Wall Street Journal*, July 16, 2022; Isaacson, *Elon Musk*, 429.
42. Isaacson, *Elon Musk*, 430; Cade Metz, "Elon Musk Backtracks, Saying His Company Will Continue to Fund Internet Service in Ukraine," *The New York Times*, October 15, 2022.
43. Alexander Vindman, *The Folly of Realism: How the West Deceived Itself About Russia and Betrayed Ukraine* (New York: PublicAffairs, 2025).
44. Isaacson, *Elon Musk*, 430; Anne Applebaum, "What Russia Got by Scaring Elon Musk," *The Atlantic*, September 11, 2023.
45. Timothy Snyder, "Elon Musk Likes to Think He Saved Us from Armageddon. He's Just Brought It Closer," *The Guardian*, September 17, 2023.
46. Isaacson, *Elon Musk*, 430–431.
47. "Putin's Politics of the Sacred and His Claim on Kyiv," seminar, Davis Center, Harvard University, March 6, 2024, https://daviscenter.fas.harvard.edu/events/putins-politics-sacred-and-his-claim-kyiv.
48. Inci Bowman, Valeri Kalabugin, and Alevtina Sedochenko, "Ethnic Composition of Crimea," International Committee for Crimea, August 12, 1999; Mark A. Green, "Crimean Tatars and Russification," *Stubborn Things* (blog), Wilson Center, September 13, 2022.
49. "The December 1, 1991, Referendum/Presidential Election in Ukraine," Commission on Security and Cooperation in Europe, 1992.
50. "Public Opinion Survey Residents of the Autonomous Republic of Crimea, May 16–30, 2013," International Republican Institute, October 20, 2013.
51. "History of the Creeping Annexation of Crimea: 2004–2010," Center for Countering Disinformation, March 14, 2023.
52. Isaacson, *Elon Musk*, 431.

53. Megan Fisher and Vitaly Shevchenko, "Ukraine Hits HQ of Russia's Symbolic Black Sea Navy," BBC, September 22, 2023.
54. Peter Dickinson, "Russia's Retreat from Crimea Makes a Mockery of the West's Escalation Fears," Atlantic Council, July 16, 2024.
55. Casey Michel, "Russia's Crimean Red Line Has Been Erased," *Foreign Policy*, October 4, 2023.
56. "War Has Arrived in Crimea," *The Economist*, September 25, 2023.
57. Isaacson, *Elon Musk*, 431.
58. Associated Press, "Elon Musk's Peace Plan for Ukraine Draws Condemnation from Zelenskyy," NPR, October 4, 2022.
59. "Ukraine Votes to Abandon Neutrality, Set Sights on NATO," Radio Free Europe/Radio Liberty, December 23, 2014.
60. David Ingram, "Musk Suggests Ukraine Should Cede Crimea, Draws Rebuke from Zelenskyy," NBC News, October 3, 2022.
61. Kelly Garrity, "Ukrainian Officials and Allies Rail Against Elon Musk Tweet," *Politico*, October 3, 2022.
62. Michelle Nichols, "Musk and Zelenskiy in Twitter Showdown over Billionaire's Ukraine Peace Plan," Reuters, October 3, 2022.
63. Thomas Grove, Warren P. Strobel, Aruna Viswanatha, Gordon Lubold, and Sam Schechner, "Elon Musk's Secret Conversations with Vladimir Putin," *The Wall Street Journal*, October 25, 2024.
64. Grove et al., "Elon Musk's Secret Conversations."
65. Akanksha Sharma and Michelle Toh, "Taiwan Hits Back at Elon Musk's Claim That It Is 'Part of China,'" CNN, September 14, 2023.
66. Reuters, "Elon Musk Suggests Making Taiwan a 'Special Administrative Zone' Similar to Hong Kong," *The Guardian*, October 7, 2022.
67. Lindsay Maizland and Clara Fong, "Why China-Taiwan Relations Are So Tense," Council on Foreign Relations, March 19, 2025.
68. Kathrin Hille, "Becoming Taiwan: In China's Shadow, an Island Asserts Its Identity," *Financial Times*, January 5, 2024.
69. Joyu Wang, "Taiwan Rebukes Elon Musk for Describing Island Democracy as China's Hawaii," *The Wall Street Journal*, September 14, 2023.
70. Michael Sobolik, interview with author.
71. Gerrit De Vynck, "Elon Musk Talks xAI, AI Superintelligence, Aliens and More on Twitter," *The Washington Post*, July 12, 2023.
72. Russel L. Honoré, "Elon Musk Is a National Security Risk," *The New York Times*, December 29, 2024.
73. David Ingram, "Elon Musk's X Is Boosting Election Conspiracy Theories with AI-Powered Trending Topics," NBC News, October 26, 2024.
74. Kirsten Grind, Eric Lipton, and Sheera Frenkel, "Elon Musk and SpaceX Face Federal Reviews After Violations of Security Reporting Rules," *The New York Times*, December 17, 2024.
75. Anita Kumar, "Real Estate Mogul Trump Sold Condos to Regime-Connected

Venezuela," *Politico*, August 5, 2019; Dustin Jones, "Foreign Officials Spent More Than $750,000 at Trump's D.C. Hotel, New Documents Show," NPR, November 15, 2022.

Section IV: Empire

1. F. Scott Fitzgerald, *The Great Gatsby* (New York: Scribner, 2004), 179.

Chapter 13: The Corruption Is the Point

1. Tyrell Davis, quoted in Eric Lipton, Theodore Schleifer, and Zolan Kanno-Youngs, "Trump Family's Cash Registers Ring as Financial Meltdown Plays Out," *The New York Times*, April 5, 2025.
2. "Elon Musk, Mark Zuckerberg, Jeff Bezos, and Sundar Pichai Attend Trump's Inauguration," YouTube, posted by Associated Press, January 20, 2025, https://www.youtube.com/watch?v=KU0U2ZESWvE.
3. A. Martinez and Obed Manuel, "More Billionaires Than Ever Ranked in *Forbes*' Annual List. Here Are the Top 10," *Morning Edition*, NPR, April 1, 2025.
4. "Who Are the Biggest Donors?," Open Secrets, https://www.opensecrets.org/elections-overview/biggest-donors, accessed November 30, 2025.
5. Gabrielle Canon, "Billionaires Spent Record Amounts During 2024 Federal Election—Report," *The Guardian*, April 1, 2025.
6. Josh Marcus, "Gamblers Spent More Than $3.3bn on Polymarket Betting on 2024 Presidential Election, Mostly for Trump," *The Independent*, November 5, 2024; Derek Saul, "Kamala Harris Has More Billionaires Prominently Backing Her Than Trump—Bezos and Griffin Weigh In (Updated)," *Forbes*, October 30, 2024.
7. Saul, "Kamala Harris."
8. "Who Are the Biggest Donors?," Open Secrets.
9. Alex Rogers, Eva Xiao, and Sam Learner, "Battle of the Billionaires: The Mega Rich Spending to Swing the U.S. Election," *Financial Times*, October 6, 2024.
10. Google Trends, search term "oligarchy": https://trends.google.com/trends/explore/TIMESERIES/1758745200?hl=en-U.S.&tz=240&date=all&geo=U.S.&hl=en&q=oligarchy&sni=3, accessed November 30, 2025.
11. George Washington, "Farewell Address," September 19, 1796, Founders Online; "President Dwight D. Eisenhower's Farewell Address (1961)," January 17, 1961, National Archives.
12. "Remarks by President Biden in a Farewell Address to the Nation," The White House, January 15, 2025.
13. U.S. Department of the Treasury, "Fact Sheet: U.S. Department of the Treasury Actions to Prevent and Disrupt Corruption," press release, December 11, 2023.
14. Attorney General Pam Bondi, "Total Elimination of Cartels and Transnational

Criminal Organizations," memorandum to all Justice Department employees, February 5, 2025.

15. Nick Cleveland-Stout, "'Poison' Ivy Lee, America's First Foreign Lobbying Tycoon," Responsible Statecraft, August 19, 2024.
16. Casey Michel, *Foreign Agents: How American Lobbyists and Lawmakers Threaten Democracy Around the World* (New York: St. Martin's Press, 2024); "Don't Forget. Michael Flynn Pleaded Guilty. Twice" (editorial), *The New York Times*, May 7, 2020.
17. "Paul Manafort: Ex-Trump Campaign Manager Jailed for Fraud," BBC, March 8, 2019.
18. "Former U.S. Senator Robert Menendez Sentenced to 11 Years in Prison for Bribery, Foreign Agent, and Obstruction Offenses," press release, United States Attorney's Office, Southern District of New York, January 29, 2025.
19. Attorney General Pam Bondi, "General Policy Regarding Charging, Plea Negotiations, and Sentencing," memorandum to all Justice Department employees, February 5, 2025.
20. Ben Freeman and Nick Cleveland-Stout, "Lobbyists Win: Bondi Memo Guts Foreign Meddling Law," Responsible Statecraft, February 7, 2025.
21. Ken Dilanian, "Pam Bondi Ends FBI Effort to Combat Foreign Influence in U.S. Politics," NBC News, February 6, 2025.
22. "Attorney General Memorandum Redirects U.S. Anti-Corruption Efforts Raising Questions and Concerns," Transparency International U.S., February 6, 2025.
23. Fatima Hussein and Eric Tucker, "Trump's Justice Department Ends Biden-Era Task Force Aimed at Seizing Assets of Russian Oligarchs," Associated Press, February 6, 2025.
24. Faarea Masud, "Trump Halts Prosecution of Firms Accused of Bribery Abroad," BBC, February 11, 2025.
25. Mariam Shenawy, "The U.S. Justice Department Narrows Scope of Anti-Bribery Laws," Organized Crime and Corruption Reporting Project, June 11, 2025.
26. "Pausing Foreign Corrupt Practices Act Enforcement to Further American Economic and National Security," The White House, February 10, 2025.
27. Jen Kirby, "The U.S. Has Made Its Biggest Anti-Money-Laundering Changes in Years," *Vox*, January 4, 2021.
28. "U.S. Beneficial Ownerships Information Registry Now Accepting Reports," Financial Crimes Enforcement Network, U.S. Department of the Treasury, January 1, 2024.
29. Sam Ellefson, "Treasury Department Won't Enforce Beneficial Ownership Rule Under the Corporate Transparency Act," International Consortium of Investigative Journalists, March 5, 2025.
30. Max de Haldevang, "Trump Sold $1.5 Billion of Condos to Potential Money Launderers Thanks to This Gaping Loophole," *Quartz*, July 20, 2022.

31. "Treasury Department Announces Suspension of Enforcement of Corporate Transparency Act Against U.S. Citizens and Domestic Reporting Companies," press release, U.S. Department of the Treasury, March 2, 2025.
32. Michael Stratford, "Treasury Will Delete Beneficial Ownership Data After Rule Rollback, FinCEN Chief Says," *Politico*, September 9, 2025.
33. "FinCEN Issues Proposed Rule to Postpone Effective Date of Investment Adviser Rule," Financial Crimes Enforcement Network, U.S. Department of the Treasury, September 19, 2025.
34. "Art II.S.3.3.1, Overview of Take Care Clause," Constitution Annotated, U.S. Congress, https://constitution.congress.gov/browse/essay/artII-S3-3-1/ALDE_00001160/, accessed November 30, 2025.
35. Tovia Smith, "Trump's $5 Million Gold Card Offers the Rich a Fast Lane to Residency," *Morning Edition*, NPR, June 2, 2025.
36. "Ending Corrupt Abuse of EU Golden Passports and Visas," Transparency International, https://www.transparency.org/en/campaigns/ending-corrupt-abuse-european-union-golden-passports-visas, accessed November 30, 2025.
37. "EB-5 Integrity Fund," U.S. Citizenship and Immigration Services, October 28, 2025.
38. Elena Giordano, "Trump: 'I Know Some Russian Oligarchs Who Are Very Nice People,'" *Politico*, February 26, 2025.
39. "The Trump Gold Card Is Here," https://trumpcard.gov, accessed November 30, 2025.
40. Louis Jacobson, "President Donald Trump's Tax Law Has 'Tax Breaks for Billionaires, Permanent; Tax Breaks for Everybody Else, Expire,'" PolitiFact, Poynter Institute, July 8, 2025.
41. Adam Campbell, Kaitlyn A. Blanchard, and Patrick T. Conner, "Estate Planning and Other Tax Strategies Under the One Big Beautiful Bill Act," Husch Blackwell, July 14, 2025.
42. Greg Iacurci, "House Republican Tax Bill Favors the Rich—How Much They Stand to Gain, and Why," CNBC, May 23, 2025.
43. Greg Leiserson and Brandon DeBot, "The Trump Administration's Proposed IRS Cuts Would Declare Open Season for High-End Tax Evasion and Deny Americans Modern Taxpayer Services," Tax Law Center, New York University School of Law, June 24, 2025.
44. Janet Holtzblatt, "Cutting the IRS Enforcement Budget Is a Disservice to Taxpayers," Tax Policy Center, Urban Institute and Brookings Institution, July 11, 2025.
45. Leiserson and DeBot, "The Trump Administration's Proposed IRS Cuts."
46. "The Revenue and Distributional Effects of IRS Funding," The Budget Lab, Yale University, March 13, 2025.
47. Corey Smith and Jens Heycke, "Dismantling the Justice Department Tax Division Will Cost U.S. Billions," *The Hill*, August 17, 2025.

48. Laton McCartney, *The Teapot Dome Scandal: How Big Oil Bought the Harding White House and Tried to Steal the Country* (New York: Random House, 2009).
49. Eric Lipton, "Trump Real Estate Deal in Oman Underscores Ethics Concerns," *The New York Times*, June 20, 2023; Pesha Magid, "Trump Organization Plans Second Saudi Arabian Tower in Regional Expansion," Reuters, December 12, 2024; Khanh Vu and Francesco Guarascio, "Exclusive: Fistful of Dollars and Rice for Vietnam Farmers Displaced for $1.5 Billion Trump Golf Club," Reuters, August 11, 2025; Brenna T. Smith, Peter Grant, and Daniel Kiss, "The Trump Organization Has Expanded Globally Since the 2024 Election. See Where," *The Wall Street Journal*, June 2, 2025.
50. Smith, Grant, and Kiss, "The Trump Organization Has Expanded Globally."
51. Brady Dale, "The Big Moments in Biden's Crypto Crackdown," *Axios*, November 5, 2024.
52. Peter Stone, "'Roadmap for Corruption': Trump Dive into Cryptocurrency Raises Ethics Alarms," *The Guardian*, May 25, 2025.
53. Ezra Klein, "A Democrat Who Is Thinking Differently," *The New York Times*, February 18, 2025.
54. Michelle Conlin, "Buyers of $TRUMP Meme Spent $148 Million to Win Dinner with President Trump," Reuters, May 12, 2025; Sarah N. Lynch and Chris Prentice, "U.S. Justice Dept Disbands Crypto Enforcement Team, Citing Trump Order," Reuters, April 8, 2025; Allison Morrow, "A Crypto Mogul Who Invested Millions into Trump Coins Is Getting a Reprieve on Civil Fraud Charges," CNN, February 28, 2025.
55. Eric Lipton, David Yaffe-Bellamy, Bradley Hope, Tripp Mickle, and Paul Mozur, "Anatomy of Two Giant Deals: The U.A.E. Got Chips. The Trump Team Got Crypto Riches," *The New York Times*, September 15, 2025.
56. Kat Lonsdorf, "Trump Administration Officially Accepts Jet from Qatar for Use as Air Force One," *Morning Edition*, NPR, May 21, 2025.
57. Dan Alexander, "How Truth Social and Crypto Helped Donald Trump Double His Fortune in Just One Year," *Forbes*, March 31, 2025.
58. Adam Serwer, "The Cruelty Is the Point," *The Atlantic*, October 2018.
59. "New York City Mayor Eric Adams Charged with Bribery and Campaign Finance Offenses," press release, United States Attorney's Office, Southern District of New York, September 26, 2024.
60. Aaron C. Davis and Carol D. Leonnig, "$10M Cash Withdrawl Drove Secret Probe into Whether Trump Took Money from Egypt," *The Washington Post*, August 2, 2024.
61. Dana Rubinstein and William K. Rashbaum, "Cheap Flights and Deleted Texts: 10 Takeaways from the Adams Indictment," *The New York Times*, September 26, 2024.
62. George Joseph, "'I'm Collaborating': How New York City's Mayor Gave In to Trump's Migrant Crackdown," *The Guardian*, February 21, 2025; Michael S.

Schmidt, William K. Rashbaum, Maggie Haberman, and Jonah E. Bromwich, "How the Justice Dept. Helped Sink Its Own Case Against Eric Adams," *The New York Times*, February 13, 2025; Paula Reid, Gloria Pazmino, and Eric Levenson, "NYC Mayor Eric Adams Thanks Justice Department After Prosecutors Directed to Drop Case Against Him," CNN, February 11, 2025.

63. Jonah E. Bromwich and William K. Rashbaum, "3 Adams Case Prosecutors Resign Rather Than Expres Regret to Justice Department," *The New York Times*, April 22, 2025.
64. George Joseph, "'Show Me the Money': How Eric Adams Made It to the Top—and Fell Back Down," *The Guardian*, October 2, 2024.

Chapter 14: Age of Empires

1. Harry S. Truman, diary entry, July 16, 1945, *American Experience*, PBS.
2. "Middle East Dialogues: Tarek Masoud in Conversation with Jared Kushner," YouTube, posted by Harvard's Middle East Initiative, March 7, 2024, https://www.youtube.com/watch?v=dtaIHr5S0ts&t=809s.
3. Alexandre Kateb, "The Abraham Accords After Gaza: A Change of Context," Carnegie Endowment for International Peace, April 25, 2025; Omar Rahman, "Five Reasons Why the Abraham Accords Are Ceding Ground to Arab-Iranian De-Escalation," Baker Institute for Public Policy, Rice University, July 11, 2023.
4. Mick Krever, Jomana Karadsheh, Ami Kaufman, and Abeer Salman, "Israel's Far-Right Wants to Move Palestinians Out of Gaza. Its Ideas Are Gaining Attention," CNN, January 17, 2024.
5. Patrick Wintour, "Jared Kushner Says Gaza's 'Waterfront Property Could Be Very Valuable,'" *The Guardian*, March 19, 2024; Ishaan Tharoor, "Trump's Plan for Gaza Is a Nonstarter, but It Reflects a Stark Reality," *The Washington Post*, February 6, 2025.
6. "Middle East Dialogues: Tarek Masoud in Conversation with Jared Kushner."
7. "Middle East Dialogues: Tarek Masoud in Conversation with Jared Kushner."
8. "Middle East Dialogues: Tarek Masoud in Conversation with Jared Kushner."
9. Joshua Leifer, "The Netanyahu Doctrine: How Israel's Longest-Serving Leader Reshaped the Country in His Image," *The Guardian*, November 21, 2023; David Isaac, "71% of Israelis Oppose Palestinian State; 68% Support Sovereignty in J&S; Poll," Jewish News Syndicate, February 2, 2025.
10. "Middle East Dialogues: Tarek Masoud in Conversation with Jared Kushner."
11. "Middle East Dialogues: Tarek Masoud in Conversation with Jared Kushner."
12. Sheila Ryan, "Constructing a New Imperialism: Israel and the West Bank," *MERIP Reports* 9 (1972): 3–11, 17; Tahani Mustafa, "Any Attempt to Run Gaza Like the West Bank Will Fail—and Hamas Will Benefit," *The Guardian*, December 7, 2023.
13. Luc Bronner, "In Israel, Rhetoric Dehumanizing Palestinians and Calls for Eradicating Gaza Have Become Commonplace," *Le Monde*, May 21, 2025.

14. Justin Elliott, "Jared Kushner by Day: Mideast Peace. Kushner Companies by Night: Donating to a West Bank Settlement," *ProPublica*, December 6, 2017.
15. Elliott, "Jared Kushner by Day."
16. Elliott, "Jared Kushner by Day"; Kali Robinson, "What Is U.S. Policy on the Israeli-Palestinian Conflict?," Council on Foreign Relations, July 12, 2023.
17. Robinson, "What Is U.S. Policy on the Israeli-Palestinian Conflict?"; Dan Williams and Galit Altstein, "Kushner's Affinity Gets Nod to Double Stake in Israel's Phoenix," Bloomberg, January 15, 2025; Judd Legum, "The Foreign Policy of an American," Popular Information, January 27, 2025.
18. Freddy Brewster and Katya Schwenk, "Jared Kushner May Profit from Expanded Israeli Settlements," *Jacobin*, January 18, 2025.
19. "Phoenix Financial," Who Profits Research Center, https://www.whoprofits.org/companies/company/7348?the-phoenix-holdings, accessed November 30, 2025; Brewster and Schwenk, "Jared Kushner May Profit."
20. Diana Hodali and Emad Hassan, "Kushner's Plan for Palestinians: What's (Not) in It?," Deutsche Welle, June 25, 2019.
21. Hodali and Hassan, "Kushner's Plan for Palestinians."
22. Tal Schneider, "For Years, Netanyahu Propped Up Hamas. Now It's Blown Up in Our Faces," *Times of Israel*, October 8, 2023.
23. Hodali and Hassan, "Kushner's Plan for Palestinians."
24. Seb Starcevic, "Trump: Gaza Could Be 'Better Than Monaco,'" *Politico*, October 8, 2024.
25. Karen DeYoung and Cate Brown, "Gaza Postwar Plan Envisions 'Voluntary' Relocation of Entire Population," *The Washington Post*, August 31, 2025; "The GREAT Trust: From a Demolished Iranian Proxy to a Prosperous Abrahamic Ally," https://www.washingtonpost.com/documents/f86dd56a-de7f-4943-af4a-84819111b727.pdf, accessed November 30, 2025; Judd Legum and Noel Sims, "Kushner Takes Millions from Saudis, Advises Trump on Middle East Policy," Popular Information, September 9, 2025.
26. Daniella Cheslow and Eric Bazail-Eimil, "About That Latest Gaza Riviera Plan," *Politico*, September 2, 2025.
27. Will Neal, "Trump Hands His Favorite Son-in-Law a New Job," *Daily Beast*, September 9, 2025.
28. Alexandra Ulmer, "Jared Kushner Advises from Afar as Ivanka Trump Opts Out of Role in Father's Second Term," Reuters, January 15, 2025.
29. Reuters, "Kushner Has Held Talks with MBS on U.S.-Saudi Diplomacy, Israel Normalization," *Times of Israel*, October 4, 2024.
30. Ulmer, "Jared Kushner Advises from Afar."
31. Ulmer, "Jared Kushner Advises from Afar."
32. "Trump's Twisted Move to Distract from Epstein," YouTube, posted by *Daily Beast*, August 12, 2025, https://www.youtube.com/watch?v=By6j7kp9R5k.
33. Julian Borger, "Steve Witkoff: From Property Developer to Global Spot-

light as Trump's Tough-Talking Troubleshooter," *The Guardian*, February 22, 2025.

34. Ulmer, "Jared Kushner Advises from Afar."
35. Monica Hunter-Hart and Giacomo Tognini, "How Jared Kushner's Bold Bets in the Middle East Made Him a Billionaire," *Forbes*, September 16, 2025; "Legal Analysis of the Conduct of Israel in Gaza Pursuant to the Convention on the Prevention and Punishment of the Crime of Genocide," United Nations Human Rights Council, A/HRC/60/CRP.3, September 16, 2025.
36. Casey Michel, "How Russia Became the Leader of the Global Christian Right," *Politico*, February 9, 2017.
37. Tim Mak, "NRA Was 'Foreign Asset' to Russia Ahead of 2016, New Senate Report Reveals," *All Things Considered*, NPR, September 27, 2019.
38. Seva Gunitsky, "One Word to Improve U.S. Russia Policy," *The New Republic*, April 17, 2018.
39. Daniel Johnson, "Trump Is Counting on a Quick Ukraine Peace Deal, Leaving Putin Rubbing His Hands," *The Telegraph*, April 6, 2025.
40. "'He Had a Lot to Do with This': Who Is Kirill Dmitriev, the Russian 'Interlocutor' Trump's Envoy Mentioned When He Returned from Moscow This Week?," Meduza, February 13, 2025.
41. Erin Banco, "Revealed: Jared Kushner's Private Channel with Putin's Money Man," *Daily Beast*, August 23, 2020.
42. Alexander Gabuev, Alexandra Prokopenko, and Tatiana Stanovaya, "Putin's Theories of Victory: Russia Sees Trump's Dealmaking as a Can't-Lose Proposition," *Foreign Affairs*, March 26, 2025.
43. Mikhail Zygar, "Russian Jared Kushner," *The Last Pioneer*, Substack, February 18, 2025.
44. "'He Had a Lot to Do with This.'"
45. Zygar, "Russian Jared Kushner"; Gabuev, Prokopenko, and Stanovaya, "Putin's Theories of Victory."
46. "Treasury Prohibits Transactions with Central Bank of Russia and Imposes Sanctions on Key Sources of Russia's Wealth," press release, U.S. Department of the Treasury, February 28, 2022.
47. Maya Mehrara, "Putin Congratulated Donald Trump on Win Through 'Mutual Friends': Report," *Newsweek*, November 6, 2024.
48. Zygar, "Russian Jared Kushner"; Irina Malkova, "Kirill Dmitriev: Economic Envoy, or Political Peace-Maker?," The Bell, April 15, 2025; "Who Is Mr. Dmitriev?"; "'He Had a Lot to Do with This.'"
49. Veronika Melkozerova, "Trump Administration Military Aid Halt Will Only Encourage Russia, Ukraine Warns," *Politico*, July 2, 2025.
50. Rikard Jozwiak, "Russia Wants Sanctions Lifted in Exchange for a Cease-Fire. The EU Isn't Ready to Do That," Radio Free Europe / Radio Liberty, April 1, 2025.

51. "U.S. Global Magnitzky Sanctions," Human Rights First, June 30, 2023; Ben Cardin, "Remembering Sergei Magnitzky," Commission on Security and Cooperation in Europe, November 18, 2021.
52. "U.S. Treasury Imposes Sanctions on Russian Federation President Vladimir Putin and Minister of Foreign Affairs Sergei Lavrov," press release, U.S. Department of the Treasury, February 25, 2022.
53. Michael A. Weber, "The Global Magnitzky Human Rights Accountability Act: Scope, Implementation, and Considerations for Congress," Congressional Research Service, R46981, December 3, 2021.
54. Jo Becker, Walter Bogdanich, Maggie Haberman, and Ben Protess, "Why Giuliani Singled Out 2 Ukrainian Oligarchs to Help Look for Dirt," *The New York Times*, November 25, 2019.
55. "U.S. Must Lift Sanctions Against Russia—Medvedev," TASS, September 23, 2025; Kateryna Denisova, "Russia Seeks Sanctions Relief, Resource Deal with U.S. via Negotiator Dmitriev, Zelensky Says," *Kyiv Independent*, April 10, 2025.
56. Paul Massaro, "Biden Might Stop a Sanctions Revolution," *Foreign Policy*, August 24, 2021.
57. Fatima Hussein, Matthew Lee, and Julia Frankel, "U.S. Sanctions 3 Israeli West Bank Settlers and Their Outposts for Violence Against Palestinians," PBS, March 14, 2024.
58. "Treasury Targets Organization with Ties to Violent Actions in the West Bank," press release, U.S. Department of the Treasury, November 18, 2024.
59. "Imposing Sanctions for Dispossession and Violence in the West Bank," U.S. Department of State, November 18, 2024; "Treasury Targets Organization."
60. "Executive Order on Imposing Certain Sanctions on Persons Undermining Peace, Security, and Stability in the West Bank," The White House, February 1, 2024.
61. Julia Frankel, "Jewish Population in West Bank Keeps Rising. Settlers Hope Trump Will Accelerate Growth," Associated Press, February 4, 2025.
62. "Pogromists Rule the West Bank" (editorial), *Haaretz*, April 3, 2025; Patrick Kingsley, Fatima AbdulKarim, and Natan Odenheimer, "With Arson and Land Grabs, Settler Attacks in West Bank Hit Record High," *The New York Times*, August 14, 2025.
63. Brad Brooks-Rubin, "What Just Happened: Trump's Termination of West Bank Settler Sanctions," Just Security, January 30, 2025; Brad Brooks-Rubin, "Do Sanctions Work? It Depends. Burma and the West Bank Might Be Models," Just Security, November 13, 2024.
64. Barak Ravid, "Trump Admin. Lifts Sanctions on Israeli Settlers Involved in Attacks on Palestinians," *Axios*, January 24, 2025.
65. Brooks-Rubin, "What Just Happened."
66. Alexander Cooley and Daniel Nexon, "Trump's Antiliberal Order: How

America First Undercuts America's Advantage," *Foreign Affairs*, January 7, 2025.

67. Reuters, "U.S. Removes Sanctions from Antal Rogán, Aide to Hungary's Viktor Orbán," *The Guardian*, April 15, 2025.
68. Eric Bazail-Eimil, "U.S. Sanctions Brazilian Judge for Prosecuting Trump Ally Bolsonaro," *Politico*, July 30, 2025; Ana Lankes, "The Untold Story of Bolsonaro's Weird and Wild Coup Attempt," *The Economist*, August 28, 2025.

Chapter 15: Turnkey Totalitarianism

1. *Thunderbolts*, directed by Jake Schreier, 2025.
2. "Elon Musk Spends Election Night with Trump at Mar-a-Lago," ABC News, November 6, 2024.
3. "Elon Musk Spends Election Night."
4. Julia Ingram and Steve Reilly, "Elon Musk Spends $277 Million to Back Trump and Republican Candidates," CBS News, December 6, 2024.
5. "Who Are the Biggest Donors?," 2020 cycle, Open Secrets, https://www.opensecrets.org/elections-overview/biggest-donors?cycle=2020, accessed November 30, 2025.
6. "Who Are the Biggest Donors?," 2016 cycle, Open Secrets, https://www.opensecrets.org/elections-overview/biggest-donors?cycle=2016, accessed November 30, 2025.
7. "Who Are the Biggest Donors?," 2012 cycle, Open Secrets, https://www.opensecrets.org/elections-overview/biggest-donors?cycle=2012, accessed November 30, 2025.
8. Kenneth P. Vogel, "2012: The Year of the Big Donor," *Politico*, February 1, 2012.
9. "Who Are the Biggest Donors?," Open Secrets, https://www.opensecrets.org/elections-overview/biggest-donors, accessed November 30, 2025.
10. Li Yuan, "Many Chinese See a Cultural Revolution in America," *The New York Times*, March 6, 2025.
11. Steve Inskeep, "Musk's DOGE Group Has Access to the Federal Payments System. What Does That Mean?," *Morning Edition*, NPR, February 4, 2025.
12. Stephen Young, "DOGE's Staff Firing Fiasco at the Nuclear Weapon Agency Means Everything but Efficiency," *Bulletin of the Atomic Scientists*, April 16, 2025.
13. Katherine Tangalakis-Lippert and Jack Newsham, "DOGE's Anti-DEI Drive Flagged These Programs. Only They Weren't DEI," *Business Insider*, March 11, 2025.
14. Kurtis D. Werner, "Edith Bolling Wilson: Madam President or Dutiful Wife?," Harry S. Truman Library and Museum, National Archives, https://www.trumanlibrary.gov/education/lesson-plans/edith-bolling-wilson-madam-president-or-dutiful-wife, accessed November 30, 2025.

15. Yuan Yang, "Why Musk Admires China," *Financial Times*, December 21, 2023.
16. Tipranks, "Why Big Brands Are Quietly Returning to X," March 30, 2025.
17. Peter Kafka, "Wait a Minute. Has Elon Musk Really Turned Twitter Around, After All?," *Business Insider*, March 19, 2025.
18. Nicole Narea, "Elon Musk's Secretive Government IT Takeover, Explained," *Vox*, February 5, 2025.
19. Todd Harrison, "Golden Dome Is a Trillion Dollar Gambit," War on the Rocks, September 19, 2025.
20. Mike Stone and Marisa Taylor, "Exclusive: Musk's SpaceX Is Frontrunner to Build Trump's Golden Dome Missile Shield," Reuters, April 17, 2025.
21. Stone and Taylor, "Exclusive: Musk's SpaceX Is Frontrunner."
22. Tara Copp and Anthony Izaguirre, "Trump Administration Tries to Bring Back Fired Nuclear Weapons Workers in DOGE Reversal," Associated Press, February 16, 2025.
23. Phelim Kine, "Radio Free Asia Set to Furlough Most U.S.-Based Staff Due to Government Funding Freeze," *Politico*, March 14, 2025.
24. Sean Collins and Gabrielle Berbey, "The Silencing of Voice of America," *Vox*, March 19, 2025.
25. Shaurir Ramanujan, "Reclaiming the Land of the Snows: Analyzing Chinese Settler Colonialism in Tibet," *Columbia Journal of Asia* 1, no. 2 (2022).
26. Joie Liu, "Mountains of Resistance: The Past and Present of Tibet's Quest for Independence," *Harvard International Review*, November 6, 2024.
27. Erich Schwartzel, *Red Carpet: Hollywood, China, and the Global Battle for Cultural Supremacy* (New York: Penguin, 2022).
28. Josh Rogin, "China Is Getting Away with Cultural Genocide in Tibet," *The Washington Post*, November 1, 2023; Terry Philpott, "Don't Ignore the Plight of Tibet Under the Chinese Communist Party" (letter), *The Guardian*, July 1, 2021.
29. "RFA Celebrates Its 25th Anniversary," Radio Free Asia, September 29, 2021; "Knowledge of China's Gulag Owes Much to American-Backed Radio," *The Economist*, October 24, 2019; Li Yuan, "Trump Could Hand China a 'Strategic Victory' by Silencing Voice of America," *The New York Times*, March 28, 2025.
30. Erin Hale, "Chinese State Media Revel in Demise of Voice of America, Radio Free Asia," Al Jazeera, March 19, 2025.
31. "Tibetans Express Concern About Gutting of RFA, but Say, 'We Still Hear You,'" Radio Free Asia, March 26, 2025; "Radio Free Asia Taken Off Air: Millions of People Deprived of Access to Reliable Information," Reporters Without Borders, April 4, 2025; Phelim Kine, "DOGE Targets Radio Free Asia," *Politico*, March 13, 2025.
32. "RFA Announces Mass Layoffs, Shutdown of Major Language Services," Radio Free Asia, May 2, 2025; Gyaltsen Choedrak, "The Silencing of Tibetan

Voices: Who Benefits and Who Loses from the Closure of VOA and RFA?," *Tibetan Review*, April 18, 2025.

33. Maya Yang, "More Than 500 Workers at Voice of America and Other Broadcasters to Be Laid Off," *The Guardian*, August 30, 2025.
34. "'China Is Your Daddy': Backlash Against Tibetan Student's Election Prompts Questions About Foreign Influence," CBC, February 14, 2019; "College Freedom Forum 2023," Universidad Francisco Marroquin, https://newmedia.ufm.edu/coleccion/college-freedom-forum-2023/in-search-of-tibetan-identity/, accessed November 30, 2025.
35. Chemi Lhamo, interview with author.
36. Chemi Lhamo, interview with author.
37. Phelim Kine, "Elon Musk's Attacks on a Group Long Backed by the GOP Prompt Republican Shrugs," *Politico*, February 13, 2025.
38. David Pierson and Berry Wang, "Cuts to U.S.-Backed Rights Groups Seen as a Win for China," *The New York Times*, February 14, 2025.
39. Pierson and Wang, "Cuts to U.S.-Backed Rights Groups."
40. Yuan, "Trump Could Hand China a 'Strategic Victory.'"
41. Pierson and Wang, "Cuts to U.S.-Backed Rights Groups."
42. Tsering Dolka Gurung, "Without Radio Free Asia, Who Will Expose China's Atrocities?," *The Diplomat*, April 1, 2025.
43. Michael Sobolik, interview with author.
44. Michael Sobolik, interview with author.
45. David Folkenflik, "A Bane for Tyrants Abroad, U.S.-Funded Networks Fear Fate Under Kari Lake," NPR, March 10, 2025.
46. Yuan, "Trump Could Hand China a 'Strategic Victory.'"
47. Yoko Kubota and Raffaele Huang, "China Looks to Musk as Conduit to Trump, Seeking to Ward Off Harsh Policies," *The Wall Street Journal*, November 24, 2024.
48. Max Rust and Sean McLain, "See How China Is Dominating the Global EV Market," *The Wall Street Journal*, September 17, 2025.
49. Chris Kirkham, "Exclusive: Tesla's Brand Loyalty Collapsed After Musk Backed Trump, Data Shows," Reuters, August 4, 2025; Chris Isidore, "Musk Caught in 'Code Red' Moment at Tesla," CNN, April 21, 2025; Jack Ewing, "Musk Vows to Spend Less Time in Washington as Tesla's Profit Drops 71%," *The New York Times*, April 22, 2025.
50. Ewing, "Musk Vows to Spend Less Time in Washington."
51. Isidore, "Musk Caught in 'Code Red' Moment."
52. Kubota and Huang, "China Looks to Musk as Conduit."
53. Michael Martina and David Brunnstrom, "U.S. Lawmakers Warn That China Could Use Musk to Influence Trump," Reuters, February 25, 2025.
54. Sun Yu, "Chinese Investors Privately Take Stakes in Elon Musk's Companies," *Financial Times*, March 8, 2025.

55. Joshua Kaplan and Justin Elliott, "How Elon Musk's SpaceX Secretly Allows Investment from China," *ProPublica*, March 26, 2025.
56. Kaplan and Elliott, "How Elon Musk's SpaceX Secretly Allows."
57. Yu, "Chinese Investors Privately Take Stakes."
58. Alexander Ward and Nancy A. Youssef, "Pentagon Prepared Briefing for Musk on Top Secret U.S. Weapons for China War," *The Wall Street Journal*, April 25, 2025.
59. Ward and Youssef, "Pentagon Prepared Briefing for Musk"; Alexander Ward, Nancy A. Youssef, and Annie Linskey, "Trump Says Elon Musk Won't Get Briefing on Pentagon's China War Plans," *The Wall Street Journal*, March 21, 2025.
60. Ward and Youssef, "Pentagon Prepared Briefing for Musk."
61. Josh Dawsey, Annie Linskey, Brian Schwartz, and Dana Mattioli, "Inside Elon Musk's Shock-and-Awe Months in the White House," *The Wall Street Journal*, April 4, 2025.
62. Ward, Youssef, and Linskey, "Trump Says Elon Musk Won't Get Briefing"; Michael M. Grynbaum, "Trump Attacks Reporting on Musk War Plans Meeting," *The New York Times*, March 21, 2025.
63. Michael Johnston, "The New American Hustle: Trump Is Changing Corruption—and Making It More Dangerous," *Foreign Affairs*, August 6, 2025.
64. Yang, "Why Musk Admires China."
65. Julia Angwin, "'This Is What We Were Always Scared Of': DOGE Is Building a Surveillance State," *The New York Times*, April 30, 2025.
66. Paul Ohm, "Don't Build a Database of Ruin," *Harvard Business Review*, August 23, 2012; Barton Gellman, "Inside the NSA's Secret Tool for Mapping Your Social Network," *Wired*, May 24, 2020.
67. Angwin, "'This Is What We Were Always Scared Of.'"
68. Ariane Ollier-Malaterre, "Digital Surveillance Is Omnipresent in China. Here's How Citizens Are Coping," *The Conversation*, March 13, 2024; Erin Baggott Carter and Brent Carter, "Exporting the Tools of Dictatorship: The Politics of China's Technology Transfers," *Perspective on Politics* 23, no. 3 (2025): 1089–1108.
69. Yang, "Why Musk Admires China."
70. George Orwell, *1984* (1949; New York: Plume, 2022).
71. Clare Duffy and Amy O'Kruk, "Here's How the Feud Between Elon Musk and Donald Trump Has Unfolded," CNN, July 3, 2025.

Chapter 16: We Own Everything

1. George Washington to James Warren, March 31, 1779, Founders Online.
2. Peter Baker, "In Assault on Free Speech, Trump Targets Speech He Hates," *The New York Times*, September 21, 2025.
3. Tom Dreisbach, "Criminal Records of Jan. 6 Rioters Pardoned by Trump

Include Rape, Domestic Violence," *Morning Edition*, NPR, January 30, 2025.

4. Jude Joffe-Block, Lisa Hagen, and Audrey Nguyen, "How Kash Patel Has Used Children's Books and Podcasts to Promote Conspiracy Theories," *All Things Considered*, NPR, December 10, 2024.
5. "American Marianas," *The New York Times*, February 27, 1976.
6. Tyler Dawson, "Donald Trump Should Apologize to Canada for 51st State Comments, Louisiana Lt.-Gov. Says," *National Post*, September 24, 2025.
7. Samantha Waldenberg and Michael Rios, "Trump Reiterates Threat to Retake Panama Canal 'Or Something Very Powerful' Will Happen," CNN, February 2, 2025.
8. Alexander Smith, "Trump's Plans for a 'Riviera of the Middle East' in Gaza Condemned," NBC News, February 5, 2025.
9. Hannah Demissie and Molly Nagle, "Trump Says 'We Can't' Do Without Greenland as Vance Tours Territory amid U.S. Takeover Controversy," ABC News, March 28, 2025.
10. Danica Kirka and Stefanie Dazio, "'We're Going to Get' Greenland, Trump Said in His Address. Prime Minister Says Island Isn't for Sale," PBS, March 5, 2025.
11. Conor Finnegan, "After Trump Tried to Buy Greenland, U.S. Gives Island $12M for Economic Development," ABC News, April 23, 2025.
12. Robert W. Merry, *A Country of Vast Designs: James K. Polk, the Mexican War and the Conquest of the American Continent* (New York: Simon & Schuster, 2010); Thomas Richards, *Breakaway Americas: The Unmanifest Future of the Jacksonian United States* (Baltimore: Johns Hopkins University Press, 2020); Dean L. May, *Three Frontiers: Family, Land and Society in the American West, 1850–1900* (New York: Cambridge University Press, 1997).
13. Daniel Immerwahr, *How to Hide an Empire: A History of the Greater United States* (New York: Farrar, Straus and Giroux, 2019); Warren Zimmermann, *First Great Triumph: How Five Americans Made Their Country a World Power* (New York: Farrar, Straus and Giroux, 2004); Amy S. Greenberg, *A Wicked War: Polk, Clay, Lincoln, and the 1846 Invasion of Mexico* (New York: Knopf, 2012).
14. Jon Meacham, *Thomas Jefferson: The Art of Power* (New York: Random House, 2013); Andrew Roberts, *Napoleon: A Life* (New York: Viking, 2014); Daniel Walker Howe, *What Hath God Wrought: The Transformation of America, 1815–1848* (New York: Oxford University Press, 2007); Ronald J. Jensen, *The Alaska Purchase and Russian-American Relations* (Seattle: University of Washington Press, 1975).
15. Jacob Gronholt-Pederson and Tom Little, "Greenland's Independence Gradualists Win Election amid Trump Control Pledge," Reuters, March 12, 2025.
16. Jeffrey Gettleman, Maya Tekeli, and Chris Buckley, "For Greenland's Minerals, the Harsh Reality Behind the Glittering Promise," *The New York Times*,

March 3, 2025; "Key Details of Greenland's Rich but Largely Untapped Mineral Resources," Reuters, January 13, 2025.

17. Sarah Derouin, "Greenland Is Getting a Lot of International Attention for Its Mineral Resources—but What Is Hiding Under the Ice?," BBC, January 22, 2005; Suhana Roy, "Balancing Environmental Protection with Economic Development: The Greenland Mining Dilemma," *Vermont Journal of Environmental Law* blog, April 2025.
18. Tom Perkins, "Trump Donors Eye Potential Bonanza If U.S. Succeeds with Greenland Land-Grab," *The Guardian*, April 15, 2025.
19. Perkins, "Trump Donors Eye Potential Bonanza."
20. Perkins, "Trump Donors Eye Potential Bonanza."
21. Benjamin Madley, *An American Genocide: The United States and the California Indian Catastrophe, 1846–1873* (New Haven, CT: Yale University Press, 2017); Claudio Saunt, *Unworthy Republic: The Dispossession of Native Americans and the Road to Indian Territory* (New York: W. W. Norton, 2020); T. J. Stiles, *Custer's Trials: A Life on the Frontier of a New America* (New York: Knopf, 2015); Robert V. Remini, *Andrew Jackson and His Indian Wars* (New York: Viking, 2001); Merry, *A Country of Vast Designs*; Scott W. Berg, *38 Nooses: Lincoln, Little Crow, and the Beginning of the Frontier's End* (New York: Pantheon, 2012).
22. Richard W. Maass, *The Picky Eagle: How Democracy and Xenophobia Limited U.S. Territorial Expansion* (Ithaca, NY: Cornell University Press, 2020).
23. Jean Edward Smith, *Grant* (New York: Simon & Schuster, 2001); Matthew Karp, *This Vast Southern Empire: Slaveholders at the Helm of American Foreign Policy* (Cambridge, MA: Harvard University Press, 2016); Kristofer Allerfeldt, "How the U.S. Has Tried to Annex Canada Before—and Why Some Canadians Wanted to Become American," *The Conversation*, March 10, 2025.
24. Kate Kelly, "Trump Is Eyeing Greenland. His Commerce Nominee Has Financial Ties There," *The New York Times*, January 29, 2025.
25. Zachary B. Wolf, "Trump Is Primed to Cash In on the Crypto Gold Rush He's Helping Create," CNN, September 3, 2025.
26. Rick Claypool, "Big Crypto, Big Spending: Crypto Corporations Spend an Unprecedented $119 Million Influencing Elections," Public Citizen, August 21, 2024; Jasper Goodman, "Crypto Firms Pour Millions into Trump Inauguration," *Politico*, January 17, 2025.
27. John Hyatt, "The Richest Crypto and Bitcoin Billionaires in the World 2024," *Forbes*, April 2, 2024.
28. Ali Breland, "A Peter Thiel–Linked Startup Is Courting New York Scenesters and Plotting a Libertarian Paradise," *Mother Jones*, September 7, 2023.
29. Dryden Brown, interview with author.
30. Margaux MacColl, "'I Went to Greenland to Try to Buy It': Meet the Founder Who Wants to Recreate Mars on Earth," *TechCrunch*, November 15, 2024.

31. Krista Mahr, "I Caught a Glimpse of the New World Order in Greenland," *The New York Times*, April 22, 2025.
32. Diana Roy and Jonathan Master, "What Would Greenland's Independence Mean for U.S. Interests?," Council on Foreign Relations, March 13, 2025.
33. Gil Duran, "The Most Powerful Crypto Bro in Washington Has Very Weird Beliefs," *The New Republic*, October 1, 2024; "The Digital Nation: Crypto's End Game," Praxis, September 18, 2024.
34. Chas Newkey-Burden, "Network States: The Tech Broligarchy Who Want to Create New Countries," *The Week*, April 22, 2025.
35. Duran, "The Most Powerful Crypto Bro in Washington."
36. "The Digital Nation: Crypto's End Game"; Zoë Bernard, "Welcome to Praxis: The High-Tech, High-Testosterone Eden That Will Save the World," *Vanity Fair*, June 4, 2025.
37. "The Digital Nation: Crypto's End Game."
38. "The Digital Nation: Crypto's End Game."
39. Duran, "The Most Powerful Crypto Bro in Washington."
40. Gustavo Palencia, "Honduras Top Court Declares Self-Governing ZEDE Zones Unconstitutional," Reuters, September 20, 2024.
41. Andy Vasoyan, "A Startup Linked to Peter Thiel Wants to Build the 'Next Great City' in Greenland," InsideHook, February 6, 2025.
42. Dryden W. T. Brown (@Dryden), "With Greenland, we have the opportunity to ring in a new age of expansion—this time peaceful and mutually beneficial, but no less invigorating," X, posted November 12, 2024, x.com/drydenwtbrown/status/1856424587652935850.
43. Breland, "A Peter Thiel–Linked Startup Is Courting."
44. Vasoyan, "A Startup Linked to Peter Thiel."
45. Rachel Corbett, "The For-Profit City That Might Come Crashing Down," *The New York Times*, August 28, 2024.
46. Rachael Levy and Alexandra Ulmer, "Exclusive: Greenland 'Freedom City'? Rich Donors Push Trump for a Tech Hub Up North," Reuters, April 10, 2025.
47. Joseph Bernstein, "Who Would Give This Guy Billions to Build His Own Utopia?," *The New York Times*, December 12, 2023.
48. Gil Duran, "Praxis: Tech Dystopia as the 'New America,'" Nerd Reich, October 12, 2024.
49. Levy and Ulmer, "Exclusive: Greenland 'Freedom City'?"
50. Levy and Ulmer, "Exclusive: Greenland 'Freedom City'?"
51. Praxis (@PraxisNation), "According to plan," posted December 22, 2024, X, https://x.com/praxisnation/status/1870965611314184646.
52. Miranda Bryant and Jennifer Rankin, "New Opinion Poll Shows 85% of Greenlanders Do Not Want to Join U.S.," *The Guardian*, January 28, 2025; Miranda Bryant, "Denmark Summons U.S. Diplomat over Alleged Greenland Influence Campaign," *The Guardian*, August 27, 2025.

53. Alan Taylor, *American Civil Wars: A Continental History, 1850–1873* (New York: W. W. Norton, 2024).
54. Berg, *38 Nooses*; Jeffrey Ostler, *Surviving Genocide: Native Nations and the United States from the American Revolution to Bleeding Kansas* (New Haven, CT: Yale University Press, 2019); "Shadows at Dawn," 2008, https://webhelper.brown.edu/giovi/Aravaipa/event.html; "Marias (Bear Creek) Massacre," Montana Historical Society, https://mhs.mt.gov/education/IEFA/IEFALessonPlans/Marias-Massacre, accessed November 30, 2025; Brigham D. Madsen, "Bear River Massacre," *Utah History Encyclopedia*, 1994; Madley, *An American Genocide.*
55. Levy and Ulmer, "Exclusive: Greenland 'Freedom City'?"
56. "Indigenous Peoples in Kalaallit Nunaat (Greenland)," IWGIA, https://iwgia.org/en/kalaallit-nunaat-greenland.html, accessed November 30, 2025.
57. Dryden Brown, interview with author.
58. Breland, "A Peter Thiel–Linked Startup Is Courting." Given the rank failures of Napoleon's dictatorship, the ongoing obsessions with his rule are especially bizarre. Napoleon's disastrous leadership resulted in France's embarrassing defeats in its efforts to reclaim Haiti, the sell-off of France's North American holdings for pennies on the dollar, and the spectacular immiseration and years-long occupation of France by foreign powers. Roberts, *Napoleon: A Life.*
59. Breland, "A Peter Thiel–Linked Startup Is Courting."
60. Breland, "A Peter Thiel–Linked Startup Is Courting"; John Gray, "Bronze Age Pervert Will Not Save the American Right," *New Statesman*, September 23, 2023.
61. "The Digital Nation: Crypto's End Game."
62. "Declaration of Ascent," Praxis, 2024, https://www.praxisnation.com/news/declaration-of-ascent.
63. Breland, "A Peter Thiel–Linked Startup Is Courting"; "Declaration of Ascent."
64. Bernstein, "Who Would Give This Guy Billions."
65. Breland, "A Peter Thiel–Linked Startup Is Courting."
66. Hadas Gold, "Curtis Yarvin Wants to Replace American Democracy with a Form of Monarchy Led by a 'CEO,'" CNN, May 30, 2025.
67. Ava Kofman, "Curtis Yarvin's Plot Against America," *The New Yorker*, June 2, 2025.
68. Breland, "A Peter Thiel–Linked Startup Is Courting."
69. Breland, "A Peter Thiel–Linked Startup Is Courting."
70. Bernstein, "Who Would Give This Guy Billions."
71. Peter Thiel, "The Education of a Libertarian," *Cato Unbound*, April 13, 2009.
72. Duran, "The Most Powerful Crypto Bro in Washington."
73. "The Future of Crypto with Brian Armstrong, CEO of Coinbase," YouTube, posted by Moment of Zen, August 17, 2024, https://www.youtube.com/watch?v=CQdaQr3EW8g&t=1305s.

74. "Brian Armstrong" (profile), *Forbes*, https://www.forbes.com/profile/brian-armstrong/, accessed November 30, 2025.
75. "The Digital Nation: Crypto's End Game."
76. Dryden Brown, interview with author.
77. Duran, "Praxis: Tech Dystopia as the 'New America.'"
78. Chris Cameron, "Army Bases That Honor Confederate Traitors Could Soon Be Renamed for These Heroes," *The New York Times*, July 4, 2022.

Chapter 17: Your Government Is on Trial

1. Quoted in Rachel Chrastil, *Bismarck's War: The Franco-Prussian War and the Making of Modern Europe* (New York: Basic Books, 2023), 169.
2. Robert S. La Forte, "Theodore Roosevelt's Osawatomie Speech," *Kansas Historical Quarterly* 32, no. 2 (1966): 187–200.
3. "William H. Taft Recalls Dispute with Theodore Roosevelt, 1922," Gilder Lehrman Institute of Amerian History, https://www.gilderlehrman.org/history-resources/spotlight-primary-source/william-h-taft-recalls-dispute-theodore-roosevelt-1922; "Bull Moose Party," *Encyclopedia Britannica*, accessed November 30, 2025.
4. "From the Archives: President Teddy Roosevelt's New Nationalism Speech," The White House, December 6, 2011.
5. La Forte, "Theodore Roosevelt's Osawatomie Speech."
6. La Forte, "Theodore Roosevelt's Osawatomie Speech."
7. La Forte, "Theodore Roosevelt's Osawatomie Speech."
8. "From the Archives: President Teddy Roosevelt's New Nationalism Speech."
9. "The New Nationalism," Theodore Roosevelt Center, https://theodorerooseveltcenter.org/Research/Digital-Library/Record?libID=o308460, accessed November 30, 2025.
10. "From the Archives: President Teddy Roosevelt's New Nationalism Speech."
11. "From the Archives: President Teddy Roosevelt's New Nationalism Speech."
12. "From the Archives: President Teddy Roosevelt's New Nationalism Speech."
13. "From the Archives: President Teddy Roosevelt's New Nationalism Speech."
14. "From the Archives: President Teddy Roosevelt's New Nationalism Speech."
15. "From the Archives: President Teddy Roosevelt's New Nationalism Speech."
16. "The New Nationalism," Theodore Roosevelt Association, https://www.theodoreroosevelt.org/content.aspx?page_id=22&club_id=991271&module_id=338365, accessed November 30, 2025.
17. "The New Nationalism," Theodore Roosevelt Association.
18. Adam Winkler, *We the Corporations: How American Businesses Won Their Civil Rights* (New York: Liveright, 2018).
19. Meg Matthias, "What Did We Call America's Elite Before the '1 Percent'?," *Encyclopedia Britannica*, June 13, 2025.
20. "Creating a Fair Wealth Tax," press release, Roosevelt Institute, 2021, https://rooseveltinstitute.org/press-releases/creating-a-fair-wealth-tax/.

21. "Jayapal Introduces Constitutional Amendment to Reverse Citizens United," press release, Office of Rep. Pramila Jayapal, February 13, 2025.
22. "State and Local Support," United for the People, https://united4thepeople.org/state-local/, accessed November 30, 2025; Ashley Balcerzak, "Study: Most Americans Want to Kill 'Citizens United' with Constitutional Amendment," Center for Public Integrity, May 10, 2018.
23. "From the Archives: President Teddy Roosevelt's New Nationalism Speech."
24. La Forte, "Theodore Roosevelt's Osawatomie Speech."
25. Stephen Fowler, "Bernie Sanders Is Drawing Record Crowds as He Pushes Democrats to 'Fight Oligarchy,'" *Morning Edition*, NPR, March 22, 2025.
26. Vivienne Walt, "The Wealth Tax Plans That Are Roiling New York and Paris," *The New York Times*, September 15, 2025.
27. Albert L. Willis to Gresham, February 8, 1895, https://history.state.gov/historicaldocuments/frus1895p2/d41.

Afterword

1. William Dalrymple, *The Last Mughal: The Fall of a Dynasty: Delhi, 1857* (New York: Vintage, 2008).
2. Barak Ravid, Dave Lawler, Marc Caputo, and Colin Demarest, "How Trump's 28-Point Plan for Ukraine Shocked the World," *Axios*, November 24, 2025.
3. Christo Grozev and Michael Weiss, "Made in Moscow: The 'U.S. Peace Plan' for Ukraine Was Substantially Formulated Months Ago by Kremlin Operative Kirill Dmitriev," *The Insider*, November 26, 2025.
4. Gram Slatter and Erin Banco, "Exclusive: U.S. Peace Plan for Ukraine Drew from Russian Document, Sources Say," Reuters, November 26, 2025.
5. Judd Legum, "Jared Kushner's Double Life," *Popular Information*, September 30, 2025.
6. Ray Furlong, Ljudmila Cvetkovic, and Valona Tela, "Serbian Parliament to Fast-Track Jared Kushner Property Development," RFE/RL, November 3, 2025; Julian Borger, "Serbia Secretly Agreed Deal with Jared Kushner Firm to Develop Protected Belgrade Site," *The Guardian*, November 13, 2025.
7. Ezra Klein, "The Israeli Right's Plan to Carve Up Gaza," *The New York Times*, October 28, 2025.
8. Robbie Gramer, Alexander Ward, and Lara Seligman, "How the U.S. Drafted a Russia-Friendly Peace Plan for Ukraine," *The Wall Street Journal*, November 24, 2025.
9. Grozev and Weiss, "Made in Moscow."
10. Grozev and Weiss, "Made in Moscow."
11. Ross Anderson, "The Nuclear Club Might Soon Double," *The Atlantic*, July 8, 2025.
12. "Who Attended Trump's Dinner for the Saudi Crown Prince?," *The New York Times*, November 18, 2025.

13. Andrew Roth, "Trump and Mr Bone Saw Stage Love-In as Saudi's $1tn Wipes the Bloody Slate Clean," *The Guardian*, November 18, 2025.
14. Harold Meyerson, "Ellisons Tap Saudis to Fund News Media Takeover," *The American Prospect*, November 20, 2025.
15. Lloyd Lee, Shubhangi Goel, and Thibault Spirlet, "The Guest List for White House Dinner for the Saudi Crown Prince Included Nearly 50 Executives," *Business Insider*, November 20, 2025.

Index

About the Author

Versha Sharma

CASEY MICHEL is one of the U.S.'s leading journalists and authors covering the world of dark money and international corruption. He is the author of *American Kleptocracy*, named by *The Economist* as one of the "best books to read to understand financial crime," and *Foreign Agents*, which received starred reviews from both *Kirkus Reviews* and *Publishers Weekly* and was described by *Foreign Policy* as one of the "biggest foreign-policy book releases of 2024."

He writes regularly on offshoring, foreign lobbying, authoritarianism, and illicit wealth for *The New York Times*, *Financial Times*, *The Wall Street Journal*, *The Atlantic*, and *Foreign Affairs*. He received his master's degree in Russian, Eurasian, and East European Studies from Columbia University's Harriman Institute, and he is currently sanctioned by the Russian regime for his work. *United States of Oligarchy* is his third book.